# FACT-FINDING BEFORE THE INTERNATIONAL COURT

*Fact-Finding before the International Court of Justice* examines a number of significant recent criticisms of the way in which the ICJ deals with facts. The book takes the position that such criticisms are warranted and that the ICJ's current approach to fact-finding falls short of adequacy both in cases involving abundant, particularly complex or technical facts and in those cases involving a scarcity of facts. The author skilfully examines how other tribunals such as the adjudicative bodies of the World Trade Organization and inter-State arbitrations conduct fact-finding and makes a number of select proposals for reform, which would enable the ICJ to address some of the current weaknesses in its approach. The proposals include, but are not limited to, the development of a power to compel the disclosure of information, greater use of provisional measures and a clear strategy for the use of expert evidence.

JAMES GERARD DEVANEY holds a PhD from the European University Institute in Florence, Italy. His doctoral research focused on international courts and tribunals but he has published on a wide range of areas of international law including self-defence and the use of force, the law of treaties and state succession. He is currently teaching at the University of Glasgow.

# FACT-FINDING BEFORE THE INTERNATIONAL COURT OF JUSTICE

JAMES GERARD DEVANEY
*University of Glasgow*

CAMBRIDGE
UNIVERSITY PRESS

# CAMBRIDGE
## UNIVERSITY PRESS

University Printing House, Cambridge CB2 8BS, United Kingdom

One Liberty Plaza, 20th Floor, New York, NY 10006, USA

477 Williamstown Road, Port Melbourne, VIC 3207, Australia

314-321, 3rd Floor, Plot 3, Splendor Forum, Jasola District Centre, New Delhi - 110025, India

79 Anson Road, #06-04/06, Singapore 079906

Cambridge University Press is part of the University of Cambridge.

It furthers the University's mission by disseminating knowledge in the pursuit of education, learning and research at the highest international levels of excellence.

www.cambridge.org
Information on this title: www.cambridge.org/9781316507025

© James Gerard Devaney 2016

This publication is in copyright. Subject to statutory exception and to the provisions of relevant collective licensing agreements, no reproduction of any part may take place without the written permission of Cambridge University Press.

First published 2016
First paperback edition 2018

*A catalogue record for this publication is available from the British Library*

*Library of Congress Cataloging in Publication data*
Names: Devaney, James Gerard.
Title: Fact-finding before the International Court of Justice / James Gerard Devaney, University of Glasgow.
Description: Cambridge, United Kingdom : Cambridge University Press, 2016. | Includes bibliographical references.
Identifiers: LCCN 2016011208 | ISBN 9781107142213 (Hardback)
Subjects: LCSH: International Court of Justice–Rules and practice. | Evidence, Criminal (International law) | Criminal investigation (International law) | International law and human rights.
Classification: LCC KZ6287 .D48 2016 | DDC 345/.052–dc23 LC record available at http://lccn.loc.gov/2016011208

ISBN 978-1-107-14221-3 Hardback
ISBN 978-1-316-50702-5 Paperback

Cambridge University Press has no responsibility for the persistence or accuracy of URLs for external or third-party internet websites referred to in this publication, and does not guarantee that any content on such websites is, or will remain, accurate or appropriate.

# CONTENTS

*Table of cases* vii
*Acknowledgements* xvi

**Introduction** 1

1 **Rules of evidence before the International Court of Justice** 14
 1.1 The fact-finding powers of the International Court of Justice 15
 1.2 *Da mihi factum, dabo tibi jus*: the Court's reactive approach to fact-finding 27
 1.3 The Court's reactive approach to fact-finding: contributing factors 30
 1.4 A natural counterpart: fact-assessment and the weighing of evidence 43
 1.5 Does the Court have unlimited discretion to pursue a more proactive approach to fact-finding? 51
 1.6 Chapter 1 summary: the Court's reactive approach to fact-finding 72

2 **Criticisms of the Court's current reactive approach to fact-finding** 73
 2.1 Group 1: Problems relating to abundant, particularly complex or technical facts 74
 2.2 Group 2: Problems arising from insufficient evidence, specifically non-appearance 115
 2.3 Chapter 2 summary: criticisms of the Court warranted 125

3 **The practice of other international courts and tribunals** 127
 3.1 Fact-finding and fact-assessment at the WTO 130
 3.2 Fact-finding and fact-assessment in recent inter-State arbitrations 150
 3.3 Chapter 3 summary 176

4 **Winds of change: the possibility of reform**     179
    4.1   Developing a power to compel the disclosure of evidence     180
    4.2   Provisional measures     202
    4.3   Developing a clear strategy for the use of experts before the Court     217
    4.4   Chapter 4 summary: realistic measures to achieve a more proactive approach to fact-finding     241

5 **A more proactive approach to fact-finding**     242
    5.1   Positive aspects of the Court's current reactive approach     242
    5.2   How to deal with factually complex cases before the Court     245
    5.3   The limits of the Court's fact-finding powers     247

*Epilogue*     254
*Bibliography*     257
*Index*     275

# TABLE OF CASES

## Permanent Court of International Justice

*Designation of the Netherlands Workers' Delegate to the Third Session of the International Labour Conference*, 1922 PCIJ, Ser. B, No. 1   4
*Mavrommatis Palestine Concessions*, 1924 PCIJ, Ser. A, No. 2   36, 42
*Certain German Interests in Polish Upper Silesia* (Merits), 1926 PCIJ, Ser. A, No. 7   4
*Denunciation of the Treaty of 2 November 1865 between China and Belgium*, 1927 PCIJ, Ser. A, No. 8   208
*Jurisdiction of the European Commission of the Danube*, 1927 PCIJ, Ser. B, No. 14   98–99
*Case Concerning the Factory at Chorzów (Germany v. Poland)* (Claim for Indemnity) (Jurisdiction), 1927 Ser. A, No. 9   23
*Case Concerning the Factory at Chorzów* (Claim for Indemnity) (Merits), 1927 Ser. A, No. 17   24, 37
*Free Zones of Upper Savoy and the District of Gex* (1932), PCIJ, Ser. A/B, No. 46   13
*Case Concerning the Administration of the Prince Von Pless (Preliminary Objection)*, PCIJ, Ser, A/B, No, 52   98
*Lighthouses Case between France and Greece, Judgment*, 1934 PCIJ, Ser. A/B, No. 62   190
*Diversion of Water from the Meuse*, Order of 13 May 1937, PCIJ, Ser. C, No. 81   17

## International Court of Justice

*Admission of a State to the United Nations (Charter, Art. 4)*, Advisory Opinion: ICJ Reports 1948, p. 57   56, 58
*Corfu Channel Case, Judgment of April 9th, 1949*: ICJ Reports 1949, p. 4   2, 4, 16, 19, 20, 24, 36, 37, 46, 60, 80, 119, 120, 122, 162, 191, 197, 201, 214, 225, 226, 227, 250
*Corfu Channel Case, Judgment of December 15th, 1949*: ICJ Reports 1949, p. 244   17, 119
*International Status of South-West Africa, Advisory Opinion*: ICJ Reports 1950, p. 128   4, 38, 80, 81, 82, 225
*Haya de la Torre Case, Judgment of June 13th, 1951*: ICJ Reports 1951, p. 71   56, 59
*Case concerning rights of nations of the United States of America in Morocco, Judgment of August 27th, 1952*: ICJ Reports 1952, p. 176   192
*Anglo-Iranian Oil Co. (jurisdiction) Judgment of July 22nd, 1952*: ICJ Reports 1952, p. 93   46

*The Minquiers and Ecrehos case, Judgment of November 17th, 1953*: ICJ Reports 1953, p. 47  192

*Nottebohm Case (second phase), Judgment of April 6th, 1955*: ICJ Reports 1955, p. 4  46, 118

*Case concerning the Aerial Incident of July 27th, 1955 (Israel v. Bulgaria), Preliminary Objections, Judgment of May 26th, 1959*: ICJ Reports 1959, p. 127  26, 215

*Certain Expenses of the United Nations (Article 17, paragraph 2, of the Charter), Advisory Opinion of 20 July 1962*: ICJ Reports 1962, p. 151  62, 66

*Case Concerning the Temple of Preah Vihear (Cambodia v. Thailand) (Merits)*: ICJ Reports 1962, p. 6  28, 80

*Northern Cameroons (Cameroon v. United Kingdom), Preliminary Objections, Judgment*: ICJ Reports 1963, p. 15  59, 62, 69, 71

*Barcelona Traction, Light and Power Company, Limited, Preliminary Objections, Judgment*: ICJ Reports 1964, p. 6  42, 162, 191, 213

*South West Africa, Second Phase, Judgment*: ICJ Reports 1966, p. 6  38, 81

*Legal Consequences for States of the Continued Presence of South Africa in Namibia (South West Africa) notwithstanding Security Council Resolution 276 (1970), Advisory Opinion*: ICJ Reports 1971, p. 16  10, 52, 66, 80, 190

*Appeal Relating to the Jurisdiction of the ICAO Council, Judgment*: ICJ Reports 1972, p. 46  26

*Fisheries Jurisdiction (Federal Republic of Germany v. Iceland), Interim Measures of Protection, Order of 17 August 1972*: ICJ Reports 1972, p. 30  204

*Fisheries Jurisdiction (Federal Republic of Germany v. Iceland), Merits, Judgment*: ICJ Reports 1974, p. 175  117, 119

*Trial of Pakistani Prisoners of War, Order of 15 December 1973*: ICJ Reports 1973, p. 347  119

*Nuclear Tests (Australia v. France), Judgment*: ICJ Reports 1974, p. 253  6, 46, 116, 118, 119, 124, 207, 246

*Nuclear Tests (New Zealand v. France), Judgment*: ICJ Reports 1974, p. 457  6, 9

*Fisheries Jurisdiction (United Kingdom v. Iceland), Merits, Judgment*: ICJ Reports 1974, p. 3  117

*Aegean Sea Continental Shelf, Judgment*: ICJ Reports 1978, p. 3  42, 46, 118–120, 190

*United States Diplomatic and Consular Staff in Tehran (United States of America v. Iran), Judgment*: ICJ Reports 1980, p. 10  20, 37, 41, 45, 46, 47, 60, 62, 119, 120, 124, 154, 207

*Continental Shelf (Tunisia/Libyan Arab Jamahiriya), Judgment*: ICJ Reports 1982, p. 18  22, 32, 80

*Delimitation of the Maritime Boundary in the Gulf of Maine Area (Canada/United States of America), (Appointment of Expert), Order of 30 March 1984*: ICJ Reports 1984, p. 165  21

*Delimitation of the Maritime Boundary in the Gulf of Maine Area, Judgment*: ICJ Reports 1984, p. 246  16, 80

*Application for Revision and Interpretation of the Judgment of 24 February 1982 in the Case concerning the Continental Shelf (Tunisia/Libyan Arab Jamahiriya) (Tunisia v. Libyan Arab Jamahiriya), Judgment*: ICJ Reports 1985, p. 192  22, 24, 32

TABLE OF CASES ix

*Continental Shelf (Libyan Arab Jamahiriya v. Malta), Judgment*: ICJ Reports 1985, p. 13   32, 80, 82

*Military and Paramilitary Activities in and against Nicaragua (Nicaragua v. United States of America) Merits, Judgment*: ICJ Reports 1986, p. 14   2, 9, 13, 17, 23, 25, 33, 39, 41, 44, 46, 48, 56, 59, 60, 80, 100, 107, 116, 117, 118, 119, 121, 122, 191, 206, 246

*Frontier Dispute, Provisional Measures*, Order of 10 January 1986: ICJ Reports 1986, p. 3   209

*Frontier Dispute, Judgment*: ICJ Reports 1986, p. 554   21, 22

*Border and Transborder Armed Actions (Nicaragua v. Honduras), Jurisdiction and Admissibility, Judgment*: ICJ Reports 1988, p. 69   26

*Applicability of the Obligation to Arbitrate under Section 21 of the United Nations Headquarters Agreement of 26 June 1947, Advisory Opinion*: ICJ Reports 1988, p. 12   97

*Elettronica Sicula SpA (ELSI), Judgment*: ICJ Reports 1989, p. 15   80, 182, 221

*Applicability of Article VI, Section 22, of the Convention on the Privileges and Immunities of the United Nations, Advisory Opinion*: ICJ Reports 1989, p. 177   52

*Arbitral Award of 31 July 1989 (Guinea-Bissau v. Senegal), Judgment*: ICJ Reports 1991, p. 53   21

*Questions of Interpretation and Application of the 1971 Montreal Convention Arising from the Aerial Incident at Lockerbie, (Libyan Arab Jamahiriya v. United States of America), Provisional Measures*, Order of 14 April 1992: ICJ Reports 1992, p. 114   55

*Land, Island and Maritime Frontier Dispute (El Salvador/Honduras: Nicaragua intervening), Judgment of 11 September 1992*: ICJ Reports 1992, p. 455   24, 33

*Application of the Convention on the Prevention and Punishment of the Crime of Genocide (Bosnia and Herzegovina/Yugoslavia [Serbia and Montenegro]), Provisional Measures*: ICJ Reports 1993, p. 3   26

*Territorial Dispute (Libyan Arab Jamahiriya/Chad), Judgment*: ICJ Reports 1994, p. 6   189, 190

*East Timor (Portugal v. Australia), Judgment*: ICJ Reports 1995, p. 90   65, 71

*Legality of the Use by a State of Nuclear Weapons in Armed Conflict, Advisory Opinion*: ICJ Reports 1996, p. 66   5, 28, 29

*Land and Maritime Boundary between Cameroon and Nigeria, Provisional Measures*, Order of 15 March 1996: ICJ Reports 1996, p. 13   208

*Legality of the Threat or Use of Nuclear Weapons, Advisory Opinion*: ICJ Reports 1996, p. 226   28, 29

*Gabčikovo-Nagymaros Project (Hungary/Slovakia), Judgment*: ICJ Reports 1997, p. 7   4, 16, 17, 33, 34, 78

*Land and Maritime Boundary between Cameroon and Nigeria (Cameroon v. Nigeria), Preliminary Objections, Judgment*: ICJ Reports 1998, p. 315   45

*Kasikili/Sedudu Island (Botswana/Namibia), Judgment*: ICJ Reports 1999, p. 1045   78

*Request for Interpretation of the Judgment of 11 June 1998 in the Case concerning the Land and Maritime Boundary between Cameroon and Nigeria (Cameroon v. Nigeria), Preliminary Objections (Nigeria v. Cameroon), Judgment*: ICJ Reports 1999, p. 31   121

x                    TABLE OF CASES

*LaGrand (Germany v. United States of America), Judgment*: ICJ Reports 2001, p. 466   204
*Maritime Delimitation and Territorial Questions between Qatar and Bahrain, Merits, Judgment*: ICJ Reports 2001, p. 40   82, 84, 85, 101, 122
*Arrest Warrant of 11 April 2000 (Democratic Republic of the Congo v. Belgium), Judgment*: ICJ Reports 2002, p. 3   3
*Land and Maritime Boundary between Cameroon and Nigeria (Cameroon v. Nigeria: Equatorial Guinea intervening) Judgment*: ICJ Reports 2002, p. 303   85
*Certain Criminal Proceedings in France (Republic of the Congo v. France), Provisional Measure*, Order of 17 June 2003: ICJ Reports 2003, p. 102   207
*Oil Platforms (Islamic Republic of Iran v. United States of America), Judgment*: ICJ Reports 2003, p. 161   187, 188, 214, 215
*Legal Consequences of the Construction of a Wall in the Occupied Palestinian Territory, Advisory Opinion*: ICJ Reports 2004, p. 136   52, 62, 63, 97, 98, 115, 122, 123, 198
*Armed Activities on the Territory of the Congo (Democratic Republic of the Congo v, Uganda), Judgment*: ICJ Reports 2005, p. 168   1, 5, 9, 29, 41, 45, 46, 47, 48, 62, 63, 64, 69, 75, 95, 96, 97, 99, 102, 104, 106, 107, 108, 109, 110, 206, 212, 213, 243
*Application of the Convention on the Prevention and Punishment of the Crime of Genocide (Bosnia and Herzegovina v. Serbia and Montenegro), Judgement*: ICJ Reports 2007, p. 43   5, 7, 26, 29, 41, 48, 64, 65, 80, 88, 89, 94, 95, 99, 109, 112, 113, 114, 162, 183, 191, 207, 209, 212, 213, 214, 215
*Application of the Convention on the Prevention and Punishment of the Crime of Genocide (Croatia v. Serbia), Preliminary Objections, Judgment*: ICJ Reports 2008, p. 413   29, 30, 90, 113, 183, 225, 235, 243
*Pulp Mills on the River Uruguay (Argentina v. Uruguay), Judgment*, ICJ Reports 2010, p. 14   2, 5, 6, 10, 19, 48, 74, 75, 79, 82, 84, 91, 92, 93, 128, 168, 191, 192, 193, 196, 198, 207, 218, 220, 224, 227, 228, 232, 234, 239
*Ahmadou Sadio Diallo (Republic of Guinea v. Democratic Republic of the Congo), Merits, Judgment*, ICJ Reports 2010, p. 639   192
*Accordance with International Law of the Unilateral Declaration of Independence in Respect of Kosovo*, Advisory Opinion, ICJ Reports 2010, p. 403   65, 66, 67, 70
*Application of the International Convention on the Elimination of all Forms of Racial Discrimination (Georgia v. Russian Federation) Preliminary Objections*, ICJ Reports 2011, p. 70   49, 50
*Certain Activities Carried out by Nicaragua in the Border Area (Costa Rica v. Nicaragua)*, Joinder of Proceedings, Order of 27 April 2013, joining the proceedings in the cases of *Certain Activities carried out by Nicaragua in the Border Area (Costa Rica v. Nicaragua)*, Application Instituting Proceedings, 18 November 2010, and *Construction of a Road in Costa Rica along the San Juan River (Nicaragua v. Costa Rica)* Application Instituting Proceedings, 21 December 2011   10, 11, 228
*Whaling in the Antarctic (Australia v. Japan: New Zealand intervening)*, Judgment, ICJ Reports 2014, p. 226   5, 225, 227, 228, 229, 234, 235
*Maritime Dispute (Peru v. Chile)*, Judgment, ICJ Reports 2014, p. 3   127

TABLE OF CASES                                  xi

## Inter-State arbitrations

*Norwegian Shipowners' Claims (Norway v. United States of America)*, Award, PCA, 13 October 1922   153

*American-Mexican General Claims Commission, William A Parker (USA) v. United Mexican States*, Award, 31 March 1926, RIAA 4 (1951)   12, 196, 197, 198, 200

*Island of Palmas (or Miangas) (United States of America v. The Netherlands)*, Award, 4 April 1928   12, 153

*Radio Corporation of America v. The National Government of the Republic of China*, Award, PCA, 13 April 1935   153

*Maritime Delimitation (Eritrea v. Yemen)*, 22 RIAA 335 (PCA 1999)   75

*Southern Bluefin Tuna (New Zealand. v. Japan, Australia v. Japan)*, 23 R.I.A.A. 2000   74

*Malaysia/Singapore*, Award on Agreed Terms, 1 September 2005   152, 210

*Barbados/Trinidad and Tobago*, Award, 11 April 2006, 45 ILM 798   75, 152

*Saluka Investments B.V. (Netherlands v. Czech Republic)*, Partial Award, para. 273 (Permanent Court of Arbitration 2006)   75

*Arbitral Tribunal Constituted Pursuant to Article 287, and in Accordance with Annex VII, of the United Nations Convention on the Law of the Sea, in the Matter of Arbitration between: Guyana and Suriname*, Award, 17 September 2007   151, 152, 158–165, 175, 176, 200, 236, 237, 255, 256

*In the Matter of an Arbitration before a Tribunal Constituted in Accordance with Article 5 of the Arbitration Agreement between the Government of Sudan and the Sudan People's Liberation Movement/Army on Delimiting Abyei Area and the Permanent Court of Arbitration Optional Rules for Arbitrating Disputes between Two Parties of Which Only One Is a State between the Government of Sudan and the Sudan People's Liberation Movement/Army*, Final Award, 22 July 2009   75, 151, 152, 158, 165–170, 176

*The Republic of Mauritius v. United Kingdom*, arbitration instituted December 2010, pending   151, 152, 236, 237

*Polis Fondi Immobilare di Banche Popolare S.G.R.p.A. v. International Fund for Agricultural development*, Case No 2010-8, para. 156   75

*In the Matter of the Indus Waters Kishenganga, Arbitration before the Court of Arbitration Constituted in Accordance with the Indus Waters Treaty 1960 between the Government of India and the Government of Pakistan Signed on 19 September 1960, between the Islamic Republic of Pakistan and the Republic of India*, Partial Award, 18 February 2013   125, 151, 169, 170–176, 236, 256

*In the Matter of the Chagos Marine Protected Area, Arbitration before an Arbitral Tribunal Constituted under Annex VII of the United Nations Convention on the Law of the Sea between the Republic of Mauritius and the United Kingdom of Great Britain and Northern Ireland*, Award, 18 March 2015   236

## The adjudicative bodies of the World Trade Organization

United States – Standards for Reformulated and Conventional Gasoline, Appellate Body Report, WT/DS2/AB/R, 26 April 1996  144

United States – Measure Affecting Imports of Woven Wool Shirts and Blouses from India, Appellate Body Report, WT/DS33/AB/R, 25 April 1997  144

Canada – Certain Measures Concerning Periodicals, Appellate Body Report, WT/DS31/AB/R, 30 June 1997  143

Argentina – Measures Affecting Imports of Footwear, Textiles, Apparel and Other Items, Panel Report, WT/DS56/R, 25 November 1997  148, 186, 187, 191, 198, 201, 216

India – Patent Protection for Pharmaceutical and Agricultural Chemical Products, Appellate Body Report, WT/DS50/AB/R, 19 December 1997  149, 191

European Communities – Measures Concerning Meat and Meat Products (Hormones), Appellate Body Report, WT/DS26/AB/R, WT/DS48/AB/R/ 16 January 1998  132, 142, 218

Argentina – Measures Affecting Imports of Footwear, Apparel and Other Items, Appellate Body Report, WT/DS56/AB/R, 27 March 1998  135, 148, 186, 187, 191

Indonesia – Certain Measures Affecting the Automobile Industry, Panel Report, WT/DS54/R, 2 July 1998  130, 149

European Communities – Measures Affecting the Importation of Certain Poultry Products, Appellate Body Report, WT/DS69/AB/R, 13 July 1998  142

Korea – Taxes on Alcoholic Beverages, Panel Report, WT/DS57/R, WT/DS84/R, 17 September 1998  145

United States – Import Prohibition of Certain Shrimp and Shrimp Products, Appellate Body Report, WT/DS58/AB/R, 12 October 1998  134, 189

Australia – Measures Affecting Importation of Salmon, Appellate Body Report, WT/DS18/AB/R, 20 October 1998  131, 142

Canada – Measures Affecting the Export of Civilian Aircraft, Appellate Body Report, WT/DS70/AB/R, 2 August 1999  135, 136, 184, 185, 186

India – Quantitative Restrictions on Imports of Agricultural, Textile and Industrial Products, Appellate Body Report, WT/DS90/AB/R, 22 September 1999  146

Japan – Measures Affecting Agricultural Products (Japan – Agricultural Products II) WT/DS76/AB/R, 19 November 1999  134

Korea – Definitive Safeguard Measure on Imports of Certain Dairy Products, Appellate Body Report, WT/DS98/AB/R, 14 December 1999  144

United States – Definitive Safeguard Measures on Imports of Wheat Gluten from the European Communities, Panel Report, WT/DS166/R, 31 July 2000  149

United States – Definitive Safeguard Measure on Imports of Wheat Gluten from the European Communities, Appellate Body Report, WT/DS166/AB/R, 22 December 2000  142

European Communities – Measures Affecting Asbestos and Asbestos-Containing Products, Appellate Body Report, WT/DS135/AB/R, 12 March 2001  142

TABLE OF CASES                                    xiii

*United States – Section 211 Omnibus Appropriations Act of 1998*, Panel Report, WT/DS176/R, 6 August 2001   145

*Chile – Price Band System and Safeguard Measures Relating to Certain Agricultural Products*, Appellate Body Report (AB/2002-3), WT/DS207/AB/R, 23 September 2002   132

*Japan –Measures Affecting the Importation of Apples*, Appellate Body Report, WT/DS245/AB/R, 26 November 2003   137

*United States – Subsidies on Upland Cotton*, Panel Report, WT/DS26/R, 8 September 2004   145

*United States – Investigation of the International Trade Commission in Softwood Lumber from Canada*, Panel Report, WT/DS277/RW, 15 November 2005   150

*European Communities – Measures Affecting the Approval and Marketing of Biotech Products*, Panel Report, WT/DS291/R, WT/DS292/R, WT/DS293/R, 29 September 2006   136

*European Communities – Selected Customs Matters*, Appellate Body Report, DT/315/AB/R, 13 November 2006   137, 138

*Brazil – Measures Affecting Import of Retreated Tyres*, Complaint by the European Communities, Appellate Body Report, WT/DS332/AB/R, 3 December 2007   19, 234

*Turkey – Measures Affecting the Importation of Rice*, Panel Report, WT/DS334/R, 21 September 2007   130

*United States – Subsidies on Upland Cotton*, Appellate Body Report, WT/DS267/AB/RW, 20 June 2008   130

*United States – Continued Existence and Application of Zeroing Methodology*, Appellate Body Report, WT/DS350/AB/R, 19 February 2009   134

*United States – Measures Affecting Trade in Large Civil Aircraft (Second Complaint)*, Appellate Body Report, WT/DS353/AB/R, 12 March 2012   140, 200

*United States – Measures Concerning the Importation, Marketing and Sale of Tuna and Tuna Products*, Appellate Body Report, WT/DS381/AB/R, 16 May 2012   147

*United States – Shrimps and Sawblades; US- Anti-Dumping Measures on Certain Shrimp and Diamond Sawblades from China*, Panel Report, WT/DS422/R, 8 June 2012   146

*China – Certain Measures Affecting Electronic Payment Services*, Panel Report, WT/DS413/R, 16 July 2012   146

## Iran–US claims tribunal

*Leila Danesh Arfa Mahmoud and Islamic Republic of Iran, Case No. 237, Chamber Two*, Order of 12 July 1982   155

*International Systems and Controls Corporation and Industrial Development and Renovation Organization of Iran et al., Case No. 439, Chamber Two*, Order of 18 November 1982   155

*Ultrasystems Incorporated and Islamic Republic of Iran et al.*, Award No. 27-84-3 (4 March 1983) reprinted in 2 Iran-U.S. C.T.R. 114, 115 (1983)   157

*William Stanley Shashoua and Government of the Islamic Republic of Iran, et al., Case No. 69*, Chamber One, Order of 14 March 1983   156, 201

*Konstantine A. Gianoplus and Islamic Republic of Iran, Case No. 314*, Chamber One, Order of 19 October 1983   155

*Henry F. Teichmann, Inc., Carnegie Foundry and Machine Company and Hamadan Glass Company, Case No. 264*, Chamber One, Order of 2 February 1984   154

*Weatherford International Inc. and the Islamic Republic of Iran, Case No. 305*, Chamber Two, Order of 15 February 1985   156, 201

*INA Corporation and the Islamic Republic of Iran*, Award No. 184-161-1 (12 August 1985) at 14, reprinted in 8 Iran-US CTR 373, 382 (1985–1)   156

*Hoshang Mostofizadeh and Government of the Islamic Republic of Iran, National Iranian Oil Company, Case No. 278*, Chamber Two, Order of 15 January 1986   154–155

*H. A. Spalding, Inc.* and *Ministry of Roads and Transport of the Islamic Republic of Iran – Tribunal*, Award No. 212-437-3 (24 February 1986) reprinted in 10 Iran-U.S. Cl. Trib. Rep. 22, 26–33   157

*Ministry of National Defence of the Islamic Republic of Iran and Government of the United States of America, Case No. B-61*, Chamber One, Order of 27 May 1987   155

*Minister of National Defence of the Islamic Republic of Iran and Government of the United States of America, Case No. B1 (claims 2 & 3)*, Full Tribunal; Order of 2 July 1987   155

*Brown & Root Inc. and the Islamic Republic of Iran, Case No. 432*, Chamber One, Order of 4 January 1993   156, 201

## Other

*Davie v. Magistrates of Edinburgh* 1953 S.C. 34 (Scottish Court of Session)   231

*Air Canada and Others Appellants v. Secretary of State for Trade and Another Respondents* [1983] 2 W.L.R. 494 (House of Lords)   9

*Daubert v. Merrel Dow Pharmaceuticals, Inc.*, 509 U.S. 579 (1993) (U.S. Supreme Court)   38, 77

*Kumho Tire Co. v. Carmichael*, 526 U.S. 137 (1999) (U.S. Supreme Court)   38, 77

*Prosecutor v. Kordic and Cerkez*, Case No. IT-95-14 (26 February 2001) (ICTY)   238, 239

*Prosecutor v. Krstić*, IT-98-33 (2 August 2001) (ICTY)   112

*The MOX Plant* case (*Ireland v. United Kingdom*) Order of 3 December 2001 (ITLOS)   159, 206

*Prosecutor v. Galić (Decision Concerning the Expert Witness Ewa Tabeau and Richard Philipps)* IT-93-29-T (3 July 2002) (ICTY)   80

*Case Concerning Land Reclamation by Singapore in and around the Straights of Johor* (*Malaysia v. Singapore*) Provisional Measures, Order of 8 October 2003 (ITLOS)   6, 206, 209, 210, 221, 222, 223, 224

*Prosecutor v. Blagojević (Decision on Prosecution's Motion for Admission of Expert Statements)* IT-02-60-T (7 November 2003) (ICTY)   80

*Prosecutor v. Blagojević and Jokić (Judgment) IT-02-60-T* (17 January 2005) (ICTY) 223

*Prosecutor v. Ndindilyimana et al. (Decision on the Prosecutor Opposing the Testimony of Witness DE4-30 as a Factual Witness) ICTR-00-56-T* (16 May 2007) (ICTR) 81

*Prosecutor v. Karemera (Decision on 'Requete de la Defense de M. Ngirumpatse en Retrait de la Deposition du Temoin GFJ et des Pieces Afferentes') ICTR-98-44-T* (6 August 2008) (ICTR) 81

*Prosecutor v. Stanišć and Simatović, IT-03-69* (30 May 2013) 112, 113

# ACKNOWLEDGEMENTS

Firstly I would like to express my gratitude to Professor Martin Scheinin, who supervised the doctoral thesis upon which this book is based. He was always there when he was needed and his calm, measured supervision allowed me to write the thesis that I wanted to write. Similarly, I would like to thank the other members of the panel who examined my PhD, Judge Giorgio Gaja and Professor Geir Ulfstein. I would also like to thank those at Cambridge University Press, in particular Finola O'Sullivan, Elizabeth Spicer and the anonymous reviewers whose comments were exceedingly helpful.

My greatest thanks go to Professor Christian J. Tams. At various times in my life I have been Professor Tams's student, research assistant, co-author and now colleague. I am indebted to him for providing me with so many opportunities and hope that we will work together for many years to come. I must also thank Therese O'Donnell who, one rainy winter afternoon in Glasgow, first sparked my interest in public international law and who has been unconditionally supportive ever since, providing guidance both academic and otherwise.

This book was written mainly in the Biblioteca Nazionale Centrale di Firenze, the Lauterpacht Centre for International Law in Cambridge and of course in the Statistics Room of the EUI library. My time in Cambridge was the most productive period of the whole process and my thanks go to Professors James Crawford, Roger O'Keefe, Philippe Sands and Iain Scobbie and Drs Brendan Plant and Akbar Rasulov who all took the time to sit down with me and listen to my thoughts on what would become this book. None of them had to, but they all did, and for that I am extremely grateful.

I would also like to thank my parents Jim and Teresa and my brother Thomas for being the best family anyone could ever wish for. My family and friends played two important roles in my life these last few years: (1) enthusiastically embracing the opportunity to visit me both in Florence and Porto which ensured I never felt too far from Glasgow and (2) never wanting to talk about international law or the ICJ. Honourable mentions go to my best friends David Ward (who wins the award for most frequent visitor), Lauren Mayberry, David McAlpine, Mark Conroy, Alex McIntyre, Jamie Scott and Sophie Battye.

Going to the EUI was one of the best decisions I have ever made and I will leave a better person with immeasurably broader horizons. Particular thanks go to Professor Francioni for his encouragement in my first year when it was very much needed. I would also like to thank Petros Mavroidis, Jonathan Chevry, Donal Hasset, Hanna Eklund, Frank McNamara, Skander Galand, Emma Nyhan, Emily Hancox, Manu De Groof, Jan Zglinski, Emma Linklater, Robin Gadbled, Philipp Sahm, Johann Leiß and Guilherme Sampaio, to mention a select few. One person who deserves a special mention is Carlo Maria Cantore – a real friend and someone who did everything in his power to make me feel at home in Italy (including an intensive crusade to make me a Juventus fan, although I daresay I enjoyed more success in making him a fan of my beloved Glasgow Celtic). Thanks too go to Luísa Lourenço who welcomed me into Via Dei Rustici and who completes what I consider my family in Florence. E finalmente à minha Benedita, sempre ao meu lado, não tenho palavras suficientes para dizer o que queria dizer. No final, do fundo do coração, este livro, como todas as outras coisas na minha vida, é para ti.

# Introduction

In 1958 Neill Alford Jr stated that the likelihood of a dispute as to the facts in any case before the International Court of Justice was fairly remote.[1] He argued that this was so due to the fact that generally neither State party to a case before the Court had sufficient evidence to question the factual assertions made by the other party.[2] However, a number of developments in the intervening fifty or so years have proved Alford wrong, as increasingly the Court has had to deal with cases in which the outcome of the case has turned not just on legal questions but also on factual determinations.[3] As Mosk has stated:

> [T]here have been dramatic changes in the availability, ascertainment and importance of facts. The technological age has produced more facts and more facts that can and must be ascertained ... it is no longer necessary to wade through a warehouse full of documents to find critical evidence ... It also may not be necessary to travel thousands of miles to find documents and interview witnesses. New methods of storing documents and of communicating have drastically affected means of investigating and ascertaining facts.[4]

Crucially, such cases requiring a heavy focus on the facts have challenged the Court's traditional approach to the facts. In the past the Court was often able to decide the outcome of a case through reliance on undisputed facts. In essence, in such cases it was not so much the facts that

---

[1] N. H. Alford Jr, 'Fact Finding by the World Court' 4 *Villanova Law Review* 37, 57.
[2] Ibid.
[3] S. Halink, 'All Things Considered: How the International Court of Justice Delegated its Fact-Assessment to the United Nations in the Armed Activities Case' 40 *NYU Journal of International Law and Politics* 13, 13; K. J. Keith, 'The International Court of Justice and Criminal Justice' 59 *International and Comparative Law Quarterly* 895, 904; R. Teitelbaum, 'Recent Fact-Finding Developments at the International Court of Justice' 6 *The Law and Practice of International Courts and Tribunals* 119, 125.
[4] R. Mosk, 'The Role of Facts in International Dispute Resolution' 203 *Receuil des Cours – Collected Courses at the Hague Academy* 11, 19.

were disputed, but rather the legal conclusions that were to be drawn from them.[5] It has been remarked that '[i]n times past, courts and arbitrators dealt with situations that were not as complex as those today'.[6] Whether or not this is so (for cases such as *Corfu Channel* and *Nicaragua* could hardly be described as straightforward in terms of the facts),[7] what is certain is that the Court is increasingly deprived of the possibility of basing its decisions on undisputed facts.

In addition to the disputes coming before the Court being consistently complicated, these complex facts are being increasingly contested. States themselves have demonstrated a willingness to use 'ever more sophisticated forms of evidence to substantiate their claims'.[8] Such developments have led to criticism of the way the Court handles factually complex cases that come before it (as we will see in greater detail in the following

---

[5] Indeed, cases before the PCIJ primarily concerned the application of treaties and as such the Court 'was in a position to establish and rely on facts that were not in dispute between the parties, obviating, in most cases, the need for detailed rules of evidence'; see E. Valencia-Ospina, 'Evidence before the International Court of Justice' 1 *International Law Forum du droit international* 202, 202; see also Rosalyn Judge Higgins, 'Speech by H. E. Judge Rosalyn Higgins, President of the International Court of Justice at the 58th Session of the International Law Commission' *International Law Commission*; Shabtai Rosenne and Yaël Ronen, *The Law and Practice of the International Court, 1920–2005* (4th edn, Leiden, Boston: Martinus Nijhoff, 2006) 1040; with regard to the ICJ, as Judge Yusuf stated in the *Pulp Mills* case, 'on many occasions in the past the Court was able to resolve complex and contested factual issues without resorting to Article 50 of the Statute' or utilising its other fact-finding powers; *Case Concerning Pulp Mills on the River Uruguay (Argentina v. Uruguay)*, ICJ Judgment (20 April 2010), Declaration of Judge Yusuf at 6.

[6] Mosk, 'The Role of Facts in International Dispute Resolution' 23.

[7] See *Corfu Channel Case (UK v. Albania)* (Merits) (1949) ICJ Rep 4; *Military and Paramilitary Activities in and against Nicaragua (Nicaragua v. United States of America)* (Merits) Judgment, ICJ Reports 1986 14.

[8] Anna Riddell and Brendan Plant, *Evidence before the International Court of Justice* (London: British Institute of International and Comparative Law, 2009) 5; Teitelbaum, 'Recent Fact-Finding Developments at the International Court of Justice' 152; Jean D'Aspremont and Makane M. Mbengue, 'Strategies of Engagement with Scientific Fact-Finding in International Adjudication', Amsterdam Law School Research Paper No. 2013-20, stating that '[i]t is commonplace that the role of science and technologies is growingly infusing all the layers of the international legal system as a whole'; Anna Riddell, 'Scientific Evidence in the International Court of Justice – Problems and Possibilities' 20 *Finnish Yearbook of International Law* 229, 229; Daniel Peat, 'The Use of Court-Appointed Experts by the International Court of Justice' 84 *British Yearbook of International Law* 271; Jacqueline Peel, 'Risk Regulation Under the WTO SPS Agreement: Science as an International Normative Yardstick?' Jean Monnet Working Paper 02/04.

chapters)[9] and have been one of the driving forces behind calls to move away from the Court's current approach to the facts.[10]

That is not to say that no such disputes where the facts are uncontroversial come before the Court today – even now the Court will occasionally be asked to deal with a case that turns almost exclusively on legal issues alone. For instance, in the *Arrest Warrant* case the Court only had to consider the legal issue of whether the arrest warrant issued by Belgium violated its international obligations to respect the immunity from criminal jurisdiction of the incumbent Minister for Foreign Affairs of the Democratic Republic of Congo.[11]

However, there is no doubt that today disputes in which the resolution of factual determinations is critical to the resolution of the legal issues in the dispute are commonplace.[12] Domestic courts with procedures for discovery or explicit powers to compel the production of evidence often have to guard against so-called 'fishing expeditions' whereby one party

---

[9] S. Mathias et al., 'The International Court of Justice at 60: Performance and Prospects' Proceedings of the Annual Meeting – American Society of International Law, Vol 100, Annual 2006, 398; Teitelbaum, 'Recent Fact-Finding Developments at the International Court of Justice' 120; Stephen M. Schwebel, *Three Cases of Fact-Finding by the International Court of Justice in International Law* (Cambridge University Press, 1994) 2; Thomas Franck, 'Fact-finding in the I.C.J.' in R. B. Lillich (ed), *Fact-finding before International Tribunals: Eleventh Sokol Colloquium* (Ardsley-on-Hudson, NY: Transnational Publishers, 1992) 21; John Crook, 'The Case Concerning Armed Activities on the Territory of the Congo (Democratic Republic of Congo v. Uganda) and its Implications for the Rules on the Use of Force' (American Society of International Law Briefing at Tillar House).

[10] C. J. Tams, 'Article 49' in A. Zimmermann (ed), *The Statute of the International Court of Justice: A Commentary* (Oxford University Press, 2006) 1107. As Tams has stated, '[g]iven the increasing number of cases brought before the Court, and the considerable length of proceedings, it is not surprising that the Court's cautious approach just described has come under strain. Especially in recent years, there has been talk about the need to "modernize the conduct of the Court's business"'; see also Caroline E. Foster, 'New Clothes for the Emperor? Consultation of Experts by the International Court of Justice' 5 *Journal of International Dispute Settlement* 139.

[11] *Arrest Warrant of 11 April 2000 (Democratic Republic of the Congo v. Belgium), Judgment, ICJ Reports 2002* 3.

[12] Rosalyn Judge Higgins, 'Speech by H. E. Judge Rosalyn Higgins, President of the International Court of Justice to the Sixth Committee of the General Assembly' *Sixth Committee of the General Assembly, 2 November 2007*; Laurence Boisson de Chazournes, 'Introduction: Courts and Tribunals and the Treatment of Scientific Issues' 3 *Journal of International Dispute Settlement* 479. Similarly, Highet stated that since the mid-1980s the Court has been 'increasingly exposed to situations involving disputed facts'; K. Highet, 'Evidence, the Court, and the Nicaragua Case' 81 *The American Journal of International Law* 1, 10.

submits often speculative requests for the disclosure of information in the possession of the other party. However, this is not a problem the ICJ has ever faced. Indeed, its reactive approach to the facts results in the 'opposite extreme'– namely the danger that the parties overwhelm the Court with thousands of pages of written submissions, annexes and reports. Whether this practice has arisen as a result of the fact that the parties are unclear as to what kind of information the Court will find probative or not, the end result is that the Court struggles to deal with the vast amounts of evidence.[13] The fear of 'documentary overload'[14] prompted the Court to adopt its Practice Directions II and III urging the parties to submit only documentary evidence that was absolutely necessary to support their case.[15]

Despite these Practice Directions the Court itself has in recent times referred to 'mass[es] of scientific and technological information',[16] 'vast

---

[13] Teitelbaum suggests that the Court is partly to blame for this: 'the Court's failure to give some guidance to the parties in terms of the burden of proof required, *prior* to the rendering of its decision, may contribute to the excessive annexes and lack of focus in the written pleadings on the part of counsel'; see Teitelbaum, 'Recent Fact-Finding Developments at the International Court of Justice' 123.

[14] Berman has referred to documentary overload being 'a real and growing problem. The urge to be complete is understandable and laudable, but it leads to the essential becoming swamped by the peripheral'; see Frank Berman, 'Remarks by Frank Berman' 106 *Proceedings of the Annual Meeting (American Society of International Law)* 162.

[15] To provide some illustration, in the Permanent Court's first case the documents submitted included only a handful of letters, memoranda and one telegram; see Nomination of the Netherlands Workers' Delegate to the Third Session of the International Labour Conference, 1922 PCIJ, Ser. B, No. 1 (Advisory Opinion of July 31). By the time of the *German Interests in Polish Upper Silesia* case, however, just a few years later, the Court was already dealing with substantial documentary evidence, more than two hundred documentary annexes being submitted at one stage or another in the course of these proceedings; see *Certain German Interests in Polish Upper Silesia (Germany v. Poland)* (Merits) 1926 PCIJ, Ser. A, No. 7, Judgment of May 25, at 11–13; see Hudson Reports at 116; Highet, 'Evidence, the Court, and the Nicaragua Case' 16. In *Corfu Channel*, the first case to come before the ICJ, 188 documents were submitted in total and by 1950 and the *South West Africa* advisory opinion the submission of documentary evidence 'had reached truly epic dimensions' – with over 27 pages required simply to list the over three hundred documents submitted; ibid. See *International Status of South-West Africa, Advisory Opinion: ICJ Reports 1950* 128.

[16] *Gabčikovo-Nagymaros Project (Hungary/Slovakia), Judgment, ICJ Reports 1997* 7 para 2 (25 September) Dissenting Opinion of Judge Skubiszewski; Judge Schwebel has also described the more than 5,000 pages of pleadings and documentary annexes as having placed a 'considerable burden on the Court's tiny translation services and on its budget'; see Stephen M. Schwebel, 'Speech of the President of the International Court of Justice to the General Assembly' A/52/PV36, 27 October 1997.

amounts of factual and scientific material containing data and analysis'[17] 'complex scientific'[18] or 'highly complex and controversial technological, strategic and scientific information'[19] and simply 'vast masses of factual material'.[20] The Court is not just referring here to the sheer quantity of information put before the Court but also to the complexity of the evidentiary issues at the heart of such cases.[21]

For instance, in the *Armed Activities* case the Court had to deal with a myriad of (often extremely complex) factual issues related to the Democratic Republic of Congo's claims that Uganda had violated the prohibition on the use of force, supported irregular Ugandan forces and occupied part of its territory as well as violated international human rights law and international humanitarian law, amongst other claims.[22] Similarly, in the *Bosnian Genocide* case the Court had to make numerous factual determinations in order to establish whether Serbia had committed the atrocities alleged by Bosnia-Herzegovina and to establish whether it had the specific intent to commit genocide.[23] Most recently, in the *Whaling in the Antarctic* case, in the course of assessing whether the taking, killing and treating of whales could be classified as being done 'for purposes of scientific research', the Court went to considerable lengths in examining such complex issues as the reasonableness of the use of lethal methods and the very design and (to some extent) implementation of Japan's JARPA II whaling programme.[24]

A further example is the *Pulp Mills* case, which was described by two judges of the Court itself as being one of the 'exceptionally fact-intensive'

---

[17] *Pulp Mills Case* para 229.
[18] Ibid., Joint Dissenting Opinion of Al-Khasawneh and Simma, para 11.
[19] Legality of the Use by a State of Nuclear Weapons in Armed Conflict, Advisory Opinion, ICJ Reports 1996 66 para 15.
[20] Ibid., Dissenting Opinion of Judge Weeramantry 451.
[21] Please note that the terms 'evidentiary' and 'evidential' are used interchangeably throughout, owing to their synonymous nature and reflecting the common use of both terms in practice. 'Evidential' is historically the older term and is more prominent in British English, with 'evidentiary' (invented by J. Bentham in his 'Elements of the Art of Packing...' in 1821 or J. Mill in his 'History of British India, Volume III' according to the Oxford English Dictionary) being used more often in American English.
[22] *Armed Activities on the Territory of the Congo (Democratic Republic of the Congo v. Uganda), Judgment, ICJ Reports 2005* 168, 239, 116 para 24.
[23] *Application of the Convention on the Prevention and Punishment of the Crime of Genocide (Bosnia and Herzegovina v. Serbia and Montenegro), Judgment, ICJ Reports 2007* 43, 91.
[24] *Whaling in the Antarctic (Australia v. Japan: New Zealand intervening)*, Judgment, 31 March 2014, at para 67.

cases that have become commonplace in recent times.[25] The factually complicated nature of the *Pulp Mills* case was summed up well in the Dissenting Opinion of Judge Cançado Trindade, who stated that 'by and large, conflicting evidence seems to make the paradise of lawyers and practitioners, at national and international levels. It seems to make, likewise, the purgatory of judges and fact-finders, at national and international levels.' However, Judge Cançado Trindade went on to say that '[c]onsideration of this issue cannot be avoided'[26] and there is no doubt that this is so. Whilst the factually complex nature of cases regularly coming before the Court might be akin to purgatory for it, it is clear that such issues can no longer be avoided. In fact, if current trends are to continue, as former President of the Court Judge Rosalyn Higgins stated in her address to the Sixth Committee of the General Assembly in 2007, such 'fact-heavy' cases are likely to be a constant feature of the Court's work in the future.[27]

Accordingly, it is a feature of modern international adjudication that complex factual issues are commonplace and that the handling of these issues is an integral part of the international judicial function.[28] It is clear that the Court's approach to the facts ought to reflect this. However, before we turn our attention to the Court's current approach to fact-finding (and recent criticisms of this approach) it is necessary to first consider just why factual determinations matter in international adjudication.

It can be anticipated that the consistently factually complex nature of contemporary international litigation will not be universally accepted as presenting any meaningful challenges for the Court and for international law as a whole. For instance, one may argue that the establishment of the

---

[25] *Pulp Mills Case*, Dissenting Opinion of Judges Al-Khasawneh and Simma at para 3.
[26] Ibid., Dissenting Opinion of Judge Cançado Trindade at para 148.
[27] Judge Higgins stated that '[t]he judicial determination of relevant facts will be an ever more important task for the Court' and cited the *Case Concerning Land Reclamation by Singapore in and around the Straights of Johor (Malaysia v. Singapore) Provisional Measures, International Tribunal for the Law of the Sea, Order of 8 October 2003*, in which 4,000 pages of annexes were put before the Court; see Higgins, 'Speech by H. E. Judge Rosalyn Higgins, President of the International Court of Justice to the Sixth Committee of the General Assembly'.
[28] In the words of Rosenne, '[t]here is no question that modern international relations, and hence modern diplomacy and modern international litigation, is daily becoming increasingly concerned with scientific and technological facts'; see 'Fact-Finding before the International Court of Justice' in S. Rosenne, *Essays on International Law and Practice* (The Hague: Martinus Nijhoff, 2007); Makane Moïse Mbengue, 'Scientific Fact-finding by International Courts and Tribunals' 3 *Journal of International Dispute Settlement* 509, 512; *Nuclear Tests (New Zealand v. France), Judgment, ICJ Reports 1974* 457 para 30.

facts is a secondary concern in inter-State adjudication where the primary task of the tribunal is to settle the dispute before it.[29] As one commentator has stated, 'it can be argued that the ultimate purpose of international adjudication is not establishing the facts, or truths, even, The Truth, but rather to settle the dispute'.[30] This is a position that has carried great weight over the years and is one which is supported by the historical preference of the Court to decide cases on questions of law rather than the facts.

In the past it has been argued that well-reasoned judgments based in the law rather than decided on technical issues of fact have traditionally been perceived as being of a higher prestige and consequently somehow less offensive to the State party on the wrong end of the judgment.[31] This argument in some way ties in with the deference shown to States as a result of their sovereign nature (a point to be examined in greater detail in Section 1.3.3. below) and the belief that in international litigation, with often so much at stake, 'technicalities are taboo'.[32] In addition, international judges, educated in one particular legal system, often hail from domestic appellate courts which in general do not deal with complex factual issues, these having been determined by the lower trial courts.[33]

---

[29] The situation being somewhat different in relation to international criminal law, see N. A. Combs, *Fact-Finding Without Facts: The Uncertain Evidentiary Foundations of International Criminal Convictions* (Cambridge University Press, 2010); R. Mackenzie et al., *The Manual on International Courts and Tribunals* (2nd edn, Oxford University Press, 2010); Tim Kelsall, *Culture under Cross-Examination: International Justice and the Special Court for Sierra Leone* (Cambridge University Press, 2009).

[30] C. Romano, 'The Role of Experts in International Adjudication' (2009) Société Française Pour le droit International.

[31] A number of reasons have been cited as potential explanations for the Court's traditional predilection for questions of law over questions of fact such as a reluctance or inability to conduct independent fact-finding and the domestic judicial experience of the judges of the Court. See R. R. Bilder, 'The Fact/Law Distinction in International Adjudication' in R. B. Lillich (ed), *Fact-finding before International Tribunals* (Irvington-on-Hudson, NY: Transnational, 1992) 97; Foster, 'New Clothes for the Emperor? Consultation of Experts by the International Court of Justice' 28.

[32] D. V. Sandifer, *Evidence Before International Tribunals*, Vol 13 (University Press of Virginia, 1975) 22; it could be argued that technical or more nuanced judgments allow both sides to claim a victory of sorts, as in the case of the *Bosnian Genocide* case; see www.nytimes.com/2007/02/26/world/europe/26cnd-hague.html.

[33] On this issue see Daniel Terris, Cesare P. R. Romano and Leigh Swigart, *The International Judge: An Introduction to the Men and Women Who Decide the World's Cases* (Oxford University Press, 2007) 20, who note that out of 215 judges in their study, approximately one third (70) came from national domestic courts, one third (85) from academia and one third (60) from civil service, both national and international.

As such, it is not difficult to imagine that this attitude towards facts – that, having already been dealt with by lower courts, they require no further attention – could easily be carried over to the International Court (even if only subconsciously).[34]

However, such arguments founder in the face of the consistent practice of the ICJ since its inception. Specifically, the submissions of the parties and the practice of the Court in every case of insisting on establishing the factual basis of the case before it necessarily shows that the Court views its own function as making judgments that are not merely legal abstractions but that in reality accord with the facts.

Article 49 of the Rules of the Court stipulates that States are required to submit a Memorial to the Court[35] that shall contain 'a statement of the relevant facts' and that the resulting Counter-Memorial must contain an admission or denial of these facts.[36] This ensures, in the words of Rosenne, 'the presentation and airing of the facts and of any arguments on them throughout the written proceedings in every contentious case'.[37] Similarly, if a case is brought before the Court on the basis of a unilateral application, it must contain a succinct statement of the facts, and the subsequent pleadings require the systematic developments of each party's statement of the facts.[38] In short, this provision explicitly confirms that facts will play a part in any case that comes before the Court in one way or another.

In addition, Article 36(2)(c) of the Court's Statute gives the Court jurisdiction over disputes concerning 'the existence of any fact which, if established, would constitute a breach of an international obligation'. Although this provision deals specifically with cases brought under the optional clause, it also gives a good indication of what would be considered a 'legal dispute' under Article 36(1) of the Statute, establishing the Court's jurisdiction.[39] Such provisions, at the heart of the operation of

---

[34] This argument has been made by Lauterpacht, who in the context of the influence on the law of evidence of the majority of judges coming from what he terms 'the Roman law systems of law' has argued that 'the probability is that they would tend to apply the rules of evidence obtaining in their own legal systems and disregard those applied by Common Law courts.' See H. Lauterpacht, 'The So-Called Anglo-American and Continental Schools of Thought in International Law' 12 *British Yearbook of International Law* 31, 37.
[35] Under Article 43 of the Statute and 45 of the Rules of the Court.
[36] Article 49(1) and 49(2) of the Rules of the Court.
[37] Rosenne, *Essays on International Law and Practice* 235.
[38] Article 38(1) of the Rules of the Court.
[39] Highet, 'Evidence, the Court, and the Nicaragua Case' 5.

the Court since 1920, highlight the centrality of facts in the Court's work. The Court cannot change the general procedural rules set out in its Statute pertaining to evidence. As the Court stated in the *Nicaragua* case, it is 'bound by the relevant provisions of its Statute and Rules relating to the system of evidence, provisions devised to guarantee the sound administration of justice, while respecting the equality of the parties'.[40] Alternatively, in the words of Georg Schwarzenberger, 'individual parties to cases before the Court have but a limited choice: they may take the Statute as they find it or leave it'.[41]

Whilst a former President of the Court once remarked that international lawyers tend to think a lot about the law and perhaps too little about procedure and the finding of facts, there is no doubt that the Court itself considers the establishment of a sound factual basis as an essential part of the judicial function.[42] Ensuring that the Court's decisions are 'founded on a sure foundation of fact'[43] has been very much a central part of the international judicial function and this can be evidenced by the time and effort dedicated to this process in each and every case before the Court.[44] The Court itself has stated that it sees the establishment of the facts as a prerequisite in any case that comes before it: '[the Court] will first make its own determination of the facts and then apply the relevant rules of international law to the facts which it has found to have existed'.[45]

The Court is one of both first and last instance meaning that unlike certain domestic Constitutional Courts, the establishment of the facts is

---

[40] See *Nicaragua Case* 39 at 59 ; I. Scobbie, 'Discontinuance in the International Court: The Enigma of the Nuclear Tests Cases' 41 *International and Comparative Law Quarterly* 808, 810; Scobbie states that the Court is bound by its rules of procedure for a good reason – to provide an element of predictability for States before the Court and to prevent ad hoc or arbitrary modifications that deny any guarantee of consistency (ibid.), 'International Court of Justice: Resolution Concerning the Internal Judical Practice of the Court' [American Society of International Law] 70 *The American Journal of International Law* 905; see further Robert Kolb, *The International Court of Justice* (Oxford: Hart, 2013) 942.

[41] Georg Schwarzenberger, *International Law – As Applied by International Courts and Tribunals* (London: Stevens & Sons, 1968) 413.

[42] Rosalyn Higgins, 'Introductory Remarks by Rosalyn Higgins' 106 *Proceedings of the Annual Meeting (American Society of International Law)* 229, 229.

[43] See Lord Justice Bingham in *Air Canada and Others Appellants v. Secretary of State for Trade and Another Respondents* (1983) 2 W.L.R. 494; A. L. Marriott, 'Evidence in International Arbitration' 5 *Arbitration International* 280, 281.

[44] Higgins, 'Introductory Remarks by Rosalyn Higgins' 229.

[45] See *Armed Activities Case* 200 para 57.

an essential part of the Court's function.[46] As the Court stated in *Pulp Mills*:

> [I]t is the responsibility of the Court, after having given careful consideration to all the evidence placed before it by the Parties, to determine which facts must be considered relevant, to assess their probative value, and to draw conclusions from them as appropriate ... the Court will make its own determination of the facts, on the basis of the evidence presented to it, and then it will apply the relevant rules of international law to those facts which it has found to have existed.[47]

And it would appear that the same goes for advisory opinions. The Court has in the past addressed arguments such as those of South Africa in the *Namibia* case, in which it was argued that since advisory opinions could only be given on legal questions, the Court ought to refuse to give an advisory opinion where doing so would entail a factual determination.[48] However, the Court in this case (and in subsequent cases) rejected this argument outright.[49]

As such, it is clear that the Court considers the determination of the facts as an essentially important part of the judicial function. This can be seen in the substantial amount of time dedicated to pleadings on the facts in cases that come before the Court and as a result the issue of how the Court deals with facts and the current deficiencies of its current approach to be considered in subsequent chapters, are issues deserving of our attention.[50]

Additionally, with a number of high-profile cases currently before the Court such as the joined cases between Costa Rica and Nicaragua[51] and

---

[46] K. Highet, 'Evidence and Proof of Facts' in Lori F. Damrosch (ed), *The International Court of Justice at a Crossroads* (Dobbs Ferry, NY: Transnational, 1987) 355; Franck, 'Fact-finding in the I.C.J.' 21; C. J. Tams, 'Article 51' in A. Zimmermann (ed), *The Staute of the International Court of Justice: A Commentary* (Oxford University Press, 2006) 1301; however see section 2.1.4. for some critical comments on how the Court often relies on fact-finding commissions in order to establish the facts and a discussion as to whether this is a delegation of the Court's judicial function.

[47] *Pulp Mills Case* para 162; see also paras 163 and 168.

[48] Pleadings, *Namibia Advisory Opinion*, Vol. 1, 143 para 45.

[49] *Legal Consequences for States of the Continued Presence of South Africa in Namibia (South West Africa) notwithstanding Security Council Resolution 276 (1970), Advisory Opinion*, ICJ Reports 1971 16, 27 para 40.

[50] Kolb, *The International Court of Justice* 928.

[51] *Cases concerning Construction of a Road in Costa Rica along the San Juan River (Nicaragua v. Costa Rica); Certain Activities carried out by Nicaragua in the Border Area (Costa Rica v. Nicaragua)*.

the recent proceedings instituted by Nicaragua against Columbia regarding delimitation of the continental shelf between these two States,[52] it would appear that the need for consideration of such issues is more pressing than ever.[53]

Different domestic legal systems employ broadly different approaches to the key issues of the law of evidence.[54] For instance, in proceedings before a court in a common law jurisdiction 'the truth is presumed to lie somewhere between the opposing positions of the two parties' and as such the judge's role is an adversarial one – that of a disinterested umpire, presiding over the enforcement of the rules of evidence and adjudicating on the competing assertions of the parties.[55] On the other hand, in proceedings before a court in a civil law jurisdiction, the role of the judge is inquisitorial – traditionally playing a much more active role in establishing the facts in any case before it.[56] One thing that all the

---

[52] See ICJ Press Release No. 2013/21, 17 September 2013, www.icj-cij.org/docket/files/154/17530.pdf.

[53] *Certain Activities Carried out by Nicaragua in the Border Area (Costa Rica v. Nicaragua)*, Joinder of Proceedings, Order of 27 April 2013, joining the proceedings in the cases of *Certain Activities Carried out by Nicaragua in the Border Area (Costa Rica v. Nicaragua)*, Application Instituting Proceedings, 18 November 2010, and *Construction of a Road in Costa Rica along the San Juan River (Nicaragua v. Costa Rica)* Application Instituting Proceedings, 21 December 2011; and indeed until the removal of the case from the docket of the Court at the request of the Republic of Ecuador, the *Aerial Spraying* case looked as if it would raise many pertinent issues in this regard also; see ICJ Press Release No. 2013/20, 17 September 2013, *Aerial Herbicide Spraying (Ecuador v. Colombia)*, www.icj-cij.org/docket/files/138/17526.pdf.

[54] Evidence defined as: 'the material submitted by a party to a dispute, on its own initiative or at the Court's request, to prove a fact alleged or a legal title claimed'; see International Court of Justice. Registry, United Nations Institute for Training and Research, *A Dialogue at the Court: Proceedings of the ICJ/UNITAR Colloquium Held on the Occasion of the Sixtieth Anniversary of the International Court of Justice, at the Peace Palace on 10 and 11 April 2006* (The Hague: International Court of Justice, Registry of the Court, 2007) 25, whereas Proof is defined as 'any effort that attempts to establish the truth or fact, something serving as evidence, a convincing token or argument; the effect of evidence; the establishment of fact by evidence'. See also 'proof is the result or effect of evidence, while "evidence" is the medium or means by which a fact is proved or disproved', F. J. Ludes and H. J. Gilbert (eds), *Corpus Juris Secundum: A Complete Restatement of the Entire American Law, Vol 31 A: Evidence* (St Paul: West Publishing, 1964) 820; F. J. Ludes and H. Gilbert, 'Corpus Juris Secundum, Vol. 35' (Brooklyn: American Law Book Company), 820 cited in Riddell and Plant, *Evidence before the International Court of Justice* 79.

[55] Riddell and Plant, *Evidence before the International Court of Justice* 1.

[56] See Roger Derham and Nicole Derham, 'From Ad Hoc to Hybrid – The Rules and Regulations Governing Reception of Expert Evidence at the International Criminal Court' 14 *International Journal of Evidence and Proof* 25, 33.

major domestic legal systems have in common, however, is that they all possess detailed and sophisticated rules of evidence that are routinely applied in civil and criminal cases which come before their judicial bodies.

Rules of evidence and procedure in international adjudication, on the other hand, were for a long time somewhat of a misnomer. As one commentator has noted, 'the typical evidentiary regime in international proceedings can be characterized by the generality, liberality and scarcity of its provisions'.[57] Several important factors explain why detailed rules of evidence of the type common to domestic legal systems never developed in international litigation including (but not limited to)[58] the influence of the evidentiary regime of international arbitration[59] and the sovereign nature of the parties to international adjudication[60] which necessitates what has been called 'an obligation to accommodate as far as possible each litigating State's notion of the most appropriate way of

---

[57] Riddell and Plant, *Evidence before the International Court of Justice* 2; M. Grando, *Evidence, Proof, and Fact-Finding in WTO Dispute Settlement* (Oxford University Press, 2009) 12.

[58] Further factors include the dual trial and appeal function of the Court, the binding nature of its decisions and the impossibility of appeal. Gattini has also suggested that courts themselves are unwilling to constrain the way they operate, being 'too unwilling to constrain themselves by the authority of a given precedent or a given set of rules, in the absence of clear indications in their statutes'; A. Gattini, 'Evidentiary Issues in the ICJ's Genocide Judgment' 5 *Journal of International Criminal Justice* 889, 899; see also G. Niyungeko and J. A. S. Salmon, *La preuve devant les juridictions internationales* (Louvain-La-Neuve, Belgium: Bruylant, 2005) 413.

[59] As Lauterpacht characterised the situation in 1931, 'no specific rules as to evidence and proof have so far evolved in international arbitration. But there has been a general tendency, sanctioned by a long series of arbitral pronouncements, to disregard elaborate restrictions upon the admissibility of evidence and to accept the principle that no evidence should be excluded a *limine* and that it should be left to the judge to appreciate the weight and persuasiveness of the evidence put before him.' In this regard, the *Parker* case of March 1926 before the American-Mexican Mixed Claims Commission (where the Commissioners expressly refused to be bound by restrictive and purely technical rules of proof and evidence) is cited as an example. Lauterpacht also notes that the same view was expressed by Professor Huber in the *Island of Palmas* Arbitration; Lauterpacht, 'The So-Called Anglo-American and Continental Schools of Thought in International Law' 42.

[60] The equality of parties is a generally accepted principle of international adjudication; see Rüdger Wolfrum, 'International Courts and Tribunals, Evidence' *Max Planck Encyclopedia of Public International Law* ; Valencia-Ospina, 'Evidence before the International Court of Justice' 202: '[w]hen litigants are sovereign States, it is perhaps only logical for them to have the main initiative and responsibility in regard to the production of evidence'. See also T. M. Franck, *Fairness in International Law and Institutions* (Oxford: Clarendon Press, 2002) 336: 'compelled disclosure is inconsistent with the nature of sovereignty'.

presenting and substantiating its own version of events'.[61] A further reason for the relative scarcity of rules of evidence in international litigation is the nature of the cases brought before it. Cases routinely centre around issues such as national security, sovereignty and other such crucially important matters. When dealing with matters of such import in international litigation technicalities are very much seen as taboo.[62] The rationale is that the outcome of a case based on a technicality relating to the law of evidence would be unlikely to aid the desired settlement of the dispute at hand.[63] As Sir Hersch Lauterpacht stated, 'the importance of the interests at stake precludes the excessive or decisive reliance upon formal and technical rules'.[64]

But what is the role of the International Court of Justice in establishing the facts in cases brought before it and can its evidentiary regime too be characterised as one governed by the generality, liberality and scarcity of its provisions? This question will be addressed in the next chapter which will evaluate the evidentiary provisions of the Court's Statute and Rules and the fact-finding powers that the Court possesses and consider the extent to which it has utilised those powers in practice.

---

[61] Riddell and Plant, *Evidence before the International Court of Justice* 2; The Court addressed equality of the parties in the *Nicaragua* case, stating '[t]he provisions of the Statute and the Rules of the Court concerning the presentation of pleadings and evidence are designed to secure a proper administration of justice, and a fair and equal opportunity for each party to comment on its opponent's contention'; see *Nicaragua Case* at para 31.

[62] Sandifer, *Evidence before International Tribunals* 22.

[63] See Court in *Free Zones of Upper Savoy and the District of Gex* (1932) PCIJ Series A/B, No 46, 155–6, in which the Court rejected Switzerland's argument that evidence presented by France late in the oral proceedings should be inadmissible, stating 'the decision of an international dispute of the present order should not depend mainly on a point of procedure'.

[64] H. Lauterpacht, *The Development of International Law by the International Court* (Cambridge University Press, 2011) 366; to this end see also Article 19 of the Nuremberg Charter which states that '[t]he Tribunal shall not be bound by technical rules of evidence. It shall adopt and apply to the greatest possible extent expeditious and non-technical procedure, and shall admit any evidence which it deems to have probative value', which is a good example in this regard.

# 1

# Rules of evidence before the International Court of Justice

This chapter evaluates the evidentiary provisions of the Court's Statute and Rules of Court and the fact-finding powers that the Court possesses in order to consider the extent to which it has utilised those powers in practice. It will be shown that whilst the Court in fact possesses relatively broad fact-finding powers, due to a number of factors it has never made use of them to any significant extent. Instead, the Court operates under extremely broad rules of admissibility of evidence that allow almost any piece of evidence to come before the Court that the State parties so choose. That the Court operates in this manner is to a large extent necessitated by the principles of State sovereignty and equality that espouse that States should be able to choose what evidence they place before the Court. Further, the Court is shackled by resource and time constraints that make independent fact-finding in each and every case largely impractical. As a result of its truncated fact-finding role, the Court's fact-assessment role takes on added significance, an issue examined in the second half of the chapter.

### (i) The development of the rules of evidence before the International Court of Justice

Rules of evidence and procedure before international courts and tribunals seek to enable them to establish a factual foundation upon which to base legal determinations, even where the parties before the tribunal cannot come to an agreement on the facts relating to the dispute.[1] The provisions of the Court's Statute relating to evidence were adopted by the First Committee on Draft Statute during the United Nations Conference on International Organization (UNCIO), being 'greatly facilitated' by the Washington Committee of Jurists who had met prior to the San

---

[1] M. Benzing, 'Evidentiary Issues' in A. Zimmermann et al. (eds), *The Statute of the International Court of Justice* (2nd edn, Oxford University Press, 2012) 1236.

Francisco Conference from 9 to 20 April 1945 to undertake an article-by-article revision of the Statute of the Permanent Court of International Justice (PCIJ).[2] The draft adopted by First Committee took the report of the Washington Committee of Jurists as the basis of its discussions and many articles ('particularly those relating to procedure') were taken over without substantial amendment.[3] In fact, the following provisions relating to the Court's fact-finding powers were adopted at the UNCIO without amendment or deliberation, as the First Commission 'unanimously approved without discussion, Articles 39–64 *en bloc* of draft Statute of the Committee of Jurists'.[4] The Court's powers are also supplemented by those contained within the Rules of the Court, most recently updated in 1978. The following section sets out to examine briefly the fact-finding powers that the Court possesses before we turn our attention to the extent to which the Court has made use of these powers in the subsequent subsections of this chapter.

## 1.1 The fact-finding powers of the International Court of Justice

The Statute of the International Court of Justice and its Rules of Procedure endow the Court with considerable fact-finding powers. Although the fact-finding powers set out in the Court's Statute and Rules are broad enough to allow the Court substantial autonomy and flexibility in terms of its evidentiary procedure, the provisions themselves are not particularly detailed.[5] This lack of specificity is most probably due to the influence of the PCIJ whose statute contained similarly sparse evidentiary provisions and the fact that, having primarily dealt with cases involving the application of

---

[2] UN Doc 875 IV/1/74, 9 June 1945 – Committee 1 – ICJ – Draft Report of Rapporteur of Committee IV/1.

[3] Report of Committee of Jurists reproduced in Annex 4. Articles 49–51 exactly the same in draft as in final edition. Text of Report omitted; reproduced in full as Jurist 86 G/73 in Vol XIV. See also 1st Meeting Commission IV, Rapporteur Progress Report, 'the Court has been empowered to promulgate rules in order to exercise its various functions especially in the field of procedure'. UN Doc. 435 IV/7, 19 May 1945.

[4] UN Doc. 264 IV/1/18, 12 May 1945, Committee 1, ICJ.

[5] E. Valencia-Ospina, 'Evidence before the International Court of Justice' 4 *International Law Forum du droit international* 202; Sir Arthur Watts, 'Burden of Proof and Evidence before the ICJ' in F. Weiss (ed), *Improving WTO Dispute Settlement Procedures: Issues and Lessons from the Practice of Other International Courts and Tribunals* (London: Cameron May, 2000) 300.

treaties, the PCIJ 'was in a position to establish and rely on facts that were not in dispute between the parties, obviating, in most cases, the need for detailed rules of evidence.'[6] That having been said, the Court is endowed with a number of significant fact-finding powers which deserve to be considered in greater detail.

### 1.1.1  The power to make orders

Article 48 of the Court's Statute is a general provision that represents a central pillar of the Court's statutory fact-finding powers, providing that the Court 'shall make orders for the conduct of the case, shall decide the form and time in which each party must conclude its arguments, and make all arrangements connected with the taking of evidence.' In utilising its statutory powers to obtain evidentiary information through site visits, requesting evidence from the parties, establishing a commission of inquiry or seeking an expert opinion, by putting questions to the parties, or by requesting a public international organisation to bring information before it,[7] (all considered below) the Court must necessarily make use of orders under Article 48. Article 48 has been described as both 'a guarantee for the orderly taking of evidence' and the 'general provision governing arrangement concerning the taking of evidence'[8] although it need not be explicitly referred to by the Court when making orders.[9] Having considered this important general provision it is necessary to take a closer look at the Court's specific fact-finding powers as set out in its Statute and Rules of Procedure.

### 1.1.2  The power to make site visits

The Court has the power to take steps to proactively 'procure evidence on the spot'. Article 44, paragraph 2 of the Court's Statute makes specific provision for the possibility of such site visits.[10] Such visits

---

[6]  Valencia-Ospina, 'Evidence before the International Court of Justice' 202.
[7]  Articles 44(2), 49, 50, 51 and 34 of the Statute respectively.
[8]  S. T. Bernárdez, 'Article 48' in A. Zimmermann (ed), *The Statute of the International Court of Justice: A Commentary* (Oxford University Press, 2006) 1097.
[9]  Examples include the commissions of inquiry established in the *Corfu Channel Case* and *Delimitation of the Maritime Boundary in the Gulf of Maine Area, Judgment, ICJ Reports 1984*, 246, and the site visit in the *Gabčikovo-Nagymaros Case*.
[10]  Article 44, paragraph 1 of the Court's Statute underlines that the Court cannot summon witnesses and experts directly but must instead act through national institutions and 'as such depends on the application of the municipal law of the State concerned'.

are limited to those undertaken by the full bench of the Court[11] as a result of a decision of the Court and must be distinguished from unofficial visits to the site and visits by experts which cannot be considered as falling under this provision.[12] The practice of the Court in this regard has meant that the importance of Article 44 is somewhat limited.[13] The rare example of a site visit in the practice of the Court is the visit made in the *Gabčikovo* case during which the agent of Slovakia invited the Court to 'visit the locality to which the case relates and there to exercise its functions with regards to the obtaining of evidence, in accordance with Article 66 of the Rules of the Court'.[14] The Court subsequently visited various sites along the river Danube that were at the heart of the dispute between Slovakia and Hungary and 'took note of the technical explanations given by the representatives who had been designated for the purpose by the Parties'.[15] Despite the fact that Judge Schwebel described the site visit in this case as providing the Court with 'a new dimension of insight into the case and what it meant to the Parties much more than could have been gleaned confining the proceedings to The Hague',[16] the site visit in *Gabčikovo* remains the exceptional case in the practice of the Court.[17]

---

[11] It is thought that a delegation or committee of judges, such as was the suggestion of Judge Schwebel in the *Nicaragua* case (see Dissenting Opinion of Judge Schwebel at para 132) would be contrary to 'general considerations of proper administration of justice', which are thought to require a visit by the full Court; see Christian Walter, 'Article 44' in A. Zimmermann (ed), *The Statute of the International Court of Justice: A Commentary* (Oxford University Press, 2006) 1043; M. Bedjaoui, 'La "Descente sur les lieux" dans la pratique de la Cour International de Justice et de sa devanciere' in Gerhard Hafner (ed), *Liber Amicorum Professor Ignaz Seidl-Hohenveldern in Honour of His 80th Birthday* (The Hague: Martinus Nijhoff, 1998) 9.

[12] Such as in the *Corfu Channel Case, Decision of the Court dated 17 January 1949*, in which the commission of experts was asked by the Court to visit the area to clarify certain aspects of the case, which would fall under Articles 48 and 50; see Walter, 'Article 44' 1042.

[13] Walter, 'Article 44' 1041.

[14] *Gabčikovo-Nagymaros Case*, para 10, although the Permanent Court did also do so in *Diversion of Water from the Meuse* (Netherlands/Belgium), Order of 13 May 1937, PCIJ, Series C, No 81, pp 53; see Higgins, 'Speech by H. E. Judge Rosalyn Higgins, President of the International Court of Justice to the Sixth Committee of the General Assembly'.

[15] *Gabčikovo-Nagymaros Case*, para 10.

[16] Schwebel, 'Speech of the President of the International Court of Justice to the General Assembly'.

[17] Ibid., stating that 'one can imagine only some contentious cases where the situation on the ground may lend itself to carrying out a site visit'.

Importantly, whilst such site visits can technically be ordered by the Court without the consent of the parties *proprio motu*,[18] in practice such a visit without the consent of the State to whose territory the Court will 'descend' will in all likelihood not be practicable (although the Court has never stated lack of consent as a reason for not ordering such a site visit).[19] These visits appear to have an 'illustrative function' in helping the Court to 'understand better the localities in question', their main advantage being that in cases in which technical or scientific facts are disputed between the parties, the visit may provide a helpful background to the complex facts.[20] To date this illustrative function of site visits has 'prevailed over any type of evidence gathering and evaluation, which one might also envisage.'[21] In light of factually complex cases coming before the Court, whilst it is possible to imagine that more use could be made of this provision in terms of gathering evidence, the utility of a bench of judges who are not necessarily experts in the particular area under investigation visiting the site could be said to be limited when compared to the establishment of a commission of experts, for example. Perhaps this could explain why this provision has not been often mentioned in relation to making greater use of the Court's statutory fact-finding powers.

### 1.1.3 The power to intervene in and direct proceedings and ask questions

Either prior to or during proceedings the Court under Article 61 of the Rules may indicate what points or issues it would like the parties to address specifically or on which issues it considers there has been sufficient argument. Articles 61(2) and (3) provide that any judge may at any time during the oral proceedings put questions to 'agents, counsel and advocates' and ask for explanations, which may be answered immediately but usually will be answered in accordance with the timeframes set by the President.[22] In practice the Court has generally limited itself to individual

---

[18] Walter, 'Article 44' 1043, Bedjaoui, 'La "Descente sur les lieux" dans la pratique de la Cour International de Justice et de sa devanciere' 7.
[19] Walter, 'Article 44' 1044.     [20] Ibid.     [21] Ibid.
[22] See Article 61(4) Rules of the Court; C. E. Foster, *Science and the Precautionary Principle in International Courts and Tribunals: Expert Evidence, Burden of Proof and Finality* (Cambridge University Press, 2011) 87, quoting Rosenne and Ronen, *The Law and Practice of the International Court, 1920–2005* 1299; Riddell and Plant, *Evidence before the International Court of Justice* 312.

judges occasionally asking questions from the bench during the oral proceedings.[23] As we will see in Chapter 3, practice before the ICJ differs substantially from that before the World Trade Organization (WTO) adjudicative bodies, which regularly put longer questions to the parties. Foster has argued the WTO panels are able for example 'to pursue the development of a thorough understanding of all aspects of the case by means of specific, direct questions to the parties after each of the oral hearings, or substantive meetings with the parties'.[24] The issue of whether the Court ought to develop a similar practice will be examined in greater detail in Chapter 4 (at Section 4.3.2).

### 1.1.4 The power to request information from the parties

Relatedly, Article 49 of the Court's Statute contains what has been called the 'central prerogative' of any international court or tribunal[25] to participate in hearings before it.[26] It must be read in conjunction with Article 62(1) of the Court's Rules which states that '[t]he Court may at any time call upon the parties to produce evidence or to give such explanations as the Court may consider to be necessary for the elucidation of any aspect of the matters in issue, or may itself seek other information for this purpose'.[27] In practical terms, Article 49 confers on the Court the ability to become actively involved in proceedings before it by conferring two distinct powers. Article 49 firstly, together with Article 50, regulates the obtaining of evidence by the Court itself (as opposed to the evidence submitted by the parties as part of their pleadings) by calling upon the parties 'to produce any document or to supply any explanations'.[28] In other words, Article 49 sets out a general power of the Court to request further documents.[29] Secondly, Article

---

[23] Riddell and Plant, *Evidence before the International Court of Justice* 88; see for instance *Pulp Mills Case*.

[24] Foster, *Science and the Precautionary Principle in International Courts and Tribunals* 88; See for instance *Brazil – Measures Affecting Import of Retreaded Tyres*, Complaint by the European Communities (WT/DS332), Report of the Appellate Body DSR 2007: IV, 1527, Report of the Panel DSR 2007: V, 1649.

[25] See also Rule 77 ITLOS Rules of Procedure, ICSID Convention Article 43(a); ICSID Arbitration Rules, Rule 34(2); Article 24(3) Rules of Procedure of the Iran-US Claims Tribunal.

[26] Article 49, ICJ Statute; Article 62, Rules of the International Court of Justice, 1978, ICJ Acts & Docs 4 (as amended 14 April 2005).

[27] Article 62(1) Rules of the Court.    [28] Pleadings, VVol IV 428 in *Corfu Channel Case*.

[29] Separate from another special means: Article 66 of the Rules.

49 provides the Court with the power to request further explanation or clarification from the parties, such as information on questions of law or fact.

As such, the scope of Article 49 is considerable, covering requests for fresh evidence and clarification of existing evidence, both documentary and testimonial evidence even before the hearing has commenced.[30] Crucially, Article 49 is silent on the issue of whether States are under a legal obligation to disclose information – an issue discussed in greater detail in Chapter 4 at Section 4.1. In relation to refusal to comply with the Court's request for information, under Article 49, 'formal note shall be taken of any refusal'.[31] However, the Court has not done so in practice thus far and whether it would choose to do so would very much depend on the circumstances of each case.[32] The merits of more regularly drawing adverse inferences as is the practice before other international courts and tribunals will also be considered in Section 4.2.6.

### 1.1.5 The power to establish an inquiry or seek expert evidence

Article 50 of the Court's Statute gives the Court the power to call upon individuals or institutions to provide expert advice or institute an inquiry.[33] The Court has never called a witness *proprio motu* and as such this issue will not be addressed in the following section although Higgins has stated that calling witnesses *proprio motu* 'is a possibility that is constantly in its view'.[34] The following section will first assess the Court's power to call upon individual experts under Article 50 before considering the related power to establish commissions of inquiry.

---

[30] See Article 62 Rules of the Court, *United States Diplomatic and Consular Staff in Tehran (United States of America v. Iran), Judgment, ICJ Reports 1980* 10 at 7, 10, para 7; see Tams, 'Article 49' 1102.

[31] Article 49 sentence 2.

[32] Tams, 'Article 49' 1106, for example, in the *Corfu Channel Case* 4 the Court stated that it accepted the reasons given for the UK's refusal to hand over requested document XCU.

[33] Article 50 states that 'The Court may, at any time, entrust any individual, body, bureau, commission, or other organization that it may select, with the task of carrying out an enquiry or giving an expert opinion.'

[34] Higgins, 'Speech by H. E. Judge Rosalyn Higgins, President of the International Court of Justice to the Sixth Committee of the General Assembly'; S. Talmon, 'Article 43' in A. Zimmermann et al. (eds), *The Statute of the International Court of Justice: A Commentary* (2nd edn, Oxford University Press, 2012), see paras 133–6.

### 1.1.5 (i)  Court-appointed experts

The Court under Article 50 of its Statute, as elaborated in Article 62(2) of its Rules, has the power to appoint an expert to advise it on the case at hand.[35] The Court has not made use of this power to date except in the *Gulf of Maine* case in which Canada and the United States specifically requested the Chamber to appoint experts to assist in determining the maritime boundary and other technical matters.[36] The Chamber appointed Commander P. B. Beazley to assist it in technical matters regarding the maritime boundary and the expert's report was annexed to the judgment (see Section 1.1.5 (ii) regarding Article 50 experts appointed by the Court).[37] The usefulness of Commander Beazley's assistance is disputed.[38]

Interestingly, in the *Case Concerning the Frontier Dispute (Burkina Faso v. Mali)* Article IV(3) of the 1983 Special Agreement in which the parties agreed to submit their frontier dispute to a Chamber of the Court requests the Chamber 'to nominate, in its Judgment, three experts to

---

[35] Article 62(2) states that 'The Court may, if necessary, arrange for the attendance of a witness or expert to give evidence in the proceedings'.

[36] See Article II(3) *Case Concerning Delimitation of the Maritime Boundary in the Gulf of Maine Area (Canada v. United States of America)*, Special Agreement, 25 November 1981.

[37] *Delimitation of the Maritime Boundary in the Gulf of Maine Area (Canada/United States of America), (Appointment of Expert, Order of 30 March 1984, ICJ Reports 1984)* 165, *Gulf of Maine Case*; see Technical Report annexed to the Judgment, ibid., 347–52, 353 para 3 (Art. II para 3 of the Special Agreement).

[38] For instance, Highet, 'Evidence, the Court, and the Nicaragua Case' 27; *Gulf of Maine Case* 273–8 states that 'the Chamber did not find that any of this technical evidence was relevant or determinative; instead, it based its opinion primarily on a geographical solution and essentially ignored the factual controversies concerning aspects other than geography', whilst Riddell, 'Scientific Evidence in the International Court of Justice – Problems and Possibilities' 238; has stated that '[t]he expert's involvement in this respect is not strictly the situation envisaged in Article 50 but seems to have worked relatively well in this case, with the expert assisting in several technical aspects of the case such as the preparation of a technical map in relation to the maritime delimitation and being available for consultation by the Chamber throughout the course of proceedings.' See also *Case Concerning the Arbitral Award of 31 July 1989 (Guinea-Bissau v. Senegal), Judgment, ICJ Reports 1991* 53, in which Article 9(2) of the Agreement between the parties stated that if the Agreement was found not to be in force then the Court would delimit the boundary: 'That decision shall include the drawing of the boundary line on a map. To that end, the Tribunal shall be empowered to appoint one or more technical experts to assist it in the preparation of such a map.' Ultimately, however, the pre-existing agreement was found to be in force that this provision did not come into play and the dispute was later removed from the Court's docket.

assist them in the demarcation operation'.[39] The Chamber accepted this request in the order nominating the experts to assist in the implementation of the Chamber's judgment; however, the Chamber did not refer to Article 50 of the Statute but to Article 48 (its power to make orders) in stating that its belief was that the parties had not asked the Chamber to utilise its Article 50 powers (the purpose of which would have been to assist the Court, and would have been paid for by the Court) but rather to exercise a power specifically conferred upon the Court by the Special Agreement.[40]

Similarly, after the Court had delivered its judgment in the *Case Concerning the Frontier Dispute (Burkina Faso v. Niger)* the parties, under Article 7(4) of the Special Agreement between Burkina Faso and Niger of 24 February 2009, asked the Court 'to nominate, in its Judgment, three experts to assist them as necessary in the demarcation'.[41] The Court, specifically referring to the previous Burkina Faso frontier case, and taking advice from the parties as to what tasks the experts could be expected to undertake, agreed to nominate experts to assist in the implementation of the Court's judgment, all the while stressing that it was not utilising its Article 50 Statute powers in doing so,[42] but again was exercising 'a power, conferred on it by Special Agreement'.[43] Just why the Court has been so hesitant to be seen to be using its Article 50 powers is unclear.

The distinction between Court-appointed and party-appointed experts remains significant since the procedure for the examination of a Court-appointed expert and a party-appointed expert differ.[44] For instance, the appointment of experts by the Court is made by an order[45] and with Court-appointed experts 'the Court is free to define the subject-matter of the testimony'.[46] It is unclear whether the Court could compel parties to co-operate with the Court-appointed expert and provide them with the

---

[39] See Article IV(3) of Special Agreement, ICJ Reports 1986 558.
[40] *Frontier Dispute, Judgment, ICJ Reports 1986* 554, 648.
[41] See Order of 12 July 2013, *Nomination of Experts, Frontier Dispute (Burkina Faso v. Niger)* 2.
[42] Referring to *Application for Revision and Interpretation of the Judgment of 24 February 1982 in the Case concerning the Continental Shelf (Tunisia/Libyan Arab Jamahiriya) (Tunisia v. Libyan Arab Jamahiriya), Judgment, ICJ Reports 1985* 192, 228 para 65.
[43] See Order of 12 July 2013 *Nomination of Experts, Frontier Dispute (Burkina Faso v. Niger)* 2.
[44] Article 51 and the relevant Rules regulate the procedure for examining Court-appointed experts.
[45] See Article 67(1) Rules.   [46] Tams, 'Article 51' 1310.

information required. Whilst this issue is discussed further in Section 4.3.2, it would appear that the utility of the Court-appointed expert will at least to some extent depend on voluntary co-operation from the parties.[47] A further crucial distinction is Article 67 of the Rules which refers to the rights of the parties in relation to experts appointed by the Court – providing that 'every report or record of an enquiry, and every expert opinion shall be communicated to the parties, which shall be given the opportunity of commenting upon it'. However, this provision does not include any right of the parties to examine the Court-appointed expert – a potentially crucial distinction which we will examine in greater detail in Chapter 4.[48]

### 1.1.5 (ii) Commissions of inquiry

The second fact-finding power conferred on the Court by Article 50 of the Court's Statute is the power to entrust an independent body or commission with the 'task of carrying out an enquiry or giving an expert opinion'.[49] Article 50 is a potentially useful provision since, as one commentator has stated '[g]iven the complexity of many of the disputes submitted to adjudication, it is highly desirable that the Court be in a position to receive independent advice'.[50]

Article 50 Commissions of Inquiry should be distinguished from site visits discussed above made by the Court as set out in Article 44(2) of the Statute of the Court. As one commentator has stated, '[w]hile a site visit will usually help to ascertain the facts of a case (and may thus constitute a specific form of inquiry), Art. 50 only covers inquiries that the Court entrusts to other bodies or institutions.'[51] Evidence sought under Article 50 is not considered *ex parte* evidence: 'evidence sought under Article 50 will usually be preferred over *ex parte* evidence, which is often seen as biased simply because it has been introduced by one party'.[52]

---

[47] Ibid.    [48] Ibid.
[49] Article 50, Statute of the International Court of Justice; see also Article 67 of Rules of the Court. The PCIJ appointed a committee of experts in the *Case Concerning the Factory at Chorzów (Germany v. Poland)* (Claim for Indemnity) (Jurisdiction), Series A, No 9; A 18 (1929) 14; ICJ appointed experts in the *Corfu Channel Case* to assess the facts and to provide an expert evaluation of the damage sustained by the UK. In the *Nicaragua* case the Court refused to use its power; 'the Court felt it was unlikely that an enquiry of this kind would be practical or desirable'. See *Nicaragua Case* para 61.
[50] Tams, 'Article 50' 1109.    [51] Ibid.
[52] Ibid., citing J. Pauwelyn, 'The Use of Experts in WTO Dispute Settlement' 51 *International and Comparative Law Quarterly* 325.

The Court has only made use of its powers under Article 50 in two cases: once in the *Chorzów Factory* case before the PCIJ to, amongst other things, 'enable the Court to fix, with a full knowledge of the facts ... the amount of the indemnity to be paid by the Polish Government to the German Government'[53] and twice in the *Corfu Channel* case before the ICJ, once to examine several factual issues including determining the visibility of the mine-laying activities in the Channel from the Albanian coast, which the Court described as a crucial factor in the case[54] and a second expert commission to determine the damages to be paid by Albania to the United Kingdom.[55] The Commission ultimately concluded that it was 'indisputable' that, all things being equal, the operation would have been visible from the coastline – and the Court subsequently praised the Commission, stating that it could not fail 'to give great weight to the opinion of the experts who examined the locality in a manner giving every guarantee of correct and impartial information'.[56]

It should be noted that parties do not have a right under Article 50 to have the Court appoint a commission of inquiry or expert in the same way that they have the right to appoint their own expert under Article 43 – the establishment of such a commission is completely at the discretion of the Court.[57] And indeed there have been no such inquiries in the last few decades.[58] Instead, the Court has 'more often than not' refused requests by one of the parties to appoint an inquiry or expert or held that it would find such action unnecessary.[59] In the past the Court has refused to appoint an expert to shed light on the delimitation of the boundary between Tunisia and Libya, noting that its 1982 judgment had left the issue to the parties' experts;[60] refused a request to send an inquiry to a disputed region on the basis that such an inquiry was not necessary in order to reach a decision on the case at hand;[61] and perhaps most famously, rejected Judge Schewbel's suggestion

---

[53] *Case Concerning the Factory at Chorzów* (Claim for Indeminty) (Merits) Series A No. 17, see Order of 13 September 1928.
[54] *Corfu Channel Case* 20; See Experts Report of 1 December 1949.
[55] See ibid., Order of 17 December 1948, and Order of 9 April 1949. [56] Ibid.
[57] Tams, 'Article 50' 1113.
[58] Higgins, 'Speech by H. E. Judge Rosalyn Higgins, President of the International Court of Justice to the Sixth Committee of the General Assembly'.
[59] Tams, 'Article 50' 1112.
[60] *Application for Revision and Interpretation of the Judgment of 24 February 1982 in the Case concerning the Continental Shelf* para 65.
[61] *Land, Island and Maritime Frontier Dispute (El Salvador/Honduras: Nicaragua intervening)*, Judgment of 11 September 1992, ICJ Reports 1992 455 paras 22 and 65.

that a fact-finding inquiry be set up in the *Nicaragua* case to gather facts in Nicaragua, the United States, El Salvador, Honduras, Costa Rica, Guatemala and Cuba on the same basis.[62] Judge Schwebel later remarked that the Court at the time had refused the request on the basis that the inquiry, in properly carrying out its function, would in all likelihood have found it necessary to go not only to Nicaragua but also to neighbouring States and even the United States, which of course, was not co-operating with the Court.[63]

Unlike provisions in other international courts, the matter on which an expert opinion is sought need not be one of a technical or scientific issue but could deal with more general matters such as an issue of linguistics.[64] It should be noted that Article 50 can only be used where States are willing to co-operate with the Court and as such, Tams concludes that 'Art. 50 is likely to remain what it has been to date: a helpful, but rarely used, means of obtaining information about the facts of a case'.[65] However, this provision was given explicit backing by a number of judges of the Court as one that could be more readily made use of by the Court to better establish the facts of a case before it – an issue considered in much greater detail in Chapter 4.

### 1.1.6 The power to request information from public international organisations

Article 34(2) of the Court's Statute provides that the Court may request relevant information from public international organisations with regard to cases before it.[66] However, Article 34(2) of the Court's Statute was neither utilised nor referred to in the early years of the

---

[62] *Nicaragua Case*, see Dissenting Opinion of Judge Schwebel, 249, 322 para 132; Specifically, Judge Jennings cited the non-appearance of the United States and stated that there was a limit to what the Court could do in such cases: '[t]here are limits to what the Court can do, in accordance with Article 53 of the Statute, to satisfy itself about a non-appearing party's case; and that is especially so where the facts are crucial'. See Judge Jennings para 69.

[63] Ibid. para 61.  [64] Tams, 'Article 50' 1114, unlike Article 13 DSU, for example.

[65] Ibid.

[66] The relevant Rules of the Court, Article 69(1) to (3) further provide that the Court can 'at any time prior to the closure of the oral proceedings, either *proprio motu* or at the request of one of the parties ... request a public international organization ... to furnish information relevant to a case before it'; C. M. Chinkin and R. Mackenzie, 'Intergovernmental Organizations as "Friends of the Court"' in L. R. Chazournes et al. (eds), *International Organizations and International Disputes Settlement: Trends and Prospects* (Ardsley, NY: Transnational, 2002) 140.

Court's operation.[67] The first use came when the Secretary-General informed the Council of the International Civil Aviation Organization (ICAO) that a case pending before the Court potentially affected its interests, namely the *Aerial Incident of 27 July 1955* case.[68] The same organisation was later informed of proceedings under Article 34(3) potentially affecting its interests, this time by the President of the Court, in the *ICAO Council* case[69] although the ICAO Council subsequently did not file any observations on the case.[70] In the following years scarce reference was made to the provision, the only other example being the *Border and Transborder Armed Actions* case in which the Court informed the OAS of the case, but once more the organisation chose not to take any action.[71]

More recently the Court's Registrar communicated to the Secretary-General, as depository, that the Convention on the Prevention and Punishment of the Crime of Genocide would form the basis of the *Bosnian Genocide* case.[72] This was the first time in which the Court had utilised Article 34(3) in relation to an organ of the UN itself.[73] Perhaps the reason that greater use of this provision has not been used to inform UN organs is due to the fact that Article 40 of the ICJ Statute already provides that the Secretary-General be informed of all cases that come before the Court, and Article 69(2) of the Rules gives the Secretary-General the right to submit information to the Court. Dupuy has made reference to 'the striking fact that on the whole, inter-governmental organizations do not seem to be particularly interested in taking the initiative, on the basis of Art. 34, para 2, of requesting the Court to receive information which they would consider as relevant to a case pending before it'.[74] The possibility of making greater use of this power

---

[67] Pierre-Marie Dupuy, 'Article 34' in A. Zimmermann (ed), *The Statute of the International Court of Justice: A Commentary* (Oxford University Press, 2006) 551.
[68] *Case concerning the Aerial Incident of July 27th, 1955 (Israel v. Bulgaria), Preliminary Objections, Judgment of May 26th, 1959: ICJ Reports 1959* 127; ICAO Doc. C-WP/2609, 21 February 1958, para 5.
[69] *Appeal Relating to the Jurisdiction of the ICAO Council, Judgrnent, ICJ Reports 1972* 46.
[70] Ibid. 48 para 5.
[71] *Border and Transborder Armed Actions (Nicaragua v. Honduras), Jurisdiction and Admissibiltiy, Judgment, ICJ Reports 1988* 69.
[72] *Application of the Convention on the Prevention and Punishment of the Crime of Genocide* (Bosnia and Herzegovina/Yugoslavia [Serbia and Montenegro]), Provisional Measures, ICJ Reports 1993 3.
[73] Dupuy, 'Article 34' 553.    [74] Ibid.

to coordinate the Court's fact-finding efforts with those of international commissions of inquiry is also critically examined in Chapter 5.

## 1.2 *Da mihi factum, dabo tibi jus*: the Court's reactive approach to fact-finding

Consequently, it can be said that the Court possesses 'powerful tools for collecting evidence, ones that could be used at any time' in the proceedings,[75] the cumulative effect of which arm the Court with the power both to request evidence itself and to direct the parties in their fact-finding efforts.[76]

Crucially, however, despite possessing such relatively broad fact-finding powers, the Court has rarely made significant use of them.[77] As we will see, a survey of the Court's practice in the previous section demonstrates this point and is perfectly summarised by former Judge Schwebel who has stated that ultimately the 'role of the full Court, in my experience, has tended to be predominantly passive'.[78] Before the ICJ, the general tendency has been to 'ask the parties to produce the evidence ... rather than to have investigations into facts led by the Court itself'.[79] Taken together, this practice constitutes what can be termed the Court's 'reactive approach' to fact-finding.

### 1.2.1 A reluctance to engage with complex factual situations?

A number of commentators have argued that the Court has traditionally employed a number of different tactics in order to avoid engaging with complex factual and scientific determinations, what might be termed 'avoidance techniques'.[80] Such commentators have argued that the Court has shown a tendency to focus on legal reasoning and to use 'legal rationality to shield itself from scientific [or factual] controversies'.[81]

---

[75] Teitelbaum, 'Recent Fact-Finding Developments at the International Court of Justice' 122.
[76] Halink, 'All Things Considered: How the International Court of Justice Delegated its Fact-Assessment to the United Nations in the Armed Activities Case' 19; Franck, 'Fact-finding in the I.C.J.' 21; K. Highet, 'Evidence, The Chamber, and the ELSI Case' in Richard B. Lillich (ed), *Fact-Finding before International Tribunals* (Ardsley-on-Hudson, NY: Transnational, 1992) 74.
[77] Benzing, 'Evidentiary Issues' para 12.
[78] Schwebel, *Three Cases of Fact-Finding by the International Court of Justice in International Law* 3.
[79] Walter, 'Article 44' 1041.
[80] J. D'Aspremont and M. M. Mbengue, 'Strategies of Engagement with Scientific Fact-Finding in International Adjudication' (Amsterdam Law School Research Paper No. 2013–20) 11.
[81] Ibid.; Franck, 'Fact-finding in the I.C.J.' 28.

One such commentator was Thomas Franck, who argued that the Court has in the past deliberately sought to shift the focus of the case to legal rather than factual issues, stating that 'in different questions of fact, the Court tends to make a complicated task of fact-finding unimportant or unnecessary by devising a rule which downgrades the importance of the elusive facts.'[82] One example given by Franck is the *Temple at Preah Vihear* case in which the Court held that whilst the map drawn up by the Mixed French-Siamese Commission in 1907 alleging to demonstrate title over the disputed area was not determinative in itself, Thailand's failure to object to it and subsequent behaviour was seen by the Court to be equitable estoppel.[83] The Court stated that '[g]iven the grounds on which the Court bases its decision, it becomes unnecessary to consider whether, at Preah Vihear, the line as mapped does in fact correspond to the true watershed line in this vicinity ... or, if not, how the watershed in fact runs'.[84] The reasoning of the Court to this end led Franck to argue that '[a] procedural or evidentiary rule thus saved the Court from having to duplicate the voyage along the Dangrek Escarpment for purposes of locating the disputed watershed line'.[85]

Rosenne has similarly criticised the apparent unwillingness of the Court to conduct its own fact-finding and implied that the Court has placed considerable emphasis on the legal issues in order to circumvent a number of factual issues.[86] Rosenne has in particular cited the *Anglo-Iranian Oil Company* and *Fisheries Jurisdiction* cases in which he characterises the behaviour of the Court as relying 'only on the facts as stated by the applicants in their written and oral pleadings' whilst making no attempt to challenge or verify those facts itself.[87]

The *Legality of Threat or Use of Nuclear Weapons* advisory opinion is another case cited in this regard given the fact that substantial amounts of information were submitted to the Court in the course of proceedings, and the Court did not consider it necessary to 'study various types of nuclear weapons and to evaluate highly complex and controversial

---

[82] Franck, 'Fact-finding in the I.C.J.' 30.
[83] *Case Concerning the Temple of Preah Vihear (Cambodia v. Thailand)*, Merits, Judgment of 15 June 1962: ICJ Reports 1962 6, 35.
[84] Ibid., 35; Franck, 'Fact-finding in the I.C.J.' 25.
[85] *Temple of Preah Vihear Case*; Franck, 'Fact-finding in the I.C.J.' 25.
[86] S. Rosenne, 'Fact-Finding before the International Court of Justice' in *Essays on International Law and Practice* (The Hague: T.M.C. Asser Press, 1999) 237.
[87] Ibid.

## 1.2 THE ICJ'S REACTIVE APPROACH TO FACT-FINDING     29

technological, strategic and scientific information'.[88] However, in this case it is difficult to argue definitively that the Court was consciously trying to avoid making factual determinations. Instead, the Court stated that it would 'simply address the issues arising in all their aspects by applying the legal rules relevant to the situation.'[89]

The accusation that the Court employs avoidance techniques in order to avoid dealing with the facts is rather difficult to substantiate definitively. In fact, having not been in the Court's position, in such cases it is often difficult to imagine how one could prove that the decision taken by the Court to focus on legal issues and not conduct further fact-finding was the wrong decision. It may be that the Court had sound reasons for not conducting its own fact-finding such as considerations of judicial economy or the fact that resolution of those factual issues was not central to the resolution of the dispute at hand.

Taking up this point, it is necessary to emphasise that there are undoubtedly positive aspects of the Court's reactive approach to fact-finding. Whilst there are a number of serious problems with this approach as set out in Chapter 2 it should be made clear that the reactive approach is not without its benefits. For instance, there are a number of practical reasons why it is sensible for the Court to place the emphasis on the parties in terms of fact-finding. This is the case since the Court is often significantly removed from the facts of the dispute, both in terms of distance and time. As such, it is arguably more prudent for the parties themselves, who are generally closer to the facts, to put such evidence before the Court, than it is for the Court to embark on a fact-finding expedition from The Hague.

Staying with the nature of the cases that come before the Court, the sheer breadth of legal and factual issues, number of potential witnesses and territory may in some way justify the Court's reactive position. For instance, in cases such as *Armed Activities*, *Bosnian Genocide* and *Croatian Genocide*, the disputes in question involved a dizzying array of factual and legal issues as well as having taken place over many years and often over many different States.[90] Similarly, the highly political nature of cases before the Court means that it may take many years for the

---

[88] *Legality of the Threat or Use of Nuclear Weapons, Advisory Opinion, ICJ Reports 1996* 226 para 15.
[89] *WHO Advisory Opinion*, 15.
[90] See Introduction (i) on the factual complexity of cases.

proceedings to get under way.[91] Furthermore, as stated above, many States see it as part of their privilege as a sovereign State to choose which pieces of evidence they put before the Court. Accordingly it would appear to make little sense for the Court to duplicate the fact-finding efforts of the parties. As such, the Court's decision to accept the evidence put before it by the parties and to concentrate on the points of contention as defined by the parties seems like the only viable option.

And indeed the Court should not completely disregard all evidence submitted by the parties in order to undertake wide-ranging fact-finding on its own accord. Rather, the following chapters will show that there are a number of deficiencies regarding the way the Court currently operates and that the practice of other international courts and tribunals in some way provides a helpful blueprint for reform in order to ensure that the Court makes factual determinations that are as accurate as they can be.

As such, rather than talking in terms of the Court using 'avoidance techniques' in order to negate the need to engage with the facts, the most that can be said is that the Court, since the days of the PCIJ,[92] has very clearly displayed a number of tendencies which, taken together, demonstrate a consistently reactive approach to the facts in cases that have come before it. It is these tendencies and their contribution to the Court's reactive approach to fact-finding which is the subject of the following section.

## 1.3 The Court's reactive approach to fact-finding: contributing factors

Such tendencies evident in the Court's jurisprudence include the predominance of, and apparent preference for reliance on, documentary evidence before the Court; extremely broad rules of admissibility; the

---

[91] In this regard see *Application of the Convention on the Prevention and Punishment of the Crime of Genocide (Croatia v. Serbia)*, the application instituting proceedings being filed in 1999 and the final judgment not delivered until 3 February 2015.

[92] The great American Judge Manley Hudson said in 1943 of the PCIJ that '[i]ssues of fact are seldom tried before the Court, and where a question of fact arises the Court must usually base its finding on statements made on behalf of the parties either in the documents of the written proceedings or in the course or oral proceedings'. This description of the practice of the PCIJ suggests that the Court's current reactive approach has been passed down genetically from its predecessor; see M. Hudson, *The Permanent Court of International Justice 1920–1942* (New York: MacMillan, 1943) 565; and Therese O'Donnell, 'Judicialising History or Historicising Law: Reflections on *Irving v. Penguin Books and Lipstadt*' 62 *Northern Ireland Legal Quarterly* 291, 300.

## 1.3 CONTRIBUTING FACTORS

sovereign nature of the parties to cases before the Court and the so-called classical approach to the judicial process – each will be assessed in turn in the following subsections.

### 1.3.1 Predominance of documentary evidence

The first and perhaps most prominent tendency of the Court which contributes to the Court's reactive approach to evidence is the clear preponderance of documentary evidence before the Court.[93] In keeping with the Court's liberal evidentiary regime, documentary proof is preferred to oral testimony before the Court,[94] being 'by far the most common and certainly the most important type of evidence in litigation before the ICJ.'[95] This preference has been credited to the influence of civil law systems 'given that there are striking similarities – especially in their emphasis on written means of proof'.[96]

Whilst there has been limited use of oral testimony and cross-examination, generally 'the use of evidence in written form is the rule ... in cases before the ICJ'.[97] The consequence of the Court's clear preference for written documentary evidence is that the Court has much greater experience in dealing with this type of evidence and as such has had many opportunities to develop a number of rough guiding principles to guide it in its evaluation of such documents, as we will see in Section 1.4.

The Court's preference for relying on historical documentary evidence can be clearly seen in myriad cases throughout the history of the Court's operation. For instance, in the *Continental Shelf* case between Tunisia

---

[93] Valencia-Ospina, 'Evidence before the International Court of Justice' 204. This preference is demonstrated before other international courts and tribunals also: see Charles Nelson Brower and Jason D. Brueschke, *The Iran-United States Claims Tribunal* (The Hague, Boston, London: Martinus Nijhoff, 1998) 186. It has existed from the birth of international criminal law at Nuremberg: see Robert H. Jackson, *The Nurnberg Case* (New York: Alfred A. Knopf, 1947) viii.

[94] Chester Brown, 'Aspects of Evidence in International Adjudication' in *A Common Law of International Adjudication* (Oxford University Press, 2007) 91; quoting J. A. Jolowicz, *On Civil Procedure* (Cambridge University Press, 2000) 211.

[95] Riddell and Plant, *Evidence before the International Court of Justice* 231.

[96] Ibid. See also Valencia-Ospina, 'Evidence before the International Court of Justice' 204; the comments of Cassese and Schabas in Marlise Simons, 'Serbia's Darkest Pages Hidden from Genocide Court' (New York) *The New York Times*, 8 April 2007, www.nytimes.com/2007/04/08/world/europe/08iht-serbia.5.5192285.html?_r=1&pagewanted=all.

[97] Riddell and Plant, *Evidence before the International Court of Justice* 231.

and Libya the Court was asked to set out the applicable principles for the delimitation of the continental shelf between these two States, and furthermore to 'specify precisely the practical way the aforesaid principles and rules apply in this particular situation so as to enable the experts of the two counties to delimit these areas without any difficulties'.[98] Although Libya called one expert, Dr A. Fabricus, a professor of Geology, who was examined and then cross-examined by Professors Bowett and Virally, the Court was able to resolve the legal issues in the case solely through reliance on maps and other documentary evidence placed before it by the parties without having to conduct any of its own fact-finding.[99] Although this case has been cited as one in which the Court employed one of its 'avoidance techniques' in order to avoid conducting its own fact-finding, it is again difficult to conclusively argue that doing so would have produced a result more satisfactory to the parties in this particular case. What can clearly be seen, however, is the Court's preference for, and adeptness at, using historical documentary evidence to resolve legal issues in cases before it.

This approach can again be seen in the other maritime delimitation case involving Libya's continental shelf during the negotiations on the United Nations Convention on the Law of the Sea (UNCLOS) – namely the case involving Libya and Malta.[100] This case was inevitably influenced not only by the earlier case involving Libya and Tunisia but also by the UNCLOS negotiations which were ongoing at that time. However it should be noted that this influence was mutual, with the Court's decisions on such issues being influential during the negotiation of the UNCLOS.[101] At the start of the 1980s Libya and Malta eventually ratified the Special Agreement to bring their case before the Court. Again the Court was able to resolve the legal issues asked of it by the parties through reliance on documentary, geographical, information put before it by the parties themselves.[102]

---

[98] *Continental Shelf (Tunisia/Libyan Arab Jamahiriya), Judgment, ICJ Reports 1982* 18, Special Agreement, Article 1.
[99] Ibid. para 62; Highet, 'Evidence, the Court, and the Nicaragua Case'; *Application for Revision and Interpretation of the Judgment of 24 February 1982 in the Case concerning the Continental Shelf* 117–18.
[100] *Continental Shelf (Libyan Arab Jamahiriya v. Malta) Judgment, ICJ Reports 1985* 13.
[101] S. Rosenne, *The World Court: What It Is and How It Works* (5th edn, The Hague: Martinus Nijhoff, 1995) 219.
[102] *Continental Shelf (Libya v. Malta)*; Highet, 'Evidence, the Court, and the Nicaragua Case' 27.

In keeping with the trend of resolving land and maritime delimitation cases solely on documentary and historical evidence placed before it by the parties rather than appointing experts of its own or conducting other forms of fact-finding, the Chamber established by the parties in the *Land, Island and Maritime Frontier Dispute* again resolved the legal issues asked of it in this way. Illustrative of the Chamber's approach was its refusal of El Salvador's request to conduct a site visit, owing to the fact it had experienced serious difficulties in providing evidence for various reasons beyond its control including the fact that information was not stored in any central archives.[103] The Chamber refused El Salvador's request to visit the site to procure the evidence of effectivités, stating simply that it 'did not consider it necessary to exercise its power to obtain evidence, nor to accede to El Salvador's request that it should arrange for an inquiry or expert opinion under Article 50 of the Statute'.[104] The Chamber provided no further explanation of this decision, before relying on the other documentary evidence that had been placed before it in carrying out the delimitation.

Further, in the *Nicaragua* case,[105] one of the cases of non-appearance that we shall discuss in the following chapter, despite being 'not as fully informed as it would wish to be' the Court took no steps to more proactively procure evidence that may have shed some light on the case.[106] The U.S. Judge Schwebel drafted a lengthy dissent from the majority in the *Nicaragua* case arguing that the Court was wrong to not make greater use of its fact-finding powers to call for additional evidence or establish a commission of inquiry in light of the United States's withdrawal from the case.[107] For example, in relation to the issue of whether El Salvador had ever requested the help of the US in self-defence, the Court merely stated that there was 'no evidence' to suggest so but never invited El Salvador to submit its further evidence nor took any steps of its own to procure further evidence. In short, the Court remained passive.[108]

Similarly, in the *Gabčikovo-Nagymaros* case in 1997 the parties put before the Court a myriad of scientific expert reports by independent

---

[103] *Land, Island and Maritime Frontier Dispute*, para 64.   [104] Ibid.
[105] *Nicaragua Case*.
[106] Ibid. 20, 123; ibid. 110–11; Schwebel, *Three Cases of Fact-Finding by the International Court of Justice in International Law* 15.
[107] Schwebel, *Three Cases of Fact-Finding by the International Court of Justice in International Law* 13.
[108] Ibid.

experts,[109] national and international non-governmental bodies[110] and a number of European Community expert studies[111] on a broad range of issues including hydrology, seismology, ecology and hydrobiology. However, even with this voluminous factual and scientific information before the Court,[112] (described by the Court as 'an impressive amount of scientific material aimed at reinforcing their respective arguments')[113] the Court held that it was 'not necessary in order to respond to the questions put to it in the Special Agreement for it to determine which of those points of view is scientifically better founded.'[114] Instead, the Court based its judgment in treaty law, State responsibility and on the respective legal obligations of the parties before it, relying on the whole on the documentary evidence placed before it by the parties.[115]

The Court's reticence with regard to the appointment of experts in this case was criticised by commentators and the dissenting opinion of one judge in particular who argued that it was unclear how the Court felt it was able to make a legal determination as to 'the immediacy and gravity of the environmental peril without taking into account the scientific data submitted by the parties intending to prove just that'.[116]

---

[109] I.C.J. Pleadings, Gabčikovo-Nagymaros, Vol I at 57 para 2.28; Counter-Memorial of Hungary, Vol 1, at para 1.30 onwards.
[110] Counter-Memorial of Hungary, at para 1.33.
[111] For instance, see I.C.J. Pleadings, Gabčikovo-Nagymaros, Vol II Annexes 12, 19, 22, Volume III Annex 33; EC Working Group of Independent Experts on Variant 'C' of project, 23 November 1992; EC Working Group of Monitoring and Water Management Experts for the project, Data Report of 2 November 1993; EC Fact-Finding Mission 31 October 1992; EC Working Group of Monitoring and Water Management Experts for the Project, 1 December 1993.
[112] Riddell, 'Scientific Evidence in the International Court of Justice –Problems and Possibilities' 245; Lee Thomson, 'The ICJ and the case concerning the G/N Project: The Implications for International Watercourses Law and International Environmental Law' Centre for Energy, Petroleum, Mineral Law and Policy, Annual Review (1999) Article 8, wwwdundeeacuk/cepmlp/car/html/car3_article8htm.
[113] Gabčikovo-Nagymaros Case para 54; 'Both Parties have placed on record an impressive amount of scientific material aimed at reinforcing their respective arguments. The Court has given most careful attention to this material, in which the Parties have developed their opposing views as to the ecological consequences of the Project. It concludes, however, that, as will be shown below, it is not necessary in order to respond to the questions put to it in the Special Agreement for it to determine which of those points of view is scientifically better founded.'
[114] Ibid. para 54.   [115] D'Aspremont and Mbengue, 'Strategies of Engagement' 15.
[116] Riddell, 'Scientific Evidence in the International Court of Justice – Problems and Possibilities' 245; Thomson, 'The ICJ and the case concerning the G/N Project'. This point was made by Judge Herczegh who stated in his dissenting opinion that 'As a judicial organ, the Court was admittedly not empowered to decide scientific questions

However, one must be careful when considering such issues since it is extremely difficult to argue that the Court should have engaged more intimately with complex factual or scientific issues, and further that any such engagement would have made any particular difference to the outcome of the case. That having been said, what we can assess is the means and methods employed by the Court and what we can confidently state is that the Court has displayed, and continues to display, a tendency to rely on documentary evidence and that it has demonstrated clear reluctance to conduct its own fact-finding.

The Court's unwillingness or inability to utilise its fact-finding powers is compounded by the fact that the Court employs remarkably broad rules of admissibility. The onus placed on States to bring evidence before the Court as a result of the Court's reactive approach to fact-finding necessitates that some consideration be given to the limitations that are placed on exactly what evidence can come before Court, or in other words the Court's rules on admissibility.

### 1.3.2 Admissibility

Consistent with the theme of scarce rules of evidence in international litigation, the admissibility of evidence before the Court is similarly unconstrained by detailed evidentiary rules and procedures. Unlike international criminal tribunals established subsequently, the ICJ has no explicit rules of evidence regarding admissibility.[117] In fact, it has been said that there exists a general rule of *liberté de la prevue* or 'the free

---

touching on biology, hydrology, and so on, or questions of a technical type which arose out of the G/N Project; but it could- and even should- have ruled on the legal consequences of certain facts alleged by one Party and either admitted or not addressed by the other, in order to assess their respective conduct in this case' See Dissenting Opinion of Judge Herczegh 177.

[117] See for instance Rule 89(C) of the International Criminal Tribunal for the former Yugoslavia (ICTY) which states that '[a] Chamber may admit any relevant evidence which it deems to have probative value', which has in fact been described as 'arguably the most frequently used provision in the Rules'; see Patricia Viseur Sellers, 'Rule 89 (C) and (D): At Odds or Overlapping with Rule 96 and Rule 95?' in Richard May et al. (eds), *Essays on ICTY Procedure and Evidence in Honour of Gabrielle Kirk McDonald* (The Hague: Martinus Nijhoff, 2001). Rule 89(D) even permits the exclusion of evidence on the grounds that it lacks probative value, although this provision has not been the subject of extensive jurisprudence. See also Gideon Boas, 'Admissibility of Evidence under the Rules of Procedure and Evidence of the ICTY: Development of the "Flexibility Principle"' in Richard May et al. (eds), *Essays on ICTY Procedure and Evidence in Honour of Gabrielle Kirk McDonald* (The Hague: Martinus Nijhoff, 2001) 265.

admissibility of evidence before the Court'[118] (with only a small number of exceptions).

Former President of the Court Rosalyn Higgins has summed up the Court's approach to the admissibility of evidence in stating that '[t]he parties are entitled to expect that we will examine every single thing that they put before us, and we do'.[119] Again, the explanation offered for this approach is familiar, as Brower asserts: '[f]or obvious diplomatic reasons international tribunals are reluctant to spurn anything proffered by a sovereign.'[120] Unlike domestic courts where there generally exist numerous and sophisticated evidentiary constraints regarding the admissibility of evidence, it has been said that they 'have no place in international adjudication, where the relevance of facts and the value of evidence tending to establish facts are left to the appreciation of the court.'[121] As a general rule it can be said that any evidence put forward by a State party in a case before the Court will be accepted by the Court unless it is challenged by the other party and is subsequently proved to fall foul of one of the limited exceptions to the principle of free admissibility.[122]

One possible explanation offered to explain the Court's flexible approach to evidence and broad powers to determine the evidentiary weight of any piece of evidence that comes before it is that '[u]nlike a common-law lay jury, this highly-qualified and experienced international bench is not considered to need "protection" from potentially unreliable evidence.'[123] The Court has, however, imposed a limited number of

---

[118] See *Mavrommatis Palestine Concessions, PCIJ, Ser. A No. 2, 34 (1924)*; Brown, 'Aspects of Evidence in International Adjudication' 90.

[119] Speech by H. E. Judge Rosalyn Higgins, President of the International Court of Justice to the General Assembly of the United Nations, 1 November 2007, www.icj-cij.org/press com/files/3/141113.pdf; in that way 'at least the state parties cannot feel that a decision rests on an incomplete presentation of the facts and law'; Franck, *Fairness in International Law and Institutions* 336.

[120] C. N. Brower, 'Evidence Before International Tribunals: The Need for Some Standard Rules' (1994) 28 *The International Lawyer* 47, 148.

[121] Rosenne and Ronen, *The Law and Practice of the International Court, 1920–2005* 557; see also C. N. Brower, 'The Anatomy of Fact-Finding Before International Tribunals: An Analysis and a Proposal Concerning the Evaluation of Evidence' in R. B. Lillich (ed), *Fact-Finding Before International Tribunals* (Irvington-on-Hudson, NY: Transnational, 1992).

[122] See Sandifer, *Evidence Before International Tribunals* 176; Valencia-Ospina, 'Evidence before the International Court of Justice' 204.

[123] Valencia-Ospina, 'Evidence before the International Court of Justice' 205; see Corfu Channel *(United Kingdom v. Albania)* Merits, 1949 ICJ Rep. 4 (Judgment of 9 April).

restrictions on the principle of free admissibility, ostensibly in order to ensure good judicial order.[124]

The first of these limitations is evidence originating from negotiations between parties seeking resolution of a particular dispute. This has been described as '[p]erhaps the only clear-cut example of evidence being considered inadmissible by the Court'.[125] The consistent practice with regard to negotiations between two States seeking to resolve a particular dispute has led to the development of a general rule that the Court will not 'consider evidence consisting of statements ... made in the course of those negotiations, so that the information or documents generated can not then be used against the parties in any pending or future litigation'.[126]

A clear example of this limitation can be seen in the *Chorzów Factory* case in which the PCIJ stated that it would not take into account 'declarations, admissions or proposals which the Parties may have made during direct negotiations between themselves, when such negotiations have not led to a complete agreement'.[127] The Court subsequently followed this reasoning in the *Burkina Faso/Mali* case.[128] Crucially, however, the Court provided a slight nuance in finding that whilst evidence originating from negotiations between the parties was inadmissible, evidence of the circumstances surrounding the agreement may in fact be admissible. This has led commentators to conclude that '[e]ven this clear rule as to inadmissibility has been closely proscribed'.[129]

A second, and more complex, limitation is that relating to illegally obtained evidence. Although the Court has never specifically rejected illegally obtained evidence, there has been academic debate on the issue centring around the *Corfu Channel* and *Tehran Hostages* cases.[130] Despite arguments to the contrary,[131] it would seem that the Court does not in fact have a rule prohibiting the admission of illegal evidence; as Highet has stated, '[t]he likely result ... is that – without specifically ruling on

---

[124] W. M. Reisman and E. E. Freedman, 'Plaintiff's Dilemma: Illegally Obtained Evidence and Admissibility in International Adjuducation, The' 76 *American Journal of International Law* 737, 739.
[125] Riddell and Plant, *Evidence before the International Court of Justice* 154.
[126] M. Kazazi, *Burden of Proof and Related Issues: A Study on Evidence Before International Tribunals*, VVol 1 (The Hague: Martinus Nijhoff, 1996) 402.
[127] See *Chorzów Factory Case* 19.     [128] *Frontier Dispute Case* para 147.
[129] Ibid. para 147; Riddell and Plant, *Evidence before the International Court of Justice* 155.
[130] See Reisman and Freedman, 'Plaintiff's Dilemma' 739; H. Thirlway, 'Dilemma or Chimera – Admissibilty of Illegally Obtained Evidence in International Adjudication' 78 *American Journal of International Law* 622, 633.
[131] Thirlway, 'Dilemma or Chimera'; Reisman and Freedman, 'Plaintiff's Dilemma'.

the matter – the Court will consider any such evidence on its own footing and weigh it accordingly, but will not exclude it from consideration on the ground of "illegality" alone'.[132] President Spender in *South West Africa* laid out position of the Court:

> The evidence will remain on the record; the Court is quite able to evaluate evidence, and if there is no value in the evidence, then there will be no value given to this part of the evidence ... This Court is not bound by the strict rules of evidence applicable in municipal courts and if the evidence ... does not sufficiently convey that the evidence is reliable in point of fact, then the Court, of course, deals with it accordingly when it comes to its deliberation.[133]

This underlines how far the Court's liberal approach to evidence extends and the subsequent importance of the weighing of evidence (the fact-assessment stage),[134] to which we will later return. It is interesting to note that amongst the myriad arguments made as to how to reform the Court's fact-finding procedure, arguments in favour of the introduction of stricter rules of admissibility are rarely made. This is perhaps due to the fact that there are a number of obvious positive aspects of the Court's policy of *liberté de la prevue*. To briefly mention one by way of example, the Court has avoided the difficulties which beset the United States Supreme Court when it attempted to move away from its traditional *Frye* test for admissibility to the more stringent *Daubert* test which cast the Supreme Court as the gatekeeper in terms of the admission of scientific evidence.[135] This move proved troublesome as the Supreme Court struggled to define purely 'scientific' evidence and ultimately in the *Kumho Tyre* case was forced to expand the test to cover 'technical' and 'other specialized' [sic] forms of knowledge.[136] The ICJ's approach to date has allowed the Court to avoid becoming embroiled in such technical disputes which could have needlessly consumed much of the Court's time and effort.

---

[132] Highet, 'Evidence, the Court, and the Nicaragua Case' 46.
[133] South West Africa, Second Phase, [1966] Pleadings-X, 122; XI, 460.
[134] Benzing, 'Evidentiary Issues' 1243 para 29.
[135] See *Daubert v. Merrel Dow Pharmaceuticals, Inc.*, 509 U.S. 579 (1993); for commentary see Eric Helland and Jonathan Klick, 'Does Anyone Get Stopped at the Gate? An Empirical Assessment of the Daubert Trilogy in the States' 20 *Supreme Court Economic Review* 1; Sophia I. Gatowski et al., 'Asking the Gatekeepers: A National Survey of Judges on Judging Expert Evidence in a Post-Daubert World' 25 *Law and Human Behavior* 433; O'Donnell, 'Judicialising History or Historicising Law'.
[136] *Kumho Tire Co. v. Carmichael, 119 S. Ct.*; Michael J. Saks, 'Banishing Ipse Dixit: The impact of Kumho Tire on Forensic Identification Science' 57 *Washington and Lee Law Review* 879, 882.

## 1.3.3 The continuing influence of the sovereign nature of the parties

A further facilitating factor is the sovereign nature of parties in cases before the Court which continues to influence the operation of the Court to this day. To elaborate, owing to the fact that the Court deals exclusively with States, there remains an extent to which the Court must take into account issues beyond the purely legal. This being the case, the ICJ is much more than a Court, since both symbolically and functionally it is concerned with more than the narrow adjudication of the legal issues raised in the case that has come before it. The Court, despite (or perhaps because of) the proliferation of international courts and tribunals in recent years, remains unrivalled in terms of informal influence and the authority of its legal pronouncements.[137]

The influence (waning or otherwise) of the principle of sovereign equality is a recurring theme in any study of international adjudication. Similarly, in the context of the ICJ's fact-finding processes, the significance of the principle of sovereign equality cannot be ignored and is a key factor in terms of explaining the Court's current reactive approach in three distinct but related senses. First of all, the Court has traditionally felt compelled to accommodate sovereign States' notions of the most appropriate way of presenting and substantiating its own version of events.[138] For instance, the Court in the *Nicaragua* case addressed the issue of sovereign equality and cited its influence as a key factor for explaining the Court's approach to the production of evidence:

> The provisions of the Statute and the Rules of the Court concerning the presentation of pleadings and evidence are designed to secure a proper administration of justice, and a fair and equal opportunity for each party to comment on its opponent's contention.[139]

---

[137] This is so despite the Court's legal pronouncements having no binding force apart from between the parties to the case before it under Article 59 of the Court's Statute, and despite there existing no formal doctrine of *stare decisis*, the Court's pronouncements have always been accorded significant respect by States, scholars and other international tribunals; see M. Shahabuddeen, *Precedent in the World Court*, Vol 13 (Cambridge University Press, 1996).

[138] Foster, *Science and the Precautionary Principle in International Courts and Tribunals* 80; Riddell and Plant, *Evidence before the International Court of Justice* 2.

[139] *Nicaragua Case* para 31.

The sovereign equality of States is part of the genetic make-up of international adjudication and the ensuing deference to the wishes of States in terms of fact-finding would appear to be a corollary.[140] This position is echoed in international legal scholarship by commentators who argue that when the parties before an international court such as the ICJ are sovereign States, 'it is perhaps only logical for them to have the main initiative and responsibility in regard to the production of evidence.'[141] It has even been argued that the failure to accurately establish the facts in an inter-State case can have more far-reaching consequences than a similar failure in a trial before a domestic court.[142] For instance, Sandifer has cited the fact that not only are the 'vital interests of states' at stake in a case before the Court that could potentially affect the lives of thousands of people, but the functioning of the international community and friendly relations between States could turn on the procedural establishment of the facts.[143] Similarly, Franck has made the link between the principle of sovereign equality and the next explanatory factor to be examined, that of compelled disclosure, which Franck argues is absolutely 'inconsistent with the nature of sovereignty'.[144]

Secondly, the sovereign nature of the parties before the Court affects its approach to fact-finding owing to the fact that the Court's jurisdiction is ultimately consensual. In other words, since the parties before the Court could in theory revoke their consent to appear before the Court at any time, the Court is forced to adopt a 'softly-softly' approach to evidence gathering in order to avoid States feeling as if their right to a fair hearing is being hindered by the Court's procedural approach to fact-finding.[145] As such, in seeking to ensure that States are not discouraged from consenting to the Court's jurisdiction it is felt that the Court must avoid narrow procedural technicalities.[146]

Finally, one of the most significant factors which facilitates the Court's reactive approach is the Court's apparent inability to compel the parties before it to produce evidence.[147] Whilst Chapter 4 will argue that the

---

[140] Wolfrum, 'International Courts and Tribunals, Evidence'.
[141] Valencia-Ospina, 'Evidence before the International Court of Justice' 202; Brower, 'Evidence Before International Tribunals: The Need for Some Standard Rules' 148.
[142] Sandifer, *Evidence before International Tribunals* 4.   [143] Ibid.
[144] Franck, *Fairness in International Law and Institutions* 336.
[145] Schwebel, *Three Cases of Fact-Finding by the International Court of Justice in International Law* 4.
[146] Watts, 'Burden of Proof and Evidence before the ICJ' 289.
[147] Highet, 'Evidence, the Court, and the Nicaragua Case' 10.

## 1.3 CONTRIBUTING FACTORS

Court can in fact be more proactive in terms of guiding the production of evidence, for now it can be said that the fact the Court does not possess an *explicit* power to compel the production of evidence has contributed to the mainstream belief that it is not competent to do so.

Neither the Court's Statute nor Rules provide any concrete guidance on when the Court should call upon States to produce evidence[148] and as a result it has only ever asked a State party to produce evidence on a handful of occasions (and has never drawn negative inferences from a State's failure to do so).[149] The Court's reluctance to draw negative conclusions from a refusal to produce requested evidence is symptomatic of the Court's general reluctance to take a proactive role in the fact-finding process.[150] Consequently, the onus falls very much on the State parties before the Court to do so.[151] As such, contributing to the Court's reactive approach to fact-finding, cases are generally defined by the evidence the parties seek to rely upon and by the facts they decide to contest.[152]

### 1.3.4 'Classical' approach to the international judicial function

A further factor that arguably could have contributed to the Court's current reactive approach to evidence is the so-called 'classical' account of the international judicial function. This account sees the process of judicial reasoning from the perspective of the 'judge in isolation, detached from his institutional surrounding and function in a juristic vacuum, freed from the restraints imposed by the requirements of evidence and procedure'.[153] As a result of this traditional conception of

---

[148] See Art. 49 ICJ Statute and Art. 62(1) Rules of the Court.
[149] Halink, 'All Things Considered: How the International Court of Justice Delegated its Fact-Assessment to the United Nations in the Armed Activities Case' 19; Teitelbaum, 'Recent Fact-Finding Developments at the International Court of Justice' 129.
[150] See Christian J. Tams, 'Article 49, 50' in A. Zimmerman (ed) *The Statute of the International Court of Justice: A Commentary* (Oxford and New York: Oxford University Press, 2006) 1099.
[151] Bernárdez, 'Article 48'; see also *Armed Activities Case* paras 58–9, (again citing the *Nicaragua Case* at 14, 50), and the practice followed in *Tehran Hostages Case* 3. See also *Bosnian Genocide Case* para 212; Halink, 'All Things Considered: How the International Court of Justice Delegated Its Fact-Assessment to the United Nations in the Armed Activities Case' 21.
[152] Article 49, Statute of the International Court of Justice, 26 June 1945, 58 Stat. 1055, 33 UNTS. 993.
[153] Scobbie, 'Discontinuance in the International Court' 808. See B. N. Cardozo, *The Nature of the Judicial Process* (Yale University Press, 1921); J. C. Hutcheson Jr, 'Judgment

adjudication the Court has in the past played down the significance of the procedural side of international adjudication. For example, the Court stated in the *Mavrommatis* case that '[t]he Court, whose jurisdiction is international, is not bound to attach to matters of form the same degree of importance which they possess in municipal law'.[154] This sentiment has been echoed again by the Court through the years in cases such as *Aegean Sea Continental Shelf* in which the Court stated that:

> Neither the Statute nor the Rules of Court contain any rule regarding the procedure to be followed in the event of an objection being taken *in limine litis* to the Court's jurisdiction. The Court therefore is at liberty to adopt the principle which it considers best calculated to ensure the administration of justice, most suited to procedure before an international tribunal and most in conformity with the fundamental principles of international law.[155]

A similar sentiment was expressed by Vice-President Wellington Koo in the preliminary objections phase of the *Barcelona Traction* case:

> [I]nternational law ... attaches less importance to form and appearance than municipal law ... International law, being primarily based upon the general principles of law and justice, is unfettered by technicalities and formalistic considerations which are often given importance in municipal law.[156]

The so-called *Mavrommatis* view that matters of form and procedure can be discounted is one which places the judge at the centre of the judicial process and sees the procedural and institutional framework of the Court as secondary to the will of the judge (who, as we have seen, is generally deferential to the sovereign nature of the State parties before the Court). This is a position that has been criticised[157] but for our purposes it

---

Intuitive: The Function of the Hunch in Judicial Decision' 14 *Cornell Law Quarterly* 274; E. Levi, 'An Introduction to Legal Reasoning' 15 *University of Chicago Law Review* 501.

[154] *Mavrommatis Palestine Concessions Case Preliminary Obejections Judgment.*

[155] *Aegean Sea Continental Shelf, Judgment, ICJ Reports 1978* 3 para 42 (see also paras 41-7).

[156] *Barcelona Traction, Light and Power Company, Limited, Preliminary Objections, Judgment, ICJ Reports 1964* 6 paras 15, 32; to this end see also Article 19 of the Nuremberg Charter which states that '[t]he Tribunal shall not be bound by technical rules of evidence. It shall adopt and apply to the greatest possible extent expeditious and non-technical procedure, and shall admit any evidence which it deems to have probative value'.

[157] For example, Scobbie argues that greater emphasis must be placed on the institutional context of judicial decision making – and highlights recent theoretical analysis of judicial activity and the restraints placed on judicial discretion by judges themselves as the main

should be noted that the traditional view of matters of procedure as a subsidiary concern is a factor which has contributed to the current reactive approach of the Court to fact-finding.[158]

The preceding subsections outlined that the Court has very clearly displayed a number of tendencies which, taken together, demonstrate a consistently reactive approach to the facts in cases that have come before it. Such tendencies evident in the Court's jurisprudence include the predominance of, and apparent preference for reliance on, documentary evidence before the Court; extremely broad rules of admissibility; the sovereign nature of the parties to cases before the Court and the so-called classical approach to the judicial process amongst a number of others. This reactive approach necessarily has a knock-on effect on the Court's fact-assessment practice, which is the subject to which we now turn our attention.

## 1.4 A natural counterpart: fact-assessment and the weighing of evidence

The preceding sections have illustrated that the Court plays a limited role in regulating the evidence that comes before it. As such, the Court is obliged to pay particularly close attention to the evaluation of this evidence (in particular if it is the basis for a legal pronouncement). As Judge Sir Hersch Lauterpacht stated, '[a] substantial part of the task of judicial tribunals consists in the examination and the weighing of the relevant facts',[159] and '[n]othing a court does affects the public perception of its fairness so clearly' as weighing of the facts.[160]

The weighing of the facts is here termed the Court's 'fact-assessment' role and is the central focus of the following sections. It is first necessary to differentiate more clearly the Court's fact-finding and fact-assessment roles by considering what exactly we mean when we talk about fact-assessment. As we have seen, evidence before the Court is not filtered in accordance with (detailed) rules of admissibility at the start of a case as it

---

driving factor for this shift in emphasis. Scobbie, 'Discontinuance in the International Court' 809. In terms of the theoretical analysis, see R. Alexy, R. Adler and N. MacCormick, *A Theory of Legal Argumentation – the Theory of Rational Discourse as a Theory of Legal Justification* (Oxford University Press, 1989); N. MacCormick, *Legal Reasoning and Legal Theory* (Oxford: Clarendon Press, 1978).

[158] Watts, 'Burden of Proof and Evidence before the ICJ' 289.
[159] Alford Jr, 'Fact Finding by the World Court' 56.
[160] Lauterpacht, *The Development of International Law by the International Court* 48.

is in many domestic legal systems. Further, there are no provisions in the Court's Statute or Rules which specifically address the probative weight that the Court should give to evidence submitted to it. In this regard the Court has substantial discretion in assessing and attributing weight to the evidence put before it.[161] As Judge Keith has stated, '[w]hat are issues of admissibility of evidence in some legal systems are often dealt with internationally as matters of weight or evaluation.'[162] As such, some forms of evidence considered inadmissible before national courts can come before the Court.[163]

The Court's own evaluation of the evidence in which it attributes weight to different forms of evidence, the 'discretionary power to assess the evidence', is described as the 'natural counterpart' of the principle of free admissibility[164] and is one of singular importance.[165] This process of weighing the probative value of the evidence put before it, the fact-assessment process in other words, is not only important in the abstract but in practical terms too since traditionally the material admissibility of evidence has 'rarely been disputed on formal grounds, with parties instead focussing on challenging the weight of evidence relied upon by the other side'[166] or 'probative value'.[167]

The Court itself has stated that it in assessing the weight of evidence before it, its task is to categorise evidence under different headings and

---

[161] Benzing, 'Evidentiary Issues' 1264.
[162] 'As mentioned, arguments that in some legal systems might lead to a court ruling that the evidence is inadmissible, for instance, as hearsay, opinion or the rulings of other courts, are generally directed instead at the weight to be given to the item', Keith, 'The International Court of Justice and Criminal Justice' 905; see also Katherine Del Mar, 'Weight of Evidence Generated through Intra-Institutional Fact-finding before the International Court of Justice' 2 *Journal of International Dispute Settlement* 393, 396.
[163] Del Mar, 'Weight of Evidence Generated through Intra-Institutional Fact-finding before the International Court of Justice' 396 gives the example of hearsay ("*preuve par oui-dire*"): the Court has stated '[n]or is testimony evidence not within the direct knowledge of the witness, but known to him only from hearsay, of much weight', *Nicaragua Case* para 68.
[164] Registry, Training and Research, *A Dialogue at the Court* 25; Rosenne and Ronen, *The Law and Practice of the International Court, 1920–2005* 257.
[165] Del Mar, 'Weight of Evidence Generated through Intra-Institutional Fact-finding before the International Court of Justice' 396; Halink, 'All Things Considered: How the International Court of Justice Delegated its Fact-Assessment to the United Nations in the Armed Activities Case' 21; Valencia-Ospina, 'Evidence before the International Court of Justice' 202.
[166] S. Rosenne, *The Law and Practice of the International Court* (3rd edn, The Hague: Martinus Nijhoff, 1985) 584.
[167] Riddell and Plant, *Evidence before the International Court of Justice* 185.

## 1.4 FACT-ASSESSMENT AND THE WEIGHING OF EVIDENCE

then allocate 'probative value to them accordingly'[168] or, in other words, to 'identify the documents relied on and make its own clear assessment of their weight, reliability and value'.[169]

The Court is the final arbiter in the assessment of the evidence that comes before it.[170] As Franck has stated, the Court must 'strive mightily to resolve cases on the facts – credible finings of fact – and avoid to the greatest degree possible the temptation to mitigate shortages of factual evidence, or lack of fact-analysis, by recourse to doctrines of law intended, wittingly or not, to bypass recourses to facts'.[171] However, just because the Court is the final arbiter of the facts, this does not mean that the Court acts in an arbitrary manner as we will see in the following subsection.

### 1.4.1 Assessment of evidence: guiding principles

In recent times several commentators have argued that there are a number of discernible principles which the Court has developed (admittedly in a piecemeal fashion and in a manner that is far from explicit)[172] in cases before it over the last thirty years which guide the Court in determining the weight, reliability and value that the Court will accord to evidence before it.[173] It has been suggested that the trend towards a clearer articulation of the principles which guide the Court in its assessment of the evidence, which has gained pace in the recent jurisprudence of the Court,[174] has its roots in the *Nicaragua* case,[175] to which we now turn.

---

[168] *Land and Maritime Boundary between Cameroon and Nigeria (Cameroon v. Nigeria), Preliminary Objections, Judgment, ICJ Reports 1998* 315, Dissenting Opinion of Judge Koroma para 8; Riddell and Plant, *Evidence before the International Court of Justice*.

[169] *Armed Activities Case* paras 58–9; the Court itself referred to *Nicaragua Case* 50, and the practice followed in *Tehran Hostages Case* 3.

[170] Registry, Training and Research, *A Dialogue at the Court* 25.

[171] Franck, 'Fact-finding in the I.C.J.'.

[172] Halink argues that a study of the practice of the Court shows that it has merely hinted at, as opposed to explicitly spelled out, exactly how it weighs evidence in case brought before it; Halink, 'All Things Considered: How the International Court of Justice Delegated its Fact-Assessment to the United Nations in the Armed Activities Case' 21.

[173] See for instance Registry, Training and Research, *A Dialogue at the Court* 25; Riddell and Plant, *Evidence before the International Court of Justice* 186; Halink, 'All Things Considered: How the International Court of Justice Delegated its Fact-Assessment to the United Nations in the Armed Activities Case' 22; S. Rosenne, *The Law and Practice of the International Court*, VVol 1 (The Hague: Martinus Nijhoff, 1965) 582.

[174] Riddell and Plant, *Evidence before the International Court of Justice* 186. [175] Ibid.

### 1.4.2 Practice of the Court

The non-appearance of the United States before the Court in the *Nicaragua* case meant that the Court was forced to 'articulate its scrutiny of the evidence in more detail than ever before'.[176] The Court acknowledged that a situation in which one party had refused to appear before the Court (a situation which the Court has faced in the past on more than eight occasions)[177] was a challenge to its traditional approach to fact-assessment in that it could not assume that the truth lay somewhere between the competing assertions of the parties before it. Despite the absence of one party, however, the Court stated that Article 53 of its Statute nevertheless obliged it to 'employ whatever means and resources may enable it to satisfy it whether the submissions of the Applicant State are well founded *in fact and law*'.[178] The Court noted that its role in such circumstances is modified somewhat and necessitates that the Court does not play a passive role but instead utilises its 'freedom in estimating the value of the various elements of evidence' (a topic that will be explored in more detail in Chapter 2 at 2.2).[179]

The Court gave careful consideration to how the facts put before the Court by Nicaragua were weighed and evaluated, in particular giving specific guidance on certain issues. The Court explicitly indicated a preference for certain types of evidence in its fact-assessment capacity, making reference to the general practice of courts and remarking that there were forms of testimony which were to be regarded as being of '*prima facie* superior credibility'.[180] The forms of evidence referred to by the Court include the evidence of a disinterested witness, defined as 'one who is not party to the proceedings and stands to gain or lose nothing from its outcome',[181] and the evidence of a party 'as is against its own interest'.[182] The Court held that such statements against the interest of

---

[176] Ibid.; Highet, 'Evidence and Proof of Facts' 2.
[177] *Corfu Channel Case, Anglo-Iranian Oil Co. (United Kingdom v. Iran), Preliminary Objection, Judgment, ICJ Reports 1952* 107; *Nottebohm Case (second phase), Judgment of April 6th, 1955: ICJ Reports 1955* 4; *Nuclear Tests (Australia v. France), Judgment, ICJ Reports 1974* 253; *Nuclear Tests Case 1974, Aegean Sea Continental Shelf Case, Tehran Hostages Case and Nicaragua Case.*
[178] *Nicaragua Case* paras 59–60 (emphasis added). C.f. the opinion of Judge Jennings who nevertheless was of the opinion that the United States had prejudiced its chances of success by not taking part in the proceedings and submitting evidence. Highet, 'Evidence, the Court, and the Nicaragua Case' 3.
[179] *Nicaragua Case* paras 59–60. [180] Ibid. paras 59–60. [181] Ibid. paras 59–60.
[182] Ibid. 14, 41; *Armed Activities Case* para 61.

## 1.4 FACT-ASSESSMENT AND THE WEIGHING OF EVIDENCE  47

the State made by 'high-ranking official political figures' are to be seen of particular probative value since they can be construed as a form of admission.[183]

Furthermore, in the absence of the United States the Court was forced to evaluate facts which were 'for the most part, matters of public of knowledge which have received extensive coverage in the world press' – an issue that the Court had previously had to consider in the *Tehran Hostages* case.[184] It was in this context that the Court expressed clear suspicion of what was termed 'evidence emanating from a single source'.[185] Instead, the Court indicated a strong preference for contemporaneous evidence from those with direct knowledge of the situation[186] stating that any evidence emanating from a single source had 'no greater value as evidence than the original source'.[187]

In stating that such forms of evidence are of superior credibility in the eyes of the Court in the process of its fact-assessment, the Court made explicit for the first time the type of consideration it takes into account when assessing evidence before it.[188] Whilst the Court only went as far as saying that such evidence was *prima facie* more credible, such guidance was significant in elucidating the Court's reasoning in fact-assessment and would subsequently be relied on and developed in later cases such as *Armed Activities*.[189]

In the *Armed Activities* case the Court gave what has been called '[t]he clearest statement of the Court's general approach to the assessment of evidence' to date, developing the position it had taken in earlier cases such as *Nicaragua*.[190] In this case the Court stated that its role in fact-assessment was to 'identify the documents relied on and make its own clear assessment of their weight, reliability and value' and crucially went on to explain what items it had eliminated from its consideration.[191] This

---

[183] *Nicaragua Case* 14, 41; *Armed Activities Case* para 61.
[184] *Tehran Hostages Case* 9, para 12.
[185] Halink, 'All Things Considered: How the International Court of Justice Delegated Its Fact-Assessment to the United Nations in the Armed Activities Case' 22; *Nicaragua Case* 14, 41.
[186] *Nicaragua Case* 14, 41.
[187] Halink, 'All Things Considered: How the International Court of Justice Delegated Its Fact-Assessment to the United Nations in the Armed Activities Case' 22; *Nicaragua Case* 14, 41.
[188] *Nicaragua Case* 41, paras 59–60.
[189] Riddell and Plant, *Evidence before the International Court of Justice* 189.
[190] See *Nicaragua Case* 85; see also *Tehran Hostages Case* 3.
[191] *Armed Activities Case* 59.

was the first time that the Court had expressly stated what pieces of evidence it had excluded due to their limited evidentiary value.[192]

The Court proceeded to elaborate on the forms of evidence that it considered to be of superior credibility, very much following the Nicaragua *dicta*, stating that it would treat with caution any evidence put before it which had been specifically prepared for the case at hand[193] and would treat with similar caution any evidentiary materials 'emanating from a single source'.[194] In giving further guidance, the Court stated that it would instead give preference to evidence from persons with direct knowledge and would give 'particular attention to reliable evidence acknowledging facts or conduct unfavourable to the State represented by the by the person making them' – making direct reference to the *Nicaragua* case in this regard.[195]

The Court went on to provide that it would give weight to evidence that has not been challenged 'by impartial persons for the correctness of what it contains' and that special attention was to be given to evidence obtained by examination of persons directly involved, and who were subsequently cross-examined 'by judges skilled in examination and experienced in assessing large amounts of factual information' (an issue to which we shall return).[196] The Court subsequently confirmed this reasoning in the *Bosnian Genocide* case in relation to this issue, stating that the Court 'should in principle accept as highly persuasive findings of fact made by [the ICTY] at trial, unless of course they have been upset on appeal'.[197]

In the *Pulp Mills* case the Court explicitly laid out its task in evaluating the evidence brought before it, stating that:

> [I]t is the responsibility of the Court, after having given careful consideration to all the evidence placed before it by the Parties, to determine which facts must be considered relevant, to assess their probative value, and to draw conclusions from them as appropriate.[198]

As Judge Keith echoed, the task of the Court is to 'decide disputes of fact which have to be resolved in determining whether a party to the proceedings has breached its legal obligations.'[199] Judges Al-Khasawneh and

---

[192] Riddell and Plant, *Evidence before the International Court of Justice* 190.
[193] *Armed Activities Case* 61.   [194] Ibid.
[195] Ibid.; see also *Nicaragua Case* para 64; Franck, *Fairness in International Law and Institutions* 338.
[196] *Armed Activities Case* para 61.   [197] *Bosnian Genocide Case* para 223.
[198] *Pulp Mills Case* para 168.   [199] Ibid., Separate Opinion of Judge Keith at para 8.

## 1.4 FACT-ASSESSMENT AND THE WEIGHING OF EVIDENCE 49

Simma further argued that 'the task of a court of justice is not to give a scientific assessment of what has happened, but to evaluate the claims of parties before it and whether such claims are sufficiently well-founded so as to constitute evidence of breach of a legal obligation'.[200]

Interestingly, in the *Georgia v. Russia* case in 2011, the Court seemed to develop what has been termed the 'legal significance' guiding principle.[201] In this case the Court set aside a large amount of evidence that had been brought before it by the parties, essentially conferring legal significance on 'only two exchanges' between Georgia and Russia in arriving at the conclusion that the crucial dispute arose between 9 and 12 August 2008.[202] In doing so the Court categorised all evidence dated earlier than 9 August 2008 as not being 'legally significant' for the purposes of showing the existence of a dispute through finding specific faults or defects with each individual piece of documentary evidence. The faults or defects with the evidence can be categorised as:

1. Formal defects, where, for example, circulation of documents to the United Nations under agenda heading items other than the crucial 'racial discrimination';[203]
2. Defects relating to authorship, such as where, for example, a document is not authored or endorsed by one or other of the parties;[204]
3. Defects due to inaction, where, for example, the judgment stated that the Georgian military did not act after complaints against Russian peacekeepers;[205]
4. Defects relating to attribution where, for example, documents did not show a clear attribution of violations to the Russian Federation;[206]
5. Defects relating to matters of notice where, for example, there appeared to be a lack of notice or proof that Russia received allegations of misconduct.[207]

---

[200] Ibid., Dissenting Opinion of Judges Al-Khasawneh and Simma at para 4.
[201] *Case Concerning Application of the International Convention on the Elimination of all Forms of Racial Discrimination (Georgia v. Russian Federation)* (Preliminary Objections) 2011, Separate Opinion of Judge Simma.
[202] These being statements of the Georgian and Russian Representatives in the Security Council debate on 10 August 2008 and a statement of the Georgian President Saakashvili in a CNN interview and the reply of the Russian Foreign Minister at the OSCE; ibid., Separate Opinion of Judge Simma at para 3.
[203] See ibid. at paras 53, 55–6, 59–62, 65–8, 70, 75–6, 78, 80–2, 84–7, 89, 91–103, 108.
[204] Ibid. at paras 54, 55, 71–3, 76, 80–1.   [205] Ibid. at paras 55, 74, 77, 79, 83, 84, 91.
[206] Ibid. at paras 51–3, 57–61, 81.   [207] Ibid. at paras 61, 104.

Taken as a whole, the statements of the Court in the cases examined demonstrate that whilst the Court is happy to delegate its fact-finding function to the parties, there are some general principles upon which the Court can draw when weighing evidence brought before the Court. Riddell and Plant, in their study on this issue (as cited by Judge Simma in his Separate Opinion in the *Georgia v. Russia* case), have suggested that the Court takes into account seven factors which can be summarised as including the following:

1. *Source*: whether the source of the evidence is independent from the parties and whether it has been corroborated;
2. *Interest*: whether the fact-finding in question has been carried out by a disinterested party;
3. *Relation to events*: whether the fact-finding is a direct observation of the events by someone who was present at the time or whether it is secondary information (or hearsay);
4. *Method*: whether the fact-finding was carried out in a methodologically sound manner;
5. *Verification*: whether the evidence has been previously cross-examined or corroborated;
6. *Contemporaneity*: less weight will be given to evidence not prepared at the time when the facts occurred due to the Court's wariness of documents provided specifically for the case before the Court;
7. *Procedure*: whether the evidence has come before the Court in accordance with its Rules of Procedure.[208]

To these seven principles it is suggested that a further two could be included. The first is that of the principle of legal significance, as relied upon by the Court in the *Georgia v. Russia* case through which, as we have seen above, a number of formal defects can deprive a piece of evidence of its evidentiary worth. The second is the principle of *executive-administrative finality*, a principle which grants greater weight to evidence originating from within the United Nations or similar organisations - a guiding principle discussed in detail in the following chapter at Section 2.2.4.

However, the main aim of this section has merely been to explore briefly the Court's current fact-assessment practice and to elucidate more clearly those guiding principles the Court has indicated it takes into consideration in cases that come before it. Having done so, considering

---

[208] Riddell and Plant, *Evidence before the International Court of Justice* 192, as cited by Judge Simma in his Separate Opinion in *Georgia v. Russia Case* at para 20.

## 1.5 A MORE PROACTIVE APPROACH TO FACT-FINDING?

the Court's reluctance to utilise those fact-finding powers that it possesses and preference for developing guiding principles for fact-assessment, a picture begins to emerge of the Court's reactive approach to fact-finding. Whilst some commentators have praised the Court's evaluation of evidence brought before it and its recent pronouncements setting out more clearly the factors it considers when assessing the facts, it is not our goal to make a judgement in this regard.[209] Rather, these principles are articulated here only in order to reinforce the point made in this chapter: the practice of the Court is to eschew its considerable fact-finding powers in favour of assessing the evidence put before it by the parties themselves.

A further question which must be asked at this preliminary stage, whilst examining the Court's current approach to fact-finding, is whether the Court's discretion to make factual determinations could ever be constrained in any way as a result of its role as principle organ of the United Nations. For instance, is the Court completely free to depart from a factual determination already made on an issue, for instance, by the Security Council of the United Nations? It is to this particular potential obstacle that we now turn in this final section of Chapter 1.

### 1.5 Does the Court have unlimited discretion to pursue a more proactive approach to fact-finding?

This part examines whether the Court's discretion to take a more proactive approach to fact-finding is in fact any way fettered by its position as part of the institutional framework of the United Nations. Not every international court and tribunal may be completely free to adopt a proactive approach to fact-finding. In fact, the institutional structure to which the court belongs may have a significant influence on how it approaches fact-finding.[210] For instance, Alvarez has argued that 'whether a court's assessment of the facts (or the law) is likely to remain the last word within the specific legal regime in which it operates is likely to influence how (or even whether) it engages in fact-finding.'[211] Ultimately, any international court or tribunal's factual determinations 'may turn on whether the court thinks it can get away with

---

[209] Paul S. Reichler, 'The Impact of the Nicaragua Case on Matters of Evidence and Fact-Finding' 25 *Leiden Journal of International Law* 149, 149.
[210] See Martin Shapiro, *Courts: A Comparative and Political Analysis* (University of Chicago Press, 1986).
[211] J. Alvarez, 'Are International Judges Afraid of Science?: A Comment on Mbengue' 34 *Loyola of Los Angeles International and Comparative Law Review* 12, 92.

such determinations, or whether it needs to pay heed to its own fragile legitimacy or jurisdiction'.[212] There has been some suggestion that the Court might not be completely free to make factual determinations. For instance, the Court in the *Namibia* advisory opinion stated that:

> A binding determination made by a competent organ of the United Nations to the effect that a situation is illegal cannot remain without consequence. Once the Court is faced with such a situation, it would be failing in the discharge of its judicial function if it did not declare that there is an obligation, especially upon Members of the United Nations, to bring that situation to an end.[213]

In a similar vein, in its written submissions in *The Wall* advisory opinion, Belgium argued that since General Assembly Resolution ES-10/13 of 21 October 2003 had already 'identified the applicable law but also expressly declared the wall to be in contradiction to international law'[214] the Court's legal opinion was not necessary, suggesting that when another organ of the United Nations has made a factual determination, the Court is precluded from examining the same factual issue.

Relatedly, Germany argued that any opinion the Court would give would be 'devoid of object and purpose',[215] since:

> [T]he question on which the opinion of the Court has been sought concerns issues where the Assembly has already taken a clear legal position. In its resolution ES-10113, the General Assembly not only *identified* the law that applies to the issue (International Humanitarian Law) but also already formally *declared* the wall to be in contradiction to international law. Thus, the General Assembly requires no guidance from the Court on the legality of the wall.[216]

Comparably, in the same case Jordan submitted that '[w]here the Security Council has decided or determined or declared that a situation is in violation of international law, and has thus considered it to be illegal, or where the General Assembly's consistent conduct over many *years* reflects an *opinio juris* to that effect, the Court cannot disregard such legal conclusions'.[217]

---

[212] Ibid.  [213] *Namibia Advisory Opinion* 52 para 117.
[214] *The Wall Advisory Opinion, Submission of Belgium* para 8.
[215] Contrary to *Applicability of Article VI, Section 22, of the Convention on the Privileges and Immunities of the United Nations, Advisory Opinion, ICJ Reports 1989* 177, 188.
[216] *The Wall Advisory Opinion, Submission of Germany* 8, stating '[w]hat is more, the General Assembly has already answered the question as to what "legal consequences" arise from the construction of the wall: in resolution ES-10113, and by applying the norms of international law on state responsibility, it *demanded* that Israel "stop and reverse" the construction of the wall'; see also *The Wall Advisory Opinion, Submission of Germany* 60, 5.63.
[217] *The Wall Advisory Opinion, Submission of Germany* 60, 5.63.

## 1.5 A MORE PROACTIVE APPROACH TO FACT-FINDING?

However, this ought not to be the case with regards to the ICJ. The Court is not bound to accept findings-of-fact made by other UN organs and in fact it is not desirable for it to do so. In examining more closely the Court's role as final arbiter of the facts, and following on from the examination of the principles that guide the Court in the course of fact-assessment, the following section will focus in greater detail on the Court's freedom to depart from findings-of-fact made by other UN organs.

### 1.5.1 Gagged and bound? The International Court of Justice and its relationship with other principal organs

Factual determinations made in Security Council and General Assembly resolutions play a significant role in the Court's assessment of the facts.[218] But how exactly is the Court affected by factual determinations made by other principal organs of the United Nations? Is it formally bound to follow findings-of-fact as espoused by the General Assembly or the Security Council for example or is it free instead to determine and assess the facts for itself in its capacity as a judicial body? In answering these questions it is suggested that conducting a static examination of the traditional roles of the principal organs based on the role envisaged for them in the UN Charter is a helpful starting point.

### 1.5.2 A static examination of the traditional roles of the principal organs

The Court is just one of six principal organs of the United Nations and all six principal organs of the Organisation are (at least) formally equal.[219] The Court's status as both principal organ and principal judicial organ is the basis for this formal equality.[220]

---

[218] Teitelbaum, 'Recent Fact-Finding Developments at the International Court of Justice' 148. This can take many forms: directly submitted to the court (such as dossiers and written statements prepared by the Secretary-General on behalf of the UN in advisory proceedings – following a request from the Court under Article 69(4) of the Statute of the Court) or by State parties before the Court bringing UN Documents to the attention of the Court (in advisory or contentious proceedings). See also Del Mar, 'Weight of Evidence Generated through Intra-Institutional Fact-finding before the International Court of Justice' 395.

[219] Mohammed Bedjaoui, *The New World Order and the Security Council: Testing the Legality of its Acts* (The Hague: Martinus Nijhoff, 1994) 13.

[220] Article 7(1) UN Charter which marks the Court out as a principal organ of the organisation must be read in conjunction with Article 92 UN Charter which refers to the Court as the principal judicial organ of the UN and Article 1 of the Court's Statute which refers

### 1.5.3   The Court: principal organ

There are a number of important legal implications of the Court's status as principal organ under Article 7(1) of the UN Charter.[221] For our purposes, however, it is first of all crucial to note that the principal organs of the UN are to a large extent interdependent and operate under a duty of co-operation with the other principal organs.[222] Furthermore, there is no hierarchy between it and the other principal organs, ('at least not between the ICJ and the Security Council and General Assembly'.[223]) As such, the Court's status as principal organ 'means that it exists on a par with the other principal organs'.[224]

### 1.5.4   The Court: judicial organ – functional distinction

Further, despite the fact the Court's status under Article 94 of the UN Charter as a judicial organ distinguishes it, and marks its independence from, the other principal organs,[225] this judicial status does not change the relationship between it and the other principal organs which continues to be governed by the principal of equality. As Gowlland-Debbas has stated:

> to the Court has having been established by the Charter of the UN as the principal judicial organ of the UN.

[221] Including the incorporation of the Court's Statute into the UN Charter and that the Court is bound to the goals and principles expressed in Articles 1 and 2 of the Charter; S. Rosenne, *The Law and Practice of the International Court* (2nd edn, The Hague: Martinus Nijhoff, 1987) 64; A. Pellet, 'Strenghtening the Role of the International Court of Justice as the Principal Organ of the United Nations' 3 *The Law and Practice of International Courts and Tribunals* 159, 161.

[222] V. Gowlland-Debbas, 'Article 7' in A. Zimmermann (ed), *The Statute of the International Court of Justice: A Commentary* (Oxford University Press, 2006) 87; see also Bedjaoui, *The New World Order and the Security Council: Testing the Legality of Its Acts* 13; Pellet, 'Strenghtening the Role of the International Court of Justice as the Principal Organ of the United Nations' 162.

[223] The Secretary General has also referred to the 'complementary relationship between the three concerned organs' (1991 Report of the SG – UN Doc. A/46/1, 1991, p. 4); see also Bedjaoui, *The New World Order and the Security Council: Testing the Legality of Its Acts* 78; Gowlland-Debbas, 'Article 7' 88; Rosenne, *The Law and Practice of the International Court 1987* 71, T. D. Gill, 'Legal and Some Political Limitations on the Power of the UN Security Council to Exercise its Enforcement Powers under Chapter VII of the Charter' 26 *Netherlands Yearbook of International Law* 33, 117.

[224] T. D. Gill and S. Rosenne, *The World Court: What It Is and How It Works*, VVol 41 (The Hague: Martinus Nijhoff, 2003) 36.

[225] Gowlland-Debbas, 'Article 7' 93.

## 1.5 A MORE PROACTIVE APPROACH TO FACT-FINDING? 55

> As a 'principal organ', the ICJ is bound to cooperate with the other principal organs and to give effect to their decisions; as a 'judicial organ' it distinguishes itself from the other organs in its composition and functions which direct it to maintain its judicial integrity and its distance from the other, politically-oriented bodies.[226]

The functional distinction between the Court and the other principal organs can be seen in relation to its responsibilities, its composition and its method of operation. The Court is an independent judicial body composed of impartial judges as opposed to appointed politicians or civil servants, and whilst it may share the ultimate goal of the maintenance of international peace and security and settlement of international disputes, the Court operates in accordance with its Statute in a legal manner in conducting purely legal proceedings.[227]

This functional distinction extends to the fact-finding and fact-assessment activities of the different UN organs. As we have seen in Chapter 1, the Court possesses broad fact-finding powers which are judicial in character. On the other hand the Security Council, as the executive arm of the UN, is political in terms of its composition and its fact-finding activities reflect this.[228] Information relied upon by the Council when passing resolutions would not necessarily be accorded any weight by the Court.[229]

The Court itself has considered the functional distinction between the UN organs, contrasting the Court's legal methods of dispute settlement with the Council's methods.[230] For instance, the Court has said that whilst Members of the Council are legally entitled to base their decisions

---

[226] Ibid. (emphasis added).
[227] V. Gowlland-Debbas, 'The Relationship between the International Court of Justice and the Security Council in the Light of the Lockerbie Case' 88 *The American Journal of International Law* 643, 653.
[228] G. Distefano and E. Henry, 'The International Court of Justice and the Security Council: Distentangling Themis from Ares' in Karine Bannelier, Théodore Christakis and Sarah Heathcote (eds), *The ICJ and the Evolution of International Law: The Enduring Impact of the Corfu Channel Case* (Oxford and New York: Routledge, 2012).
[229] Ibid., citing *Case Concerning Questions of Interpretation and Application of the 1971 Montreal Convention Arising from the Aerial Incident at Lockerbie, (Libyan Arab Jamahiriya v. United States of America), Provisional Measures*, Order of 14 April 1992, ICJ Reports 1992 114, paras 42–3.
[230] Lockerbie, 1992 ICJ Rep. at 22, 134, and 34, 144, respectively; Gowlland-Debbas, 'The Relationship Between the International Court of Justice and the Security Council in the Light of the Lockerbie Case' 653; see also 1992 ICJ Rep at 96, 201 (El-Kosheri, J., Dissenting), ibid.

on political considerations,[231] the Court's judicial function prohibits it from making decisions based on practicability or political expediency.[232] As such, in the words of Judge Weeramantry, the Court's 'tests of validity and the bases of its decisions are naturally not the same as they would be before a political or executive organ of the United Nations.'[233] The position of the Court as set out in the Charter is well summarised by Judge Schwebel in the *Nicaragua* case:

> [W]hile the Security Council is invested by the Charter with the authority to determine the existence of an act of aggression, it does not act as a court in making such a determination. It may arrive at a determination of aggression – or, as more often is the case, fail to arrive at a determination of aggression – for political rather than legal reasons. However compelling the facts which could give rise to a determination of aggression, the Security Council acts within its rights when it decides that to make such a determination will set back the cause of peace rather than advance it. In short, the Security Council is a political organ which acts for political reasons. It may take legal considerations into account but, unlike a court, it is not bound to apply them.[234]

As such, the Court's role as both principal and judicial organ puts it in a position of both interdependence and independence. The records of the UNCIO confirm that the position of equality between organs created by Articles 7(1) and 94 UN Charter was envisaged by the drafters of the Charter.[235] Despite the fact 'there appears to have been no [explicit] discussion at San Francisco of the mutual relations of the different principal organs established by the Charter'[236] the protracted debate regarding the role that the principal organs should play in interpretation of the Charter provides valuable guidance as to the way in which the drafters envisaged the relationship between the principal organs and the Court.

By way of illustration, a proposal that would have seen the inclusion of a provision explicitly addressing the issue of Charter interpretation in the

---

[231] *Admission of a State to the United Nations (Charter, Art 4), Advisory Opinion: ICJ Reports 1948* 57, Basdevant, Winiarski, McNair and Read, J. J., dissenting.
[232] *Haya de la Torre Case, Judgment of 13 June1951: ICJ Reports 1951* 71, 79.
[233] 1992 ICJ Rep. at 56, 166. See also Elihu Lauterpacht, 'Aspects of the Administration of International Justice' 42–3 (1991).
[234] *Nicaragua Case*.
[235] Del Mar, 'Weight of Evidence Generated through Intra-Institutional Fact-finding before the International Court of Justice' 395.
[236] Rosenne, *The Law and Practice of the International Court 1987* 64.

## 1.5 A MORE PROACTIVE APPROACH TO FACT-FINDING? 57

body of the UN Charter itself was not adopted by the Subcommittee.[237] Rather, the Subcommittee favoured a decentralised approach whereby no single principal organ was given exclusive authority to interpret the Charter.[238] The Subcommittee Report stated that 'in the course of the operations from day to day of the various organs of the Organization, it is inevitable that each organ will interpret such parts of the Charter as are applicable to its functions.'[239] The Subcommittee Report further stated that States and competent UN organs were free to interpret the Charter in a whole number of ways 'including by reference to the International Court of Justice'[240] in the course of contentious or advisory proceedings.[241] Consequently, whilst the Court has a role in Charter interpretation like all other principal organs, the role of the Court, or of any other principal organ for that matter, is not exclusive or definitive.[242]

In lieu of any principal organ having exclusive domain over interpretation of the Charter, the concept of 'general acceptance' plays a central role. To elaborate, if any organ were to interpret the Charter in a way that was not conceived as of as being 'generally acceptable' by the other organs, that particular interpretation would be rendered without binding force.[243] This ensures that the equality of principal organs is respected and that the power of interpreting the Charter is

---

[237] Doc. 933, IV/2/42(2), Documents of the United Nations Conference on International Organization, San Francisco, 1945, (Volume 13, Commission IV, Judicial Organization, Library of Congress, United Nations Information Organizations) 709.

[238] B. Martenczuk, 'The Security Council, the International Court and judicial review: What lessons from Lockerbie?' 10 *European Journal of International Law* 517, 526.

[239] Doc. 933, IV/2/42(2), Documents of the United Nations Conference on International Organization, San Francisco, 1945, (Volume 13, Commission IV, Judicial Organization, Library of Congress, United Nations Information Organizations) 709.

[240] Martenczuk, 'The Security Council, the International Court and judicial review: What lessons from Lockerbie?' 526; c.f. G. R. Watson, 'Constitutionalism, Judicial Review, and the World Court' 34 *Harvard International Law Journal* 1, 8.

[241] Article 96(1) UN Charter; see also Doc. 933, IV/2/42(2), Documents of the United Nations Conference on International Organization, San Francisco, 1945 (Volume 13, Commission IV, Judicial Organization, Library of Congress, United Nations Information Organizations) 709.

[242] N. Singh, *The Role and Record of the International Court of Justice* (The Hague: Martinus Nijhoff, 1989) 39; Martenczuk, 'The Security Council, the International Court and judicial review: What lessons from Lockerbie?' 526.

[243] Article 96(1) UN Charter; see also Doc. 933, IV/2/42(2), Documents of the United Nations Conference on International Organization, San Francisco, 1945 (Volume 13, Commission IV, Judicial Organization, Library of Congress, United Nations Information Organizations) 709; Doc. 933, at 710.

dispersed.[244] Taken together, this results in a situation in which 'there is no institutional hierarchy as between these [principal] organs'[245] as 'each of the principal organs possesses its own interpretation of certain elements of the Charter'.[246]

Furthermore, in interpreting the Charter each organ must balance its freedom to interpret the Charter with the principle of legality,[247] a general limitation on the power of UN organs,[248] which essentially provides that UN organs must operate 'in accordance with the present Charter'.[249] In the absence of judicial review of the acts of UN organs to determine their legality, this decentralised system for ensuring compliance with the law is the only one that is truly 'compatible with the reality of the Charter as a treaty and with the consensual character of the underlying relations' at this stage of development in the international legal order.[250]

### 1.5.5 *Functional parallelism*

However, it is clear that the relationship of equality between principal organs brings with it considerable potential for conflict. As Pellet has stated, '[t]o be blind to the tensions which might arise from this requires a large amount of angelism or naïvité'.[251] In such cases the question arises as to whether, for example, in acting under Chapter VII of the Charter, the Council can bind the Court. As we have seen,

---

[244] Doc. 933, at 710; see also Watson, 'Constitutionalism, Judicial Review, and the World Court' 12; Bedjaoui, *The New World Order and the Security Council: Testing the Legality of Its Acts* 11.

[245] M. N. Shaw, 'The Security Council and the International Court of Justice: Judicial Drift and Judicial Function' in A. S. Muller (ed), *The International Court of Justice: Its Future Role After Fifty Years*, VVol 3 (The Hague: Martinus Nijhoff, 1997) 237.

[246] Bedjaoui, *The New World Order and the Security Council: Testing the Legality of Its Acts* 11.

[247] F. Francioni, 'Multilateralism à la carte: The Limits to Unilateral Withholdings of Assessed Contributions to the UN Budget' 11 *European Journal of International Law* 43, 52.

[248] See *Admission of a State to the UN Advisory Opinion* 64 in which the Court stated: 'The political character of an organ cannot release it from the observance of the treaty provisions established by the Charter when they constitute limitations on its power or criteria for its judgment'.

[249] To use the terminology of Article 25(5) of the Charter.

[250] Francioni, 'Multilateralism à la carte' 58.

[251] Pellet, 'Strenghtening the Role of the International Court of Justice as the Principal Organ of the United Nations' 159.

## 1.5 A MORE PROACTIVE APPROACH TO FACT-FINDING? 59

however, a static examination of the Charter system reveals that this is not so and that in formal terms no organ is entitled to bind the other. Rather, the Charter envisages that the Court and the Council co-operate in matters that are of concern to both organs in tandem. The Court has echoed this sentiment, stating in the *Nicaragua* case that 'the Council has functions of a political nature assigned to it whereas the Court exercises purely judicial functions. Both organs can therefore perform their separate but complementary functions with respect to the same events.'[252]

Consequently the functional distinction between the organs is clear-cut: '"the function of the Court is to state the law"[253] and it can decide only on the basis of law'[254] meaning that 'no objection of *lis pendens* or *res judicata* may be raised against the ICJ acting simultaneously ... in a case pending before the SC'.[255] As a result, whilst the Court will always apply the law to the case at hand, 'its power of action and decision is subject to no limitation deriving from the fact that the dispute before it might also be within the competence of some other organ.'[256]

Whilst Article 12 UN Charter fetters the competence of the General Assembly to make recommendations on matters of international peace and security when a particular situation is already before the Security Council,[257] 'the ICJ has not generally considered itself to be similarly constrained.'[258] On the other hand, it is clear that just as the Council cannot bind the Court, the fact that a matter is before the Court does not prevent the Council from also dealing with the matter – 'the ICJ does not benefit from any privilege of primacy in the exercise of its law-adjudicating function'[259] – and consequently 'the Court is not bound to defer to the Council in a particular case and vice versa'.[260] As Rosenne

---

[252] Ibid.
[253] *Northern Cameroons (Cameroon v. United Kingdom), Preliminary Objections, Judgment,* ICJ Reports 1963 33; see also Shaw, 'The Security Council and the International Court of Justice' 238.
[254] *Haya de la Torre Case* 79; see also Shaw, 'The Security Council and the International Court of Justice' 238.
[255] J. Delbrück, 'Article 24' in B. Simma (ed), *Charter of the United Nations: A Commentary* (Oxford University Press, 2002) 447.
[256] Rosenne, *The Law and Practice of the International Court 1987* 118.   [257] Ibid.
[258] K. R. Cronin-Furman, 'The International Court of Justice and the United Nations Security Council: Rethinking a Complicated Relationship' 106 *Columbia Law Review* 435, 442.
[259] Distefano and Henry, 'Distentangling Themis from Ares' 68.
[260] *Nicaragua Case* 392.

has famously stated, this 'well illustrates the functional parallelism of two principal organs of the United Nations, each of which has competence, under the combined Charter and Statute, to deal with the same "dispute"'.[261]

Article 36(3) of the UN Charter provides another example of a clear functional distinction between the organs and the fact that action by one organ does not preclude action by another: again we see functional parallelism. Article 36(3) of the Charter sets out that the Security Council should take into account the fact that 'legal disputes should as a general rule be referred by the parties to the Court'.[262] As the Court confirmed in the *Tehran Hostages* case,[263] whilst the Court ought not to be precluded from addressing the legal issues that arise in the settlement of an international dispute, and whilst the juxtaposition of Articles 36(1) and (3) hints at a distinction between legal and political disputes, any suggestion that the Council should be legally obliged to refrain from dealing with a dispute on the fact it is 'purely legal' is not feasible in practice.[264] The Court itself said as much in the *Nicaragua* case, questioning whether the Council should shy away from a case brought before it because it has legal implications.[265] Indeed, nothing in the Charter imposes a binding obligation on the Council (Article 36(3) uses 'should' rather than 'shall'),[266] to refer a dispute to the Court on the basis that it has legal implications, in all likelihood since it is almost impossible to imagine any

---

[261] Rosenne and Ronen, *The Law and Practice of the International Court, 1920–2005* 87; see also I. Petculescu, 'The Review of the United Nations Security Council Decisions by the International Court of Justice' 52 *Netherlands International Law Review* 167, 170; in practice, the Court has abided by this conception of parallelism. In the *Nicaragua* case, the Court stated that 'even after a determination under Article 39, there is no necessary inconsistency between Security Council action and adjudication by the Court'; see also Stein and Richter, 'Article 36' in Bruno Simma and Hermann Mosler (eds), *The Charter of the United Nations: A Commentary* (Oxford University Press, 1996) 545.

[262] Recommendations of the SC made under Art 36(1) (made only once in practice – in the Corfu Channel case) are not binding and do not establish the jurisdiction of the Court: and, 'to interpret Art 36(6) as suggested above would amount to a recognition of compulsory jurisdiction because the parties themselves would be forced to abstain from voting in the SC under Art 27(3)'; see also Stein and Richter, 'Article 36' .545.

[263] In the *Tehran Hostages* case the Court stated that it was for the Court itself as the principal judicial organ of the UN 'to resolve any legal questions that may be in issue between parties to a dispute; and the resolution of such legal questions by the Court may be an important and sometimes decisive, factor in promoting the peaceful settlement of the dispute. This is indeed recognized by Article 36 of the Charter, paragraph 3' *Tehran Hostages Case* 22 para 40.

[264] Stein and Richter, 'Article 36' 545.   [265] *Nicaragua Case* 435 para 96.

[266] Stein and Richter, 'Article 36' 545.

international dispute that did not have legal implications. At most it could be said that Article 36(3) obligates the Council to consider other procedures for settlement of the dispute.[267] It would appear that the only way in which the traditional distinction between the political and the legal has any relevance is in whether the Council, in exercising its considerable discretion, feels that the behaviour of the parties to any dispute would benefit from judicial settlement of the dispute through referral to the Court or whether the political powers of the Council itself would be better suited.[268]

### 1.5.6 A dynamic examination of the roles of the principal organs: jurisprudence of the Court

The significance of the practice of the Court and factual determinations made by its resolutions lies in the fact that it is possible that through the acquiescence of States, a 'subsequent practice' in terms of Article 31(3)(b) of the Vienna Convention on the Law of Treaties could be formed.[269] But is there a basis to the argument that the practice of the Council brings into question the formally equality of the two organs? In other words; is there any evidence that the Court has considered its own discretion fettered by Security Council action? In order to answer these questions, it is essential to consider a number of significant cases.

The jurisprudence of the Court brings out very clearly the theme of the absence of any hierarchy between the principal organs (at least between the Court and the Council). In the cases that have come before the Court in which there have been issues of concurrent exercise of powers, there has never been any suggestion from either the Council or

---

[267] Gowlland-Debbas, 'The Relationship between the International Court of Justice and the Security Council in the Light of the Lockerbie Case' 656; see also H. Kelsen, *The Law of the United Nations: A Critical Analysis of Its Fundamental Problems* (New York: Frederick A. Praeger, 1950) 405, T. J. H. Elsen, *Litispendence between the International Court of Justice and the Security Council* (The Hague: TMC Asser Instituut, 1986) 54.

[268] *WHO Advisory Opinion*, para 25.

[269] Article 31(3)(b) Vienna Convention on the Law of Treaties 1969, Done at Vienna on 23 May 1969, United Nations Treaty Series, VVol 1155. p. 331; see also Watson, 'Constitutionalism, Judicial Review, and the World Court' 15; S. Lamb, 'Legal Limits to United Nations Security Council Powers' in Guy S. Goodwin-Gill and Stefan Talmon (eds), *The Reality of International Law: Essays in Honour of Ian Brownlie* (Oxford University Press, 1999) 365.

the Court that the simultaneous exercise of their respective functions would be problematic.[270] To give but one example, the Court in *Certain Expenses* stated that:

> It is not to be assumed that the General Assembly would ... seek to fetter or hamper the Court in the discharge of its judicial functions; the Court must have full liberty to consider all relevant data available to it in forming an opinion on a question posed to it for an advisory opinion.[271]

As such, the position is that as stated by the United States during the *Tehran Hostages* crisis: '[t]here is absolutely nothing in the United Nations Charter or in this Court's Statute to suggest that action by the Security Council excludes action by the Court, even if the two actions might in some respects be parallel.'[272] But what of factual determinations more specifically?

Whilst the Court has considered factual determinations made by the Security Council and General Assembly on a number of occasions, its pronouncements could not accurately be described as particularly coherent or enlightening until relatively recently. In the *Northern Cameroons* case the Court found that the case before it was non-justiciable since the legal issue in question, the legal status of the territory, had already been determined by the General Assembly.[273] In addition, at the merits stage of the *Armed Activities* case the Court held that the Uganda Peoples' Defence Forces (UPDF) had violated territorial sovereignty 'on the Security Council's determination that the conflict constituted a threat to peace, security and stability in the region and that the Security Council

---

[270] *Hostages Case*, 1980 ICJ Rep. at 21–2; the Court stated that '[t]he reasons are clear. It is for the Court, the principal judicial organ of the United Nations, to resolve any legal questions that may be in issue between parties to a dispute; and the resolution of such legal questions by the Court may be an important, and sometimes decisive, factor in promoting the peaceful settlement of the dispute.'

[271] *Certain Expenses of the United Nations (Article 17, paragraph 2, of the Charter)*, Advisory Opinion of 20 July 1962: ICJ Reports 1962 157.

[272] Gowlland-Debbas, 'The Relationship Between the International Court of Justice and the Security Council in the Light of the Lockerbie Case' 656; see also the oral proceedings in *The Wall* in which Palestine made the compelling argument that the Court should bear in mind that its task is not simply to give 'just another political opinion' but as principal judicial organ of the United Nations, the Court ought to remain 'faithful to the requirements of its judicial character' and give a legal judgment that necessarily entails autonomous factual determinations; see *The Wall Advisory Opinion, Submission of Palestine* 33, para 14.

[273] *Northern Cameroons Case* 21.

called for States concerned "to bring to an end the presence of these uninvited forces".[274] It has been said that the Court in *Armed Activities* 'seemed to consider some of the Security Council Resolutions as providing a factual basis from which the Court could draw legal conclusions, almost as if a Security Council Resolution constituted fact-findings of a lower court'.[275]

Similarly, in *The Wall* advisory opinion the Court's argument that the territories in question remained occupied was based on Security Council Resolutions that condemned the occupation and action taken by Israel.[276] Further, in relation to the applicability of the Geneva Convention IV to the Occupied Territory the Court expressly referred to General Assembly and Security Council resolutions as authority.[277] The Court also employed, albeit as subsidiary authority, resolutions in relation to the right of the Palestine to self-determination[278] and that the settlements breach the Geneva Convention IV.[279] It was in relation to this last issue, the illegality of the settlements, however, that the Court was most heavily reliant on UN resolutions – referring exclusively to Security Council Resolutions 446 (22 March 1979), 452 (20 July 1979) and 456 (1 March 1980) for legal justification.[280] Criticism of *The Wall* advisory opinion for precluding itself from participating in any fact-finding and accepting that the SG's Report mentioned in the question provided for a 'given factual situation.'[281] Commentators at the time remarked upon the fact that it is surprising that the Court would rely so heavily on resolutions that were not

---

[274] *Armed Activities Case* 224 para 151; UNSC Resolution 1234, 9 April 1999; Del Mar, 'Weight of Evidence Generated through Intra-Institutional Fact-finding before the International Court of Justice' 408.

[275] Teitelbaum, 'Recent Fact-Finding Developments at the International Court of Justice' 149.

[276] UNSC Resolution 242 (1967), 22 November 1967; UNSC Resolution 298 (1971), 25 September 1971; UN SC Resolution 478 (1980), 20 August 1980. See the Separate Opinion of Judge Higgins, *Legal Consequences of the Construction of a Wall (Advisory Opinion)* 2004 136, paras 74–5.

[277] Ibid. paras 98–9.

[278] Ibid. paras 118, 88, 156; I. Scobbie, 'Unchart(er)ed Waters?: Consequences of the Advisory Opinion on the Legal Consequences of the Construction of a Wall in the Occupied Palestinian Territory for the Responsibility of the UN for Palestine' 16 *European Journal of International Law* 941, 943.

[279] *The Wall Advisory Opinion* para 120.

[280] Ibid. paras 99, 120. Despite, as Scobbie has pointed out, other material being available on this point; Scobbie, 'Unchart(er)ed Waters?' 943.

[281] See *The Wall Advisory Opinion* para 37.

technically binding under Chapter VII, and with no reference to the interpretation of this provision in State practice.[282]

The combination of Article 25 UN Charter and Article 103 UN Charter render Security Council Resolutions binding on all Member States and create obligations that take precedence over all other legal norms (save, perhaps, for *jus cogens* norms). Whilst clearly intended to cover inter-State relations, these fundamentally important provisions of the UN Charter nevertheless mean that is 'difficult ... for the Court to deviate from an assessment of fact by the Security Council that forms the basis of measures adopted by the Council acting under Chapter VII of the UN Charter'.[283]

In addition, Pellet's suggestion that 'the resolutions of other principal organs, whether of the General Assembly or the Security Council, are not relied on that much by the Court unless they have a compulsory nature'[284] seems questionable. For example, one commentator has pointed out that 'the Court attributes weight to both binding and non-binding paragraphs of General Assembly and Security Council Resolutions' citing the Court's reliance on a preambular paragraph of Security Council Resolution 1304 (2000) in aiding its determination that massive human rights violations and grave breaches of International Humanitarian Law (IHL) had taken place[285] and the Court's reliance on a preambular paragraph of a General Assembly Resolution which referred to the 'abhorrent policy of ethnic cleansing being carried out in Bosnia-Herzegovina' as examples.[286] Further, it has been shown that 'the Court referred to and quoted from a number of preambular and operative paragraphs of Security Council and General Assembly resolutions that referred to sexual violence', which were 'based on reports before the General Assembly and Security Council, such as Reports of the Secretary-General, the

---

[282] Such as international legal scholarship, including the work of the ICHRC, and statements of parties to the Geneva Convention; Scobbie, 'Unchart(er)ed Waters?'.

[283] Del Mar, 'Weight of Evidence Generated through Intra-Institutional Fact-finding before the International Court of Justice' 407.

[284] Pellet has argued that criticism of the Court's reliance on General Assembly and Security Council resolutions is 'not well-founded' since 'it is normal and legitimate that the principal judicial organ of the United Nations demonstrates that it is particularly attentive to the "trends" expressed in the resolutions of the political organs.' Pellet, 'Strenghtening the Role of the International Court of Justice as the Principal Organ of the United Nations' 169.

[285] *Armed Activities Case* paras 206–7 and UNSC Resolution 1304 (2000), 16 June 2000.

[286] *Bosnian Genocide Case* para 190.

## 1.5 A MORE PROACTIVE APPROACH TO FACT-FINDING? 65

Commission of Experts, the Special Rapporteur for Human Rights ... and various United Nations agencies in the field.'[287]

Whilst the Court in the past has stated that any factual or legal determinations made by the Security Council 'had the same legal force as the provision of the resolution in which it was contained' until the *Kosovo* Advisory Opinion of 2010 the Court had not squarely addressed the issue in any case that had come before it .[288] The Court has on several occasions in the past made a distinction between resolutions that have binding legal effects, known as decisions, and resolutions that do not have such binding effect, known as recommendations.[289] As such, it could be said that any factual determination contained in a decision was legally binding on the addressee of the situation whilst a determination made in a recommendation would not have the same binding character, and so on. However, the Court has never given any guidance on whether any factual determination made in a decision of the Council or the General Assembly would be binding on the Court.[290] The closest that the Court has come to addressing the issue before the *Kosovo* opinion was in its rejection of Portugal's argument in the *East Timor* case that certain factual determinations contained within resolutions of the General Assembly and Security Council should be taken as 'givens'.[291] The Court highlighted conflicting State practice in coming to the conclusion that the resolutions in question could not be considered as factual 'givens' capable of settling the dispute.[292]

---

[287] Del Mar, 'Weight of Evidence Generated through Intra-Institutional Fact-finding before the International Court of Justice' 409; *Bosnian Genocide Case* 109 paras 301–5.

[288] *Accordance with International Law of the Unilateral Declaration of Independence in Respect of Kosovo* (Advisory Opinion) 2010 General List No. 141, at para 85; the Court's statement in para 85, 'Resolution 1244 (1999) was expressly adopted by the Security Council on the basis of Chapter VII of the United Nations Charter, and therefore clearly imposes international legal obligations', should not be misunderstood. A Security Council resolution does not need to be adopted under Chapter VII to have binding legal effect, and can contain language that does not create binding effect. See M.D. Öberg, 'The Legal Effects of Resolutions of the UN Security Council and General Assembly in the Jurisprudence of the ICJ' 16 *European Journal of International Law* 879, 884.

[289] Öberg's definition of a resolution as one that 'may create obligations, rights, and powers; contain factual and legal determinations that trigger such effects; and establish how and when they operate' is helpful in this regard; see Öberg, 'The Legal Effects of Resolutions of the UN Security Council and General Assembly in the Jurisprudence of the ICJ' 82.

[290] See ibid. 890–923.

[291] *East Timor (Portugal v. Australia)*, Judgment, ICJ Reports 1995 90, 103, paras 30–2.

[292] Ibid. paras 30–2.

The *Kosovo* advisory opinion is undoubtedly the Court's most significant contribution to the Court's jurisprudence in this regard, addressing the issue squarely for the first time.[293] In the *Kosovo* Advisory Opinion the Court rejected suggestions that it should not give an opinion because doing so would require interpreting or applying a number of decisions of the Security Council, stating that it has done so in the past in both advisory and contentious proceedings.[294] The relevance of the *Kosovo* opinion lies in its reformulation of the scope of the question requested of the Court by the General Assembly. In its request for the *Kosovo* advisory opinion, the General Assembly stated that the unilateral declaration of independence had been adopted by the Provisional Institutions of Self-Government of Kosovo. However, the factual assertion that the declaration had been adopted by the Provisional Institutions of Self-Government of Kosovo was challenged by a number of parties.[295]

In doing so, the question arose as to whether in formulating the question in this manner the General Assembly had already predetermined a particular factual element of the case – namely the identity of the authors of the declaration.[296] The Court itself noted that the factual issue of the identity of the authors of the declaration of independence could have had an important effect on the answer to the question posed by the General Assembly.[297] However, this did not deter the Court from exercising its inherent right to reformulate the question asked of it. The Court explained its decision to do so, arguing that '[i]t would be incompatible with the proper exercise of the judicial function for the Court to treat that matter as having been determined by the General Assembly.'[298] The Court went on to elaborate on its reasoning, stating that as an independent judicial organ 'the Court must be free to examine the entire record and decide for itself whether that declaration was promulgated by the Provisional Institutions of Self-Government or some other entity.'[299]

---

[293] Öberg, 'The Legal Effects of Resolutions of the UN Security Council and General Assembly in the Jurisprudence of the ICJ' 82.

[294] *Kosovo Advisory Opinion* para 46; here the Court cited *Certain Expenses Advisory Opinion* 175 and *Namibia Advisory Opinion* 51–4 paras 107–16; also provisional measures in *Lockerbie Provisional Measures* 15 paras 39–41, although note that Judge Stotnikov criticised the use of these precedents as he said they do not support the argument that the Court has interpreted acts and decisions of the Security Council; Juan J. Quintana, 'Procedural Developments at the International Court of Justice' 10 *The Law & Practice of International Courts and Tribunals* 135, 197.

[295] *Kosovo Advisory Opinion* para 52.   [296] Ibid. paras 49–56.   [297] Ibid. para 52.
[298] Ibid. para 52.   [299] Ibid. para 52.

In the course of the advisory opinion the Court found that the General Assembly's identification of the authors of the declaration of independence had been incorrect and made a contrasting factual finding. This finding constituted a crucial step in the Court's reasoning on the way to the conclusion that Security Council Resolution 1244 did not bind the authors of the declaration.[300] This bold step from the Court, denying that factual determinations made in resolutions of the General Assembly has been praised for a number of reasons to which we will turn our attention presently.[301] However, a caveat must be added here in relation to the scope of the Court's pronouncements. It would seem unlikely that the Court would adopt a practice of making contradictory factual findings from its fellow organs. In fact, in the *Kosovo* opinion the Court qualified its reformulation of the facts of the case stating that the General Assembly had not intended to fetter the Court's jurisdiction in this regard.[302] This begs the question as to whether the Court would take the same step of reformulation were the requesting organ to explicitly determine the facts in the question asked of the Court.[303]

In addition, doubt remains surrounding the application of the Court's pronouncements beyond the facts of the *Kosovo* case. To elaborate, the factual determination overturned by the Court in the *Kosovo* case 'was contained in an authorization rather than an obligation, and was made by the General Assembly rather than the Security Council (let alone under Chapter VII of the Charter).'[304] As such, doubt remains as to whether the Court would consider itself similarly unconstrained by a binding determination of a threat to the peace made by the Security Council under Article 39 of the UN Charter, for instance.[305]

Taken as a whole, where does this examination of the practice of the Court leave us? The preceding section has sought to illustrate that the position taken by the Court on factual determinations made by other UN organs has not to date been unequivocal. Nevertheless, there is a sufficient suggestion in the pronouncements of the Court to suggest that the Court would not consider itself bound by such factual determinations in

---

[300] Ibid. paras 113–21.    [301] Distefano and Henry, 'Distentangling Themis from Ares' 81.
[302] *Kosovo Advisory Opinion* para 53.    [303] Ibid. para 53.
[304] See also T. O'Donnell, 'Naming and Shaming: The Sorry Tale of Security Council Resolution 1530 (2004)' 17 *European Journal of International Law* 945.
[305] Öberg, 'The Legal Effects of Resolutions of the UN Security Council and General Assembly in the Jurisprudence of the ICJ' 83.

most cases. As such, the concluding section of this chapter examines the policy implications of the Court taking this position and indeed, whilst it is not asserted that the Court is necessarily best placed to definitively determine the facts, it is nonetheless argued that as an independent judicial organ it should not be bound by other political organs.

### 1.5.7 The policy argument: functional parallelism and functional distinction

The preceding examination of the Court's discretion to take a more proactive approach to fact-finding in light of its place in the institutional structure of the United Nations has confirmed one crucially important point. The Court should not consider itself bound by factual determinations made by the Court's fellow principal organs so long as the Security Council does not take action under Chapter VII of the Charter which 'sets aside, rules out or renders impossible the juridical solution expected of the Court.'[306]

As the preceding sections sought to illustrate, whilst nothing in the Charter precludes the functional parallelism of the Court and other principal organs, and whilst the Court has rejected any notion of litispendence in cases that have come before it (staunchly defending the Court's ability to operate in tandem with the Council) it is unavoidable that the adoption of a decision under Chapter VII of the Charter by the Council may deprive the situation before the Court of all meaning.[307]

Whilst such a dose of realism is essential regarding the Chapter VII powers of the Council, it should nonetheless be emphasised that short of such frustration or material change in circumstances with regard to a dispute before the Court, the Court should in no way consider itself bound by a factual determination made by the Council.[308] The Court

---

[306] *Lockerbie Provisional Measures* 44, 154; 1992 ICJ REP 44, 154; see also Gowlland-Debbas, 'The Relationship Between the International Court of Justice and the Security Council in the Light of the Lockerbie Case' 659.

[307] Gowlland-Debbas, 'The Relationship between the International Court of Justice and the Security Council in the Light of the Lockerbie Case' 661; see also H. D. de Vabres, *L'action publique et l'action civile dans les rapports de droit pénal international* (Leiden, Boston and Brill: Nijhoff, 1929) 207.

[308] Gowlland-Debbas, 'The Relationship between the International Court of Justice and the Security Council in the Light of the Lockerbie Case' 674; Benzing, 'Evidentiary Issues' 1242, para 24.

## 1.5 A MORE PROACTIVE APPROACH TO FACT-FINDING? 69

should not consider itself unable to contradict the Council in relation to a factual determination for reasons of judicial propriety nor consider it an inherent limitation of the judicial function.[309] In other words, the relationship between the Court and other principal organs should be 'one of coordination and functional cooperation in the attainment of the aims of the Organization, not one of competition or mutual exclusion'[310] in all but the most extreme circumstances (those being the frustration of the case before the Court by the action of the Council under Chapter VII). That the principle of litispendence does not operate in relation to the principal organs is due to the fact that each organ does not try to avoid the duplication of proceedings as in domestic law but rather seeks to operate as different processes within the framework of an 'integrated structure for the peaceful settlement of disputes on the international plane.'[311]

In addition, the fact-finding processes of the General Assembly and Court are substantially different and could in theory lead, and in fact in practice have led, to different results. Such criticisms of the Council's fact-finding have come up in cases before the Court. For instance, Uganda challenged the Court's reliance on a factual determination made by the Security Council in Resolution 1304 in the course of the *Armed Activities* case, contending that 'it is evident that in reaching its conclusions about the law the Security Council has not acted in a way that would normally be recognised as judicial. The Security Council emphasis is on political adhesion rather than impartial conclusions based on unbiased consideration of the facts and the objective examination of the law'.[312]

Furthermore, were the Court to consider its discretion fettered by other organs of the United Nations its judicial independence would be detrimentally affected. The principle of *compétence de la compétence*, that the Court 'determines the limits of its own jurisdiction, and it decides on challenges to it', is fundamentally important to the independence of

---

[309] Gowlland-Debbas, 'The Relationship between the International Court of Justice and the Security Council in the Light of the Lockerbie Case' 674; as referred to by the Court in the Northern Cameroons case for example; see Northern Cameroons 1963 ICJ REP. at 29.

[310] Ibid. See also Judge Ni, 1992 ICJ Rep. at 22, 134.

[311] See E. McWhinney, *Judicial Settlement of International Disputes: Jurisdiction, Justiciability, and Judicial Law-Making on the Contemporary International Court* (The Hague: Martinus Nijhoff, 1991) 39.

[312] Counter Memorial of the Republic of Uganda, Case Concerning Armed Activities on the Territory of the Congo, (*Democratic Republic of the Congo v. Uganda*) 2001 ICJ at 191 para 191.

international judicial organs. Should an international court's jurisdiction be defined by another organ it is difficult to imagine how that court could be described as independent in any way. The same might be said for factual determinations: if the Court's ability to make such determinations were subject to those of another organ, that court's judicial independence would be called into question. As Geroges Abi-Saab has stated, '[i]f you are not the one who has the final word, it makes you always look behind your back, which greatly undermines independence.'[313]

And indeed it is clear the there are significant differences between the fact-finding procedures of the Court (as outlined in this chapter) and those of the Council, mainly due to the different goals that the two organs seek to achieve. As a political organ the Council has different, more political, priorities and as a judicial organ, fact-finding lies at the heart of the judicial function. On this issue, it should be noted that the Security Council has a history of making inaccurate factual findings; see, for example, Resolution 1530 of 2004 which incorrectly attributed the Madrid bombings to the 'terrorist group ETA' after the incident when in fact it later emerged that the attacks were the work of an Al-Qaeda cell.[314]

As a result of such errors a more proactive judicial approach to the facts could be an advantage in this regard. Of course in cases of functional parallelism it is not beyond the realms of possibility that, for example, the Court and the Council may come to conflicting factual determinations but such conflicts must be dealt with as they arise whilst all the while bearing in mind that both organs ultimately operate as part of the same institutional apparatus and are seeking to achieve the same goals, albeit by different means.

### 1.5.8 *Summary: the Court's discretion unfettered*

In sum, to a greater or lesser extent the principles of equality and functional parallelism apply equally to both findings-of-fact and interpretations of the Charter. Just as the Court does not have a Charter-based

---

[313] Georges Abi-Saab, 'Independence of the Judiciary from Political Organs' in L. Boisson de Chazournes, C. Romano and R. Mackenzie (eds), *International Organizations and International Dispute Settlement: Trends and Prospects* (Ardsley, NY: Transnational, 2002) 246; Daniel Müller, 'The Question Question' in M. Milanović and M. Wood (eds), *The Law and Politics of the Kosovo Advisory Opinion* (Oxford University Press, 2015) 122.

[314] Distefano and Henry, 'Distentangling Themis from Ares' 81.

## 1.5 A MORE PROACTIVE APPROACH TO FACT-FINDING? 71

power to review the legality of acts of the Security Council as a result of the functional parallelism envisaged by the drafters of the Charter, the corollary is that the Security Council cannot formally bind the Court in relation to determinations of fact made by it.

The Court is not formally bound by assertions of fact contained within resolutions of the General Assembly or Security Council, regardless of whether they relate to an issue being concurrently dealt with by the Council in the course of maintaining or restoring international peace and security under Chapter VII of the UN Charter (except in those cases in which the Council frustrates the action of the Court by materially affecting the dispute by means of a decision under Chapter VII).[315] Even in such circumstances the Court 'must at all times preserve its independence in performing the functions which the Charter has committed to it as the United Nations' principal judicial organ'.[316] This independence is key – flowing from both the UN Charter, the Court's Statute and from the very nature of the judicial function.[317] The Court itself must at all times ensure the proper administration of justice, maintain its high juridical character and integrity[318] whilst safeguarding its judicial function.[319] The significance of the Court's independence in relation to its assessment of the facts cannot be overstated. As such, the Court should ensure at all times that it strictly evaluates the probity of evidence before it in order to ensure the proper administration of justice.

Ultimately, we can answer the fundamentally important question posed at the start of this subsection, namely whether or not the Court's discretion in relation to fact-finding is in any way fettered by its position within the institutional machinery of the United Nations, in the negative. The foregoing examination has shown that there is nothing in either the Court's constitutive instruments or practice which would fetter the Court's discretion and that accordingly the Court, as an independent tribunal, possesses the discretion required in order to adopt a more proactive approach to fact-finding, should it choose to do so.

---

[315] See Öberg, 'The Legal Effects of Resolutions of the UN Security Council and General Assembly in the Jurisprudence of the ICJ' 892; Del Mar, 'Weight of Evidence Generated through Intra-Institutional Fact-finding before the International Court of Justice' 405.
[316] *Lockerbie Provisional Measures*, Dissenting Opinion of Judge Weeramantry, at 58.
[317] Shaw, 'The Security Council and the International Court of Justice' 245; Singh, *The Role and Record of the International Court of Justice* 173.
[318] *Northern Cameroons Case* 29.
[319] Ibid. at 38; see also Dissenting Opinion of Judge Skubiszewski in the *East Timor Case* at 258.

## 1.6 Chapter 1 summary: the Court's reactive approach to fact-finding

This chapter examined the evidentiary provisions of the Court's Statute and Rules and the fact-finding powers that the Court possesses in order to consider the extent to which it has utilised those powers in practice. It was shown that whilst the Court in fact possesses relatively broad fact-finding powers in its Statute and Rules of Procedure, due to a number of factors it has never made use of them to any significant extent. Instead, the Court operates under extremely broad rules of admissibility of evidence that allow almost any piece of evidence to come before the Court that the States' parties so choose. In addition, it was shown that the Court's discretion to make factual determinations is in no way fettered by its institutional position as a principal organ of the United Nations.

These factors taken together, the apparent reluctance to conduct fact-finding, the broad rules of admissibility and the emphasis on fact-assessment, amount to what can accurately be described as the Court's reactive approach to evidence. This is an approach that, as shown above, was developed for a number of reasons including the sovereign nature of the parties before the Court, the Court's inability to compel evidence and what could be termed the 'classical' approach to judicial reasoning. However in recent times the reasons underpinning this reactive approach have begun to be questioned and the approach as a whole has come in for criticism. These criticisms of the current reactive approach to fact-finding form the basis of the following chapter.

# 2

# Criticisms of the Court's current reactive approach to fact-finding

### (i) Introduction: is the ICJ factually challenged?[1]

Chapter 1 assessed the Court's traditional reactive approach to fact-finding. It was argued that the Court's approach has been influenced by a number of factors including its status as an international judicial body with no compulsory jurisdiction, and by the sovereign nature of the States party to cases that come before it. However, in recent times there has been considerable criticism of the Court's reactive approach to fact-finding. Whilst it is acknowledged that there are a number of reasons that explain why the Court has historically taken this reactive approach to fact-finding, and that in some situations the Court's reactive approach is justifiable, it is these recent criticisms that this chapter sets out to assess. The criticisms explored in this chapter at the very least merit a re-examination of the Court's approach to the facts. To what extent these deficiencies can be overcome is a topic to which we will return in Chapter 4.

Recent criticisms can be divided into two main groups: (i) those relating to abundant or particularly complex or technical facts before the Court and (ii) those relating to a lack of evidence before the Court. The first group of criticisms are diverse and relate to the Court's difficulties in dealing with copious, complex or scientific evidence that are increasingly prevalent in international adjudication. Criticisms of the Court's reactive approach when faced with this kind of evidence will be considered in the first half of this chapter.

The second group of criticisms, concerning the lack of evidence before the Court, includes (but is not limited to) the non-appearance of States before the Court. In cases where a party fails to appear before the Court its reactive approach to fact-finding is found wanting due to the fact that it only has the evidence of one party upon which to make its findings-of-fact.

---

[1] 'Factually challenged' is a turn of phrase used by Alvarez, 'Are International Judges Afraid of Science?: A Comment on Mbengue' 83.

74  CRITICISMS OF THE ICJ'S CURRENT REACTIVE APPROACH

Without conducting its own investigations into the factual background of the case at hand the Court's reactive approach, which makes it dependent on States to submit the facts to it, is a handicap for the Court. In such cases the Court is forced to cast its net wider to obtain facts from fact-finding commissions or to rely on public knowledge in order to attempt to fill the void in the evidentiary record left by the non-appearing party.

### 2.1 Group 1: problems relating to abundant, particularly complex or technical facts

The first group of criticisms are diverse and relate to the Court's difficulties in dealing with cases involving abundant, particularly complex or technical facts that are increasingly prevalent in international adjudication. In other words, the issues explored in the following section do not arise out of a lack of facts before the Court, but rather result from the difficulty of assessing those facts.[2]

First of all, a preliminary word must be said regarding what exactly is meant by abundant, particularly complex or technical facts, including the nature of 'scientific' evidence. Whilst this issue has been addressed in detail elsewhere[3] and it is not the intention of the author to address it in a definitive manner, it ought to be emphasised that the Court has never taken the position that complex factual or scientific issues are non-justiciable, as has occasionally been argued before other adjudicative bodies.[4] Such arguments have not been made often and have never been explicitly endorsed by an international tribunal.[5]

---

[2] Bruno Simma, 'The International Court of Justice and Scientific Expertise' 106 *Proceedings of the Annual Meeting (American Society of International Law)* 230; see for instance J. G. Sandoval and E. Sweeney-Samuelson, 'Adjudicating Conflicts over Resources: The ICJ's Treatment of Technical Evidence in the Pulp Mills Case' 3 *Goettingen Journal of International Law* 447, 449 stating that '[t]he Court's current reactive approach means that it might not be properly equipped to solve disputes'; Peat, 'The Use of Court-Appointed Experts by the International Court of Justice'.

[3] See for instance Foster, *Science and the Precautionary Principle in International Courts and Tribunals* and Jacqueline Peel, *Science and Risk Regulation in International Law* (Cambridge University Press, 2013).

[4] For instance, in the *Southern Bluefin Tuna* case Japan argued that 'questions of scientific judgment ... are not justiciable'. See *Southern Bluefin Tuna (New Zealand v. Japan, Australia v. Japan)*, 23 R.I.A.A. 2000 1 at 40(a); on justiciability see Ian Brownlie, 'The Justiciability of Disputes and Issues in International Relations' 42 *British Yearbook of International Law* 123.

[5] D'Aspremont and Mbengue 11.

## 2.1 ABUNDANT, COMPLEX OR TECHNICAL FACTS

It has been suggested that the Court struggles to deal in particular with issues that are scientifically controversial since science is 'irresolutely oriented towards the unknown – i.e. the "not known yet": the uncertain.'[6] As a result there is a conflict between the objectives that scientists and judges are trying to achieve: international adjudicators aim to 'freeze' the 'facts' and talk of 'findings' and 'veracities' whilst scientific fact-finding talks of 'probabilities'.[7] And indeed various international courts and tribunals have at different times described their *modus operandi* as being to 'establish which relevant facts [they] regard as having been convincingly established by the evidence',[8] to rely on facts 'not suggesting the slightest doubt'[9] or 'clear and compelling evidence'[10] in order to determine the 'established facts'.[11] By the same token they have been reluctant to engage in claims based on unconvincing evidence[12] and have refused to 'weigh intangible and elusive points of proof'.[13]

As such, the argument goes that since international adjudicators have shown a preference for relying on 'those facts which they have found to have existed',[14] they are somewhat stumped 'in situations in which the facts

---

[6] Mbengue, 'Scientific Fact-finding by International Courts and Tribunals' 513; Mbengue states that scientific facts 'are precisely typified by their volatility, their circularity, their paucity, their impalpability', ibid. Foster, *Science and the Precautionary Principle in International Courts and Tribunals* 5: '[i]n disputes involving scientific uncertainty and potential future harm, international courts and tribunals are called upon to make judicial decisions in circumstances where potentially decisive facts about future events clearly cannot be obtained at the time of adjudication ... Here the concept of "certainty" is to be taken literally: an absence of certainty has to be accepted from the start'.

[7] Mbengue, 'Scientific Fact-finding by International Courts and Tribunals' 513.

[8] *Armed Activities Case* para 72.

[9] *Fisheries Jurisdiction (Germany v. Iceland), Judgment,* 1973 ICJ 49 para 18 (2 February), Jurisdiction of the Court para 24.

[10] *Saluka Investments B.V. (Netherlands v. Czech Republic), Partial Award* para 273 (Permanent Court of Arbitration 2006).

[11] *Polis Fondi Immobiliare di Banche Popolare S.G.R.p.A. v. International Fund for Agricultural development, Case No 2010-8* para 156.

[12] *Abyei Arbitration (Sudan/Sudan People's Liberation Movement/Army)* para 489 (Permanent Court of Arbitration 2009); *Delimitation of Maritime Boundary (Guyana v. Suriname)* para 424 (Permanent Court of Arbitration 2007); *Delimitation of the Exclusive Economic Zone and Continental Shelf (Barbados v. Trinidad and Tobago)* 27 RIAA 147 (Permanent Court of Arbitration 1910), *Delimitation of the Border (Eritrea v. Ethiopia)* 25 RIAA 83 (Permanent Court of Arbitration 2002); *Delimitation of the Exclusive Economic Zone and Continental Shelf (Barbados v. Trinidad and Tobago)* 27 RIAA 147 (Permanent Court of Arbitration 1910) para 266.

[13] *Maritime Delimitation (Eritrea v. Yemen)* 22 RIAA 335 (Permanent Court of Arbitration 1999).

[14] *Pulp Mills Case,* Joint Dissenting Opinion of Judges Al-Kasawneh and Simma paras 167-8.

in question are so uncertain that they have not been "found to exist"'[15] which in turn results in judicial caution.[16] Undoubtedly there are a number of aspects of this argument that ring true.

The nature of the process of scientific fact-finding differs from that of legal fact-finding. As Foster, whose work in this area is extremely influential, has stated, '[s]cientific disputes must be adjudicated in the knowledge that all scientific assertions are subject to the possibility of being discarded should they prove to be false ... [t]oday's "minority science" could become tomorrow's "mainstream science."'[17] As such, all disputes involving specifically scientific issues must be adjudicated with this in mind. In practical terms this means that even if good evidentiary practice is perfectly observed in the manner proposed in Chapter 4 there is nevertheless the chance that a scientific fact established beyond the standard of proof could become open to challenge once more. Foster has correctly argued that for this reason it is clear that 'the possibility of subsequent scientific developments must be accommodated within international legal procedure' through reassessment proceedings, for example.[18]

However the problematic nature of 'scientific evidence' should not be overstated. Judges are regularly asked to engage in similar 'probabilistic' assessments when dealing with complex economic or public policy issues in cases that come before them. Similarly, as in science, standards and burdens of proof vary from case to case and court to court in international law. As such, in the words of Alvarez, '[d]eciding on the basis of uncertainty is what international and domestic courts do every day'[19] and the legal fact-finding process should be able to make allowances for issues of scientific uncertainty.[20]

In addition, it is not clear to what extent international courts can be criticised for their handling of scientific evidence in particular. The main question in this regard becomes; what exactly is 'scientific' evidence? It is difficult to justify why 'scientific' evidence per se is the only form of

---

[15] Mbengue, 'Scientific Fact-finding by International Courts and Tribunals' 515.
[16] Lauterpacht, *The Development of International Law by the International Court* .
[17] Foster, *Science and the Precautionary Principle in International Courts and Tribunals* 10. This is not to mention the problem of areas in which little or no scientific research has been done and where there are acknowledged gaps in scientific knowledge.
[18] See Chapter 8 of Foster, *Science and the Precautionary Principle in International Courts and Tribunals* for a detailed discussion of this issue.
[19] Alvarez, 'Are International Judges Afraid of Science?: A Comment on Mbengue' 88.
[20] Foster, *Science and the Precautionary Principle in International Courts and Tribunals* 11.

## 2.1 ABUNDANT, COMPLEX OR TECHNICAL FACTS

evidence which poses problems for the Court as a result of its complexity. For instance, extremely complex International Centre for Settlement of Investment Dispute (ICSID) awards dealing with injury to investors, or WTO cases dealing with countervailing duties or zeroing may be just as complex factual issues as any controversial scientific issues.[21] The example of the U.S. Supreme Court is a cautionary tale in this regard. As mentioned above in Section 1.3.2., the U.S. Supreme Court in recent years has faced major difficulties in seeking to define purely 'scientific' knowledge in implementing the famous *Daubert* test for the admissibility of scientific evidence before U.S. courts.[22] Ultimately the U.S. Supreme Court in the *Kumho Tyre* case was forced to expand the test to cover 'technical' and 'other specialized' [sic] forms of knowledge.[23] In this case Judge Breyer conceded that:

> [I]t would prove difficult, if not impossible, for judges to administer evidentiary rules under which a gatekeeping obligation depended upon a distinction between 'scientific' knowledge and 'technical' or 'other specialized' knowledge. There is no clear line that divides the one from the others. Disciplines such as engineering rest upon scientific knowledge. Pure scientific theory itself may depend for its development upon observation and properly engineered machines. And conceptual efforts to distinguish the two are unlikely to produce clear legal lines capable of application in particular cases.[24]

Consequently, the focus in the following chapters will be on how the ICJ and other inter-State tribunals deal with factually complex cases which, as Alvarez has stated, necessarily require the assistance of experts who have specific skills that can help to shed light on these issues which are beyond the comprehension of the average judge, learned as they are.[25] As such, reference will not be made to the narrow term of 'scientific

---

[21] Alvarez argues that '[m]any, perhaps most, such decisions involving sophisticated investors in complex, on-going enterprises require heavily expert-laden assessments of fair market or going concern value', 'Are International Judges Afraid of Science?: A Comment on Mbengue' 86.

[22] See *Daubert v. Merrel Dow Pharmaceuticals, Inc.,* 509 U.S. 579 (1993); for commentary see Helland and Klick, 'Does Anyone Get Stopped at the Gate?'.

[23] *Kumho Tire Co. v. Carmichael, 119 S. Ct.*; M. J. Saks, 'Banishing Ipse Dixit: The impact of Kumho Tire on Forensic Identification Science' 57 *Washington and Lee Law Review* 879, 882.

[24] *Kumho Tire Co. v. Carmichael, 119 S. Ct.* at 1174; Edward J. Imwinkelried, 'Evaluating the Reliability of Nonscientific Expert Testimony: A Partial Answer to the Questions Left Unresolved by *Kumho Tire Co. v. Carmichael*' 52 *Maine Law Review* 19, 25.

[25] Alvarez, 'Are International Judges Afraid of Science?: A Comment on Mbengue' 86.

evidence' or 'scientific fact-finding' but rather to the broader category of factually complex evidence for the reasons just explained.

Criticisms of the Court's reactive approach when faced with this kind of evidence generally relate to: (i) the problematic practice of experts appearing as counsel, (ii) the Court's unwillingness to appoint its own experts or request necessary information and (iii) problematic reliance on international commissions of inquiry. Each of these issues is discussed in turn in the following sections.

### 2.1.1 Blurred lines: the practice of experts appearing as counsel

The present subsection examines the problematic consistent practice of the Court to date regarding a blurring of the distinction between counsel and experts.[26] As we have seen, the practice of the Court is essentially reactive with the onus being very much placed on the parties to put whatever information they so choose before the Court. However, instead of putting forward their own experts under Article 43(5) of the Court's Statute, States in the past have tended to include experts as counsel or have their counsel present complex factual and scientific evidence to the Court themselves.[27]

This practice can be seen consistently throughout the jurisprudence of the Court, even in technical cases such as *Botswana/Namibia*.[28] In this case experts appeared as counsel to give evidence as to whether the northern channel of the River Chobe around the Kasikili/Sedudu Island ought to be considered its main channel (and ultimately which state had sovereignty over the island).[29] Similarly, in the *Gabčikovo-Nagymaros* case scientific experts for Hungary appeared as counsel (for instance Slovakia's scientists were listed as 'counsel and experts';[30] whereas in

---

[26] Rosenne and Ronen, *The Law and Practice of the International Court, 1920-2005* 1137; Riddell, 'Scientific Evidence in the International Court of Justice – Problems and Possibilities' 236; Riddell and Plant, *Evidence Before the International Court of Justice* 321.

[27] In fact the Registrar of the Court has described this as traditionally the most common means through which experts have appeared before the Court; see Philippe Couvreur, 'Le Règlement Juridictionel' in Institut du droit économique de la mer (ed), *Le processus de délimitation maritime étude d'un cas fictif: colloque international Monoco 27-29 mars 2003* (Paris: Pedone, 2004) 380; Rosenne and Ronen, *The Law and Practice of the International Court, 1920-2005* 1137; Riddell, 'Scientific Evidence in the International Court of Justice – Problems and Possibilities' 236; Riddell and Plant, *Evidence before the International Court of Justice* 321

[28] *Kasikili/Sedudu Island (Botswana/Namibia), Judgment, ICJ Reports 1999* 1045.

[29] Ibid.    [30] *Gabčikovo-Nagymaros Case*.

*Pulp Mills* both parties listed members of their delegation as 'scientific advisors and experts') – speaking as advocates rather than experts *stricto sensu*.[31] Given the somewhat unclear position of individuals appearing before the Court in the past, it is necessary to examine more carefully the distinction between witnesses, experts and counsel.

What guidance can be gleaned from the Statute of the Court? Given the traditional focus on documentary evidence before the Court (see Section 1.3.1), it is perhaps not surprising that the provisions of the Court's Statute relating to the hearing of witnesses and experts have been described as rudimentary.[32] This is especially the case in relation to individuals put forward by the parties in support of their case with the Statute providing very little guidance in this respect.[33] That having been said, taking into account the few provisions in the Court's Statute, the Rules of the Court, and the practice of the Court, something meaningful can be said about the position of witnesses and experts before the Court. First of all, Article 42(1) and (2) of the Statute states that parties 'shall be represented by agents' and 'may have the assistance of counsel or advocates before the Court'. In addition, Article 43(5) states that proceedings before the Court will consist of a written and an oral part and that 'the oral proceedings shall consist of the hearing by the Court of witnesses, experts, agents, counsel, and advocates'.[34] Whilst stipulating that witnesses and experts must take different oaths before appearing before the Court,[35] somewhat unhelpfully neither the Court's Statute nor its Rules define any of these positions, leaving it open for the common understanding of these terms to be inferred.[36]

The approach of the Court to date has been simply to accept that any individual put forward by the parties as counsel, advocate, expert or witness appears as such.[37] The Court's approach in this respect is similar

---

[31] *Pulp Mills Case*; see oral proceedings 22 September 2009.   [32] Tams, 'Article 51' 1301.
[33] Ibid.   [34] See Article 43(5) ICJ Statute.
[35] Under Article 64(a) Rules of the Court a witness must make a solemn declaration to speak the truth, but under Article 64(b) an expert makes a declaration as to his or her solemn belief.
[36] Whilst the position of 'agent' can be considered somewhat unique: it should be noted that the agent is not restricted to representing the State politically and may for instance act as counsel and examine witnesses and experts (Article 65 Rules of Court); the agent has the role of reading the party's final submissions (Article 60(2) Rules) and to make or authorise binding statements regarding procedure during proceedings (Fifth Annual Report, PCIJ, Series E, No. 5, 250); see Talmon, 'Article 43'.
[37] Sir Arthur Watts, 'Enhancing the Effectiveness of Procedures of International Dispute Settlement' 21 *Max Planck Yearbook of United Nations Law* 21, 25.

to the procedure before civil law systems where it is 'entirely within the discretion of the court to determine who can be qualified as an expert'.[38] The Court's 'relaxed view of the matter' is illustrated well by the fact the Court has not insisted that 'counsel' be members of the bar of their domestic State, or indeed that persons who appear as counsel be a qualified lawyers at all.

Consequently, the task of the witnesses has been interpreted as being to speak to facts that they experienced first hand.[39] In contrast, the task of experts is to speak to their own specialised knowledge, training or skill.[40] Whilst a witness's testimony must be limited to issues they witnessed first hand, experts can give opinions on the issues in question and present conclusions on the basis of their expertise.[41]

In practice parties have put forward experts in support of their case for examination before the Court in a number of cases.[42] In the course of the oral pleadings during the *South West Africa* case, one of the grounds on which Mr Gross for Liberia and Ethiopia sought to challenge the evidence given by Mr P. J. Cillie, editor of the newspaper *Die Burger*, put forward by South Africa as a 'witness and expert', was that he was

---

[38] Ilias Bantekas and Susan Ntah, *International Criminal Law* (London: Cavendish, 2003), 307–16.

[39] Colleen M. Rohan, 'Rules Governing the Presentation of Testimonial Evidence' in Karim A. A. Khan, Caroline Buisman and Christopher Gosnell (eds), *Principles of Evidence in International Criminal Justice* (Oxford University Press, 2010) 529. In the *Corfu Channel* case, for instance, the parties both called and cross-examined witnesses, with the UK presenting naval officers as witnesses who made submissions regarding the damage done to the British fleet and the source of the mines that were alleged to have done the damage, and Albania also presenting naval officers as witnesses to contest these claims; see also Article 62 Rules, *Corfu Channel Case*, *Temple of Preah Vihear Case*, *Namibia Advisory Opinion*, *Nicaragua Case* and the *Elettronica Sicula SpA (ELSI), Judgment, ICJ Reports 1989* 15.

[40] See Article 64(a) and (b) of the Rules; Higgins, 'Speech by H. E. Judge Rosalyn Higgins, President of the International Court of Justice to the Sixth Committee of the General Assembly'; this definition comes from *Prosecutor v. Galić (Decision Concerning the Expert Witness Ewa Tabeau and Richard Philipps)* IT-93-29-T (3 July 2002) at 2; see also *Prosecutor v. Blagojević (Decision on Prosecution's Motion for Admission of Expert Statements)* IT-02-60-T (7 November 2003) at 19.

[41] Watts, 'Enhancing the Effectiveness of Procedures of International Dispute Settlement' 25; Rohan, 'Principles of Evidence in International Criminal Justice' 529.

[42] Experts and witnesses were called by the parties in *Corfu Channel*, Pleadings, Vol III 425–694, Vol IV 9–468; *Temple of Preah Vihear*, Pleadings, Vol II 331–442; *South West Africa* cases, Pleadings, Vol X 88–182, 238–558, Vol XI 3–708, 300–4, 313–25; *Bosnian Genocide Case* 43, 60 para 57. Experts only in *Tunisia/Libya Continental Shelf*, 155, Pleadings, Vol V 182–98; *Gulf of Maine*, Pleadings, Vol VI 393–435; *Libya/Malta Continental Shelf*, Pleadings, Vol IV 197–282.

speaking to issues on which he had no formal qualifications.[43] However, President Spender rejected this position, stating that the issue is often the weight to be given to the opinion presented rather than the qualification of the individual:

> Experts may qualify in other fields than that which is their normal qualification, if they reveal a special knowledge which is far in excess of that which is normally held by a lay person and, where a witness so qualifies, it is a question of the weight to be accorded to his opinion, not a question of the admissibility of the expert view which is expressed.[44]

In addition, the practice of the Court reveals that parties have put forward so-called expert witnesses – in other words an individual who is both an expert and someone who has witnessed the relevant event personally.[45] Expert witnesses have troubled the ad hoc international criminal tribunals in the past, but the main point to bear in mind for our purposes is that expert witnesses can be examined before the Court not only on events that they have witnessed first hand but their expertise and prior statements relating to their area of expertise can also be questioned (in the same way that an ordinary expert can).[46] The practice of presenting such witnesses, arguably blurring the distinction between witnesses and experts, is not inherently problematic since the expert witness will be examined in open Court where both testimony as to events witnessed first hand and opinion given on the basis of the witness's expertise can be tested by the parties.

---

[43] *South West Africa, Second Phase, Judgment, ICJ Reports 1966* 6, Pleadings, Vol X 514.

[44] Ibid., Vol. X 525; see also Talmon, 'Article 43' 1146.

[45] Avi Singh, 'Expert Evidence' in Karim A. A. Khan, Caroline Buisman and Christopher Gosnell (eds), *Principles of Evidence in International Criminal Justice* (Oxford University Press, 2010) 623.

[46] Rohan, 'Principles of Evidence in International Criminal Justice' 529. See, for instance, *Ndindiliyimana* in which 'it was held that when a party chooses to call a witness as a factual witness rather than an expert witness, it implicitly makes the choice to limit the witness' testimony to matters that he personally saw, heard or experienced, and any irrelevant details and matters of personal opinion or expertise beyond the remit of factual witness must be excluded'; *Prosecutor v. Ndindiliyimana et al (Decision on the Prosecutor Opposing the Testimony of Witness DE4-30 as a Factual Witness)* ICTR-00-56-T (16 May 2007) at 9; see also *Prosecutor v. Karemera (Decision on 'Requete de la Defense de M. Ngirumpatse en Retrait de la Deposition du Temoin GFJ et des Pieces Afferentes')* ICTR-98-44-T (6 August 2008) at 4 citing *Prosecutor v. Ndindiliyimana (Decision on the Prosecution's Motion Opposing the Testimony of Witness DE4-30 as a Factual Witness)* ICTR-00-56-T (16 May 2007) at 9.

However, leaving the issue of expert witnesses aside, the failure to properly maintain the distinction between counsel and experts appearing before the Court is problematic. The blurring of the distinction between experts and counsel has presented the Court with a number of difficulties in relation to fact-finding in practice. The most significant of these difficulties relates to the fact that experts appearing as counsel, despite presenting *ex parte* evidence, due to their status as counsel and not as experts cannot be cross-examined by the other party in the course of oral proceedings.[47] Only those experts put forward by the parties under Article 43(5) of the Court's Statute (as opposed to Court-appointed experts or experts appearing as counsel[48]) come within the scope of Articles 57, 58, 63 and 64 of the Rules of the Court.[49] In practical terms this means that only those individuals put forward as experts under Article 43(5) of the Statute are required to make a solemn declaration under Article 64(b) of the Rules of the Court, and only they can present statements that may be treated as evidence and crucially, can be cross-examined.[50]

As Boyle and Harrison have pointed out, denying the opposing party the opportunity to cross-examine witnesses prevents the achievement of the main goal of cross-examination: to test the credibility of the expert or witness.[51] Cross-examination is a crucial tool in testing the credibility of experts, providing real scrutiny of their 'professional aura' that might not otherwise be questioned.[52] Providing a concrete example of the problems this practice creates, Judge Simma has criticised the proceedings in the *Pulp Mills* case, stating that the evidence given by the party-appointed experts was diminished by the fact the experts appeared as counsel and

---

[47] Tams, 'Article 51' 1303; Watts, 'Burden of Proof and Evidence before the ICJ' 299; see Libya/Malta Continental Shelf Case, Pleadings, Vol IV 518–19; Talmon, 'Article 43' 1136.
[48] Talmon, 'Article 43' 1146.
[49] Article 63(1), added to the Rules of the Court after the Court's experience in the *South West Africa* case; S. Rosenne, *Procedure in the International Court: A Commentary on the 1978 Rules of the International Court of Justice* (The Hague: Martinus Nijhoff, 1983) 136. It should be noted that the right of parties to call experts may be waived; see *Maritime Delimitation and Territorial Questions* case, Qatar and Bahrain 112–14 para 8.
[50] See Rosenne and Ronen, *The Law and Practice of the International Court, 1920–2005* 1137; Talmon, 'Article 43' 1146; this also means that only experts appearing before the Court at the request of a party must make a solemn declaration that they will speak in accordance with their sincere belief under Article 64(b) of the Rules of the Court.
[51] Alan Boyle and James Harrison, 'Judicial Settlement of International Environmental Disputes: Current Problems' 4 *Journal of International Dispute Settlement* 245, 271.
[52] O'Donnell, 'Judicialising History or Historicising Law' 311.

## 2.1 ABUNDANT, COMPLEX OR TECHNICAL FACTS 83

not experts, meaning that they were not subject to examination by their own party and cross-examination by the other party. As such, the experts, their professional aura intact, simply 'merrily contradicted each other' leaving the Court none the wiser.[53]

Consequently, when experts appear as counsel their credibility will potentially escape scrutiny. The issue of cross-examination before the Court and the significant change in practice regarding the presentation of experts by parties that has occurred in recent times are considered in greater detail in Chapter 4. However, for our purposes, it should be noted that this practice, in circumscribing the examination of experts, is potentially problematic and has been criticised as such.[54] In addition to the problematic practice of experts appearing as counsel before the Court, the following section argues that the Court has made a number of clear factual errors arguably as a result of its current reactive approach to fact-finding.

### 2.1.2 Factual inaccuracies arguably made as a result of the Court's reactive approach to fact-finding

First of all it should be clarified that this section only speaks of a reluctance of the Court to make explicit use of the fact-finding powers it possesses in order to assist it in the assessment of complex facts. That we can only talk of explicit reluctance is due to the fact that we know that, to some extent, the Court does in fact informally consult experts to assist in the assessment of the facts. As Sir Robert Jennings openly stated:

> [T]he Court has not infrequently employed cartographers, hydrographers, geographers or linguists, and even specialised legal experts to assist in the understanding of the issues in a case before it; and it has not on the whole felt any need to make this public knowledge or even to apprise the parties.[55]

---

[53] Simma, 'The International Court of Justice and Scientific Expertise' 231.
[54] Shotaro Hamamoto, 'Procedural Questions in the Whaling Judgment: Admissibility, Intervention and Use of Experts' *Japanese Society of International Law, The Honorable Shigeru Oda Commemorative Lectures* 1, 12.
[55] Sir Robert Jennings, 'International Lawyers and the Progressive Development of International Law' in J. Makarczyk (ed), *Theory of International Law at the Threshold of the 21st Century: Essays in Honour of Krzysztof Skubiszewski* (The Hague: Kluwer Law International, 1996) 413; similarly, the current Registrar of the Court has admitted the use of such experts, explaining that: '[a]ucune mention de leur intervention n'apparaît donc dans la decision ou dans un autre document public. Leur role est d'assister la Cour en tant que telle, ses membres à titre individuel , et le Greffe à des fins techniques diverses,

84  CRITICISMS OF THE ICJ'S CURRENT REACTIVE APPROACH

It is thought that the Court has chosen to seek expert assistance from so-called *experts fantômes* informally rather than appointing its own experts under Article 50 of the Statute in order to avoid the procedure set out in Article 50 and Articles 67 and 68 of the Rules which could be perceived as cumbersome, especially in relation to a minor point on which the Court needs clarification.[56]

However, in not informing the parties that it is seeking expert assistance and by circumventing the procedure set out in its Statute and Rules 'the Court disregards a procedural right of the parties – namely the right to comment on the results of independent expert advice envisaged in Art. 67, para. 2 of the Rules.'[57] Accordingly, the use of informal expert evidence is extremely problematic. Such criticisms have in recent years been raised by members of the Court, with Judges Al-Khasawneh and Simma arguing that whilst use of such experts may be pardonable if the scientific issue in dispute forms part of the margins of the case, the situation is different if the scientific issue forms part of the crux of the case.[58] As such, it has been argued that the use of informal expert evidence is extremely problematic and that in the interests of the proper administration of justice the practice of the Court in seeking informal advice from experts should be restricted.[59]

In addition to the problematic use of *experts fantômes*, Anna Riddell has written of fact-finding errors made by the Court in a number of cases. One example cited by Riddell is that of *Qatar v. Bahrain* in which the Court was called upon to determine whether there had been a channel navigable even at low tide between the islands of Fasht al Azm and Sitrah Island.[60] Neither party was able to produce evidence relating to the state of the channel before 1982 and the party-appointed experts produced conflicting evidence.[61] As such, aware that unless the Court were to utilise its own fact-finding powers in order to shed more light on the

---

telles que par exemple l'étude du matériau cartographique fourni par les parties ou l'établissement de cartes ou de croquis particuliers'; Couvreur, 'Le Règlement Juridictionel' 384.

[56] Tams, 'Article 50' 1118.   [57] Ibid.
[58] *Pulp Mills Case*, Dissenting Opinion of Judges Al-Khasawneh and Simma at para 14; see also Simma, 'The International Court of Justice and Scientific Expertise' 231.
[59] Tams, 'Article 50' 1118.
[60] Riddell, 'Scientific Evidence in the International Court of Justice – Problems and Possibilities' 243.
[61] Ibid.; *Maritime Delimitation and Territorial Questions between Qatar and Bahrain, Merits, Judgment, ICJ Reports 2001* 40, at 98 para 189.

## 2.1 ABUNDANT, COMPLEX OR TECHNICAL FACTS 85

issue it would be extremely difficult for it to make a factual finding on this issue, 'in the end the Court chose to base its decision on other matters without coming to a conclusion as to the existence of the channel'.[62] The Court's decision not to conduct its own fact-finding or to choose to favour one expert over the other could arguably have been overlooked had the Court not subsequently, in drafting the maritime boundary, drawn the boundary over dry land that belonged to both parties – an aberration which, Riddell has argued, could 'have been avoided if experts had been recruited to help with the task'.[63]

Similarly, Riddell cites the factual errors made by the Court in its judgment in the *Cameroon v. Nigeria* case. In this case the Court drew a land and maritime boundary that could not be applied due to errors in the drafting and delimitation 'because of the Court's apparent failure to understand that latitudes and longitudes cannot be applied without defining the geodetic datum on which they are based'.[64] Riddell has suggested that the errors made by the Court in its delimitation of the land boundary can be attributed to an erroneous use of the 'Minna Datum' – a particular model of the earth used in this part of the world used for topographical or, as in the this case, delimitation purposes. However, even if the Minna Datum is taken into account 'the boundary line as described by the Court is still difficult to demarcate because of further errors made in the coordinates'.[65] For example, the judgment states that the Court was convinced by Cameroon's argument regarding the position of the river but confusingly gave the coordinates of the source of the river being at 13° 44' 24' longitude east and 10° 59' 09' latitude north[66] – the coordinates submitted by Nigeria.[67] In addition, the Court's sketch map shows the source of the river as around 1.5 km from where the coordinates in the judgment cite it as being.[68]

---

[62] *Qatar v. Bahrain, Judgment*, para 218; Riddell, 'Scientific Evidence in the International Court of Justice – Problems and Possibilities' 243.

[63] Riddell, 'Scientific Evidence in the International Court of Justice – Problems and Possibilities' 243; see Tim Daniel, 'Expert Evidence before the ICJ', Paper presented at the Third Bi-Annual Conference of ABLOS (2003) at 5.

[64] Ibid.    [65] Ibid.

[66] *Land and Maritime Boundary between Cameroon and Nigeria (Cameroon v. Nigeria: Equatorial Guinea intervening) Judgment, ICJ Reports 2002* 303 para 102.

[67] Riddell, 'Scientific Evidence in the International Court of Justice – Problems and Possibilities' 246.

[68] Ibid.

86    CRITICISMS OF THE ICJ'S CURRENT REACTIVE APPROACH

Riddell's work clearly highlights the uncertain factual foundations upon which the Court's judgment was based, and in fact there were a number of other substantial errors in the judgment. For instance, paragraph 102 of the judgment describes the boundary between Cameroon and Nigeria as following the course of the River Kohom 'until it reaches the peak ... of 861m' before joining the River Bogaza.[69] However, in actual fact, the height of 861m refers to a point on the River Bogaza and not to the 'peak' and, crucially, the map drawn by the Court does not correspond with the coordinates given in the judgment – the location 'annotated on the sketch map [being] roughly 3 km away from the point the Court clearly intended to describe'.[70]

In relation to the maritime boundary the Court based its delimitation on the 'largest scale chart available to it', namely British Admiralty Chart 3433, demarcating the median line and 'basepoints' from this chart alone (without geographical coordinates) which means that it was impossible to demarcate the boundary with any precision.[71] Riddell has noted that in doing so the Court did not comply with Articles 16(1), 75(1) and 84(1) UNCLOS which explicitly require geodetic datum to be specified where geographic coordinates regarding boundary lines are provided.[72] The Court made a further error in the location of so-called Point X – which it said should be equidistant between two specified basepoints, West Point and East Point, at 8° 21' 20' longitude east and 4° 17' 00' latitude north.[73] However in actual fact the position of Point X in the judgment is around 330 metres to the west of the equidistant point between the given basepoints.[74]

---

[69] *Land and Maritime Boundary between Cameroon and Nigeria* case 303 para 102.

[70] Riddell, 'Scientific Evidence in the International Court of Justice – Problems and Possibilities' 247; see also Riddell and Plant, *Evidence before the International Court of Justice* 348.

[71] See Riddell, 'Scientific Evidence in the International Court of Justice – Problems and Possibilities' 247; C. H. Schofield and C. M. Carleton, 'Technical Considerations in Law of the Sea Dispute Resolution' in A. Elferink and D. R. Rothwell (eds), *Oceans Management in the 21st Century: Institutional Frameworks and Responses* (The Hague: Martinus Nijhoff, 2004) 251.

[72] See Schofield et al. – criticising the fact that the Court did not mention datum to accompany the coordinates that it gave – 'This suggests that either the Chart was not examined properly by the Court or that none of the Judges at the ICJ was aware that coordinates need to be referred to a datum to be meaningful'; Schofield and Carleton, 'Technical Considerations in Law of the Sea Dispute Resolution' 251.

[73] *Land and Maritime Boundary between Cameroon and Nigeria* case para 307.

[74] Ibid. para 292; Schofield and Carleton, 'Technical Considerations in Law of the Sea Dispute Resolution' 245.

## 2.1 ABUNDANT, COMPLEX OR TECHNICAL FACTS

As such the Court inadvertently drew a line 'straight through a Nigeria-operated oil field which is not, it is thought, the result that the Court intended'.[75] As Riddell concludes in her extremely important work on this topic, whilst some errors are understandable in relation to extremely complicated subject matter before it, simple factual errors that are not the result of a lack of evidence and could have been prevented by greater reliance on experts are less forgivable.[76] It is concerning that the Court made so many factual errors in its judgment and one must seriously question whether had the maps been prepared (or at the very least fact-checked)[77] 'by someone who could combine a sufficient knowledge of cartography with an ability to understand and comment on the geographical aspects of the judgment' there would have been so many errors.[78]

The errors in the judgment contributed materially to the substantial difficulties that the two States have encountered in implementing the judgment. In fact, after the Court's judgment was handed down in 2002 the UN Secretary-General, at the request of the parties, established the Cameroon/Nigeria Mixed Commission to implement the judgment. However more than ten years and thirteen meetings later the Commission has still to complete the delimitation of the boundary (although the parties agreed on the maritime boundary in 2007). The parties recently agreed to appoint a Joint Technical Team of surveyors and experts in 2013 in attempts to expedite the troubled process.[79] Riddell has stated that '[t]he fact that such a lengthy and detailed procedure has to be carried out in order to render the judgment of the ICJ of any practical effect is rather telling of the suitability of the Court at present to deal with such technically complex cases.'[80] This much seems clear: any judgment of the Court's containing numerous factual errors and requiring the establishment of a further Mixed Commission to implement its flawed judgment, entailing additional expense (in this case incurred by the UN) and delays speaks to a less than optimal handling of the factual issues in the case.

---

[75] Tim Daniel, 'Expert Evidence before the ICJ' 7; Schofield and Carleton, 'Technical Considerations in Law of the Sea Dispute Resolution' 247.
[76] Riddell, 'Scientific Evidence in the International Court of Justice – Problems and Possibilities' 248.
[77] Ibid.   [78] Ibid.
[79] See unowa.unmissions.org/Default.aspx?tabid=804 and www.un.org/apps/news/story.asp?NewsID=43779&Cr=cameroon&Cr1=nigeria#.Uja9kxaZbww.
[80] Riddell, 'Scientific Evidence in the International Court of Justice – Problems and Possibilities' 249.

However, such blatant factual errors are not the only manifestation of the problems generated by the Court's approach to fact-finding – it is not always possible to point to a factual determination and determine it to be erroneous. Rather, many other problematic aspects of the Court's approach to fact-finding are harder to quantify, although this does not mean that they are any less real, as we will see in the following subsections.

### 2.1.3 Other problems arising out of the Court's reactive approach to fact-finding

A further example of the problems that may arise from the Court's current reactive approach to fact-finding can be found in the recent controversy surrounding the Court's failure to utilise its fact-finding powers to pursue items of redacted evidence presented by Serbia to the International Criminal Tribunal for the Former Yugoslavia (ICTY) in the *Bosnian Genocide* case before the Court.[81] Bosnia and Herzegovina did not have access to these documents due to the fact they had been protected by a confidentiality order at the ICTY under the terms of an agreement signed between Serbia and the Prosecutor of the ICTY.[82] Consequently Bosnia and Herzegovina requested that the Court utilise its Article 49 ICJ Statute powers to request that Serbia disclose a number of redacted documents.[83] It has been subsequently argued that the Court's decision to rule on the merits of the case (and specifically on whether Serbia had incurred State responsibility for its role in relation to the genocide at Srebrenica) without seeking access to a considerable amount of redacted evidence put before the ICTY by Serbia is a critical weakness in the Court's judgment and represents a clear failure of the Court's judicial fact-finding responsibility.[84]

The Court described these documents as 'the "redacted" sections of documents of the Supreme Defence Council of the Respondent, i.e. sections in which parts of the text had been blacked out so as to

---

[81] *Bosnian Genocide Case*.
[82] Richard J. Goldstone and Rebecca J. Hamilton, 'Bosnia v. Serbia: Lessons from the Encounter of the International Court of Justice with the International Criminal Tribunal for the Former Yugoslavia' 21 *Leiden Journal of International Law* 95, 107.
[83] The original request was made by a letter dated 28 December 2005, then refined in subsequent letters dated 19 and 24 January 2006; see *Bosnian Genocide Case* para 44.
[84] Marlise Simons, 'Genocide Court Ruled for Serbia without Seeing Full War Archive' *The New York Times*, 9 April 2007.

be illegible'.[85] Serbia had claimed that these documents were redacted 'by decision of the Council as a military secret, and by a confidential decision of the Council of Ministers of Serbia and Montenegro as a matter of national security interest'.[86] However, the Court refused to call on Serbia to produce these documents,[87] merely stating that Bosnia and Herzegovina had 'extensive documentation and other evidence available to it, especially from readily accessible ICTY records' and noted the use already made by Bosnia and Herzegovina of such evidence and the testimony of one of its witnesses, General Sir Richard Dannatt who gave evidence on the relationship between the authorities in the Federal Republic of Yugoslavia and those in the Republika Srpska.[88]

In addition, the Court refused to draw adverse inferences from Serbia's failure to put the redacted documents before the Court. Bosnia and Herzegovina had argued, whilst accepting that as the applicants they principally carried the burden of proof, that in relation to 'the attributability of alleged acts of genocide to the Respondent' the burden should be reversed 'given the refusal of the Respondent to produce the full text of certain documents'.[89] The Court, however, rejected this argument, somewhat elliptically concluding its statement on this matter by stating that '[a]lthough the Court has not agreed to either of the Applicant's requests to be provided with unedited copies of these documents, it has not failed to note the Applicant's suggestion that the Court may be free to draw its own conclusions.'[90]

Just what the Court meant by this statement is unclear. It would appear that the Court, whilst reluctant to draw explicit adverse inferences, is suggesting that the significance of these documents not being produced is not lost on it. However, it is suggested that this is a needlessly convoluted way of dealing with the situation and a number of commentators have criticised the failure of the Court to request the documents in this regard. For instance, Goldstone and Hamilton argue that this line of argument is 'hardly persuasive, given that Bosnia and Herzegovina's reason for requesting unredacted versions of these documents was that it believed these documents would provide evidence on the issue of attribution that was not clear from the documentation it already had available to it.'[91]

---

[85] *Bosnian Genocide Case* para 205.    [86] Ibid. para 205.
[87] By letters dated 2 February 2006; see ibid. para 44.    [88] Ibid. para 204.
[89] Ibid. para 204.    [90] Ibid. para 204.
[91] Goldstone and Hamilton, 'Bosnia v. Serbia: Lessons from the Encounter of the International Court of Justice with the International Criminal Tribunal for the Former Yugoslavia' 108.

Bosnia and Herzegovina had, during the oral pleadings, argued that the documents would show orders given by the Federal Republic of Yugoslavia (FYR) and records of payments made to Bosnian Serb forces which would have been potentially crucial to proving the State responsibility for the commission of, or at least complicity in, genocide.[92] Diane Orentlicher seconded this position, stating that 'the fact that they [the documents in question] were blacked out clearly implies these passages would have made a difference'.[93] A number of lawyers, under strict conditions of anonymity, confirmed that the redacted documents shed light on key issues such as the extent of Serbian influence over the Bosnian Serb forces.[94] In fact, this is a position echoed from within the Court itself. The dissenting opinion of Judge Al-Khasawneh stated that 'it is a reasonable expectation that those documents would have shed light on the central questions' and criticised not only the Court's failure to act, but also its elliptical reasoning which he described as 'worse than its failure to act'.[95] Similarly, the dissenting opinion of Judge Mahiou argued that the reasons given for the Court for not pursuing the evidence more thoroughly were not convincing and attributed its failure to act to a desire to avoid encroaching on Serbia's sovereignty and to avoid potential embarrassment were Serbia to refuse to comply with the Court's request.[96] Ultimately, Goldstone and Hamilton describe the Court's refusal to even request the documents as 'a sad legacy to leave following 14 years of litigation on this case.'[97]

It should be emphasised that the significance of this affair lies not in the particular facts of the *Bosnian* and *Croatian Genocide* cases.[98] Indeed, it may even be the case that, contrary to the views of those mentioned above, the Defence Council minutes are revealed to be relatively unimportant in terms of the legal issues in the two genocide cases. Rather, the

---

[92] *Bosnia v. Serbia* Case, CR 2006/30, 18 April 2006 para 19 (Beisen); ibid.
[93] Simons, 'Genocide Court Ruled for Serbia without Seeing Full War Archive'.     [94] Ibid.
[95] *Bosnian Genocide Case*, Dissenting Opinion of Judge Al-Khasawneh at 35.
[96] Ibid., Dissenting Opinion of Judge Mahiou at 59.
[97] Goldstone and Hamilton, 'Bosnia v. Serbia: Lessons from the Encounter of the International Court of Justice with the International Criminal Tribunal for the Former Yugoslavia' 110.
[98] Relatedly, in the recent preliminary objections phase of the *Croatian Genocide* case, the Court refused a similar request made by Croatia, stating that it was 'not satisfied that the production of the requested documents was necessary for the purpose of ruling on preliminary objections'; *Application of the Convention on the Prevention and Punishment of the Crime of Genocide (Croatia v. Serbia), Preliminary Objections, Judgment, ICJ Reports 2008* 413, 416 paras 13–15.

## 2.1 ABUNDANT, COMPLEX OR TECHNICAL FACTS 91

significance of this affair for our purposes is the fact that, apparently deprived of crucially significant information requested by one of the parties, the Court seemed unwilling to take any steps towards acquiring this information through use of its fact-finding powers in order to determine their significance for itself.[99] Such high-profile criticism of the Court's handling of the evidence, and the Court's behaviour in these circumstances, is a cautionary tale for similar cases that may arise in the future and begs the question as to whether a more proactive approach to fact-finding could avoid future incidents.

As we have already seen, the Court has also encountered significant criticism in relation to its use of evidence and experts in the *Pulp Mills* case. In particular the Court's approach to evaluating the complex and scientific evidence put before it by the parties was heavily criticised by Judges Al-Khasawneh and Simma in their joint dissenting opinion as being 'flawed methodologically'.[100] The main thrust of the judges' criticism of the Court was that the Court 'omitted to resort to possibilities provided by its Statute' leading to a constricted approach to the evaluation of the disputed scientific facts.[101] In not fully utilising its statutory fact-finding powers, the Court's approach has been criticised for failing to do what was 'necessary in order to arrive at a basis for the application of the law to the facts as scientifically certain in possible in a judicial proceeding'.[102]

Despite considerable amounts of conflicting scientific evidence placed before the Court by the parties, the Court in this case also maintained its reactive approach, examining and weighing the scientific evidence in relation to the impact of the discharge of dangerous chemicals from the mills on the environment itself without utilising its own powers to appoint experts or a commission of inquiry.[103] The Court's decision in this regard was questioned by a number of judges such as Judge ad hoc

---

[99] Alternatively there is the possibility that the Court did indeed have access to, or information about, these documents that it did not disclose to the parties on the basis of which the decision was taken that the information would not play a decisive role in proceedings. If this were the case, however, this would be equally concerning, violating the principles of transparency and due process.
[100] *Pulp Mills Case*, Dissenting Opinion of Judges Al-Khasawneh and Simma at para 2.
[101] Ibid., Dissenting Opinion of Judges Al-Khasawneh and Simma at para 2.
[102] Ibid, Dissenting Opinion of Judges Al-Khasawneh and Simma at para 2; Simma, 'The International Court of Justice and Scientific Expertise' 232.
[103] *Pulp Mills Case* para 236; Riddell, 'Scientific Evidence in the International Court of Justice – Problems and Possibilities' 250.

Vinuesa who questioned 'the Court's ability to make appropriate determinations of fact ... based on sound scientific findings'[104] despite the 'lack of specialized expert knowledge'.[105] In particular Judge ad hoc Vinuesa took umbrage with the Court making legal determinations whilst clearly being unable to speak in certain terms about the scientific issues.[106] In particular it was the Court's method that was the object of the judges' negative assessments. Criticism was voiced of the Court's practice of hearing the arguments of the parties, 'asking a few token questions' then retiring to deliberate *in camera*.[107] It is for this reason that Judges Al-Khasawneh and Simma censured the Court for 'clinging to the habits it has traditionally followed in assessing and evaluating evidence'.[108]

These judges criticised sections of the majority judgment which state that the Court 'sees no need'[109] and 'is not in a position' to arrive at specific conclusions,[110] that 'there is no [clear] evidence to support' certain claims,[111] that 'certain facts have not been established to the satisfaction of the Court'[112] or that certain evidence 'does not substantiate the claims'.[113] The judges criticised the practice of the Court in obliging Argentina to substantiate certain claims on issues that the Court, without specific expert assistance, could not 'fully comprehend'. The judges rejected the suggestion that scientific expertise ought to only come before the Court through experts acting as counsel on behalf of the parties under Article 43 of the Court's Statute outright.[114]

That the judges went so far as to describe the methodological approach taken by the Court as having the potential to 'increase doubts in the international legal community whether it, as an institution, is well-placed to tackle complex scientific questions' is undoubtedly significant.[115] The

---

[104] *Pulp Mills Case*, Dissenting Opinion of Judge Ad Hoc Vinuesa at para 44.
[105] Ibid., Dissenting Opinion of Judge Ad Hoc Vinuesa at para 71.
[106] Ibid., Dissenting Opinion of Judge Ad Hoc Vinuesa at para 70. At various points the Court states that 'Argentina has not convincingly demonstrated that Uruguay' (*Judgment* para 189); 'the Court is not in a position to conclude that Uruguay' (ibid. para 228); it has 'not been established to the satisfaction of the Court' (ibid. para 250); 'there is insufficient evidence' (ibid. para 254); 'there is no clear evidence to link' (ibid. para 259); 'a clear relationship has not been established' (ibid. para 262); 'the record does not show any clear evidence' (ibid. para 264).
[107] Ibid., Dissenting Opinion of Judges Al-Khasawneh and Simma at para 5.
[108] Ibid., Dissenting Opinion of Judges Al-Khasawneh and Simma at para 2.
[109] Ibid. para 213.   [110] Ibid. para 228.   [111] Ibid. paras 225, 239, 259.
[112] Ibid. para 250.   [113] Ibid. para 257.
[114] Ibid., Dissenting Opinion of Judges Al-Khasawneh and Simma at para 6.
[115] Ibid., Dissenting Opinion of Judges Al-Khasawneh and Simma at para 3.

judges argued that the Court ought to cease 'willingly depriving itself of the ability fully to consider the facts submitted to it' – and instead advocated that the Court make better use of inquiries and experts before the Court in an open and public manner, in contrast to the practice of relying on *experts fantômes* as has been the case in the past.

Such criticism from within the Court illustrates that the current weaknesses of the Court's approach to fact-finding are known to those on the bench and suggests a growing awareness that in cases in which the facts are particularly complex the Court's reluctance to undertake its own fact-finding is an increasingly real concern. Despite the wide range of criticisms made by judges Simma, Al-Khasawneh, Vinuesa and Yusuf in the *Pulp Mills* case, there are in fact several problematic aspects of the Court's approach to fact-finding which they did not address.

One such additional problematic issue is the Court's reliance on publicly available information such as information contained in UN Commissions of Inquiry. The Court's considerable reliance on this type of information in recent times in addition to the facts presented by the parties themselves is a corollary of the Court's reactive approach to fact-finding. For this reason it is necessary to turn our attention to this aspect of the Court's reactive approach to fact-finding.

### 2.1.4 From our own correspondent: the Court's deference to UN fact-finding

A further weakness brought about by the Court's current reactive approach to fact-finding is its problematic reliance on commissions of inquiry, particularly those conducted under the auspices of the UN.[116] Katherine Del Mar's analysis of the Court's jurisprudence reveals that the Court has always tended to attribute 'significant weight' to factual determinations made by UN fact-finding commissions and to the factual determinations included in the resolutions of

---

[116] A preliminary word of clarification regarding terminology is necessary: the terms 'commission of inquiry', 'international investigatory process', 'inquiry', 'enquiry', 'fact-finding mission' and 'investigation' have all traditionally been used interchangeably in international legal scholarship to refer to the same process. This semantic variety, however, is not of any great significance. Instead, we must focus our attention on the substance of these inquiries to consider the substantial development of the concept over the years; Christine Chinkin, 'U.N. Human Rights Council Fact-Finding Missions: Lessons from Gaza' in Arsanjani et al. (eds), *Looking to the Future: Essays on International Law in Honour of W. Michael Reisman* (Boston: Martinus Nijhoff, 2011) 476.

the General Assembly and Security Council.[117] It is this issue that is critically examined in the following section, starting with consideration of the practice of the Court in the *Bosnian Genocide* case.

Akin to the Court's elucidation of the principles which guide it in assessing facts put before it generally (see Chapter 1 at Section 1.4), the Court has in a number of recent cases addressed the issue of how it assesses fact-finding reports from official or independent bodies. The Court in *Bosnian Genocide* provided explicit guidance on the factors it takes into consideration when assessing the facts brought before it that have been gathered by a UN body, stating:

> Their value depends, among other things, on (1) the source of the item of evidence (for instance partisan, or neutral), (2) the process by which it has been generated (for instance an anonymous press report or the product of a careful court or court-like process), and (3) the quality or character of the item (such as statements against interest, and agreed or uncontested facts).[118]

The Court stated that these factors were cumulative, to be taken together to determine the weight to be attributed to certain fact-finding reports. One commentator has praised the enunciation of such guiding principles and has argued that if applied consistently they have the potential to 'greatly improve the quality of the Court's fact-assessment.'[119]

Commentators have pointed out that whilst the Court in *Bosnian Genocide* explicitly stated that it was to make its own determination of the facts,[120] almost all of the Court's treatment of the facts in the judgment could be termed 'second hand', coming from reports of fact-finding bodies or decisions of judicial bodies such as the ICTY (a point to which we will return in Section 2.2.4).[121]

Reliance on factual determinations made in UN fact-finding reports is demonstrated in relation to the issue of the weight that ought to be attributed to a UN report disputed by the parties before the Court (the

---

[117] Del Mar, 'Weight of Evidence Generated through Intra-Institutional Fact-finding before the International Court of Justice'.
[118] *Bosnian Genocide Case* para 227.
[119] Halink, 'All Things Considered: How the International Court of Justice Delegated Its Fact-Assessment to the United Nations in the Armed Activities Case' 23.
[120] *Bosnian Genocide Case* para 212.
[121] José E. Alvarez, *Burdens of Proof* (ASIL 2007); see also Gattini, 'Evidentiary Issues in the ICJ's Genocide Judgment' 900.

*Fall of Srebrenica* Report).[122] The Court's factual determinations relied significantly on this report, (a report to the General Assembly by the Secretary-General) with the Court highlighting that: 'the care taken in preparing the report, its comprehensive sources and the independence of those responsible for its preparation all lend considerable authority to it. As will appear later in this Judgment, the Court has gained *substantial assistance from this report.*'[123]

The Court further demonstrated a preference for findings-of-fact made by UN reports in stating that 'the authoritative evidentiary status of UN documents is a clear reflection of the fact that the UN has, above all other institutions, public or private, the resources and political access to produce reports of this calibre.'[124] This can be seen in the considerable reliance on the UN Commission of Experts[125] and the report of the Special Rapporteur of the Commission on Human Rights.[126] For example, in relation to the establishment of mass killings having taken place in various locations throughout Bosnia and Herzegovina during the conflict, and the fact that the majority of those killed in this way were members of a protected group but that the specific intent (*dolus specialis*) required was not present, the Court relied almost exclusively on those UN reports mentioned, stating that it believed that it had 'established by conclusive evidence' the points it needed to in order to make its subsequent legal determinations in relation to the perpetration of genocide.[127] As we will see in Section 2.1.5, the Court dealt with the particular case of the massacre at Srebrenica in much the same way, although in this case relied to a greater extent on the jurisprudence of the ICTY. The *Bosnian Genocide* case is not, however, an isolated example of this kind of reliance on findings-of-fact made in UN Commissions of Inquiry, as the *Armed Activities* case demonstrates.

---

[122] Report of the Secretary-General pursuant to General Assembly Resolution 53/35, 'The Fall of Srebrenica', 15 November 1999, UN Doc A/54/549; see Riddell and Plant, *Evidence before the International Court of Justice* 240.
[123] *Bosnian Genocide Case* para 230 (emphasis added).
[124] Riddell and Plant, *Evidence Before the International Court of Justice* 240.
[125] Final Report of the United Nations Commission of Experts (S/1994/674/Add.2).
[126] Report of the Special Rapporteur of the Commission on Human Rights, 22 August 1995 (E/CN.4/1996/9); *Bosnian Genocide Case*, see, by way of illustration, paras 246, 250, 252, 253, 255, 258, 259, 260, 262, 271; Goldstone and Hamilton, 'Bosnia v. Serbia: Lessons from the Encounter of the International Court of Justice with the International Criminal Tribunal for the Former Yugoslavia' 104.
[127] *Bosnian Genocide Case* paras 276, 277; for particular locations see paras 242–76.

96  CRITICISMS OF THE ICJ'S CURRENT REACTIVE APPROACH

In the course of proceedings of the *Armed Activities* case the Court placed considerable reliance on several UN fact-finding reports. For example, in relation to the issue of whether Uganda had breached human rights law and international humanitarian law, the Court based its conclusions entirely on the facts as they were set out in reports by the Secretary-General, United Nations Mission in the Democratic Republic of the Congo (MONUC) and the Special Rapporteur of the then Commission on Human Rights.[128] Similarly, the Court held that there was 'clear evidence of the fact that Uganda established and exercised authority in Ituri as an occupying Power' – relying heavily on the Sixth Report of the Secretary-General on MONUC[129] and that there had been massive human rights violations and grave breaches of International Humanitarian Law (IHL) the Court relying on 'credible sources'[130] including the Third Report of the Secretary-General on MONUC.[131]

In general terms the Court stated that it had established the facts upon which it based its legal determinations on 'the coincidence of reports from credible sources'[132] including UN reports, 'to the extent that they are of probative value and are corroborated, if necessary by other credible sources'.[133] The Court gave no further detail on what reports had to be corroborated and went on to state that 'it is not necessary for the Court to make findings of fact with regard to each individual incident alleged',[134] instead appearing to adopt a cumulative approach to the evidence.[135] This would suggest that the Court does not enquire into the methods of UN fact-finding or question related issues such as the standard of proof

---

[128] Halink, 'All Things Considered: How the International Court of Justice Delegated its Fact-Assessment to the United Nations in the Armed Activities Case' 27; Report of the Special Rapporteur of the Commission on Human Rights, 18 January 2000, the Third Report on the United Nations Mission in the Democratic Republic of Congo (MONUC), Security Council Resolution 1304 (2000) and the Report of the Special Rapporteur of the Commission on Human Rights 1 February 2001 and January–December 2000, Special Report by MONUC, *Armed Activities Case* paras 34–5, 60, 182; Riddell and Plant, *Evidence before the International Court of Justice* 237.

[129] UN Doc S/2001/128, 12 February 2001.

[130] UN Doc S/2001/128, 12 February 2001 para 207.

[131] Third Report of the Secretary-General on the United Nations Organisation Mission in the Democratic Republic of the Congo, 12 June 2000, UN Doc S/2000/566 paras 79, 206; see 'Convincing Evidence' consisting of two reports of the SG and a special report by MONUC – Sixth Report of the Secretary-General on the United Nations Organisation Mission in the Democratic Republic of the Congo, 12 February 2001, UN Doc S/2001/128 paras 56, 209, 239.

[132] *Armed Activities Case* para 207.    [133] Ibid. para 205.    [134] Ibid. para 237.

[135] Ibid. para 237.

applied. Commentators have criticised the Court's approach in this regard for obfuscating the individual evidentiary significance of each report by simply referring to 'reports from credible sources', 'sufficient evidence of a reliable quality', and 'persuasive evidence' and consequently making it near-impossible to assess the relevance of one report over another.[136] We will return to such criticism of the Court's use of UN fact-finding reports in the following sections.

In short, from the guidance given by the Court on individual reports it is clear that the Court placed considerable emphasis on the significance on UN reports.[137] In fact, the Court was so lenient in its review of fact-finding carried out by other UN bodies that one commentator has argued that in cases such as *Armed Activities* the Court effectively delegated its fact-assessment to the United Nations.[138] Whereas the Court was dismissive of much of the secondary evidence presented by the parties,[139] stating that it did not rely on numerous items of evidence proffered by the DRC finding them 'uncorroborated, based on second-hand reports, or not in fact saying what they are alleged to say by the DRC, or even partisan'[140] the Court found evidence contained within UN reports, in the words of one commentator, 'virtually conclusive'.[141]

UN reports are also of considerable value to the Court in advisory proceedings.[142] In *The Wall* advisory opinion the Court stated that it believed its task to be to determine the obligation of the State in question 'in light of the facts which had been reported to the General Assembly at the time'.[143] Crucially, however, the Court also stated that this did not

---

[136] Halink, 'All Things Considered: How the International Court of Justice Delegated Its Fact-Assessment to the United Nations in the Armed Activities Case' 28; *Armed Activities Case* paras 207–9.
[137] *Armed Activities Case* para 176.
[138] Halink, 'All Things Considered: How the International Court of Justice Delegated Its Fact-Assessment to the United Nations in the Armed Activities Case' 26.
[139] *Armed Activities Case* paras 64–5, 72–91 and 106–47.   [140] Ibid. para 159.
[141] Halink, 'All Things Considered: How the International Court of Justice Delegated Its Fact-Assessment to the United Nations in the Armed Activities Case' 27
[142] The question being 'what are the legal consequences ... as described in the report of the Secretary-General'; this was also the case in *Applicability of the Obligation to Arbitrate under Section 21 of the United Nations Headquarters Agreement of 26 June 1947, Advisory Opinion, ICJ Reports 1988* 12, 22 para 23 in which the question similarly directed the court to take particular account of the reports of the Secretary-General; UN Doc. A/42/915 and Add.1; see Del Mar, 'Weight of Evidence Generated through Intra-Institutional Fact-finding before the International Court of Justice' 405; Riddell and Plant, *Evidence Before the International Court of Justice* 240.
[143] *Applicability of the Obligation to Arbitrate Advisory Opinion* 22 para 23.

mean that it should 'close its eyes to subsequent events of possible relevance to, or capable of throwing light on, that question'.[144] Regardless of the fact this is an advisory opinion as opposed to a contentious case the Court remains under the same obligation to make solid factual determinations upon which to base its legal determinations.

The Court relied on factual qualifications made by both UN Commissions of Inquiry and by the principal organs.[145] Arguments were made by States time and time again during the oral proceedings that the Court would be justified in relying on UN fact-finding commissions in order to make its factual determinations.[146] The Court's reliance on UN Documentation (at least partly) as a result of Israel's refusal to participate in the oral proceedings led judge Burgenthal to argue that the Court should have refused to offer an advisory opinion on the basis that the Court 'did not have before it the requisite factual bases for its sweeping findings.'[147]

However, Judge Burgenthal was alone in finding so, and the rest of the Court had little trouble in attributing significant weight to the factual qualifications made by the UN organs. The Report of the Secretary-General especially was relied upon in providing the basis for the Court's finding that the building of the wall 'led to increasing difficulties for the population concerned regarding access to health services, educational establishments and primary sources of water' to give but one example.[148]

But what is the significance of the Court's practice of relying on factual determinations made in UN Commissions of Inquiry? The Court's practice is a manifestation of what has been termed executive administrative finality[149] and can be traced as far back as the PCIJ to cases such as *Prince of Pless*[150] and *Jurisdiction of the European Commission*

---

[144] Ibid. 22 para 23.
[145] Although they did present a Written Statement on 30 January 2004, thus participating in the written stage; this is available at www.icj-cij.org.
[146] See for instance *I.C.J. Pleadings, The Wall A.O.*, CR 2004/1, 24/2/2004 52 para 27; *I.C.J. Pleadings, The Wall A.O.*, CR 2004/1, 25/2/2004 25-6.
[147] See Declaration of Judge Burgenthal in *The Wall Advisory Opinion* 240 para 1.
[148] Ibid., Separate Opinion of Judge Higgins 189-90 para 133; for further reliance on the Secretary-General's Report and Written Statement by the United Nations see 168-71, paras 80-85 and 184 para 122.
[149] Alford Jr, 'Fact Finding by the World Court' 52.
[150] *Case Concerning the Prince Von Pless (Preliminary Objection) PCIJ Ser. A/B No. 52* (Order of Feb 4, 1933) 16, in which the Court agreed to uphold the argument made by Poland that the Court ought to delay its consideration of the case before it until the Polish Administrative Tribunal had published its decision. In agreeing to do so the Permanent Court stated that it would 'certainly be an advantage to the Court, as regards

of the Danube.[151] The Court's preference for executive-administrative finality as seen in recent cases such as *Armed Activities* and *Bosnian Genocide* illustrates that the Court continues to lend 'greater weight to UN reports than to other types of secondary evidence such as press reports' ostensibly due to the presumption that such UN reports are based on solid, objective and impartial fact-finding.[152]

However, in recent times doubt has been cast upon the precise reliability of such reports and the Court's use of them in a number of cases that have come before it.[153] Whilst reliance on findings-of-fact made in UN Commissions of Inquiry is not problematic per se, a number of significant issues regarding their operation taint their factual determinations and should caution the Court against singular reliance on such commissions of inquiry. This point is further explored in the following sections.

### 2.1.4 (i) Are weaknesses in UN fact-finding undermining the Court's factual findings?

The previous section attempted to highlight what has been termed the Court's preference for executive-administrative finality, or, in other words, its deference to findings-of-fact made by UN bodies. However, in tandem with increasingly prevalent UN fact-finding activity a number of criticisms have begun to be voiced regarding the operation of such bodies. Consequently, fundamental weaknesses in UN fact-finding have the potential to seriously undermine the Court's factual findings.

UN fact-finding is carried out by a range of bodies for a range of different purposes – at times for monitoring, at times for assessing

---

the points which have to be established in the case, to be acquainted with the final decisions' of the domestic administrative tribunal.

[151] *Jurisdiction of the European Commission of the Danube between Galatz and Braila*, PCIJ Ser. B No. 14 (1927).

[152] Teitelbaum, 'Recent Fact-Finding Developments at the International Court of Justice' 145, Riddell and Plant, *Evidence before the International Court of Justice* 237. Further, it has been suggested that a case recently removed from the Court's docket, the *Aerial Spraying* case, would also have raised issues of reliance on evidence emanating from UN sources, namely UN Special Rapporteurs appointed to examine the Ecuador-Colombia border; see Boyle and Harrison, 'Judicial Settlement of International Environmental Disputes: Current Problems' 270.

[153] Teitelbaum, 'Recent Fact-Finding Developments at the International Court of Justice' 146; C. Van den Wyngaert, 'International Criminal Courts as Fact (and Truth) Finders in Post-Conflict Societies: Can Disparities with Ordinary International Courts Be Avoided?' Proceedings of the Annual Meeting-American Society of International Law, Vol. 100, Annual 2006.

allegations of violations of international humanitarian law or even for assessing the existence of a threat to international peace and security in the case of the Security Council.[154] There are a number of positive aspects of the Court's reliance on findings-of-fact made by UN fact-finding bodies.[155] The first relates to the establishment of UN inquiries. The establishment of such bodies is not dependent solely on the individual States involved in the matter but comes about as a result of a majority decision of a UN body. These UN inquiries are also (in theory) composed of impartial experts with no interest in the outcome of the inquiry. As such, it could be presumed that findings-of-fact made by such bodies have a relatively strong claim to credibility and could arguably even be said to 'represent the views of disinterested witnesses in proceedings before the Court'[156] – defined as 'one who is not a party to the proceedings and stands to gain or lose nothing from its outcome'.[157] One commentator has argued that, on the basis of being considered a disinterested witness, findings-of-fact made by UN organs should be considered to have '*prima facie* superior credibility'.[158]

The case for considering UN bodies as disinterested witnesses rests on the argument that these bodies are unable to be party to any proceedings before the Court and as such arguably have no material interest in the case at hand. For instance, there can be no parties to advisory proceedings and whilst the Secretary-General might participate by submitting a dossier of documents and a written statement (and by participating in the oral proceedings), he does so not on behalf of the Secretariat or in his personal capacity but under Article 97 of the UN Charter as 'the chief administrative officer of the Organization'. Further, in contentious cases, organs of the UN cannot be parties to the case. One commentator has

---

[154] For more detailed information on United Nations Fact-Finding see J. G. Devaney, 'Killing Two Birds with One Stone: Can Increased use of Article 34(2) of the ICJ Statute Improve the Legitimacy of UN Commissions of Inquiry & the Court's Fact-Finding Procedure?' *STALS Research Paper n 2/2013*; M. Bothe, 'Fact-finding as a Means of Ensuring Respect for International Humanitarian Law' (Berlin, New York: Springer, 2007) 258.

[155] A. Cassese, 'Fostering Increased Conformity with International Standards: Monitoring and Institutional Fact-Finding' in A. Cassese (ed), *Realizing Utopia: The Future of International Law* (Oxford University Press, 2012) 302.

[156] For a succinct summary of some of the advantageous and problematic aspects of UN Commissions of Inquiry, see Devaney, 'Killing Two Birds with One Stone'; see also Del Mar, 'Weight of Evidence Generated through Intra-Institutional Fact-finding before the International Court of Justice' 398.

[157] *Nicaragua Case* para 64.    [158] Ibid. para 64.

argued that whilst an individual member of the General Assembly or Security Council may have a vested interest in the outcome of an advisory opinion or a contentious case, 'these organs cannot be said to "stand to gain or lose" from the judicial proceedings in the same way as an individual state ... may gain or lose from the outcome of a case'.[159]

Secondly, although obvious, it should be noted that '[t]here has never been an instance where a document generated by the Security Council, the General Assembly or the Secretariat has been questioned by the Court on the basis of its authenticity, in contrast to the evidence produced by parties to a contentious case.'[160] Taking the above into account, Del Mar argues that since States have such a huge influence on the evidence that comes before the Court otherwise, the factual qualifications made by the principal organs of the UN are even more important: '[s]uch factual qualifications constitute *prima facie* credible and reliable evidence.'[161]

However, doubt has been cast upon the reliability of such reports and the suggestion that *prima facie* credibility be accorded to findings-of-fact made by UN bodies, which leads us to the more troublesome legal implications of their operation.[162] There are a number of deficiencies that deserve highlighting. Firstly, on a purely procedural level, a number of difficulties present themselves. For instance, it has been pointed out that after fifty years of UN fact-finding there is no standard operating procedure regarding organisation and planning for fact-finding missions,[163] preventing the development of a consistent

---

[159] Del Mar, 'Weight of Evidence Generated through Intra-Institutional Fact-finding before the International Court of Justice' 398.

[160] Del Mar, 'Weight of Evidence Generated through Intra-Institutional Fact-finding before the International Court of Justice' 402; for instance see the problematic evidence in *Maritime Delimitation and Territorial Questions between Qatar and Bahrain (Qatar v. Bahrain) (Order of 30 March 1998)* ICJ Rep 243, 246; CR 2000/5 (Dr Al Muslemmi, Agent for Qatar) 29 May 2000, 16, 17.

[161] Del Mar, 'Weight of Evidence Generated through Intra-Institutional Fact-finding before the International Court of Justice' 402.

[162] Teitelbaum, 'Recent Fact-Finding Developments at the International Court of Justice' 146; C. Van den Wyngaert, 'International Criminal Courts as Fact (and Truth) Finders in Post-Conflict Societies: Can Disparities with rdinary International Courts be Avoided?', 100 *Proceedings of the Annual Meeting, American Society of International Law* 55.

[163] Bassiouni, 'Appraising UN Justice-Related Fact-Finding Missions', 5 *Washington University Journal of Law and Policy* 35, 40. As Bassiouni has said, 'there is nothing to guide, instruct, or assist the heads and appointees to these missions of how to better carry out their mandates.'

standard of practice.[164] The Office of the High Commissioner for Human Rights (OHCHR) which has reviewed the practice of UN commission of inquiries does have an internal set of guidelines dealing with operational issues but these have not been made public and as such cannot be utilised in order to improve the operation of UN Commissions of Inquiry.[165]

In practice there are a number of ways in which the procedural legitimacy of fact-finding inquiries can be adversely affected, such as where the particular way in which a mandate has been worded suggests a prejudging of certain factual elements of the situation under investigation.[166] Similar factors adversely affecting the procedural legitimacy of fact-finding inquiries include allegedly disproportionate focus on some situations (such as the Middle East Conflict),[167] and criticism in the composition of the panel[168] such as those surrounding the appointment of certain members to the Goldstone Panel which prompted its authors to publicly defend their personal impartiality and the impartiality of the report itself.[169]

Secondly, although the consent of States is not required for the initial establishment of a fact-finding inquiry, it is usually required in order to

---

[164] Bassiouni 41–2.
[165] Rob Grace and Claude Bruderlein, 'On Monitoring, Reporting, and Fact-finding Mechanisms' 1 *ESIL Reflections* 1, 4.
[166] See Chinkin, 'U.N. Human Rights Council Fact-Finding Missions: Lessons from Gaza' 494; see for instance the criticism of the Security Council's Panel Reports in the *Armed Activities* case; I.C.J. Pleadings, Armed Activities, CR 2005/09, 20/4/2005 14 para 29: 'apparently "putting the cart before the horse", the Security Council created a "Panel of Experts on the *Illegal* Exploitation of the Natural Resources of the Congo". This suggests that the facts had been characterized as "illegal" even before it was known whether they actually existed!'
[167] T. M. Franck and H. S. Farley, 'Procedural Due Process in Human Rights Fact-Finding by International Agencies' 74 *American Journal of International Law* 308, 312; Chinkin notes that by early 2009, five out of ten special sessions had been directed towards criticising Israel (a trend that has continued), echoing the shortcomings of the Commission on Human Rights; Chinkin, 'U.N. Human Rights Council Fact-Finding Missions: Lessons from Gaza' 494.
[168] For example, see the Commission set up after the Six-Day War in 1968, GA Res 2443 (XXIII) (19 December 1968) in which, due to the allegedly partisan makeup of the commission, Israel refused to co-operate.
[169] See www.guardian.co.uk/commentisfree/2011/apr/14/goldstone-report-statement-un-gaza; for an interesting account of Goldstone's thinking, see Richard J. Goldstone, 'Quality Control in International Fact-Finding Outside Criminal Justice for Core International Crimes', in Morten Bergsmo (ed), *Quality Control in Fact-Finding* (Florence: Torkel Opsahl, 2013) 35; see also Wu Xiaodan, 'Quality Control and the Selection of Members of International Fact-Finding Mandates', in ibid.

## 2.1 ABUNDANT, COMPLEX OR TECHNICAL FACTS

gain entry to the territory of a State.[170] The dispatch of a fact-finding inquiry could, after all, be seen as an 'intrusive act' which 'may be resented as unwarranted interference into events deemed to be within a state's own domestic jurisdiction'.[171] In practice it is not uncommon that consent is denied meaning that reports in such cases have to be compiled based on interviews with victims outside the territory itself and information from NGOs without any members of the panel ever having travelled to the State in question, as was the case in relation to the Human Rights Council's recent report on Syria.[172]

Furthermore, whilst ostensibly entitled 'fact-finding' missions, in reality these inquiries often make determinations on points of international law[173] such as determining that a certain factual situation amounts to a violation of IHL or human rights.[174] For example, the Goldstone Report established by the Human Rights Council in April 2009 to 'investigate all violations of international human rights law and international humanitarian law' committed in Gaza between 2008 and 2009 has been praised for providing an incisive analysis of the role that IHL and International Human Rights Law (IHRL) play in the conflict.[175] Similarly, the Legal Annex of the Palmer Report established by the Secretary-General on 2 August 2010 following the Gaza Flotilla Incident carefully manages the difficult distinction between

---

[170] Despite the Declaration on Fact-Finding urging States to adopt a policy of allowing such fact-finding missions into their territory; GA Res 46/59, (Declaration on Fact-Finding) paras 6, 21.

[171] Chinkin, 'U.N. Human Rights Council Fact-Finding Missions: Lessons from Gaza' 488. Such refusal of admittance is in fact commonplace in practice; see D. Weissbrodt and J. McCarthy, 'Fact-Finding by International Nongovernmental Human Rights Organizations' 22 *Virginia Journal of International Law* 1, 59: 'the great bulk of human rights fact-finding by both IGOs and NGOs is accomplished without on-site visits'. See also, for example, Israel's refusal to allow the Human Rights Council's fact-finding mission to visit the Occupied Palestinian Territory under HRC Resolution S-1/1. Similarly, the high-level fact-finding mission to Darfur was unable to obtain visas from the government of Sudan. HRC Res 4/8 (30 March 2007).

[172] See for example HRC Resolution S-17/1, 23 August 2011; see First Report A/HRC/S-17/1/2/Add.1 and Second Report A/HRC/19/69, 22 February 2012.

[173] Dapo Akande and Hannah Tonkin, 'International Commissions of Inquiry: A New Form of Adjudication?' EJIL: Talk!

[174] Ibid.; B. G. Ramcharan, International Law and Fact-Finding in the Field of Human Rights (The Hague: Martinus Nijhoff, 1982) 1, 6.

[175] See *Report of the United Nations Fact-Finding Mission on the Gaza Conflict, Human Rights in Palestine and Other Occupied Arab Territories, Human Rights Council, 12th Session, 25 September 2009*, A/HRC/12/48 (2009) at paras 379–436.

IHL and IHRL in relation to whether Israeli soldiers had used 'excessive force'.[176]

In making findings on legal issues the question arises as to what standard of proof the commissions of inquiry, being at most quasi-judicial, ought to apply when making legal determinations.[177] In reality the standard of proof applied is often ambiguous and the judicial skills and experience demonstrated by some commissions dubious.[178] Research shows that in the practice the standard of proof applied has varied widely between different commissions of inquiry.[179] To be clear, it is not argued that UN Commissions of Inquiry should apply the same rigorous standard of proof as would be expected of a judicial body. Rather it is argued that the considerable variation in standards of proof between inquiries threatens the development of a consistent standard of practice. Concerted focus on this important issue from the outset and throughout is essential for the future operation of such commissions of inquiry.

Relatedly, there exists a tendency to provide cursory consideration of the relevant legal issues and legal arguments of dubious soundness. A few examples illustrate this potentially problematic practice. The Goldstone Report asserted that, despite ostensibly disengaging in 2005, Israel retained effective control over the Gaza strip and that 'the international community continues to regard [Israel] as the occupying Power'.[180] In support of this position the Goldstone Report cited a Security Council Resolution[181] and a Human Rights Council Resolution.[182] In doing so, the Goldstone Report presented the legal issues as straightforward and generally accepted whilst failing to note a significant number of competing legal positions or considering the precise legal effect of the resolutions

---

[176] See The Palmer Report, 'Report of the Secretary-General's Panel of Inquiry on 31 May 2010 Flotilla Incident, July 2011' at paras 117, 134.

[177] T. Boutruche, 'Credible Fact-Finding and Allegations of International Humanitarian Law Violations: Challenges in Theory and Practice' 16 *Journal of Conflict and Security Law* 105.

[178] Halink, 'All Things Considered: How the International Court of Justice Delegated Its Fact-Assessment to the United Nations in the Armed Activities Case' 32.

[179] Stephen Wilkinson, 'Standards of Proof in International Humanitarian and Human Rights Fact-Finding and Inquiry Missions', Geneva Academy of International Humanitarian Law and Human Rights 25.

[180] HRC Resolution A/HRC/12/48, 25/9/2009 para 277.

[181] Security Council Resolution 1860, 8 January 2009.

[182] Human Rights Council Resolution S-9/1, 12 January 2009.

## 2.1 ABUNDANT, COMPLEX OR TECHNICAL FACTS 105

relied upon by the Report.[183] The report also stated that 'non-State actors that exercise government-like functions over a territory have a duty to respect human rights' without providing any State practice or *opinio juris* in support of this position.[184]

Similarly, the Philips Report established by the Human Rights Council following the Gaza Flotilla Incident[185] made the legal determination that Gaza was occupied by Israel relying solely on the findings of the Goldstone Report[186] and that it was under an illegal blockade without considering the relationship between Israel's status as an Occupying Power and the legality of the blockade.[187] This is significant since an Occupying Power need not invoke the concept of a naval blockade in international law to justify its barring access to a territory it effectively controls.[188]

Another example is the Palmer Report's straightforward characterisation of the Middle East Conflict as an international armed conflict[189] without providing any justification for this determination. This report simply states that its determination to this effect was 'based on facts as they exist on the ground'[190] and that the conflict had 'all the trappings of

---

[183] Including a strict reading of Article 42 of the Hague Regulations.
[184] *Report of the United Nations Fact-Finding Mission on the Gaza Conflict, Human Rights in Palestine and Other Occupied Arab Territories, Human Rights Council, 12th Session, 25 September 2009*, A/HRC/12/48 (2009) at para 305. In actual fact, it is far from clear that non-State actors who exercise government-like functions over a territory have a duty to respect human rights. Marko Milanovic, 'Goldstone Report on Gaza: A Question of Trust' EJIL: Talk! Whilst reference to a former Special Rapporteur and one commentator are made earlier in the report, these do not provide adequate support for such a broad assertion that is open to criticism. Disagreement is also evident in international legal scholarship on this issue; c.f. E. Samson, 'Is Gaza Occupied? Redefining the Status of Gaza under International Law' 25 *American University Law Review* 915, 923; Y. Shany, 'Faraway, So Close: the Legal Status of Gaza after Israel's Disengagement' 8 *Yearbook of International Humanitarian Law* 369.
[185] *Report of the International Fact-Finding Mission to Investigate Violations of International Law, Including International Humanitarian and Human Rights Law, Resulting from the Israeli Attacks on the Flotilla Ships Carrying Humanitarian Assistance, Human Rights Council, 15th Session, 27 September 2010*, A/HRC/15/21 (2010) – Human Rights Council Resolution 14/1 of 2 June 2010.
[186] Ibid. para 64.   [187] Ibid paras 59–61.
[188] Yuval Shany, 'Know Your Rights! The Flotilla Report and International Law Governing Naval Blockades' EJIL: Talk!
[189] The Palmer Report, 'Report of the Secretary-General's Panel of Inquiry on 31 May 2010 Flotilla Incident, July 2011' para 73; Tamar Feldman, 'A Tale of Two Closures: Comments on the Palmer Report Concerning the May 2010 Flotilla Incident' EJIL: Talk!
[190] Palmer Report para 73.

an international armed conflict'.[191] Similarly, both the Palmer and the Philips reports[192] suggested that Israel had a right to self-defence under the UN Charter in these circumstances despite the fact the doctrine of self-defence is traditionally considered a concept of the *jus ad bellum* applicable only in inter-State conflicts.[193]

Similar concerns were raised regarding the Court's reliance on reports of the 'Panel of Experts' established by the Security Council in the *Armed Activities* case (see above at Section 2.1.4(i)). The Court's reliance on these reports to make legal determinations can be seen as problematic owing to the fact that the Security Council itself stated that the Panel was not set up to gather facts for judicial purposes.[194] Further, the Panel was criticised for 'failing even to respect the methodology which it claimed to be seeking to apply and, in its first report, betraying a degree of bias which provoked criticism from a number of States.'[195] Additionally, the Security Council in paragraph 15 of Resolution 1457 (24 January 2003) urged all States:

> [T]o conduct their own investigations, including as appropriate through judicial means, in order to clarify credibly the findings of the Panel, taking into account the fact that the Panel, which is not a judicial body, does not have the resources to carry out an investigation whereby these findings can be considered as established facts.

As such we can see that the Panel reports were not intended to be fact-finding instruments and as such the Court's reliance on them to this end is somewhat problematic.[196]

---

[191] Ibid. para 73. The Panel justifies this position by highlighting the thousands of rockets fired into Israel from Gaza; D. Guilfoyle, 'The Palmer Report on the Mavi Marmara Incident and the Legality of Israel's Blockade of the Gaza Strip' EJIL: Talk! . Whether or not the Middle-East Conflict can be characterised as international in nature or not, it is clear that simply classifying rocket fire as 'all the trappings of an international armed conflict' is problematic legal reasoning; ibid. The Report's Legal Annex uses different reasoning in reaching the same conclusion. The Annex relies on the US Civil War *Prize Cases* as the sole basis for its assertion that a blockade can be invoked against a non-State actor. However, a major weakness of the legal reasoning displayed in the Annex is its sole reliance on this authority – as it has been noted, 'the idea that the modern law can be completely exposed by reference to a single set of national proceedings 150 years old is dubious at best', D. Guilfoyle, 'The Mavi Marmara Incident and Blockade in Armed Conflict' 81 *British Yearbook of International Law* 171.

[192] Palmer Report at para 73.

[193] For a fuller discussion of this issue, see C. J. Tams and J. G. Devaney, 'Applying Necessity and Proportionality to Anti-Terrorist Self-Defence' 45 *Israel Law Review* 91.

[194] I.C.J. Pleadings, Armed Activities, CR 2005/09, 20 April 2005 6 para 14; see also Opinion of Judge Kateka at para 52.

[195] I.C.J. Pleadings, Armed Activities, CR 2005/09, 20 April 2005 6 para 15.

[196] The Porter Report itself criticised the Panel Reports, stating that 'it would seem that the majority of evidence likely to be obtained by such a methodology [of flexible data

Crucially, the Court did add an important caveat that whilst UN reports are of course persuasive, 'it should be borne in mind that the Court's ultimate assessment of them depended on their concordance with other evidentiary sources presented during the proceedings'.[197] Further, the Court found parts of the Secretary-General's MONUC Report that relied on second-hand reports in the passages concerning the issue of whether or not the Congo Liberation movement had been created by Uganda to be unreliable.[198] And it has been argued that the Court's statement that it would only take into account evidence contained within UN reports 'to the extent that they are of probative value and are corroborated, if necessary, by other credible sources'[199] shows that it appreciates that some doubt exists with regard to the evidentiary weight to be attributed to them.[200]

However, these qualifications are not enough to spare the Court from criticism. Indeed, there was even some limited criticism from within the Court regarding its over-reliance on UN reports such as Judge Kateka's dissenting opinion in the case which described the UN reports methodological approach as so flexible that its findings 'would be either hearsay, biased or pure gossip, all untested'.[201] Judge Kateka urged caution in relation to reliance on just one source (as has been the practice of the Court consistently over many years) even if that source was a UN source.[202]

On this issue, Halink has called into question whether reliance on numerous reports, such as those of the Secretary-General and MONUC, could truly be said to come from 'multiple sources'. This commentator

---

collection] would be either hearsay, biased or pure gossip, all untested'; Porter Commission Report 7.
[197] Riddell and Plant, *Evidence before the International Court of Justice* 238.
[198] *Armed Activities Case* 225 para 159; although Del Mar has stated that such action is 'a rare occurrence', Del Mar, 'Weight of Evidence Generated through Intra-Institutional Fact-finding before the International Court of Justice' 407.
[199] *Armed Activities Case* paras 237–50; examples of corroboration related to UN Reports in Halink, 'All Things Considered: How the International Court of Justice Delegated its Fact-Assessment to the United Nations in the Armed Activities Case' at footnote 70.
[200] Halink, 'All Things Considered: How the International Court of Justice Delegated its Fact-Assessment to the United Nations in the Armed Activities Case' 28, Teitelbaum, 'Recent Fact-Finding Developments at the International Court of Justice' 147.
[201] See the Dissenting Opinion of Judge Kateka in *Armed Activities Case* para 53.
[202] The Court operates a rule that evidence should not come completely from one single source: see 'widespread reports of fact may prove on closer examination to derive from a single source, and such reports, however numerous, will in such case, have no greater value than their original source'; *Nicaragua Case* 40–1.

argues that since these reports all operate as part of the same apparatus doubts surround 'possible overlap in mandate and potential mutual reliance of missions in reporting on overlapping areas, thus creating a false impression of confirmation and reliability'.[203] And indeed as we have seen already such reports do cite each other as authority (see Section 2.1.4 (vi)).

This makes it all the more surprising that the Court has placed such importance on them in recent cases. In acknowledging that flaws in the reports potentially exist but in not subjecting UN reports to the same scrutiny as other items of evidence the Court is open to criticism.[204] As Van den Wyngaert has stated, '[i]t would be interesting to see what the result ... would have been had the ICJ applied the same test to the MONUC report and other documentary evidence on which (some of) its holdings were based'.[205]

The Court has also been criticised for basing so many of its findings on the Porter Commission (a domestic judicial fact-finding commission established by Uganda).[206] In the course of proceedings, the Court stated that it:

> [H]ad already expressed its view with regard to the evidentiary role of the Porter Commission materials in general ... and considers that both the Porter Commission Report, as well as the United Nations Panel reports, to the extent that they have later proved to be probative, furnish sufficient and convincing evidence for it to determine whether or not Uganda engaged in acts of looting.[207]

In its judgment the Court claimed that its considerable reliance on the Porter Commission was justified by the fact that it had obtained evidence from people under oath 'by examination of persons directly involved, and who were subsequently cross-examined by judges skilled in

---

[203] Halink, 'All Things Considered: How the International Court of Justice Delegated its Fact-Assessment to the United Nations in the Armed Activities Case' 33, cites M. C. Bassiouni, 'Appraising UN Justice-Related Fact-Finding Missions' 5 *Washington University Journal of Law and Policy* 35, 41.

[204] Halink, 'All Things Considered: How the International Court of Justice Delegated its Fact-Assessment to the United Nations in the Armed Activities Case' 28; see also Teitelbaum, 'Recent Fact-Finding Developments at the International Court of Justice' 147.

[205] Van den Wyngaert, 'International Criminal Courts as Fact (and Truth) Finders in Post-Conflict Societies: Can Disparities with Ordinary International Courts Be Avoided?' 67.

[206] Halink, 'All Things Considered: How the International Court of Justice Delegated Its Fact-Assessment to the United Nations in the Armed Activities Case' 27.

[207] *Armed Activities Case* 273.

examination and experienced in assessing large amounts of factual information' and since neither party had challenged the Report's credibility.[208]

However, the Court has been criticised for relying on the Commission's findings 'in the way an appellate body would rely on the fact findings of a trial court'[209] since any allegation confirmed by a finding of the Porter Commission appeared to be accepted by the Court as 'having met a clear and convincing standard of proof'.[210] Whilst it could be said that the Porter Commission fulfils the criteria for favoured evidence set out in paragraph 214 of the *Bosnian Genocide* judgment (that of being 'evidence obtained by examination of persons directly involved' and tested by cross-examination, the credibility of which has not been challenged subsequently)[211] the Porter Commission itself had admitted that it had serious flaws and as such it is surprising that the Court attributed it so much weight.[212]

Furthermore, Uganda criticised the Security Council's decision to name the Panel as the 'Panel of Experts on the *Illegal* Exploitation of the Natural Resources of the Congo' which it argued clearly pre-empted the outcome of the report.[213] Uganda argued that whilst the Security Council is not a judicial body, such determinations acquire 'a certain force, even in this Court, having been used in the reports of the Security Council's "Panel of Experts", as well as in the Memorial, Reply and oral argument of the DRC, in which Uganda is accused of "illegal" exploitation of the DRC's natural resources.'

The evidentiary value of the MONUC report, also heavily relied upon by the Court (see above at Section 2.1.4 (ii)) was also questioned by Uganda, who described it as 'inappropriate as a form of assistance accompanied by judicial rigour'.[214] In particular Uganda argued that

---

[208] Ibid. paras 60-1; see Teitelbaum, 'Recent Fact-Finding Developments at the International Court of Justice' 152.
[209] Teitelbaum, 'Recent Fact-Finding Developments at the International Court of Justice' 154; citing paras 114 and 115 of the *Armed Activities Case*.
[210] Teitelbaum, 'Recent Fact-Finding Developments at the International Court of Justice' 153.
[211] *Armed Activities Case* 35 para 61; see also paras 78-9, 114 and 237-42.
[212] Teitelbaum, 'Recent Fact-Finding Developments at the International Court of Justice' 151. See Report of the Judicial Commission of Inquiry into Allegations of Illegal Exploitation of Natural Resources and Other Forms of Wealth in the Democratic Republic of Congo 2001, 3.
[213] I.C.J. Pleadings, Armed Activities, CR 2005/09, 20 April 2005 14 para 29.
[214] I.C.J. Pleadings, Armed Activities, CR 2005/09, 20 April 2005 9 para 8.

MONUC had not been given an appropriate mandate to investigate facts in a way that they could be utilised in future judicial proceedings and that the Panel had encountered significant problems accessing the area in question, amongst other arguments.[215]

Potentially troublesome treatment of international law can also be seen more recently in the reports of the Human Rights Council (HRC) inquiries which were established to investigate alleged breaches of international human rights law and to identify those responsible in relation to the situation in Syria in 2012.[216] For instance, in its February 2012 report, the Commission went further than the Goldstone Report in finding that the Free Syrian Army, an armed group opposed to the government, was bound to comply with human rights obligations.[217] The Commission stated that 'at a minimum, human rights obligations constituting peremptory international law (*jus cogens*) bind States, individuals and non-State collective entities, including armed groups.'[218] In taking such a position on this issue of international law, the report leaves itself open to contradiction on the basis that, as stated above, human rights obligations are traditionally only thought to apply to States, or non-State entities carrying out the functions of a State or those having effective control over territory.[219] Although armed groups are arguably under a duty not to commit breaches of norms constituting *jus cogens* at the very least under contemporary international law, it is unclear whether a fact-finding commission is the ideal forum in which to determine whether acts breaching *jus cogens* norms have been committed, or indeed whether such acts could be attributed to the group in question and any subsequent responsibility arising out of such a breach being found.

The issue of whether armed groups are bound by certain human rights obligations is currently an unsettled issue in international law and one

---

[215] *I.C.J. Pleadings, Armed Activities*, CR 2005/09, 20 April 2005 9, para 10.
[216] See First Report A/HRC/S-17/1/2/Add.1; Second Report A/HRC/19/69, 22 February 2012.
[217] See A/HRC/19/69 at 20.   [218] A/HRC/19/69 at 20.
[219] In this regard see the legal position taken in the Report of the International Commission of Inquiry to Investigate all the alleged violations of international human rights law in the Libyan Arab Jamahiriya, A/HRC/17/44, 1 June 2011, para 72; and UN Secretary General, *Report of the Secretary-General's Panel of Experts on Accountability in Sri Lanka*, 31 March 2011, para 188. For a detailed discussion of this issue see Jean-Marie Henckaerts, and Cornelius Wiesener, 'Human Rights Obligations of Non-State Armed Groups: A Possible Contribution from Customary International Law?' in Robert Kolb and Gloria Gaggioli (eds) *Research Handbook on Human Rights and Humanitarian Law* (Cheltenham: Edward Elgar, 2013) 148.

## 2.1 ABUNDANT, COMPLEX OR TECHNICAL FACTS 111

commentator has argued that the Commission's position could be seen as an attempt to progressively develop the law on this issue.[220] However, doubt surrounds the prudence of such a course of action. To elaborate, it could be argued that the law is being broadened in order to be applicable to entities it was not intended to apply to and that, perhaps more importantly, it is being done so in a manner lacking in procedural rigour and legal justification. To give one example, it has been noted that the Commission did not examine a number of potentially important factors such as the organisational make up of the Free Syrian Army, the extent to which it controlled territory on the ground or any of the non-military functions that the entity was also engaged in. Whilst such omissions from the Commission's report are perhaps understandable due to the fact it was not permitted entry to Syria and as such was forced to rely on accounts of others within the country, it is nevertheless argued that in attempting to extend the law to armed groups, it is problematic that so little attention was paid to legal argumentation in the Commission's report.

The aforementioned examples serve to highlight that a clear trend of cursory treatment of complex legal issues can be discerned and recent subsequent developments are in keeping with this trend. For instance, in December 2014 the UN Commission of Inquiry on the Central African Republic demonstrated questionable legal reasoning, including, in the words of one commentator, the repeated conflation of the *actus reus* and *mens rea* elements of genocide.[221] Whilst no position is taken on these legal issues at this stage, it should be pointed out that issues such as the occupation of Gaza and the human rights obligations of Palestine or the Free Syrian Army are extremely complex legal issues. In making such broad-brush generalisations without proper substantiation, acknowledging different legal positions or authority, the reports potentially undermine their legitimacy, making reliance on them by the Court problematic.[222] We should also note that the Court's reliance on findings-of-fact made by other entities is not just problematic in the context of UN Commissions of Inquiry but also raises significant problems in the

---

[220] Tilman Rodenhäuser, 'Progressive Development of International Human Rights Law: The Reports of the Independent International Commission of Inquiry on the Syrian Arab Republic', EJIL: Talk!

[221] See *The International Commission of Inquiry on the Central African Republic*, Final Report, S/2014/928, 22 December 2014 para 457; Patryk Labuda, 'What Lies Beneath the "G" Word? Genocide-Labelling and Fact-Finding at the UN' EJIL: Talk!

[222] Ibid.

112   CRITICISMS OF THE ICJ'S CURRENT REACTIVE APPROACH

context of reliance on the jurisprudence of other courts and tribunals – an issue which is the subject of the following subsection.

### 2.1.5   Certain aspects of the Court's reliance on factual determinations made by other international courts

A further potentially problematic aspect of the Court's approach to fact-finding is its reliance on factual determinations made by other international courts, in particular those established under the auspices of the United Nations. The most prominent example of this to date can be found in the *Bosnian Genocide* case in which reliance on factual determinations made in cases before the ICTY is evident throughout the judgment, and to a large extent the Court is deferential to findings-of-fact made by the ICTY.[223] Whilst this practice has not been widespread in the jurisprudence of the Court to date, it is clear that there is scope for this issue to recur in the future and as such the Court's problematic handling of facts in this regard it is worthy of our attention.

In the course of the *Bosnian Genocide* case the Court went to some lengths to highlight the specific weight it would accord to factual determinations made at different stages of cases before the ICTY, for instance stating that it would accord less weight to findings-of-fact made in pre-trial decisions since the standard of proof applied in such cases was lower than that the Court was applying in the present case.[224] For example, factual determinations made by the ICTY in the *Krstić* case were central to the determination that the *dolus specialis* required for genocide was not present in any situation apart from Srebrenica.[225] Crucially, the Trial and Appeals Chambers in *Krstić* did, however, find that the *dolus specialis* was present at the massacre in Srebrenica and that as such genocide had been perpetrated; this factual determination seemed to be deferentially accepted by the Court, which paused only to say that it 'sees no reason to disagree with the concordant findings of the Trial Chamber and the Appeals Chamber'.[226] The Court even made reference to a case pending before the ICTY at the time, the *Stanišć and Simatović* case,

---

[223] *Bosnian Genocide Case*; see, by way of illustration, paras 248, 254, 261, 264, 266, 268, 272–4, 278–81, 283–318; Goldstone and Hamilton, 'Bosnia v. Serbia: Lessons from the Encounter of the International Court of Justice with the International Criminal Tribunal for the Former Yugoslavia' 104.
[224] *Bosnian Genocide Case* para 219.     [225] See ibid. paras 277, 319, 334, 354.
[226] Ibid. para 296.

## 2.1 ABUNDANT, COMPLEX OR TECHNICAL FACTS 113

which it said could shed crucial light on the relationship between Serbia and the Bosnian Serb forces.[227]

In addition, it would appear that findings-of-fact made by the ICTY will be similarly influential in the *Croatian Genocide* case with substantial reliance being placed on a number of recent ICTY cases in the oral proceedings by the parties. As Sir Keir Starmer, counsel for Croatia, stated, 'ICTY judgements [sic] are rich in ... factual findings that are highly relevant to the present proceedings. The Applicant will refer in particular to the judgements in *Mrkšić* and *Martić*; and the sentencing remarks in *Babić*.'[228]

It has been suggested that the Court's reliance on fact-finding carried out by other bodies in the *Bosnian Genocide* case is not inherently problematic practice since 'most of the allegations made before the Court had already been the subject of lengthy trials before the ICTY'.[229] Undoubtedly there is some merit to this argument due to the fact that the ICTY is an independent and impartial judicial organ. In actual fact, if the Court had disputed any of the factual determinations made by the ICTY it would have to go to great lengths to do so.[230]

Certainly the Court ought to pay the 'greatest respect' to any judgments made by international judicial bodies such as the ICTY.[231] In general a distinction ought to be drawn between facts which had been arrived at after a 'painstaking adversarial process' and those which have been gathered as part of a UN fact-finding mission (which as we have seen, operate under much less strict evidentiary working methods). Furthermore, it is of course the case that 'it would have been unnecessarily duplicative for the ICJ itself to determine those facts which had already been authoritatively established by the ICTY, and especially when there is general acceptance regarding the rigour of the ICTY's own fact-finding process.'[232]

However, the most that can be said is that factual determinations made in cases before other international courts is that they are persuasive, but not that they are determinative. This is so due to the fact that

---

[227] *Prosecutor v. Stanišić and Simatović*, IT-03-69.
[228] Case No. IT-95-13/1-T, Judgment, 27 September 2007; Case No. IT-95-11-T, Judgment, 12 June 2007; Case No. IT-03-72-S, Sentencing Judgment, 29 June 2004 respectively; *Croatian Genocide Case* 4 March 2014, Oral Proceedings, Verbatim Record 32–3 para 12.
[229] Gattini, 'Evidentiary Issues in the ICJ's Genocide Judgment'.  [230] Ibid.  [231] Ibid.
[232] Goldstone and Hamilton, 'Bosnia v. Serbia: Lessons from the Encounter of the International Court of Justice with the International Criminal Tribunal for the Former Yugoslavia' 106.

unquestioning reliance on factual findings made before another court, one with the goal of trying individual crimes, is potentially problematic:

> The problem with the Court's reasoning is that the question before it at that stage was whether genocide had occurred in Bosnia and Herzegovina, not whether genocide was committed by the relative handful of individuals who have to date been prosecuted by the ICTY ... Furthermore, the ICTY was never judging whether genocide occurred at a given location or time, but rather whether an individual before it was responsible for a particular act of genocide or not.[233]

Furthermore, relying on factual determinations made in cases before the ICTY is potentially problematic due to the possibility that the Prosecutor may have taken the decision not to prosecute a certain crime (the Prosecutor's decision to 'not include or to exclude' a genocide charge being specifically cited as significant by the Court in the *Bosnian Genocide* case)[234] as part of a plea bargain and as such 'may have nothing at all to do with the absence of evidence that genocide was committed in any particular situation.'[235]

Sir Keir Starmer, in the *Croatian Genocide* case, also argued that 'a prosecutorial decision not to prosecute should be given little or no probative value in respect of the establishment of facts',[236] highlighting a number of additional factors including the inherent link between investigative decisions and prosecutorial decisions as well as problems in locating key witnesses and also time constraints.[237] By the same token, Starmer correctly argued that decisions *to include* a charge of genocide 'can be regarded merely as different – negative and positive – outcomes of the decision-making process; that is, the decision *whether* to include a particular charge. Neither outcome involves a finding of fact; therefore, no evidential inferences should be drawn either way.'[238]

In sum, whilst of course the Court ought to draw upon fact-finding carried out by others, it should not do so in a wholesale manner as the

---

[233] Ibid.; see also *Croatian Genocide Case* 4 March 2014, Oral Proceedings, Verbatim Record 40 para 39.
[234] *Bosnian Genocide Case* para 217.
[235] Goldstone and Hamilton, 'Bosnia v. Serbia: Lessons from the Encounter of the International Court of Justice with the International Criminal Tribunal for the Former Yugoslavia' 106.
[236] *Croatian Genocide Case* 4 March 2014, Oral Proceedings, Verbatim Record 33 para 17.
[237] Ibid. 4 March 2014, Oral Proceedings, Verbatim Record 32–3 paras 26, 29, 30.
[238] Ibid. 4 March 2014, Oral Proceedings, Verbatim Record 39–40 para 38.

Court was criticised for in the present case.[239] As one commentator has stated, more is demanded of the Court than this.[240] The Court ought to 'actively engage' with such findings-of-fact, to attempt to carefully assess the value and weight of the evidence that it seeks to rely upon and clearly spell out to what extent the Court has relied upon it in making its legal determinations.[241]

Moving now to the second group of criticisms of the Court's current reactive approach to fact-finding, we turn our attention to those cases in which the Court has encountered difficulties due to insufficient evidence.

## 2.2 Group 2: problems arising from insufficient evidence, specifically non-appearance

As stated above, the second group of cases which expose the Court's current approach to fact-finding as not fit for purpose are those in which there is insufficient evidence before the Court for it to base a decision upon. A prominent example of a situation that leads to a paucity of evidence is non-appearance of one kind or another, be it complete or partial.[242] Non-appearance can be defined as the situation in which one party to a case fails to appear before the Court, to submit a counter-memorial or withdraws from proceedings at any stage before the final judgment is rendered. Non-appearance is explicitly addressed in Article 53 of the Court's Statute, which states:

1. Whenever one of the parties does not appear before the Court, or fails to defend its case, the other Party may call upon the Court to decide in favour of its claim.
2. The Court must, before doing so, satisfy itself, not only that it has jurisdiction in accordance with Articles 36 and 37, but also that the claim is well founded in fact and law.

---

[239] The Court has been criticised for demonstrating a 'timid readiness to accept these accounts and go no further – even when these sources do not purport to resolve the actual points at issue in this case'; see Alvarez, *Burdens of Proof*.

[240] Ibid. footnote 2, referencing the Declaration of Judge Burgenthal in *The Wall Advisory Opinion*.

[241] Alvarez, 'Burdens of Proof'.

[242] For more detailed statistics on non-appearance, see Jonathan Charney, 'Disputes Implicating the Institutional Credibility of the Court: Problems of Non-Appearance, Non-Participation, and Non-Performance' in Lori F. Damrosch (ed), *The International Court of Justice at a Crossroads* (Dobbs Ferry, NY: Transnational, 1987).

Article 53 of the Court's Statute is a near word-for-word reproduction of the corresponding provision of the Statute of the PCIJ.[243] The drafters of the PCIJ Statute deliberately went further than most domestic legal systems in providing a specific duty for the Court to satisfy itself not only that it had jurisdiction but also that the claim was well founded in fact and law before handing down a judgment.[244] Applying this underlying rationale to the corresponding provision in the Statute of the ICJ, Article 53 of the Statute accordingly seeks to protect the due process rights of the non-appearing party,[245] and at the same time heavily implies that there is no duty to appear before the Court beyond the obligation to adhere to the Court's decisions under Articles 59 and 60 of the Statute and Article 94(1) of the Charter.[246] Nevertheless, Article 53 permits the Court, once it has established that it has jurisdiction, to decide the case in the absence of the non-appearing party, the rationale being that non-appearance by one party should not obstruct the proper administration of justice.[247]

In relation to the Article 53 duty to ensure that the case is well founded in law, the operation of the principle *jura novit curia* provides that the Court is presumed to know the law. The operation of this principle, coupled with the fact that the Court is not confined to only consider the arguments made by the parties,[248] make the duty to ensure the case is well founded in law less onerous than the duty to ensure it is well founded in fact.[249]

---

[243] See Article 53 Statute of the Permanent Court of International Justice.
[244] H. Thirlway, *Non-Appearance before the International Court of Justice* (Cambridge University Press, 1985) 123.
[245] *Nicaragua Case* 28 para 24; Mosk, 'The Role of Facts in International Dispute Resolution' 86; Jerome B. Elkind, *Non-Appearance before the International Court of Justice: Functional and Comparative Analysis* (The Hague, Boston: Martinus Nijhoff, 1984) 100.
[246] On this debate see Thirlway, *Non-Appearance before the International Court of Justice* ; Elkind, *Non-Appearance before the International Court of Justice*; H. W. A. Thirlway, 'Normative Surrender and the Duty to Appear before the International Court of Justice: A Reply' 11 *Michigan Journal of International Law* 912; see also fourth paragraph of the Resolution of the Institut de Droit International on non-appearing States (Basel, 1991).
[247] Article 45 ICSID Convention is a similar provision providing that 'the other party may request the Tribunal to deal with the questions submitted to it and to render the award' whilst also stating that failure to appear 'shall not be deemed an admission of the other party's assertions'; Eric De Brabandere, *Investment Treaty Arbitration as Public International Law: Procedural Aspects and Implications*, Vol 112 (Cambridge University Press, 2014).
[248] *Nuclear Tests Case* 31–2 at 263–4; *Nicaragua Case* 30 at 25.
[249] As the Court stated in the *Nicaragua* case, 'the absence of one party has less impact'. The Court's duty to know the law was addressed by the Court in the *Fisheries Jurisdiction*

The situation is not as straightforward in relation to the facts, since Article 53 obliges the Court to perform a delicate balancing act. On the one hand, in seeking to ensure the case is decided on a solid factual basis, the Court may in certain cases feel obliged to undertake steps to obtain information or adapt its approach to the fact-finding process. On the other hand, however, the Court must not step in to take the place of the non-appearing State by conducting fact-finding and making legal arguments on its behalf. To do so would place a considerable burden on the Court and provide an incentive for non-appearance to States.[250]

On the face of it, Article 53 obliges the Court to take some proactive steps with regard to fact-finding in cases of non-appearance to ensure that it is satisfied that the claim is well founded in fact and law. It is important to emphasise at the outset that the following sections do not consider Article 53 problematic in itself – it is not the provision but rather the way the Court has applied the provision in practice which is problematic. What is troublesome is the effect produced by the combination of non-appearance and the Court's reactive approach in such cases. As we shall see in the following sections, faced with a lopsided evidentiary record and traditionally taking a reactive approach to the facts, the Court has made conflicting statements on the standard that must be achieved in order to fulfil its Article 53 duty. Ultimately, doubt is expressed as to whether the Court can in fact ever fulfil Article 53 in cases of non-appearance whilst maintaining its current reactive approach to fact-finding.

To elaborate, uncertainty surrounds Article 53 with regard to the exact standard to which the Court should satisfy itself.[251] In cases of

---

case in which the Court stated that it must 'consider on its own initiative all rules of international law which may be relevant to the settlement of the dispute ... the burden of establishing or proving rules of international law cannot be imposed upon any of the parties, for the law lies within the judicial knowledge of the Court'. *Fisheries Jurisdiction Case Fisheries Jurisdiction (United Kingdom v. Iceland), Merits, Judgment, ICJ Reports 1974* 3, 13, 17 at 9; see Stanimir A. Alexandrov, 'Non-appearance before the International Court of Justice' 33 *Columbia Journal of Transnational Law* 41, 59; see also *Nicaragua Case* para 29.

[250] H. Von Mangoldt and A. Zimmermann, 'Article 53' in B. Simma and others (eds), *The Statute of the International Court of Justice: A Commentary* (Oxford University Press, 2006) 1346.

[251] Thirlway, *Non-Appearance Before the International Court of Justice* 123. In 1981 Sir Gerald Fitzmaurice argued that a *prima facie* case is enough to fulfil the Court's Article 53(2) obligations: Gerald Fitzmaurice, 'The Problem of the "Non-Appearing" Defendant Government' 51 *British Yearbook of International Law* 89, 113; Fitzmaurice argues in favour of taking a tougher line against non-appearing States, presuming validity of

non-appearance, does Article 53 require the Court to make its own independent verification of the facts or 'may the Court, in the absence of challenge by the absent State, take the facts to be as they have been presented, and concentrate its attention on the legal deductions made therefrom by the active State?'[252] This is a question that the Court has struggled to answer in the past. At different times the Court seems to have deviated between two main positions: (i) that non-appearance places a greater fact-finding burden on the Court to establish a sound factual foundation, and the contrary position (ii) that non-appearance does not affect the Court's approach to fact-finding and the Court need not necessarily take additional fact-finding action to fulfil its Article 53 duty. However, as will be shown in the following sections, in cases of non-appearance the Court has in fact struggled to provide the most basic guarantees that the case is well founded in fact.

### 2.2.1 Cases of non-appearance

Non-appearance is a not-uncommon occurrence in the history of the Court.[253] In particular in the thirty or so years between the establishment of the ICJ and the *Nicaragua* case there were nine cases of non-appearance.[254] A brief survey of these cases highlights that the Court's

certain instruments as long as they were not contradicted; for example, arguing that in doing so 'the whole non-appearance technique would be stopped dead in its tracks – or at least it would no longer pay, would no longer serve any real purpose'. See also 'suffisamment fondée' or 'fondée', *Procès-verbaux* of the Proceedings of the Advisory Committee of Jurists (1920).

[252] Thirlway suggests that judges used to the adversarial system would be more readily prepared to accept that an ostensibly plausible argument not contested by the other party is a reliable basis upon which to make a judgment, whilst judges from inquisitorial backgrounds would be 'more haunted by the fear that the truth may lie elsewhere'; Thirlway, *Non-Appearance before the International Court of Justice* 123.

[253] The problem of non-appearance was seen as so persistent so as to warrant a resolution by the Institut de Droit International which stated that non-appearance before the Court tends to 'hinder the conduct of the proceedings, and may affect the good administration of justice' and creates difficulties for the other parties and for the Court in particular in relation to 'the acquisition by the Court of knowledge of facts which may be relevant for the Court's pronouncements on interim measures, preliminary objections or the merits'; preamble, Institut de Droit International (Basel, 1991), Rapporteur: Arrangio-Ruiz.

[254] In two, *Anglo-Iranian Oil Company (Anglo-Iranian Oil Co. Case)* and *Aegean Sea Continental Shelf (Aegean Sea Continental Shelf Case)* the Court dismissed the case for lack of jurisdiction. Similarly *Nottebohm (Nottebohm Case)* was dismissed for lack of standing. In the *Nuclear Tests* case the Court relied on statements made by French officials who had stated that they would be moving the tests underground, and held that

## 2.2 INSUFFICIENT EVIDENCE AND NON-APPEARANCE 119

traditionally reactive approach to fact-finding has caused it considerable difficulty in cases of non-appearance.

The Court's statements in the final phase of the *Corfu Channel* case after the withdrawal of Albania have had a profound influence on how it has approached the issue of non-appearance in cases before it over the years. In *Corfu Channel* the Court stated that Article 53 only obliges the Court to 'consider the submissions of the Party which appears, it does not compel the Court to examine their accuracy in all their details; for this might in certain unopposed cases prove impossible in practice'.[255]

As such, the Court seemed to suggest that in cases of non-appearance it was unproblematic for the Court to satisfy itself that the submissions were well founded on the basis of the facts put before it by the appearing party.

In *Nuclear Tests,* however, the Court appeared to suggest that in cases of non-appearance there was an additional burden on the Court to fulfil its Article 53 duty, stating that in such cases it was 'especially incumbent upon the Court to satisfy itself that it is in possession of all the available facts'.[256] Despite this statement, the Court stuck to its reactive approach and did not undertake any of its own fact-finding. Instead, the Court went to 'curious lengths' to include statements of French officials in the press and elsewhere that had not been put before the Court.[257] This illustrates that the approach of the Court at this time in attempting to ensure that it could fulfil its Article 53 duty was to, as far as it could, incorporate irregular procedural communications such as the statements of French officials in this case, rather than conducting its own fact-finding.

Similarly, in light of the non-appearance of Turkey in the *Aegean Sea Continental Shelf* case the Court relied on a number of informal

---

this was sufficient to end the dispute; *Nuclear Tests Case 1974*. The *Trial of the Pakistani Prisoners of War* case was discontinued by mutual agreement; *Trial of Pakistani Prisoners of War, Order of 15 December 1973, ICJ Reports 1973* 347. Of the nine cases only four reached the merits stage: the *Corfu Channel* case, the *Fisheries Jurisdiction* case, the *Tehran Hostages* case and the *Nicaragua* case.

[255] *Corfu Channel Case* 248; *Corfu Channel Case, Judgment of December 15th 1949 (Compensation), ICJ Reports 1949* 244.

[256] *Nuclear Tests Case* 253, 263 para 31, 457, 468 para 32.

[257] Ian Sinclair, 'Some Procedural Aspects of Recent International Litigation', 30 *International and Comparative Law Quarterly* 338, 349; Foreword by Judge Jessup in Sandifer, *Evidence before International Tribunals*, at x.

submissions to substantiate its arguments instead of conducting its own fact-finding.[258] Again, the Court's reluctance to move away from its reactive approach and conduct its own fact-finding meant that its only option was to cast its net wider to incorporate informal submissions or public sources of evidence in an attempt to fulfil its Article 53 duty,[259] insisting that such practice was necessitated by Article 53(2).[260]

In the *Tehran Hostages* case the issue of Article 53 arose once more.[261] Again the Court stuck to its traditional approach and avoided conducting its own investigations into the facts.[262] However, the Court's interpretation of its Article 53 duty in this way saw it run into trouble as the United States complained that due to events inside Iran it had been unable to access the information upon which it sought to rely.[263] In response, the Court addressed the objections of the United States that the it did not have sufficient factual information regarding the treatment of hostages from derailing the case by arguing that the 'essential facts' of the case were public knowledge and that 'the Court has available to it a massive body of information from various sources concerning the facts and circumstances of the present case'.[264] This position is open to criticism. Not only did the Court's reactive approach and reluctance to undertake its own fact-finding force it to rely on public information, but the Court's approach raises the question of whether it is 'legally permissible to rely on the silence of the absent party, in view of the clear intention of the draftsmen of the Statute that non-appearance should not be taken as an admission of the other party's case'.[265] As such, placing reliance on the absence of contradiction by a non-appearing party would 'constitute exactly what Article 53 was intended to forbid: the treatment of non-participation in

---

[258] James D. Fry, 'Non-Participation in the International Court of Justice Revisited: Change or Plus Ça Change' 49 *Columbia Journal of Transnational Law* 35, 64.
[259] On this see the famous comments of O'Connell in oral pleadings in *Aegean Sea*: 'while Article 53, by implication, requires that the Court be adequately informed, this can *ex hypothesi* never formally be achieved in the case of a default, although a default is precisely what the Article is supposed to provide for'; Fitzmaurice, 'The Problem of the "Non-Appearing" Defendant Government' 114.
[260] *Aegean Sea Continental Shelf Case* 3, 20 para 47; *Tehran Hostages Case* 3, 18 para 33.
[261] Sinclair, 'Some Procedural Aspects of Recent International Litigation' 351.
[262] *Corfu Channel Case* 248; Thirlway, *Non-Appearance before the International Court of Justice* 127.
[263] *Tehran Hostages Case* 9 para 11.   [264] Ibid. 10 para 13.
[265] Von Mangoldt and Zimmermann, 'Article 53' 1348; Thirlway, *Non-Appearance before the International Court of Justice* 128.

the proceedings as in itself an implied admission'[266] and threatens the equality of the parties before the Court.[267]

The *Nicaragua* case was also significant in terms of non-appearance. Whilst Judge Sir Robert Jennings noted in his dissenting opinion that the withdrawal of the United States was inevitably prejudicial to the United States itself,[268] it is clear that the withdrawal also damaged the Court in preventing it from adopting its usual reactive approach to the facts. The non-appearance of the United States posed a number of considerable difficulties for the Court's reactive approach to fact-finding. Most significantly, the Court was deprived of the oral and documentary evidence of the United States, meaning that it had a necessarily lopsided evidentiary record to draw upon[269] and consequently found itself 'required to deal with this extraordinarily complex evidence entirely on its own'.[270] The withdrawal of the United States meant that witnesses put forward by Nicaragua were only examined by its own counsel and not cross-examined by counsel for the United States. In this respect, the role of Judge Schwebel was particularly significant as he took it upon himself to conduct (at times painstaking) examination of counsel and witnesses himself.[271]

It is interesting to note that the Court was 'ill-served by its natural proclivity to say that the outcome would be the same regardless of whose versions of the facts were true',[272] being obliged to theorise more than it normally would have done in order to justify its factual determinations.[273] As such, and as we have seen in relation to earlier cases, the non-appearance of one party, in this case the United States, had a significant impact on the Court due to its traditionally reactive approach

---

[266] Thirlway, *Non-Appearance before the International Court of Justice*.
[267] As the Court stated in *Nicaragua Case* para 31, each party must be granted 'a fair and equal opportunity ... to comment on its opponent's contentions' including in relation to the facts. See also *Request for Interpretation of the Judgment of 11 June 1998 in the Case concerning the Land and Maritime Boundary between Cameroon and Nigeria (Cameroon v. Nigeria), Preliminary Objections (Nigeria v. Cameroon)*, Judgment, ICJ Reports 1999 31, 39 para 15.
[268] *Nicaragua Case*, Dissenting Opinion of Judge Sir Robert Jennings at 544.
[269] Ibid. para 67, Dissenting Opinion of Judge Sir Robert Jennings at 528.
[270] Highet, 'Evidence, the Court, and the Nicaragua Case'.
[271] See *Nicaragua Case*, Dissenting Opinion of Judge Schwebel; see also Highet, 'Evidence, the Court, and the Nicaragua Case' 28.
[272] Alvarez, 'Are International Judges Afraid of Science?: A Comment on Mbengue'; Franck, 'Fact-finding in the I.C.J.' 29.
[273] Highet, 'Evidence, the Court, and the Nicaragua Case' 4.

to fact-finding. Despite the non-appearance of the United States, however, the Court was adamant that it 'must attain the same degree of certainty as in any other case that the claim of the party appearing is sound in law, and, so far as the nature of the case permits, that the facts on which it is based are supported by convincing evidence'.[274] Highet described the Court as being caught in a vicious circle: 'the Court's job under Article 53 was made almost impossible by the complexity of the facts, just as the ability of the Court to deal with those complex facts was rendered almost impossible by the need for the Court to proceed under its Statute'.[275]

Consequently, the Court's factual findings in *Nicaragua* and the interpretation of its Article 53 duty came in for considerable criticism.[276] For instance, Reisman argued that the Court did not in fact satisfy its Article 53 duty but rather lowered 'the burden of Article 53 by selectively quoting *Corfu Channel,* citing only one-half of the relevant sentences in the *Corfu Channel* case and, in so doing, created the impression that *Corfu* was holding something it did not hold'.[277] Reisman argued that by leaving out the sentence that '[i]t is sufficient for the Court to convince itself by such methods as it considers suitable that the submissions are well founded',[278] the Court misconstrued *Corfu Channel* to avoid the necessity of resorting to 'such methods' to which the Court in *Corfu Channel* referred.

More generally, such cases raise doubts as to whether the Court can ever fulfil its Article 53 duty under its current reactive approach to fact-finding. These doubts resurfaced again after the *Nicaragua* case as instances of non-appearance continued to occur.[279] The most significant case of non-appearance in recent times is *The Wall* advisory opinion.[280] In the course of proceedings, Israel's failure to participate again placed considerable strain on the Court's approach to fact-finding.[281]

Despite the deft phrasing of the question asked of the Court by the General Assembly, the refusal of Israel to participate in the proceedings

---

[274] *Nicaragua Case* para 29.
[275] Highet, 'Evidence, the Court, and the Nicaragua Case' 5.
[276] See Statement on the U.S. Withdrawal from the Proceedings Initiated by Nicaragua in the International Court of Justice, 18 January 1985, 24 I.L.M. 246 (1985).
[277] W. Michael Reisman, 'Respecting One's Own Jurisprudence: A Plea to the International Court of Justice' 83 *The American Journal of International Law* 312, 313.
[278] *Corfu Channel Case* 248.
[279] See for example *Qatar v. Bahrain* in which Qatar was put in a difficult position given that Bahrain did not submit a Counter-Memorial; *Qatar v. Bahrain, Judgment.*
[280] *The Wall Advisory Opinion.*     [281] Ibid.

meant that the Court nonetheless was faced with familiar difficulties of a lopsided factual record. The Court sought to fill the evidentiary gap left by Israel by relying on the Fact-Finding Report of the UN Secretary-General referred to in the request for the advisory opinion.[282] However, the Court was nonetheless faced with the same difficulties as in any other case of non-appearance, namely 'a serious problem with regard to its factual record'.[283] And indeed the facts were crucial in the case, despite the legal nature of the advisory opinion sought, in determining whether Israel's construction of the wall in occupied Palestinian territory was contrary to international law.

Judge Burgenthal in his dissenting opinion went so far as to argue that the Court did not have sufficient facts upon which to base its decision, and that the Court ought to have made this explicit,[284] going on to say that 'Israel's non-participation, coupled with the ill-suited format of advisory proceedings, meant that the court would be hard pressed to develop a factual record sufficient to enable the court to properly answer the question'.[285] In addition, the Court's opinion was criticised for not taking into account legal justifications that could have been advanced by Israel[286] and for over-reliance on abstract legal principles rather than the facts[287] – both arguably a consequence of the Court's one-sided factual record. Similarly, Judge Owada in his separate opinion expressed concern about whether the Court's fact-finding approach could enable it to properly assess whether the wall in question was necessary to obtain Israel's security objectives.[288] Judge Owada lamented that the Court simply expressed a 'lack of conviction' that the wall was necessary based on 'the material before it' rather than making an 'in-depth effort ...

---

[282] See Report of the Secretary-General prepared pursuant to General Assembly resolution ES-10/13, A/E-10/248, 24 November 2003.
[283] Fry, 'Non-Participation in the International Court of Justice Revisited' 65.
[284] Ibid.; see also *WHO Advisory Opinion* para 95, Dissenting Opinion of Judge Burgenthal at para 10; *The Wall Advisory Opinion*, where the Court stated that 'The Court considers that it does not have sufficient elements to enable it to conclude with certainly that the use of nuclear weapons would necessarily be at variance with the principles and rules of law applicable in armed conflict in any circumstance'.
[285] Fry, 'Non-Participation in the International Court of Justice Revisited' 65.
[286] See Submissions of the United States of America and United Kingdom of Great Britain and Northern Ireland, available at: www.icjcij.org/docket/index.php?p1=3&p2=4&k=5a&case=131&code=mwp&p3=1.
[287] I. Scobbie, 'Regarding/Disregarding: The Judicial Rhetoric of President Barak and the International Court of Justice's Wall Advisory Opinion' 5 *Chinese Journal of International Law* 269 at footnote 111.
[288] *The Wall Advisory Opinion*, Dissenting Opinion of Judge Owada at para 23.

*proprio motu*, to ascertain the validity of this argument'.[289] Such expressions of concern from judges in cases of non-appearance bring into sharp focus the problems facing the Court as a result of its current reactive approach to fact-finding.

### 2.2.2 The Court's role in cases of non-appearance and resulting difficulties

The Court's reactive approach to fact-finding significantly impedes the Court in its attempts to fulfil its Article 53 duty. Of course the negative impact on the workings of the Court due to non-appearance is hard to quantify in exact terms but the practice of the Court shows that in cases of non-appearance, where it has a lopsided evidentiary record, the Court has historically sought to rely to a greater extent on public information and more often resorted to drawing inferences[290] rather than conducting its own fact-finding.[291] However, this approach has only aided the Court to a limited extent and in practice it has continued to experience difficulties. The limitations of a more proactive approach are examined in greater detail in Chapter 5 at Section 5.3. but for now it can be said that cases of non-appearance are particularly problematic for the Court, which is likely to always encounter significant difficulties faced with the non-co-operation of parties to cases that come before it.

It would appear that a potentially high-profile instance of non-appearance looms on the horizon.[292] On 22 January 2013 the Republic of the Philippines instituted arbitral proceedings against the People's Republic of China under Annex VII of UNCLOS. The Philippines specifically limited its claim to matters 'other than those on territorial sovereignty, boundary delimitation or historic title',[293] taking into

---

[289] Ibid., Dissenting Opinion of Judge Owada at para 30.
[290] *Tehran Hostages Case* paras 12–13; *Nuclear Tests Case 1974* paras 40–1.
[291] Fry, 'Non-Participation in the International Court of Justice Revisited' 64.
[292] For detailed historical background to the dispute and thorough assessment of the law of the sea issues involved see Zhiguo Gao and Bing Bing Jia, 'The Nine-Dash Line in the South China Sea: History, Status, and Implications' 107 *The American Journal of International Law* 98; Florian Dupuy and Pierre-Marie Dupuy, 'A Legal Analysis of China's Historic Rights Claim in the South China Sea' 107 *The American Journal of International Law* 124; and Robert Beckman, 'The UN Convention on the Law of the Sea and the Maritime Disputes in the South China Sea' 107 *The American Journal of International Law* 142.
[293] See Robert Beckman, 'The Philippines v. China Case and the South China Sea Disputes' Asia Society, LKY SPP Conference, South China Sea: Central to Asia-Pacific Peace and Security, New York, 13–15 Mar 2013: Centre for International Law.

account China's 1996 Declaration under Article 298 of UNCLOS which excluded these issues from compulsory dispute settlement under the Convention.[294] Nevertheless, on 19 February 2013 China rejected the Philippines' Notification and indicated it would take no part in the proceedings.[295]

Some commentators have argued that it is in China's best interest to either enter into negotiations with the Philippines, participate in the proceedings or risk being the subject of an unfavourable award.[296] Whether or not this is the case, the Arbitral Tribunal passed a procedural order setting dates for a hearing on jurisdiction and admissibility, controversially deciding that in the face of China's refusal to submit a counter-memorial it would treat a previous Position Paper published by China as a plea with regard to the jurisdiction of the Tribunal (despite China's explicit statement that this paper did not constitute its acceptance of or participation in the arbitration).[297] All this is to say that the issue of non-appearance is not merely historical and that given its problematic handling of the facts in such cases the fact that the Court may at any time find itself faced with an instance of non-appearance should be of great concern.[298]

## 2.3 Chapter 2 summary: criticisms of the Court warranted

This chapter set out in a systematic manner the main criticisms of the Court's current reactive approach to fact-finding. These criticisms were divided into two main groups: (i) those relating to abundant, particularly complex or technical facts and (ii) those relating to a lack of evidence before the Court. In relation to the first group of criticisms, the Court's reactive approach to fact-finding in cases which involve 'highly complex, factually intensive inquiries requiring the application of particular forms

---

[294] Article 298(1) UNCLOS.
[295] Jawad Ahmad, 'The *Indus Waters Kishenganga Arbitration* and State-to-State Disputes' 29 *Arbitration International* 507, 534.
[296] Ibid.
[297] See Permanent Court of Arbitration, Fourth Press Release, 22 April 2015, available at: www.pca-cpa.org/showpage.asp?pag_id=1529.
[298] Beckman, 'The Philippines v. China Case and the South China Sea Disputes'; similarly, at the time of writing there is some suggestion that Japan may bring its long-running dispute with China over the Senkaku-Diaoyu islands in the East China Sea before an Annex VII UNCLOS arbitral tribunal; Ahmad, 'The Indus Waters Kishenganga Arbitration and State-to-State Disputes' 535.

of expertise outside the ken of respective adjudicators' can be a recipe for an unsure factual foundation upon which to make legal judgments.[299] The Court's approach to expert evidence and use of *experts fantômes*, cross-examination, and over-reliance on UN Commissions of Inquiry all have problematic aspects which undermine the Court's fact-finding process.

In relation to the second group of criticisms, in cases where a party fails to appear before the Court, its reactive approach to fact-finding is found wanting due to the fact it only has the evidence of one party upon which to make its findings-of-fact. Without conducting its own investigations into the factual background of the case at hand the Court's reactive approach, which makes the Court dependent on States to submit the facts to it, is a handicap. These criticisms having been set out, the next chapter looks to other inter-State courts and tribunals in order to assess how they approach the problems the ICJ currently faces and asks whether the ICJ can learn anything from these other courts and tribunals in order to remedy some of the weaknesses set out in this chapter.

---

[299] Alvarez, 'Are International Judges Afraid of Science?: A Comment on Mbengue' 87.

# 3

# The practice of other international courts and tribunals

## Introduction

The preceding chapter set out a number of recent criticisms of the ICJ's current reactive approach to fact-finding. It was argued that the Court's current reactive approach to fact-finding is not fit for purpose both (i) where there are abundant, particularly complex or technical facts, since the Court's reluctance to appoint experts or conduct cross-examination impede the Court in its attempts to effectively assess the evidence presented and (ii) where there is a paucity of facts, since the Court struggles to fulfil its Article 53 ICJ Statute obligation to satisfy itself the case is sound in fact and in law.

It might be said that this much is uncontroversial. As such, this chapter takes the next step and explores whether it is possible to envisage an approach that would allow the Court to conduct fact-finding more effectively. In doing so, this chapter takes advantage of the much-discussed proliferation of international courts and tribunals and draws upon the substantial body of practice in this area.[1] The ICJ itself has 'shown increased openness to drawing insights from other international courts and tribunals' in recent judgments and the practice of other courts and tribunals suggests a number of procedural mechanisms that the Court could adopt in order to, in the words of Judge Donoghue in the recent *Maritime Dispute (Peru v. Chile)* case, 'further enrich its practice and jurisprudence'.[2]

By way of clarification, due to the fact that the ICJ deals exclusively with inter-State cases, the focus of Chapter 3 is likewise limited to inter-State adjudicatory bodies. Of course, various other (less exclusively State-centric)

---

[1] For a thorough overview of the proliferation of international courts and tribunals, see C. Romano, 'A Taxonomy of International Rule of Law Institutions' 2 *Journal of International Dispute Settlement* 241.

[2] *Maritime Dispute (Peru v. Chile)*, 27 January 2014, Judgment, Dissenting Opinion of Judge Donoghue.

areas of international law such as investment arbitration and human rights law regularly deal with interesting and important issues relating to fact-finding. However, focusing exclusively on inter-State cases ensures the most meaningful comparisons possible. For example, it was felt that drawing conclusions from a dispute between an individual and a State, such as a case before the European Court of Human Rights, would be of dubious utility as a comparison owing to the fact that the courts seek to achieve such different goals, deal with parties of a diverse nature and apply significantly different law and procedure.

Consequently, Chapter 3 is limited to a survey of the World Trade Organization (WTO) adjudicative bodies and recent inter-State arbitrations. As we will see in the following sections, this survey reveals that these adjudicatory bodies generally take a more proactive approach to fact-finding. Chapter 3 sets out the main noteworthy aspects of these more proactive tribunals, notably the most popular international tribunals in terms of case load at the moment. Doing so is a necessary first step before Chapter 4 asks whether the adoption of similarly proactive approach by the ICJ could potentially help to remedy some of the fact-finding deficiencies the Court has been criticised for in recent times.

### (i) Fact-finding and fact-assessment before the adjudicative bodies of the WTO

This section sets out to examine the handling of issues of fact-finding and fact-assessment in cases before the Panels and Appellate Body (AB) of the WTO, often referred to as representing 'best practice' in terms of international judicial fact-finding.[3] A survey of the practice of the Panels indicates that they take a broadly reactive approach to evidence. Panels have not fully utilised the relatively broad statutory fact-finding powers given to them by the Dispute Settlement Understanding (DSU). Instead, Panels have demonstrated a preference for relying on the facts as presented to them by the parties. However, on the whole it can be said that Panels and the AB play a more active fact-finding role than the ICJ. This is so due to a number of interesting aspects of the Panels and AB's approach to evidence that are examined *infra* in detail. These include the use of expert evidence, a distinctive burden of proof and the drawing

---

[3] *Pulp Mills Case*, Dissenting Opinion of Judges Al-Khasawneh and Simma at para 16; Foster, 'New Clothes for the Emperor? Consultation of Experts by the International Court of Justice' 28.

of adverse inferences amongst others. Sections 3.1.1 and 3.1.2 will examine the situation before the Panels before moving on to consider issues of fact and law that have arisen before the AB in Section 3.1.3. Finally, Section 3.1.4 examines a number of crosscutting evidentiary issues that apply to both Panels and the AB.

## (ii) Background

The WTO Dispute Settlement Body (DSB) was created during the Uruguay Round to deal with disputes that arose out of the operation of the Agreements in practice. The DSB is made up of representatives of every WTO Member and governed by the Understanding on Rules and Procedures Governing the Settlement of Disputes (DSU). The DSB is endowed with the competence to make rulings and recommendations, establish Panels, oversee the AB, adopt Panel and AB reports and even impose sanctions for non-compliance.[4] Reports of Panels and the AB are adopted by the DSB automatically unless there is consensus to the contrary.[5]

Under Article 3.2 DSU Panels and the AB are given the (relatively narrow) mandate of preserving the rights and obligations of WTO Members and of clarifying the provisions of the Agreements.[6] This can be contrasted with the broader mandate of the ICJ which also contains the task of progressive development of international law.[7] Any member can request the establishment of a Panel to adjudicate on a dispute with another WTO Member under the Agreements. The following section examines how the Panels of the WTO deal with issues of fact-finding in cases that have come before them. In turning to consider how the Panels have dealt with issues of fact-finding and fact-assessment in cases that

---

[4] See Articles 21 and 22 of the DSU regarding surveillance of implementation of recommendations and rulings and compensation and the suspension of concessions respectively.

[5] In accordance with the so-called 'negative consensus' principle; see P. C. Mavroidis, George A. Bermann and Mark Wu (eds), *The Law of the World Trade Organization: Documents, Cases and Analysis*, American Casebook Series (Eagan, MN: West, 2010).

[6] D. Steger, 'Amicus Curiae: Participant or Friend? The WTO and NAFTA Experience' in A. von Bogdandy, P. C. Mavroidis and Y. Mény (eds), *European Integration and International Coorindation: Studies in Honour of Claus-Dieter Ehlermann* (The Hague: Kluwer, 2011) 423.

[7] R. Higgins, *Problems and Process: International Law and How We Use It* (Oxford: Clarendon Press, 1995) 202; see C. J. Tams and J. Sloan (eds), *The Development of International Law by the International Court of Justice* (Oxford University Press, 2013).

have come before them, it is necessary to first examine the relevant evidentiary practice and statutory provisions as set out in the DSU. The relevant AB statutory provisions will be examined in detail below in Section 3.1.3.

## 3.1 Fact-finding and fact-assessment at the WTO

### General provisions

As with the ICJ's statutory fact-finding powers (examined in detail in Chapter 1), before the specific fact-finding provisions of the DSU can be examined, it is first of all necessary to consider a number of general provisions which apply in all cases before the WTO adjudicative bodies.

### (i) Article 12.7 DSU

Article 12.7 DSU provides that 'the report of a Panel shall set out the findings of fact, the applicability of relevant provisions and the basic rationale behind any findings and recommendations that it makes'. In doing so, a duty to respect due process and provide logical and transparent reasoning behind both the establishment of the facts and the law is imposed upon Panels. No Panel has yet been censured for failing to meet the Article 12.7 duty although the AB has criticised Panels in the past for a lack of transparency such as in in *US - Upland Cotton* in which the Appellate Body stated that the Panel could have provided a more detailed explanation of its analysis of the complex facts.[8]

---

[8] *US - Subsidies on Upland Cotton*, Appellate Body Report, WT/DS267/AB/RW, 20 June 2008 para 448; however it should be noted that there are limits to transparency such as considerations of confidentiality. The DSU makes all dispute settlement proceedings confidential including written and oral submissions and although it does not comprehensively set out procedural rules for the treatment of confidential information in the course of proceedings. In relation to information that a party claims is confidential, the Panel in *Indonesia - Autos* stated that parties may not 'invoke confidentiality as a basis for their failure to submit the positive evidence required, see; *Indonesia - Certain Measures Affecting the Automobile Industry*, Panel Report, WT/DS54/R, 2 July 1998 at para 14.235; see also *Turkey - Measures Affecting the Importation of Rice*, Panel Report, WT/DS334/R, 21 September 2007. Information not in the public domain by virtue of business confidentiality or government privilege frequently comes before Panels and the AB; and this is recognised by the WTO Agreements; see Article 12.4 SCM Agreement, Article 6.5 Anti-Dumping Agreement, Article 3.2 Agreement on Safeguards.

## (ii) Article 11 DSU

Article 11 DSU states that a Panel must 'make an objective assessment of the matter before it, including an objective assessment of the facts of the case and the applicability of and conformity with the relevant covered agreements'. As such, guided by the procedural provisions set out in Article 12 and Appendix 3[9] each and every Panel is required to assess issues of both fact and law in cases that come before it in order to establish a solid factual basis upon which to make legal determinations.[10]

What exactly does the Article 11 DSU duty to provide an objective assessment of the facts entail? Although the wording of Article 11 could potentially be interpreted in such a way as to provide the Panels with a broad mandate to carry out fact-finding activities in order to make an objective assessment of the facts, in reality the AB has taken a limited view of the duty imposed on the Panels by Article 11.[11] Rather than justifying a broad fact-finding mandate Article 11 has been interpreted to mean simply that the Panels are required to observe due process considerations of conclusion.[12]

In other words, it would appear that the objective assessment of facts simply requires that the Panel treat the evidence placed before it by the parties objectively and reach a conclusion that logically follows from the

---

[9] The power of the panel to intervene in the adjudicative process before it is provided for by Article 12.1 which gives the panel a broad power to adopt Special Working Procedures for cases that come before it after consultation with the parties. Articles 12.4 and 12.5 allow the panel control over the timeframe and deadlines of the proceedings.

[10] James Cameron and Stephen J. Orava, 'GATT/WTO Panels Between Recording and Finding Facts: Issues of Due Process, Evidence, Burden of Proof, and Standard of Review in GATT/WTO Dispute Settlement' in F. Weiss (ed), *Improving WTO Dispute Settlement Procedures: Issues and Lessons from the Practice of Other International Courts and Tribunals* (London: Cameron May, 2000) 226.

[11] M. Bronckers and N. McNelis, 'Fact and Law in Pleadings Before the WTO Appellate Body' in F. Weiss (ed), *Improving WTO Dispute Settlement Procedures: Issues and Lessons from the Practice of Other International Courts and Tribunals* (London: Cameron May, 2000) 321; see *Australia – Measures Affecting Importation of Salmon*, Appellate Body Report, WT/DS18/AB/R, 20 October 1998 para 261, in which the AB had limited itself to more of a fact-assessment role rather than fact-finding – considering the 'credibility' and 'weight' of evidence submitted to the panels by the parties – and that it was not for the AB to intervene and second-guess the panels.

[12] As Gabrielle Z. Marceau and Jennifer K. Hawkins, 'Experts in WTO Dispute Settlement' 3 *Journal of International Dispute Settlement* 493, 494 state; Article 11 'requires that panels objectively assess the matter so that there are rational bases for their decisions'.

evidence produced.[13] Whilst the Panel has complete discretion to decide what evidence to focus on in its analysis,[14] it must always ensure that its ultimate decision is reasoned and grounded in the evidence submitted by the parties.[15] The principle that decisions follow reasonably and logically from the evidence submitted by the parties is an important limit on the judicial function and prevents complete unfettered judicial discretion.[16] Nevertheless, whilst Article 11 has not been interpreted in such a manner as to justify a broad fact-finding duty placed on the Panels, there is little doubt that the Panels possess such powers, as set out in Article 13 DSU and there is an intimate relationship between these two provisions to which we shall return momentarily.[17]

### 3.1.1 *Evidentiary practice before Panels*

#### 3.1.1.1 Evidence put before Panels by the parties

Panels rely to a great extent on the evidence provided by the parties themselves.[18] In this regard, Panels take a reactive approach similar to that of the ICJ, as examined in Chapter 1. Whilst in the case of technical or scientific disputes, as we shall see, Panels have made regular use of individual experts in relation to technical issues, on the whole they establish the facts upon which their legal determinations are made on the basis of the evidence put before them by the parties without utilising the fact-finding powers the Panels possess.[19] By leaving fact-finding to the parties the Panel's assessment of the facts becomes even more important. As such, the general practice is to establish the facts by weighing the submissions of the parties to the dispute before the Panel

---

[13] M. Matsushita, T. J. Schoenbaum and P. C. Mavroidis, *The World Trade Organization*, Vol 127 (Oxford University Press, 2006) 128. As the Appellate Body stated in *Chile – Price Band System and Safeguard Measures Relating to Certain Agricultural Products*, Appellate Body Report, WT/DS207/AB/R (AB/2002-3), 23 September 2002.

[14] See *EC – Measures Concerning Meat and Meat Products (Hormones)*, Appellate Body Report, WT/DS26/AB/R, WT/DS48/AB/R/ 16 January 1998, at para 156.

[15] Articles 12.7, 14.2 DSU; Grando, *Evidence, Proof, and Fact-Finding in WTO Dispute Settlement* 56.

[16] Ibid. at footnote 230; see Mirjan R. Damaska, *Evidence Law Adrift* (New Haven: Yale University Press, 1997) 22.

[17] Marceau and Hawkins, 'Experts in WTO Dispute Settlement' 494.

[18] T. Christoforou, 'WTO Panels in Face of Scientific Uncertainty' in F. Weiss (ed), *Improving WTO Dispute Settlement Procedures: Issues and Lessons from the Practice of Other International Courts and Tribunals* (London: Cameron May, 2000) 258.

[19] Ibid.

on the basis of the evidential support for the legal positions defended by one party or the other.[20]

#### 3.1.1.2 Experts appearing on behalf of the parties

WTO Members appearing before Panels have the right to appoint their own experts to provide evidence in support of their case and they do so in practice. No Rules of Procedure govern the appointment of individual experts or regulate who can be appointed in terms of expertise.[21] It is perhaps obvious to state that the reports of Panel-appointed individual experts or expert review groups, an issue to which we shall return, will generally be accorded greater weight as a result of a perception of greater impartiality.[22] Rightly or wrongly, experts appearing on behalf of the parties are often perceived as being 'hired guns' – willing to express their expert opinion on a matter in such a way that most closely accords with the interests of the party by whom he or she has been appointed.[23]

Whilst Panels may most often establish the facts on the basis of the information put before them by the parties, this evidence put before the Panels 'should not be understood as the frontiers of truth'.[24] Article 13 DSU is an acknowledgement that there may be information that will not be revealed to the Panels through the adversarial process, for one reason or another,[25] and accordingly provides Panels with the authority to seek information on its own initiative.

### 3.1.2 WTO fact-finding powers: traversing the frontiers of truth

#### 3.1.2.1 Information that can be gathered by the Panel: Article 13 DSU

Article 13(1) and (2) DSU provide Panels with the power to 'seek information and technical advice from any individual or body which it deems

---

[20] Ibid.
[21] It is likely that through cross-examination of the expert, any doubts regarding competence would be exposed; see Section 4.3.1 below. Pauwelyn, 'The Use of Experts in WTO Dispute Settlement' 51 *International and Comparative Law Quarterly*, 325, 334; further, Marceau and Hawkins have argued that a general practice can be described in this regard; see Marceau and Hawkins, 'Experts in WTO Dispute Settlement' 502.
[22] Pauwelyn, 'The Use of Experts in WTO Dispute Settlement' 334.
[23] Ibid.; see also Marceau and Hawkins, 'Experts in WTO Dispute Settlement' 505.
[24] Steger, 'Amicus Curiae: Participant or Friend?' 421.
[25] Note that Article 13 DSU is contingent on panel informing authorities of Member within which the individual or body is situated.

appropriate' and 'seek information from any relevant source and ... consult experts to obtain their opinion on certain aspects of the matter' respectively. Articles 12 and 13 DSU together represent an extremely broad fact-finding power.[26] This 'significant investigative authority'[27] is comprised of a number of constituent powers such as the power to ask questions, the power to request information and the power to mandate both individual experts and expert review groups.[28] Each falls to be considered in turn.

### 3.1.2.2 Power to ask questions

Firstly, Article 13 DSU broadly provides for what could be called the 'central prerogative' of any international court or tribunal to participate in hearings before it.[29] In practical terms, like Article 49 of the Statute of the ICJ, Article 13 DSU confers on the Panel the ability to become actively involved in proceedings before it by conferring two distinct powers. Firstly, Article 13 gives Panels the right to put questions to the parties in the course of proceedings in order to clarify any aspect of their factual or legal contentions. As such, under Article 13, Panels have the power to ask questions of the parties appearing before them in the course of proceedings – and they regularly do so in practice. Appendix 3(8) of the DSU confirms that Article 13 DSU is a general judicial power to gather information that has not been put before the Panel by the parties themselves, through asking questions, relevant to the case before it.[30]

Further, Article 13 DSU regulates the obtaining of evidence by the Court itself as opposed to the evidence submitted by the parties as part of

---

[26] As the AB stated in *United States – Import Prohibition of Certain Shrimp and Shrimp Products*, Appellate Body Report, WT/DS58/AB/R, 12 October 1998 para 106.

[27] *Japan –Measures Affecting Agricultural Products* (Japan – Agricultural Products II), Appellate Body Report, WT/DS76/AB/R, 19 November 1999 para 129.

[28] A. W. Shoyer and E. M. Solovy, 'The Process and Procedure of Litigating at the World Trade Organization: A Review of the Work of the Appellate Body' 31 *Law and Policy in International Business* 677, 683.

[29] The AB described the power to ask questions as 'part and parcel of the investigative function and duty of panels'; *US – Continued Existence and Application of Zeroing Methodology*, Appellate Body Report, WT/DS350/AB/R, 19 February 2009 para 260; See also Article 49 ICJ Statute, Article 62, Rules of the International Court of Justice, 1978, ICJ Acts & Docs 4 (as amended 14 April 2005); Rule 77 ITLOS Rules of Procedure, ICSID Convention Article 43(a); ICSID Arbitration Rules, Rule 34(2); Article 24(3) Rules of Procedure of the Iran–US Claims Tribunal.

[30] Mavroidis, Bermann and Wu, *The Law of the World Trade Organization*; Pauwelyn, 'The Use of Experts in WTO Dispute Settlement'.

their pleadings. In other words, Article 13 sets out a general power of the Court to request further information.

### 3.1.2.3 Power to request information under 13 DSU

Article 13 DSU formally grants Panels a broad power to request information from parties appearing before them:

Right to Seek Information

1. Each panel shall have the right to seek information and technical advice from any individual or body which it deems appropriate. However, before a panel seeks such information or advice from any individual or body within the jurisdiction of a Member it shall inform the authorities of that Member. A Member should respond promptly and fully to any request by a panel for such information as the panel considers necessary and appropriate. Confidential information which is provided shall not be revealed without formal authorization from the individual, body, or authorities of the Member providing the information.
2. Panels may seek information from any relevant source and may consult experts to obtain their opinion on certain aspects of the matter. With respect to a factual issue concerning a scientific or other technical matter raised by a party to a dispute, a panel may request an advisory report in writing from an expert review group. Rules for the establishment of such a group and its procedures are set forth in Appendix 4.

As such, Article 13 provides the Panels with an investigative power that is not limited to scientific or technical evidence or even to expert evidence.[31] In fact, the AB has held that Panels can seek information from any relevant source it so chooses[32] and that in principle there are no limits to this discretionary authority.[33] In the words of the AB in *Canada Aircraft*, each Panel is 'vested with ample and extensive discretionary authority to determine *when* it needs information to resolve a dispute and *what* information it needs'.[34] In practice Panels have made use of this broad fact-finding power contained in Article (1) and (2) although at times reference has merely been made to 'Article 13' generally.

---

[31] Pauwelyn, 'The Use of Experts in WTO Dispute Settlement'.
[32] *Argentina – Measures Affecting Imports of Footwear, Apparel and Other Items*, Appellate Body Report, WT/DS56/AB/R, 27 March 1998 para 84.
[33] See *Canada – Measures Affecting the Export of Civilian Aircraft*, Appellate Body Report, WT/DS70/AB/R, 2 August 1999 para 185.
[34] *Canada – Measures Affecting the Export of Civilian Aircraft*, Appellate Body Report, WT/DS70/AB/R, 2 August 1999 para 192; in this same case the Appellate Body held that a *prima facie* case did not need to be established before a panel had the right to seek information about the allegations; see para 185.

On the face of it, it would appear that the use of the term 'should' rather than 'shall' in Article 13.1 gives requests an exhortatory character rather as opposed to binding legal effect.[35] Consequently, requests for information made of parties under Article would not compel WTO Members to place information before the Panel, and similarly individuals would be under no binding obligation to provide information (nor would members themselves be obliged to require individuals provide the requested information).[36]

However, despite the fact that a straightforward reading of Article 13 does not appear to impose a binding legal obligation on the parties to comply with requests for information there has been some suggestion in recent times that Article 13 nevertheless places a binding duty on parties. For instance, in *Canada – Civilian Aircraft* the AB stated that although the term 'should' has an exhortatory character, it could also 'express a duty or obligation'.[37] This is a significant innovation in terms of fact-finding and one that will be considered in greater detail in Chapter 4 at Section 4.1.

### 3.1.2.4 Power of Panels to mandate individual experts and expert review groups under Article 13 DSU

Panels have the power to seek expert assistance under Article 13 DSU whenever any issue of fact is raised that requires more extensive expertise than the Panel possesses.[38] The procedure in general (which has been fairly consistent despite some criticism)[39] has been comprised of a three-stage process: the selection of experts, written questions to experts, and meetings with experts.[40] During the written submissions a list of

---

[35] P. Lichtenbaum, 'Procedural Issues in WTO Dispute Resolution' 19 *Michigan Journal of International Law* 1195, 1252.

[36] Ibid.

[37] *Canada – Measures Affecting the Export of Civilian Aircraft*, Appellate Body Report, WT/DS70/AB/R, 2 August 1999 para 187; see R. Behboodi, '"Should" means "Shall": A Critical Analysis of the Obligation to Submit Information Under Article 13.1 of the DSU in the Canada-Aircraft Case' 3 *Journal of International Economic Law* 563.

[38] See also the affirmation of this power in Article 11.2 SPS Agreement and Article 14.2 TBT Agreement, Article 19.4 Agreement on Customs Valuations and Article 4.5 of the Agreement on Subsidies and Countervailing Measures; see Marc Iynedjian, 'The Case for Incorporating Scientists and Technicians into WTO Panels' 42 *Journal of World Trade* 279, 285.

[39] See *EC – Asbestos*, Appellate Body Report, para 147.

[40] See *EC – Measures Affecting the Approval and Marketing of Biotech Products*, Panel Report, WT/DS291/R, WT/DS292/R, WT/DS293/R, 29 September 2006, paras 7.20 ff; *EC – Asbestos*, *EC –Hormones*.

questions is typically submitted to the experts who are asked to submit a written reply. Whilst the parties are closely consulted at every stage of the process the consent of both parties is not required for the consultation of experts by the Panels.[41]

The use of expert evidence is an important difference between the practice of the International Court of Justice and the Panels and AB of the WTO. Whilst the practice of the ICJ until very recently has been that experts have appeared as counsel for one of the parties before the Court, in the context of the WTO (individual) experts are mandated to provide evidence on a regular basis. Expert evidence is information of such a specialised nature that, by virtue of its nature, cannot be effectively gathered or fully appreciated by the Panels themselves. In other words, it comes from a source that is more knowledgeable than the Panel.[42]

It should be made clear at the outset that under Article 13(1) and (2) DSU Panels have the option of consulting both individual experts and expert review groups. The perception of both individual experts and expert review groups as a tool for the Panel to utilise in order to establish a sound factual basis upon which it can make legal determinations[43] is supported by the Panel's broad fact-assessment responsibility, the power to 'appreciate the weight and persuasiveness of the evidence before it'.[44] Panels are endowed with the power to establish and consult expert review groups to provide information on certain aspects of the case before it in the form of a written report submitted to the Panel.[45] Importantly, these reports are of an advisory nature and do not bind the Panels but of course their findings necessarily carry great weight and could not be easily overlooked by any Panel.

---

[41] Foster, *Science and the Precautionary Principle in International Courts and Tribunals* 114; The *EC – Hormones* case provides a good example of the procedure for consulting experts before the WTO adjudicative bodies. In this case there was both tribunal-appointed and party-appointed experts, who were actively engaged throughout the case; see ibid. Annex, Transcript of the Joint Meeting with Experts, attached to the Panel reports in both the complaint by Canada and the complaint by the United States. See also *Japan – Agricultural Products* paras 10.87, 10.257 and *EC – Asbestos*, 359.

[42] Pauwelyn, 'The Use of Experts in WTO Dispute Settlement' 330.

[43] *EC – Selected Customs Matters*, Appellate Body Report, DT/315/AB/R, 13 November 2006 para 258; *Japan – Measures Affecting the Importation of Apples*, Appellate Body Report, WT/DS245/AB/R, 26 November 2003 para 232; *Australia – Salmon*, Appellate Body Report, WT/DS18/AB/R, 20 October 1998 para 267.

[44] Ibid. [45] See Appendix 4 to the DSU and Annex 2 to the TBT Agreement.

Notwithstanding the numerous reasons that go some way to explaining the preference of Panels to appoint individual experts, there are advantages to be gained from utilising the statutory power to establish expert review groups. For instance, Panels, being made up of lawyers, jurists and other non-scientific professions are arguably not the best placed forum to effectively assess and weigh technical and scientific opinions of experts.[46] For example, what may appear to be two contradictory positions taken by experts causing Panels to choose between one side or another may not conflict in the eyes of the experts who could ultimately find a common position.[47] For this reason, commentators have argued that that use of expert review groups would be preferable to ensure the most accurate possible outcome for WTO fact-finding.[48] However, to date Panels have not established any such expert review groups.

Instead, the clear preference of Panels has been to appoint individual experts under Article 13(1) DSU.[49] The procedure regarding individual expert advice is not regulated by the Agreements or DSU but parties are normally given fair opportunity to comment upon the findings of the expert both orally at the time of the investigation and formally during the proceedings.[50]

---

[46] Pauwelyn, 'The Use of Experts in WTO Dispute Settlement' 329.   [47] Ibid.

[48] Ibid.; T. Christoforou, 'Settlement of Science-Based Trade Disputes in the WTO: a Critical Review of the Developing Case Law in the Face of Scientific Uncertainty' 8 *NYU Environmental Law Journal* 622.

[49] Marceau and Hawkins, 'Experts in WTO Dispute Settlement' 497. In accordance with DSU Annex 4, *EC – Selected Customs Matters*, Appellate Body Report at para 258; *Japan – Measures Affecting the Importation of Apples*, Appellate Body Report, WT/DS245/AB/R, adopted 10 December 2003, DSR 2003:IX, 4391 para 22; *Australia – Salmon*, Appellate Body Report para 267.

[50] *EC – Selected Customs Matters*, Appellate Body Report at para 258; *Japan – Measures Affecting the Importation of Apples*, Appellate Body Report, WT/DS245/AB/R, adopted 10 December 2003, DSR 2003:IX, 4391 at para 22; *Australia – Salmon*, Appellate Body Report, above n 100 at para 267. There is the possibility of cross-examination; however, it should be noted that this process before the WTO DSB is somewhat under-developed. Pauwelyn, 'The Use of Experts in WTO Dispute Settlement' 348. See Christoforou, 'Settlement of Science-Based Trade Disputes in the WTO: a Critical Review of the Developing Case Law in the Face of Scientific Uncertainty' 632, who advocates this strongly. However, as with other international courts and tribunals, there has been some doubt expressed as to whether the conditions for cross-examination are right, as system is not purely adversarial; Pauwelyn, 'The Use of Experts in WTO Dispute Settlement' 348. See Sheila Jasanoff, 'What Judges Should Know about the Sociology of Science', 32 *Jurimetrics Journal* 345, 353–4.

### 3.1.2.5 Special permanent expert bodies

In addition to the Panel's fact-finding powers, a number of expert bodies exist under the WTO dispute settlement system that operate in relation to specific WTO agreements. Such bodies have not been widely used thus far but nevertheless form part of the WTO's fact-finding apparatus.

Perhaps the most important example is Article 11.2 of the Agreement on the Application of Sanitary and Phytosanitary Measures (SPS Agreement) which *obliges* Panels to seek expert advice although discretion remains as to what form this advice can take. As such, experts have been appointed in every SPS case except one to date.[51] One option is resort to the Permanent Group of Experts established by the Committee on Subsidies under Article 24 of the SPS Agreement. The Permanent Group, composed of five impartial experts, can provide a non-binding advisory opinion at the request of the Committee and, interestingly, submit a report to the Panel with the question of whether a measure is a prohibited study which must be accepted by the Panel – the Panel has no discretion in this respect.[52] However, no Panel to date has ever requested the Permanent Group of Experts to submit a report, perhaps due to a desire to retain control of the proceedings.[53]

Further, the WTO SCM Committee under the Agreement on Subsidies and Countervailing Measures (SCM Agreement) can establish a Permanent Group of Experts. The SCM Agreement provides that the Permanent Group of Experts must review the evidence and report its conclusions to the Panel. However, no Panel has ever made use of this provision to establish a permanent expert group, perhaps due to the obligation to accept its conclusions 'without modification'.[54]

Similarly, Article 18.2 (see Annex 2) of the Agreement on Customs Valuation provides for the establishment of the Technical Committee on Customs Valuation under the Customs Co-operation Council. Article 19.4 permits Panels to 'request the Technical Committee to carry out an

---

[51] Marceau and Hawkins, 'Experts in WTO Dispute Settlement' 501; see footnote 4, with the exception of *US–Certain Measures Affecting Imports of Poultry from China (US – Poultry (China))*, WT/DS392/R, adopted 25 October 2010.

[52] Pauwelyn, 'The Use of Experts in WTO Dispute Settlement' 336; the Group can also 'be asked for a confidential advisory opinion (that cannot be used in any dispute settlement proceedings) by any WTO Member 'on the nature of any subsidy proposed to be introduced or currently maintained by that member'.

[53] Ibid.

[54] See SCM Agreement Article 4.5; Marceau and Hawkins, 'Experts in WTO Dispute Settlement' 499.

examination of any question requiring technical consideration'. Again, the Committee must submit a report to the Panel but unlike the Subsidies Permanent Group of Experts the report is not binding on the Panel. Despite this, no use has been made of the advisory procedure to date.[55]

Such expert bodies have been said to represent an important symbol of the WTO's commitment to factual accuracy and expert advice.[56] The significance of permanent bodies as opposed to ad hoc ones, made up of experts as opposed to jurists or politicians, is important and means that they are neither judicial nor political and 'epitomise the "expert group" called in to assist both the political and the judicial decision-maker'.[57] Nevertheless, it can be said that their practical significance is limited.

One final fact-finding mechanism that is deserving of mention due to its potential utility is Annex V of the SCM Agreement. Under this Annex, entitled 'Procedures for Developing Information Concerning Serious Prejudice' there exists an information-gathering procedure for disputes in which it is claimed that a member has, through subsidisation, caused adverse effects in the form of serious prejudice to the interests of another member.[58] This process is initiated by the DSB and carried out by a member of the DSB known as a 'facilitator' within sixty days of the dispute being established and is intended to help the Panel elucidate the facts.

This remains a contested procedure in one particular area of WTO law and one that has not to date been put to use. However, at the very least it has the potential to act as a form of centralised evidence-gathering mechanism.

### 3.1.2.6 Summary: the fact-finding approach of WTO Panels

Panels possess broad statutory fact-finding powers but in practice have not made full use of them. Instead, as a result of broad rules of admissibility, almost any piece of evidence is allowed to come before the Panels that the parties so choose. As we have seen, the general tendency of the

---

[55] Pauwelyn, 'The Use of Experts in WTO Dispute Settlement' 337; see also Article 8 of the Textiles Agreement, providing establishment of the Textiles Monitoring Body. Although unable to provide expert advice to panels, Article 8 provides that before parties can come before a panel, they must argue their case before the Textiles Monitoring Body. Whilst the panels are not bound by the findings of the Textiles Monitoring Body, they are naturally influential.

[56] Ibid.      [57] Ibid.

[58] *US – Measures Affecting Trade in Large Civil Aircraft (Second Complaint)*, Appellate Body Report, WT/DS353/AB/R, 12 March 2012 para 480.

Panels has been to 'ask the parties to produce the evidence and operate with rules concerning burden of proof, rather than to have investigations into facts led by the Court itself'.[59] As such it can be said that the maxim *da mihi factum, dabo tibi jus* (give me the facts, I will give you the law) accurately governs the practice of the Panels, which it is suggested can be described as relatively reactive in terms of fact-finding.[60] Nevertheless, there are a number of factors that mark the WTO adjudicative bodies out as more proactive in terms of fact-finding than the majority of other international courts and tribunals. First, however, it is necessary to examine the treatment of facts by the AB.

### 3.1.3 *Evidence before the Appellate Body – Article 17 DSU*

The Appellate Body is remarkable in international law as one of the few standing appellate bodies. Article 17.6 of the DSU states that the Appellate Body 'shall be limited to issues of law covered in the Panel report and legal interpretations developed by the Panel', formally restricting the AB to the evidence put before the Panels and precluding it from seeking additional evidence at the appeal stage.[61] In so providing, the DSU established a system of appeal on points of law only, at least theoretically, that is in line with the majority of courts of appeal in domestic legal systems.[62] Whilst the AB may receive expert evidence in some limited circumstances, it can only hear such evidence relating to purely legal issues, such as '*amici curiae strictly limited to legal arguments* in support of the applicant's legal position on the issues of law or legal interpretations in the Panel report with respect to which the applicant has been

---

[59] Walter, 'Article 44' 1041.
[60] Or, as Huber once stated, '[t]he parties may present any proof that they judge useful and the Court is entirely free to take evidence into account to the extent that it deems pertinent'. Acts and Documents Concerning the Organization of the Court, Judgment (1926), PCIJ Series D, Addendum to No. 2 *Revision of the Rules of the Court* 250; closely related to the principle of *jura novit curia*.
[61] Pauwelyn, 'The Use of Experts in WTO Dispute Settlement' 334. The terms of DSU Article 13 do not apply to the Appellate Body.
[62] See P. J. Kuyper, 'The Appellate Body and the Facts' in M. Bronckers and Reinhard Quick (eds), *New Directions in International Economic Law, Essays in Honour of John H. Jackson* (The Hague: Kluwer Law International, 2000) 312, discussing in particular the Court of Justice of the European Union, which does not remand cases back to the Court of First Instance if the issue is capable of being decided by the Court itself ('*en état d'être jugé*'); see Opinion of Advocate General Van Gerven in Case C-404/92 P, X v. Commission (1994) ECR, 4737 point 4.

granted leave to file a written brief'.[63] Despite these formal restrictions, however, issues of fact-finding and fact-assessment frequently arise in cases before the AB, but how can this be?

First of all, it is clear that the separation of fact from law is and has always been a fiendishly difficult endeavour.[64] The AB itself has openly grappled with this distinction[65] and a number of commentators have remarked upon the apparent futility of attempting to do so in the context of the AB.[66] Aside from this fundamental conceptual difficulty, issues of fact-finding and fact-assessment most often come into play before the AB as a result of two separate but related factors: (i) allegations that the Panel has failed in its Article 11 DSU duty to make an 'objective assessment of the facts' and (ii) the consequences of a finding of a failure in this regard and the practice of 'completing the legal analysis'.

Whether a Panel has failed to make an objective assessment of the facts under Article 11 DSU necessarily raises the question of whether the Article 11 duty to make an 'objective assessment of the facts' should be considered an 'issue of law' under Article 17.6 DSU. On the whole, the AB has generally given Panels extremely broad discretion when dealing with fact-assessment.[67] As one commentator has put it, '[i]n its actual application of its task "as a trier of facts" the Panel must go very far astray before the Appellate Body will do anything about it'.[68]

Secondly, Article 17.3 sets out that the AB has the power to 'uphold, modify or reverse the legal findings and conclusions of the Panel'; however, the application of this provision, which happens at the end of

---

[63] *EC – Measures Affecting Asbestos and Asbestos-Containing Products*, Appellate Body Report, WT/DS135/AB/R, *amicus curiae* procedures, para 7(c) (emphasis added); see Section 3.1.5 above.

[64] G. Yang, B. Mercurio and Y. Li, *WTO Dispute Settlement Understanding: A Detailed Interpretation*, Vol 7 (The Hague: Kluwer Law International, 2005) 206; see *EC – Measures Concerning Meat and Meat Products (Hormones)*, Appellate Body Report, WT/DS26/AB/R, WT/DS48/AB/R/ 16 January 1998, at 132.

[65] Ibid.

[66] Grando, *Evidence, Proof, and Fact-Finding in WTO Dispute Settlement* 58; Lichtenbaum, 'Procedural Issues in WTO Dispute Resolution' 1267.

[67] See *EC – Measures Concerning Meat and Meat Products (Hormones)*, Appellate Body Report, WT/DS26/AB/R, WT/DS48/AB/R/ 16 January 1998, paras 132–5; *European Communities – Measures Affecting the Importation of Certain Poultry Products*, Appellate Body Report, WT/DS69/AB/R, 13 July 1998, paras 133–5, to mention just two.

[68] Kuyper, 'The Appellate Body and the Facts' 317; see *United States – Definitive Safeguard Measure on Imports of Wheat Gluten from the European Communities*, Appellate Body Report, WT/DS166/AB/R para 151; see also *Australia – Measures Affecting Importation of Salmon*, Appellate Body Report, WT/DS18/AB/R, 20 October 1998 para 267.

the appeal procedure, has been problematic in practice. Generally, in the case that the AB finds that an error of law has been made, the practice to date has been to proceed to 'complete the legal analysis' by applying a correct legal interpretation to the factual record.[69] This practice is most likely the result of the AB not possessing any power to remand the case back to the Panel. In doing so, the AB has in practice proceeded to apply the revised legal determination to the facts as they were established before the Panel, as if it were the first instance court.[70]

### 3.1.4 Notable crosscutting evidentiary issues affecting both Panels and the AB

This section will focus on a number of crosscutting evidentiary issues that affect both the Panels and the AB. These include the burden of proof, the *prima facie* case requirement and the practice of drawing adverse inferences.

#### 3.1.4.1 Burden of proof

A significant crosscutting evidentiary aspect of the practice of the Panels and AB of the WTO that is of potential significance is the treatment of the burden of proof. In contrast to the vague position on the burden of proof taken by the International Court of Justice, Panels and the AB have consciously attempted to address this issue in cases that have come before them. However, this increased attention has not brought about increased clarity.

---

[69] R. Howse, 'The Most Dangerous Branch? WTO Appellate Body Jurisprudence on the Nature and Limits of the Judicial Power' in T. Cottier, P.C. Mavroidis and P. Blatter (eds), *The Role of the Judge in International Trade Regulation: Experience and Lessons for the WTO*, Vol 4 (University of Michigan Press, 2009) 17.

[70] See *Canada – Certain Measures Concerning Periodicals*, Appellate Body Report, WT/DS31/AB/R, 30 June 1997 24. However, the judicially created practice of completing the analysis, in effect substituting the AB's reasoning into the decision, has not been uniformly applied in practice and as such has created somewhat disjointed case law; Yang, Mercurio and Li, *WTO Dispute Settlement Understanding* 212. Jan Kuyper has suggested that the drafters of the DSB acknowledged that giving the AB a power of remand was desirable or even necessary but believed it to be 'a bridge too far' for the Members; see Kuyper, 'The Appellate Body and the Facts' 310. Such remand authority exists in other international tribunals such as the EU Legal Order, Article 177; Cameron and Orava argue that having such a power might benefit the WTO as they could send the case back for more fact-finding or ask the panel to try the case again. Cameron and Orava, 'GATT/WTO Panels Between Recording and Finding Facts' 231.

Neither the General Agreement on Tariffs and Trade (GATT) nor the DSU specifically address the issue of the burden of proof in cases before the dispute settlement apparatus of the WTO. As such, this fundamentally important issue has been left to the Panels and AB themselves to clarify and develop in piecemeal fashion in cases that they are asked to deal with.

In international adjudication generally the approach to the burden of production would appear to be governed by the principle *actori incumbit probatio* (that the party making the legal claim bears the burden of proving it), whilst the party invoking an exception to a general rule bears the burden of justifying it (*quincumque exceptio invokat ejusdem probare debet*).[71] However, whilst the notional burden may lie with the complaining party in cases in the context of the WTO, in reality both parties generally put forward evidence in support of their position simultaneously at the start of each case.[72]

Consistent case law reveals that in cases that come before the dispute settlement apparatus of the WTO the party bearing the burden of proof is required to make a *prima facie* case that its claim is meritorious, after which it will fall to the defendant party to effectively refute this claim.[73] Whilst this requirement may appear straightforward in theory, in practice the ambiguity surrounding what exactly constitutes a *prima*

---

[71] P. C. Mavroidis, *Trade in Goods* (2nd edn, Oxford University Press, 2012) 291; G. M. Grossman, H. Horn and P. C Mavroidis, 'Legal and Economic Principles of World Trade Law: National Treatment' IFN Working Paper No 917 85; see invocation of Art XX GATT *US – Gasoline* 22–3; *US – Wool, Shirts and Blouses* 15–16; *US – FSC (Article 21.5-EC)* § 133 – see Section 4.2.2. These principles are applied in tandem with the *dubio mitius* principle that WTO Members' actions should be presumed legitimate unless proven otherwise. Of course all of this assumes that discerning between a general rule and an exception is a feasible task. However, it has been shown that due to a number of factors, in WTO law this distinction is in fact extremely difficult to make; see Grando, *Evidence, Proof, and Fact-Finding in WTO Dispute Settlement* 151 onwards.

[72] Mavroidis, *Trade in Goods* 294.

[73] Grossman, Horn and Mavroidis, 'Legal and Economic Principles of World Trade Law: National Treatment' 86; this requirement, nowhere mentioned in the DSU, apparently a creation of the WTO dispute settlement bodies themselves, is not unique to WTO dispute settlement, but nevertheless 'most other international tribunals do not expressly employ this concept in determining whether the burden of proof has been discharged'; Brown, 'Aspects of Evidence in International Adjudication' 96. The AB, in *Korea – Definitive Safeguard Measure on Imports of Certain Dairy Products*, Appellate Body Reports, WT/DS98/AB/R, 14 December 1999 para 145, stated that the Panel is under no obligation under the DSU to rule on whether a *prima facie* case has been made.

*facie* case has created much uncertainty.[74] The case law reveals that there are a number of plausible ways that the *prima facie* case requirement could be construed.

A number of Panel reports have suggested that the *prima facie* case requirement operates as a threshold for evidence that must be met before the case can proceed or before the Panel can examine the evidence placed before it.[75] However, the main problem with conceiving the *prima facie* case requirement as a form of threshold that must be met after the submission of some preliminary evidence before the Panel will proceed with its determinations is that in practice Panels do not issue intermediate rulings stating whether party has met *prima facie* case or not. As stated above, the WTO adjudicative bodies do not wait for the production of evidence from the claimant party before requesting evidence from the defendant party but instead asks for all the relevant evidence both parties wish to place before it.[76]

The second conception of the *prima facie* case requirement that is plausible from a reading of the case law is that it represents a presumption which if raised by the claimant party shifts the burden of proof to the defendant party.[77] However, conceiving of the *prima facie* case as the initial standard of proof sets the bar very low in terms of the quantum of proof required of the claimant party. This is so since, after a mere *prima facie* case is established by the claimant party, its evidence is taken as a given whilst the burden of proof shifts to the defendant party to

---

[74] Grossman, Horn and Mavroidis, 'Legal and Economic Principles of World Trade Law: National Treatment' 86 suggest that it is difficult to say anything more than that some sort of reasonableness standard will attach itself to the determination of when a *prima facie* case has been made.

[75] See, for example, *United States – Section 211 Omnibus Appropriations Act of 1998*, Panel Report, 6 August 2001, WT/DS176/R paras 8.17, 8.18, 8.19; *Korea – Taxes on Alcoholic Beverages*, Panel Report, WT/DS57/R, WT/DS84/R, 17 September 1998 para 10.57; and *United States – Subsidies on Upland Cotton*, Panel Report, WT/DS26/R, 8 September 2004, at paras 7.959, 7.974; Grando, *Evidence, Proof, and Fact-Finding in WTO Dispute Settlement* 108.

[76] As Åhman has pondered, '[w]hy would the Appellate Body talk about a party's obligation to establish a prima facie case if a panel will never determine whether such a case has been established ... It is difficult to find a satisfactory answer to this question'; see J. Åhman, *Trade, Health, and the Burden of Proof in WTO Law* (The Hague: Kluwer Law International, 2012) 89; see also Grando, *Evidence, Proof, and Fact-Finding in WTO Dispute Settlement* 114, who has argued in support of an interim pronouncement of this kind.

[77] J. Pauwelyn, 'Evidence, Proof and Persuasion in WTO Dispute Settlement: Who Bears the Burden?' 1 *Journal of International Economic Law* 227, 254.

conclusively rebut.[78] Such a conception, accepting the claim of a party based on a *prima facie* case rather than the preponderance of evidence or some other higher standard would clearly be weighted in favour of the claiming party.[79]

The third possible conception is that the *prima facie* case requirement represents the final standard of proof that must be met by the claiming party. In a number of cases, when considering all the evidence submitted to it and sought by the Panel itself, there has been some suggestion that either establishing or failing to establish a *prima facie* case is in some way or other the final determinative standard of proof.[80] Such pronouncements that appear to treat the establishment of a *prima facie* case after considering all the evidence together as the standard of proof beg the question: 'why use the cryptic language of "establishing a prima facie case", instead of just describing it as "reaching the required standard of proof" (which is the normal way of describing it in most legal systems)?'[81] Again, the main issue is that it creates a bias in favour of the claimant party.[82] As such, conceiving of the *prima facie* case as the determinative standard of proof creates a situation whereby defendant parties have a much more onerous task than claimants which carries with it its own problems such as the possibility of encouraging spurious claims.

A lack of conceptual clarity persists to this day and is evident in the most recent case law.[83]

---

[78] Grando, *Evidence, Proof, and Fact-Finding in WTO Dispute Settlement* 126.  [79] Ibid.
[80] *India – Quantitative Restrictions on Imports of Agricultural, Textile and Industrial Products*, Panel Report, WT/DS90/R, 6 April 1999 para 5.201 onwards; confirmed by the AB in *India – Quantitative Restrictions on Imports of Agricultural, Textile and Industrial Products*, Appellate Body Report, WT/DS90/AB/R (22 September 1999) para 142; see also *Canada – Measures Affecting the Export of Civilian Aircraft*, Panel Report, WT/DS70/R, 14 April 1999 and *Japan – Measures Affecting Agricultural Products*, Panel Report, WT/DS76/R para 8.72.
[81] Åhman, *Trade, Health, and the Burden of Proof in WTO Law* 89.
[82] Grando, *Evidence, Proof, and Fact-Finding in WTO Dispute Settlement* 131.
[83] For instance, In *China – Electronic Payment Services* the panel stated that 'in WTO dispute settlement, once a party has made a *prima facie* case, the burden of proof moves to the responding party, which in turn must counter or refute the claimed inconsistency'. *China – Certain Measures Affecting Electronic Payment Services*, Panel Report, WT/DS413/R, 16 July 2012 para 7.6S. The same approach was taken by the panel in *US – Shrimps and Sawblades*; *US – Anti-Dumping Measures on Certain Shrimp and Diamond Sawblades from China*, Panel Report, WT/DS422/R, 8 June 2012 para 7.7, whereas a contrasting position was taken by the AB in *US – Tuna II*. The AB set out that '[w]here the complaining party has met the burden of making its *prima facie* case, it is then for the

None of the aforementioned possible conceptions of the *prima facie* case requirement satisfactorily describes the operation of the burden of proof in the case law. As has been pointed out, in practice Panels do not actively shift the burden of proof from one party to the other as if the parties were opponents in a tennis match.[84] Indeed, the shifting of the burden of proof has no basis in the text of the DSU, and, in representing an exception to the approach taken to the burden of proof by the clear majority of other international courts and tribunals, such explicit provision in the DSU might have been warranted. The traditional approach in international adjudication of *actori incumbit probatio*, that the party alleging the claim bears the burden of providing adequate evidence to back up its claim, is a general position that provides a degree of clarity to parties considering international litigation.

It is difficult to provide any further clarity on this issue, other than to say that it is a concept that introduces 'considerable confusion' into WTO adjudication.[85] Whilst it may represent to some extent the very least that is required from the claimant party in terms of evidence, it is most likely to refer to when the tactical burden shifts in procedural terms.[86] It is customary to separate the burden of proof into the two constituent functions it plays; the burden of production (determining which party must provide evidence in support of their legal claim) and the burden of persuasion (determining which party must satisfy the standard of proof).[87] However, the extent to which the separation of

---

responding party to rebut that showing'. See *US – Measures Concerning the Importation, Marketing and Sale of Tuna and Tuna Products*, Appellate Body Report, WT/DS381/AB/R, 16 May 2012 para 216 (which, ultimately, the AB found was not even handed; see para 298). See also the discussion by the AB in *US – Clove Cigarettes* regarding the *prima facie* case at paras 289–92 specifically relating to the TBT Agreement.

[84] Grossman, Horn and Mavroidis, 'Legal and Economic Principles of World Trade Law: National Treatment' 86.

[85] J. Barceló, 'Burden of Proof, Prima Facie Case and Presumption in WTO Dispute Settlement' 42 *Cornell International Law Journal* 23, 26.

[86] Ibid.; David Unterhalter, 'Allocating the Burden of Proof in WTO Dispute Settlement Proceedings' 42 *Cornell International Law Journal* 209, 220; David Unterhalter, 'The Burden of Proof in WTO Dispute Settlement' in M. E. Janow, V. Donaldson and A. Yanovich (eds), *The WTO: Governance, Dispute Settlement & Developing Countries* (Huntington, NY: Juris Publishing, 2008); P. Van den Bossche and W. Zdouc, *The Law and Policy of the World Trade Organization* (3rd edn, Cambridge University Press, 2013).

[87] G. M. Grossman, H. Horn and P.C. Mavroidis, 'Legal and Economic Principles of World Trade Law: National Treatment'; Michelle T. Grando, 'Allocating the Burden of Proof in WTO Disputes: A Critical Analysis' 9 *Journal of International Economic Law* 615, 615.

the two constituent elements of the burden of proof is helpful is also debatable given the approach taken by the Panels and AB.

Although the requirement may take on greater relevance in cases where one party refuses to submit evidence, in general the requirement 'will most likely never be of any practical importance for as long as the WTO proceedings continue to have the same form as today'.[88]

To date the International Court of Justice has somewhat shied away from making explicit statements on the burden and standard of proof in cases that have come before it. Whilst increasingly complex cases come before the Court may call for a clearer articulation of the burden of proof and related issues, it is suggested that the practice of the adjudicative bodies of the WTO should be a somewhat cautionary tale for the Court.

### 3.1.4.2 Adverse inferences

A further notable aspect of the practice of the WTO Panels and AB is the practice of drawing adverse inferences from the refusal of a party to provide information requested of it by the other parties or that is generally relevant to the legal issues in consideration before the Panel – something that the ICJ has to date refrained from doing.[89] For example, in *Argentina – Footwear* the Panel drew an adverse inference from Argentina's refusal to provide information requested by the United States, stating this this refusal taken together with the evidence presented by the United States favoured their position.[90] The sole reference to adverse inferences in the WTO Agreements is Article 7 of the SCM Agreement, paragraph 7, Annex 5 which states that '[i]n making its determination, the Panel should draw adverse inferences from instances of non-cooperation by any person involved in the information gathering process'.

The power to draw adverse inferences more generally flows from the duty of collaboration found in international adjudication generally which requires that States co-operate in good faith in providing the Panel with

---

[88] Åhman, *Trade, Health, and the Burden of Proof in WTO Law* 90. This use of this conception of the *prima facie* case requirement has been confirmed in recent case law; see *US – Anti-Dumping Measures on Certain Shrimp and Diamond Sawblades from China*, Panel Report, WT/DS422/R, 8 June 2012 paras 7.9, 7.31–32.

[89] See for example *Canada – Measures Affecting the Export of Civilian Aircraft*, Appellate Body Report, WT/DS70/AB/RW, 2 August 1999 para 203.

[90] *Argentina – Measures Affecting Imports of Footwear, Textiles, Apparel and Other Items*, Panel Report, WT/DS56/R, 25 November 1997 para 6.40.

the required evidence.[91] In relation to the duty of collaboration, although the parties are free to submit or not submit any piece of evidence they so choose, the AB has in the past urged that parties be 'fully forthcoming from the very beginning both as to the claims involved in the dispute and as to the facts relating to those claims ... Claims must be stated clearly. Facts must be disclosed freely.'[92] This is an issue considered in much greater detail in Chapter 4.

The practice of drawing adverse inferences is simply another way to aid the Panels in determining the facts through flushing out the facts it needs that have not been placed before them by the parties themselves,[93] or in the words of one commentator 'the real value of an adverse inference lies in its capacity to induce cooperation rather than the inference itself'.[94] The Panel in *US – Wheat Gluten* demonstrated that the power to draw adverse inferences is discretionary by refusing to do so despite being requested to do so, owing to the fact it felt the factual record it possessed was sufficient to fulfil its Article 11 DSU duty.[95]

There are drawbacks to the practice of drawing adverse inferences, such as the fact that where neither the Panel nor the other party are aware of information that has been withheld from the Panel, the power is rendered useless.[96] Nonetheless, the tendency for governments to ignore requests for information in cases before Panels,[97] coupled with the uncertain nature of the power to compel the production of evidence

---

[91] P. C. Mavroidis, 'Development of WTO Dispute Settlement Procedures' in F. Ortino and E. Petersmann (eds), *Development of WTO Dispute Settlement Procedures*, Vol 18 (The Hague: Kluwer Law International, 2004) 174.

[92] *India – Patent Protection for Pharmaceutical and Agricultural Chemical Products*, Appellate Body Report, WT/DS50/AB/R, 19 December 1997 para 94; see D. P. Steger and P. Van den Bossche, 'WTO Dispute Settlement: Emerging Practice and Procedure' 92 *Proceedings of the American Society of International Law* 79, 84.

[93] D. Collins, 'Institutionalized Fact-Finding at the WTO' 27 *University of Pennsylvania Journal of International Economic Law* 367, 372; Cameron and Orava, 'GATT/WTO Panels Between Recording and Finding Facts'.

[94] Grando, *Evidence, Proof, and Fact-Finding in WTO Dispute Settlement* 266; Kuyper, 'The Appellate Body and the Facts' 321.

[95] *United States – Definitive Safeguard Measures on Imports of Wheat Gluten from The European Communities*, Panel Report, WT/DS166/R, 31 July 2000 para 8.12.

[96] Cameron and Orava, 'GATT/WTO Panels Between Recording and Finding Facts'.

[97] Ibid.; In relation to information that a party claims is confidential, the Panel in *Indonesia – Autos* states that parties may not 'invoke confidentiality as a basis for their failure to submit the positive evidence required; see *Indonesia – Certain Measures Affecting the Automobile Industry*, Panel Report, WT/DS54/R, 2 July 1998 para 14.235.

150   THE PRACTICE OF OTHER INTERNATIONAL TRIBUNALS

suggest that the practice of drawing adverse inferences from a failure to comply with requests for information made by other parties can potentially play an important role in fact-finding before the Panels.[98]

### 3.1.5   WTO concluding remarks

This survey of the operation of the issues of fact-finding and fact-assessment reveals a number of aspects of WTO dispute settlement that are innovative and potentially influential outside the confines of the WTO. For instance, the WTO dispute settlement bodies have interpreted their Article 13 DSU power to request information in a manner that allows it to almost compel the production of evidence from parties (and the drawing of adverse inferences from any failure to do so). Furthermore, there is a much greater willingness to appoint experts by the Panels. Although there are a number of less-than-satisfactory elements of WTO fact-finding and fact-assessment such as an unclear burden of proof, on the whole it can be said that there is much that is innovative and could potentially influence older courts and tribunals. A selection of these innovative and proactive fact-finding practices will be examined in Chapter 4.

## 3.2   Fact-finding and fact-assessment in recent inter-State arbitrations

This section sets out to examine the handling of issues of fact-finding and fact-assessment in a number of recent inter-State arbitrations conducted under the auspices of the Permanent Court of Arbitration (PCA).[99] Inter-State arbitration as means of dispute settlement has experienced a

---

[98] *United States – Investigation of the International Trade Commission in Softwood Lumber from Canada*, Panel Report, WT/DS277/RW, 15 November 2005 para 7.21.
[99] In 1916 James Brown Scott famously remarked upon the misnomer that is the PCA: 'it is difficult to call a court "permanent", which does not exist, and which only comes into being when it is created for the trial of a particular case, and goes out of existence as soon as the case is tried. It is difficult to consider as a court, a temporary tribunal, which is not composed of judges ... The Conference did not call the creature of their hands a court of justice. It was to be one of arbitration ... [T]he decision is to be on the basis of respect for law, which does not mean necessarily that the decision is to be reached by the impartial and passionless application of principles of law ... but the decision is to be reached "on the basis of respect for law", which may be very a different matter'; James Brown Scott, *The Hague Court Reports* xvii–xviii (Oxford, 1916).

## 3.2 RECENT INTER-STATE ARBITRATIONS

renaissance in recent times.[100] In fact, there are now more pending inter-State arbitrations than cases in the docket of the ICJ.[101] Given the increasing use being made of inter-State arbitration, this section will attempt to discern whether any broad approach to fact-finding issues can be identified from the work of three prominent inter-State arbitrations conducted in the last few years: the *Guyana/Suriname, Abyei* and *Kishengana* arbitrations.[102] The selection of these arbitral disputes is based on the fact that they are timely, high profile and, unlike some

---

[100] In the 1990s several commentators remarked upon what they saw as the decline of inter-State arbitration since the Second World War. For instance, Stuyt's 1990 survey noted that despite the fact there were 178 inter-State arbitrations between 1900 and 1945, in the forty-five years following the Second World War there were only forty-three; see A. Alexander Marie Stuyt, *Survey of International Arbitrations: 1794–1989* (The Hague: Martinus Nijhoff, 1990); further, Gray and Kingsbury noted that '[t]he vast increase in the number of States [following the Second World War] and the corresponding increase in international transactions is accompanied by a decline in the number of arbitrations'; Christine Gray and Benedict Kingsbury, 'Developments in Dispute Settlement: Inter-State Arbitration Since 1945' 63 *British Yearbook of International Law* 97, 100. On this renaissance see Jacomijn J. van Haersolte-van Hof, 'The Revitalization of the Permanent Court of Arbitration' 54 *Netherlands International Law Review* 395; Bette E. Shifman, 'Revitalization of the Permanent Court of Arbitration' 23 *International Journal of Legal Information* 284; see also C. Romano, 'Trial and Error in International Judicialization' in C. Romano, K. Alter and Y. Shany (eds), *The Oxford Handbook of International Adjudication* (Oxford University Press, 2013) 12; see also PCA Arbitral Tribunal *Iron Rhine ('IJzeren Rijn') Railway (Belgium/Netherlands), Award 24 May 2005* para 235, where the arbitral tribunal 'established a committee of independent experts to determine the costs of reactivating the railway route in question and adequate measures to achieve compliance with the required levels of environmental protection. In the award, the tribunal explicitly considered that "These issues are appropriately left to technical experts"'; Francesca Romanin Jacur, 'Remarks on the Role of *Ex Curia* Scientific Experts in International Environmental Disputes' in Nerina Boschiero and others (eds), *International Courts and the Development of International Law* (Berlin: Springer, Asser Press, 2013) 450.

[101] The website of the PCA lists at the time of writing fourteen pending inter-State or mixed arbitrations (see www.pca-cpa.org/showpage.asp?pag_id=1029) whilst the website of the ICJ lists ten pending cases (including a number of high-profile arbitrations such as the Arbitration Between the Republic of Croatia and the Republic of Slovenia, having an extremely high-profile group of arbitrators), the status of at least two of which could perhaps more accurately be described as inactive (www.icj-cij.org/docket/index.php?p1=3&p2=1). Of particular interest is the case of *The Republic of Mauritius v. The United Kingdom of Great Britain and Northern Ireland* currently pending before the PCA, brought under Article 287 and Annex VII of UNCLOS on 20 December 2010; see www.pca-cpa.org/showpage.asp?pag_id=1429; S. W. Schill, 'The Overlooked Role of Arbitration in International Adjudication Theory' 4 *ESIL Reflections*.

[102] Boyle and Harrison, 'Judicial Settlement of International Environmental Disputes: Current Problems' 275.

other arbitrations, completely available to the public. Furthermore, it is significant that these are inter-State arbitrations since disputes before the ICJ are similarly limited to State parties. So-called 'mixed arbitrations' (involving States and non-State actors) are of more limited value in terms of providing guidance for procedural improvements that the purely State-centric ICJ could implement.

The recent revitalisation of inter-State arbitration can be attributed to two main factors.[103] The first is the dispute settlement procedure set out in Annex VII of the United Nations Convention on the Law of the Sea (UNCLOS)[104] and the second is the adoption of the series of Optional Procedural Rules as part of the New Directions Initiative of the PCA.[105] Indeed, of the three arbitrations examined in this section, the *Abyei* Arbitration utilises a particular set of Optional PCA Rules and the *Guyana/Suriname* arbitration is a result of a dispute arising under UNCLOS.[106] As such, they serve as clear examples of how the PCA is increasingly relevant in contemporary international dispute settlement.

To elaborate on the first rejuvenating factor, Article 287(1) UNCLOS provides that States may make a declaration stipulating their preferred means of settling any dispute that arises under the Convention, including ad hoc arbitration in accordance with Annex VII UNCLOS. In addition to the fact that arbitration is looked upon favourably by States as providing a degree of flexibility (in relation to the selection of arbitrators, for example),[107] Article 287(5) provides that arbitration is the default

---

[103] It should be noted that the revitalisation of inter-State arbitration should not be equated with the revitalisation of the Permanent Court of Arbitration per se. The significant number of investment disputes between States and private parties have also contributed to the full docket of the PCA in recent times – a point not addressed in this section.

[104] T. Van den Hout, 'Resolution of International Disputes: The Role of the Permanent Court of Arbitration – Reflections on the Centenary of the 1907 Convention for the Pacific Settlement of International Disputes' 21 *Leiden Journal of International Law* 643.

[105] van Haersolte-van Hof, 'The Revitalization of the Permanent Court of Arbitration' 400; Shifman, 'Revitalization of the Permanent Court of Arbitration' 286.

[106] In total six UNCLOS cases have been, or at the time of writing are currently being, arbitrated under the auspices of the PCA: *MOX Plant Case (Ireland v. United Kingdom)* instituted November 2006, terminated by Tribunal Order of June 6 2008, available at https://pcacases.com/web/allcases/; *Malaysia/Singapore* (Award on Agreed Terms of 1 September 2005), available at http://wwwpca-cpaorg. For other Annex VII Arbitrations see *Barbados/Trinidad and Tobago* (Award of 11 April 2006) 45 ILM 798, available at https://pcacases.com/web/allcases/; *Bangladesh v. India*, instituted October 2009, pending; *The Republic of Mauritius v. United Kingdom*, instituted December 2010, pending.

[107] See Article 3 Annex VII UNCLOS, Van den Hout, 'Resolution of International Disputes: The Role of the Permanent Court of Arbitration'; see Shabtai Rosenne and Louis

means of settling disputes where parties fail to agree to any alternative means. As such, it can be said that the UNCLOS system of dispute settlement is somewhat predisposed to arbitration.

In relation to the second factor contributing to the revitalisation of the PCA, the Optional Procedural Rules have their roots in the United Nations Commission on International Trade Law Rules (UNCITRAL Rules).[108] Following the codification of the arbitration procedure in The Hague Conventions of 1899 and 1907 a number of high profile arbitrations had taken place before the procedure fell in to decades of desuetude.[109] In seeking to reverse the fortunes of the PCA, the UNCITRAL Rules were a major influence in the drafting of the Optional Rules in 1992 following the New Directions initiative.[110] The Working Group opted to give (a revised version of) the UNICTRAL Rules a central place in the PCA system due to their perceived flexibility and ability to apply to both States and non-State parties.[111] The success of the UNCITRAL Rules and resulting influence on the revitalisation of the PCA is also bound up with the operation of the Iran–US Claims Tribunal which significantly increased awareness of them.[112]

### 3.2.1 The influence of the Iran–US Claims Tribunal

Whilst the Iran–US Claims Tribunal is not an inter-State arbitral body, its operation to at least some extent influenced the adoption of the series

---

B. Sohn, *United Nations Convention on the Law of the Sea, 1982: A Commentary*, Vol 5 (The Hague: Martinus Nijhoff, 1989), V, at 42 referring to statements in Plenary fourth session France (1976), 59th meeting, paras 8–10, V Off. Rec. 14; and Madagascar, 61st meeting, para 44, V Off. Rec. 34. See also Natalie Klein, *Dispute Settlement in the UN Convention on the Law of the Sea*, Vol 39 (Cambridge University Press, 2005) 56.

[108] The UNCITRAL rules must be seen in the context of other arbitral rules of practice such as International Bar Association's Rules on the Taking of Evidence in International Commercial Arbitration.

[109] See for example *Island of Palmas (or Miangas) (United States of America v. The Netherlands)*, Award, 4 April 1928; *Norwegian Shipowners' Claims (Norway v. United States of America)*, Award, 13 October 1922 and the notable arbitration between China and an American corporation, *Radio Corporation of America v. The National Government of the Republic of China*, Award, 13 April 1935.

[110] van Haersolte-van Hof, 'The Revitalization of the Permanent Court of Arbitration' 400; Shifman, 'Revitalization of the Permanent Court of Arbitration' 286.

[111] *The Permanent Court of Arbitration: New Directions, Working Group on Improving the Functioning of the Court*, 13 May 1991 – Peace Palace, The Hague (The Hague: International Bureau of the Permanent Court of Arbitration in co-operation with the T.M.C. Asser Institut, 1991) 8.

[112] van Haersolte-van Hof, 'The Revitalization of the Permanent Court of Arbitration' 403.

of Optional Procedural PCA Rules and has in turn logically influenced the way that modern inter-State arbitrations operate. The Iran–US Claims Tribunal is a product of the diplomatic crisis between the United States and Iran that encompassed the hostages crisis, the imposition of economic sanctions on Iran and the subsequent judgment by the ICJ that Iran had breached its international obligations towards the diplomatic and consular staff taken hostage.[113] The Claims Settlement Declaration, part of the Algiers Accords designed to bring the diplomatic crisis to an end, provides for the establishment of the Iran–US Claims Tribunal, its competence, composition and Rules of Procedure.

The Algiers Accords stipulated that the Iran–US Claims Tribunal would follow the UNCITRAL Rules, approved by the General Assembly only a few years before in 1976, with necessary amendments since these Rules were designed for ad hoc commercial arbitration between two private parties.[114] Crucially, in terms of fact-finding, the UNCITRAL Rules are significant for a number of reasons. For instance, particularly noteworthy is the fact that the Rules provide for a more proactive role for the tribunal when compared with the existing inter-State court at the time, the ICJ.

### 3.2.1 (i) The extent to which the Iran–US Claims Tribunal takes an active role in investigating facts

From its early days the Tribunal has taken an active role in investigating the facts.[115] Generally in cases where the Tribunal feels the information put before it by the parties themselves is not adequate to establish the facts of the case it issues orders informing the parties of what information the Tribunal feels it lacks.[116] Such orders are often made after pre-

---

[113] *Tehran Hostages Case.*
[114] See Claims Settlement Agreement, Algiers Accords, 81 Dep't St. Bull. § (1981), 20 ILM 223 (1981), Art III (2); Declaration of the Government of the Democratic and Popular Republic of Algeria Concerning the Settlement of Claims by the Government of the United States of America and the Government of the Islamic Republic of Iran, Art III, para 2, reprinted in IRAN-U.S. C.T.R. 9, 10 (1981–2); Karl-Heinz Böckstiegel, 'The Relevance of National Arbitration Law for Arbitrations Under the UNCITRAL Rules' 1 *Journal of International Arbitration* 223, 227.
[115] Order of 20 December 1982 in Flexi-Van Leasing, Inc. and Islamic Republic of Iran, Case No. 36, Chamber One, reprinted in 1 Iran-U.S. C.T.R. 455 (1981–2); Order of 21 January 1983 in General Motors Corporation et al. and Government of the Islamic Republic of Iran et al., Case No. 94, Chamber One, reprinted in 3 Iran-U.S. C.T.R. 1 (1983).
[116] See for example Order of 2 February 1984 in Henry F. Teichmann, Inc., Carnegie Foundry and Machine Company and Hamadan Glass Company, Case No. 264, Chamber One; Order of 15 January 1986 in Hoshang Mostofizadeh and Government of the

hearing conferences with the parties. Such pre-hearing conferences are a notable aspect of the Tribunal's approach to fact-finding and have been described as an effective tool in alerting the Tribunal to what documents it requires to be produced.[117] As practice evolved, 'the Tribunal has continued to be quite activist and to issue detailed orders requiring parties to submit specifically described evidence'.[118]

### 3.2.1 (ii)  Production of documents: Article 24(3)

The most significant fact-finding provision in the Rules of Procedure of the Iran–US Claims Tribunal is Article 24(3) (based on the corresponding UNCITRAL provision), which states that '[a]t any time during the arbitral proceedings the arbitral tribunal may require the parties to produce documents, exhibits or other evidence within such a period of time as the tribunal shall determine'.[119]

Article 24 is significant in providing a binding power of discovery in an international arbitration involving a sovereign State.[120] A number of caveats must be added, however. Firstly, the standard of discovery at the Iran–US Claims Tribunal is much stricter compared to the traditional common law form of discovery and the Tribunal retains discretion as to whether or not it is granted.[121] Secondly, the Tribunal has developed a number of safeguards against so-called 'fishing requests' whereby one party would speculatively request a broad category of information from the other, without specifically identifying the evidence or how it will aid

---

Islamic Republic of Iran, National Iranian Oil Company, Case No. 278, Chamber Two; Order of 19 October 1983 in Konstantine A. Gianoplus and Islamic Republic of Iran, Case No. 314, Chamber One; Order of 12 July 1982 in Leila Danesh Arfa Mahmoud and Islamic Republic of Iran, Case No. 237, Chamber Two; Order of 18 November 1982 in International Systems and Controls Corporation and Industrial Development and Renovation Organization of Iran et al., Case No. 439, Chamber Two; Howard M. Holtzmann, 'Fact-Finding by the Iran–United States Claims Tribunal' in R. B. Lillich (ed), *Fact-Finding Before International Tribunals* (Ardsley-on-Hudson, NY: Transnational, 1991) 106.

[117] Ibid.
[118] Ibid., Order of 2 July 1987 in Minister of National Defence of the Islamic Republic of Iran and Government of the United States of America, Case No. B1 (claims 2 & 3), Full Tribunal; Order of 27 May 1987 in Ministry of National Defence of the Islamic Republic of Iran and Government of the United States of America, Case No. B-61, Chamber One.
[119] UNCITRAL Rules, Art 24(3).
[120] UNCITRAL Rules, Art 28(3); Holtzmann, 'Fact-Finding by the Iran–United States Claims Tribunal' 575.
[121] Mosk, 'The Role of Facts in International Dispute Resolution' 97; Holtzmann, 'Fact-Finding by the Iran–United States Claims Tribunal' 574.

the resolution of the dispute (instead merely seeking to use the procedure as a way to procure evidence to bolster its own case). In guarding against such requests, the practice emerged that the request made must be firstly 'necessary',[122] 'warranted', or 'appropriate'[123] and that secondly the party had already taken 'all reasonable steps' to obtain the requested information.[124]

### 3.2.1 (iii)   Enforcement of production orders

Once the Tribunal is satisfied that the request for disclosure is necessary, warranted or appropriate and that the requesting party has already taken 'all reasonable steps' to obtain the information, the Tribunal hands down a production order for disclosure. McCabe has estimated that only half are complied with.[125] UNCITRAL Rules provide no sanctions for non-compliance stating only in Article 28(3) that, as noted above, 'the arbitral tribunal may make the award on the evidence before it'; however, this may in some cases benefit the party withholding the information since it can keep damaging evidence from coming before the Tribunal. As such, the possibility of drawing adverse inferences from any failure to produce requested information has been described as 'most effective response to a party's failure to comply with a discovery order'.[126]

### 3.2.1 (iv)   Adverse inferences

Generally, in situations where a party has access to information relevant to the case, the Tribunal is authorised to draw adverse inferences from

---

[122] *Weatherford International Inc. and the Islamic Republic of Iran*, Case No. 305, Chamber Two, Order of 15 Feb 1985.
[123] *Brown & Root Inc. and the Islamic Republic of Iran*, Case No. 432, Chamber One, Order of 4 Jan 1993.
[124] See, for example, Order of 14 March 1983 in *William Stanley Shashoua and Government of the Islamic Republic of Iran et al*, Case No. 69, Chamber One.
[125] Monica Petraglia McCabe, 'Arbitral Discovery and the Iran–United States Claims Tribunal Experience' 20 *The International Lawyer* 499, 518.
[126] Holtzmann, 'Fact-Finding by the Iran–United States Claims Tribunal' 121; McCabe, 'Arbitral Discovery and the Iran–United States Claims Tribunal Experience' 528. See UNCITRAL commentary 570 (although in international commercial arbitration there is always the possibility of enforcement through domestic courts); see *INA Corporation and the Islamic Republic of Iran*, Award No. 184-161-1 (12 August 1985) at 14, reprinted in 8 Iran-US CTR 373, 382 (1985–I); *Brown & Root Inc. and the Islamic Republic of Iran*, Case No. 432, Chamber One, Order of 4 January 1993 para 3; *Frederica Lincoln Riahi*, Concurring and Dissenting Opinion of Judge Brower para 20; see ibid.

the failure of that party to disclose it.[127] And in practice the Tribunal has used its Article 24(3) power to draw adverse inferences from the failure of a party to comply with a request for evidence.[128] However, the Tribunal has generally been reluctant to draw adverse inferences in practice, often because one of the main prerequisites to drawing adverse inferences – 'namely showing that the missing documents are in the possession of the opposing party' – has not been established.[129] Further, even where the prerequisite is established, the Tribunal has been remarkably reluctant to draw adverse inferences.[130]

### 3.2.1 (v)  The use of experts

Experts have been appointed both by the parties and by the Tribunal itself. Brower has described the use of experts appointed by the parties as 'invaluable' to the Tribunal in relation to factually complex issues – not just scientific issues – but also in relation to property valuation and assessing accounting standards, for example.[131] Whilst parties regularly appoint experts, the Tribunal's power to appoint its own experts at the request of the parties or on its own initiative under Article 27 has been used sparingly.[132] Since parties regularly appoint experts it is sometimes not necessary for the Tribunal to appoint its own. And even in those rare cases where the Tribunal does so, it will most often only do so after the parties' own witnesses have been heard. However, it is nonetheless significant that the Tribunal appointed experts itself at all – something the ICJ has only done in a small number of cases.[133]

---

[127] Concurring Opinion of Richard M. Mosk in *Ultrasystems Incorporated and Islamic Republic of Iran et al.*, Award No. 27-84-3 (4 March 1983) reprinted in 2 Iran-U.S. C.T.R. 114, 115 (1983).

[128] Holtzmann, 'Fact-Finding by the Iran–United States Claims Tribunal' 104.

[129] Brower and Brueschke, *The Iran-United States Claims Tribunal* 194. For instance in the case of *H. A. Spalding, Inc. and Ministry of Roads and Transport of the Islamic Republic of Iran – Tribunal*, Award No. 212–437-3 (24 February 1986) reprinted in 10 Iran-U.S. Cl. Trib. Rep. 22, 26–33, at 31–2.

[130] This reluctance has provoked some criticism not only from commentators but from judges themselves, lamenting the reluctance to draw adverse inferences from failure to co-operate fully with the Tribunal in the establishment of the factual record. See *William J. Levitt and Islamic Republic of Iran*, Award No. 520-210-3 (29 August 1991) reprinted in Iran-U.S. Cl. Trib. Rep. 145 at 165.

[131] See *Chas. Main International, Inc. and Kluzestan Water and Power Authority*, Interlocutory Award No. ITL-, 23-120-2 (27 July 1983) reprinted in 3 Iran-U.S. Cl. Trib. Rep 156, 164–7; see ibid.

[132] Ibid. footnote 949 for extensive case law examples.      [133] Ibid.

### 3.2.1 (vi) The Iran–US Claims Tribunal in the round

On the whole the Iran–US Claims Tribunal takes a proactive approach to fact-finding, 'actively seeking to elucidate the facts, rather than simply evaluating what the parties put before it'.[134] But what is the significance of this brief summary of the practice of the Iran–US Claims Tribunal to our consideration of recent inter-State arbitrations? The practice of the Iran–US Claims Tribunal, operating under a modified version of the UNCITRAL Rules that influenced the revitalisation of the PCA, highlights some of the most significant aspects of modern inter-State arbitration that we will see recur when considering the following arbitrations.

To reiterate, whilst the Iran–US Claims Tribunal is not an inter-State arbitral body, its operation to at least some extent influenced the adoption of the series of Optional Procedural PCA Rules and has in turn logically influenced the way that modern inter-State arbitrations operate. The noteworthy fact-finding aspects of the Iran–US Claims Tribunal, such as its binding power of discovery, use of adverse inferences, its generally proactive approach regarding pre-hearing conferences, asking questions, requesting information and appointing experts, are all innovative when compared to the approach of the ICJ at this time, and to a large extent this remains the case even today. A similarly more proactive approach to fact-finding is evident in the following inter-State arbitrations to which we now turn our attention.

### 3.2.2 *Guyana/Suriname*

First, a preliminary word on the statutory basis for the fact-finding powers that modern inter-State arbitrations possess. Whilst the arbitral Panel most commonly has the discretion to adopt its own Rules of Procedure (through consultation with the parties),[135] in the end the Rules of Procedure relating to fact-finding are often similar. Arbitrations constituted under Annex VII of UNCLOS such as *Guyana/Suriname* most often adopt Rules of Procedure based on the PCA Optional Rules[136] meaning that there is a degree of commonality between such arbitrations and those brought on an ad hoc basis that opt to base their Rules of Procedure on the PCA Optional Rules also, such as the *Abyei*

---

[134] Holtzmann, 'Fact-Finding by the Iran–United States Claims Tribunal' 132.
[135] See Article 5 Annex VII UNCLOS.
[136] Which, as we noted above, are themselves based on the UNCITRAL Rules.

Arbitration. To elaborate, the 2012 PCA Rules of Procedure, Optional Rules for Arbitrating Disputes Between Two States and Optional Rules for Arbitrating disputes between Two Parties of which Only One Is a State all contain broadly similar provisions, based on the corresponding UNCITRAL provisions, to the effect that the Arbitral Tribunal may at any time call on the parties to produce any information it requires and may draw adverse inferences for any failure to do so.[137] The vast majority of modern inter-State arbitrations adopt Rules of Procedure containing such provisions or slight variations thereof.

The 2007 Guyana/Suriname arbitration has a number of notable fact-finding elements including the appointment of experts and a Tribunal actively engaging with a dispute over disclosure of documents.

### 3.2.2 (i) Introduction

On 24 February 2004 Guyana initiated arbitration proceedings with Suriname concerning the delimitation of its maritime boundary and related alleged breaches of international law by Suriname in disputed maritime territory. Guyana brought proceedings under Articles 286 and 287 of UNCLOS and in accordance with Annex VII of the Convention.[138] Neither party had made a declaration regarding their preferred method of dispute settlement under Article 287(1). In its Notification of Claim, Guyana stated that both parties had accepted arbitration in accordance with Annex VII through Article 287(3) of UNCLOS. The

---

[137] See Article 27(3) PCA Arbitration Rules 2012, Article 24(3) PCA Optional Rules for Arbitrating a Dispute Between Two States, Article 24(3) PCA Optional Rules for Arbitrating a Dispute between Two Parties of Which Only One is a State, Article 11 (2) Rules of Procedure Arbitral Tribunal Constituted Pursuant to Article 287, and in Accordance with Annex VII, of the United Nations Convention on the Law of the Sea, in the Matter of Arbitration Between: Guyana and Suriname, Award, 17 September 2007, Article 12(2) Rules of Procedure *MOX Plant Arbitration*, Article 24(3) UNCITRAL Arbitration Rules, General Assembly Resolution 31/98 1976 or Article 27(3) UNCITRAL Arbitration Rules 2010.

[138] Under the dispute settlement regime of UNCLOS, Art 279 provides that parties are to settle disputes peacefully in accordance with Art 2(3) UN Charter. Art 280 sets out that there is nothing to prevent States from settling disputes by their own means. Art 280(1) contains an obligation to proceed to exchange of views once dispute arises. Art 281 provides that where parties have chosen preferred means of dispute settlement then this applies. Only when no agreement that further procedure is needed. If no agreement is reached then Section 2 of Part XV 'Compulsory Procedures Entailing Binding Decisions' comes into play States can make declaration choosing ITLOS, ICJ, arbitral tribunal or special arbitral tribunal as preferred means under Art 287. Where no agreement is met then arbitration is initiated to find agreement.

Tribunal adopted its Rules of Procedure with the consent of the parties on 30 July 2004.

### 3.2.2 (ii)  Hydrographic expert

By Order No. 6 of 27 November 2006, after consultation with the parties, the Tribunal appointed an expert, more specifically a hydrographer, to assist it in the course of proceedings 'in the drawing and explanation of the maritime boundary line or lines in a technically precise manner'.[139] The hydrographer appointed by the Tribunal played a notably active part in the proceedings requesting information he felt necessary to effectively carry out his task.[140] In addition, through Order No. 8 the hydrographer undertook a site visit to inspect the position of Marker 'B' on 31 May 2007.[141] The appointment by the Tribunal of an expert to assist it clearly indicates that it wished to engage proactively with the evidence to establish a sound factual basis upon which to make a judgment rather than simply relying on the information submitted by the parties, or even on the expert evidence presented by the parties themselves. Furthermore, in contrast to the ICJ's practice of consulting the *experts fantômes* criticised in the previous chapter, the Tribunal was transparent in actively consulting with an independent expert in assisting it in the course of proceedings.[142]

### 3.2.2 (iii)  Dispute over disclosure of documents

On 4 November 2004, Guyana alleged that Suriname had objected to its requests for access to a number of files located in the archives of the Netherlands Ministry of Foreign Affairs,[143] and later requested the Tribunal to 'require Suriname to take all steps necessary to enable the parties to have access to historical materials on an equal basis and immediately advise The Netherlands that it withdraws its objection to disclosure of 7 December [2004]'.[144] Suriname justified its objection, saying that this

---

[139] 3.1. Order No. 6; *Guyana v. Suriname Arbitration* para 108, Order No. 6.

[140] Namely: 'the position of Marker "B", and other points in this 1960 survey within the geographic area of the mouth of the Courantyne River, their geodetic datum, and the WGS-84 datum position of these points if they have been determined by re-computation of the 1960 survey'; ibid. para 110, confirmed by Order No. 7, 12 March 2007, that the information had been received.

[141] Order No. 7, 21 May 2007.

[142] Van den Hout, 'Resolution of International Disputes: The Role of the Permanent Court of Arbitration' 652.

[143] *Guyana v. Suriname Arbitration* para 16.    [144] Ibid. para 17.

was not an issue of equal access to public records for the records were not public, owing to the fact they related to matters of national security and that it was the policy of the Netherlands to restrict material relating to ongoing boundary disputes.[145]

By letter to the President of 4 January 2005 Guyana again requested that the Tribunal 'adopt an Order requiring both parties to co-operate and to refrain from interference with each other's attempts to obtain documents or other information ... and ... to take all necessary steps to undo the effects' of interference that had already taken place.[146] The Tribunal, in asking for Suriname's views on Guyana's letter, reminded the parties of the importance of the principles of equality of arms and co-operation in the course of international proceedings, citing Articles 5 and 6 of Annex VII of UNCLOS as well as Articles 7(1) and (2) of the Tribunal's own Rules of Procedure in support of this position.[147] It is a significant and bold move for the Tribunal to explicitly remind the parties of their duty to collaborate with the Tribunal and this is another indicator of a Tribunal actively engaged in the fact-finding process seeking to achieve as close an approximation of the objective truth as possible.

In order to resolve the impasse the President of the Tribunal asked Guyana to submit a 'list of specific documents and information in the archives of the Netherlands Ministry of Foreign Affairs it is seeking to access, indicating in general terms the relevance of each item solely as it pertains to the maritime boundary before this tribunal' and asked Suriname to communicate its position on 'whether the specific items sought by Guyana in that list should be released to Guyana, and if not, on what basis they should be withheld'.[148]

Subsequently Suriname complained that Guyana had not specified the information it required as requested by the Tribunal, nor explained why the information it had requested was necessary and stated that it believed that 'none of the items on Guyana's list ... is a file or document that Suriname has an obligation under international law to make available to Guyana'.[149] Predictably, Guyana argued that since it had been denied access to the information it could provide no further clarification or details about the evidence it sought.[150]

---

[145] Ibid. para 18; letter to the President 27 December 2004.   [146] Ibid. para 19.
[147] Ibid.    [148] 7 February 2005, ibid. para 26.
[149] 21 February 2005, letter to President, ibid. para 28.
[150] 2 March 2005, letter to President, ibid. para 30.

### 3.2.2 (iv)  The Tribunal's approach to fact-finding

After extended disagreement over access to documents, the Tribunal issued Order No. 1 on 18 July 2005, entitled 'Access to Documents', which addressed a number of interesting fact-finding issues. First of all, the Order stated that the Tribunal would not consider any document from the archives of the Netherlands to which Guyana had been denied access.[151] This was a proactive move by the Tribunal to counteract the difficulties and apparent reluctance of Suriname to co-operate with the Tribunal in relation to this evidence.

Secondly, the Order made clear that each party had the right to 'request the other Party, through the Tribunal, to disclose relevant files or documents, identified with reasonable specificity, that are in the possession or under the control of the other Party'.[152] In this statement the Tribunal reminded the parties of their duty to collaborate with the Tribunal and sought to facilitate the disclosure of information between the parties – taking a more active role than the ICJ has to date. However the Tribunal chose its words carefully, referring not to a general right of discovery but to a right to 'documents, identified with reasonable specificity, that are in the possession or under the control of the other party'. As such the Tribunal places two important limitations – firstly referring only to information within the possession or under the control of the other party and laying down the condition that the information must be 'identified with reasonable specificity', to prevent so-called fishing expeditions.[153] It is suggested that in this the influence of the Iran–US Claims Tribunal can be discerned.

### 3.2.2  (v) Independent expert

The Order was also notably innovative in establishing an independent expert, under Article 11(3) of the Tribunal's Rules of Procedure whose task was, at the request of a party disclosing information, to review any proposal by that party to 'remove or redact parts of that file or document'[154] in light of the fact that that a party may have a right to non-disclosure for valid reasons.[155] Importantly, any dispute as to the failure

---

[151] Order No. 1 Operative Paragraph 1.    [152] Order No. 1 Operative Paragraph 3.
[153] See *Corfu Channel* on this.    [154] Order No. 1 Operative Paragraphs 4 and 5.
[155] Such as that the information does not relate to the present dispute or national security considerations or 'prejudice to governmental interest', as recognised by Judge Jessup in his Separate Opinion in the *Barcelona Traction Preliminary Objections* case para 97; see also *Corfu Channel Case* 4 and *Bosnian Genocide Case* para 205.

to produce a document, in whole or part, was to be resolved by the expert, with whom, under Article 11(4) of the Tribunal's Rules of Procedure, the parties are under a duty to co-operate.[156]

Through a letter to the President on 20 July 2005 Guyana requested a number of 'relevant files' in the possession or under the control of Suriname, pursuant to Order No. 1. On 25 July 2005 Suriname asked the Tribunal to reject Guyana's request, but stated that it was willing to comply with its obligations under paragraph 2 of the order.[157] On 27 July Suriname wrote to the President setting out the way in which it intended to provide the information to Guyana, in implementation of Order No. 1, paragraph 2. After some equivocation, Suriname agreed to submit the documents to the independent expert.[158]

The Tribunal's Order No. 3 provides that the Tribunal will retain ultimate control over the evaluation of the evidence.[159] The Order provides that if a party invokes paragraph 5 to remove or redact information requested of it, 'the Party proposing removal or redaction shall produce the entire un-redacted file or document for the Expert's inspection.'[160] The expert is then to invite the party to justify why it ought to be redacted or removed.[161]

Subsequently the Tribunal issued Order No. 4, by which it ordered Suriname to co-operate with the independent tribunal in accordance with Order No. 3[162] and ordered the independent expert to review Suriname's proposals for removal or redaction[163] and to determine whether Guyana's request for information had been made with 'reasonable specificity and appear[ed] relevant.'[164] This corresponding obligation is a clear attempt to prevent any 'fishing expeditions' from Guyana. Both parties interacted with the Tribunal and the independent expert extensively in attempting to reach common ground regarding the submission of a number of documents and attempts to withhold or redact them.[165] The independent expert, after reviewing the relevant files, submitted a report to the Tribunal which was made available to the parties.[166] Guyana completely agreed with the findings of the Report

---

[156] Order No. 1 Operative Paragraph 7.
[157] 25 July 2005, letter to the President, *Guyana v. Suriname Arbitration* para 50.
[158] Files 161 and 169A. Professor Hans van Houtte was appointed as independent expert; see Order No. 3, 12 October 2005, ibid. paras 59–60.
[159] Order No. 3, 2.0.   [160] Order No. 3, 2.3.   [161] Order No. 3, 2.3.
[162] Order No. 4, 1(a).   [163] Order No. 4, 1(b).   [164] Order No. 4, 2(a).
[165] See *Guyana v. Suriname Arbitration* paras 64–70.
[166] Ibid. para 76, 18 January 2006.

and pushed for disclosure of the documents mentioned. Suriname, on the other hand, concurred with everything apart from the disclosure of one specific document, File 161, which it insisted ought not to be disclosed.

On 16 February 2006 the Tribunal issued Order No. 5 'adopting' the recommendations of the independent expert's report in sections 5 and 6 relating to Files 161 and 169A stated that Suriname was 'hereby requested to grant Guyana immediate access to the files in accordance with those recommendations'. In relation to other documents, the Tribunal ordered that Suriname either disclose them to Guyana or submit them to the expert for redaction, as it so chose – a course of action that Suriname pursued, providing a number of documents to the expert along with a memorandum containing reasons why they ought to be redacted.[167]

The wording of the evidentiary Orders is significant and deserves closer attention. Although the Tribunal phrases the order in terms of 'requesting' information from the parties, it is unclear what the exact legal force of their orders is. The Tribunal's authority to compel the production of evidence of course stems from its constitutive instruments, in this case UNCLOS and its Rules of Procedure adopted by the parties. Neither of these instruments clearly sets out that the Tribunal possesses a power to compel the disclosure of information and unlike the WTO adjudicative bodies, as we have seen, no clear attempt has been made to develop such a power in this context. As such the exact legal nature of the Tribunal's requests remains unclear. However the possibility of developing a binding power drawing on the duty of collaboration that all States are under once they accept the jurisdiction of an international tribunal is one that remains open and is an issue that is examined in greater detail in relation to the ICJ in Chapter 4 at Section 4.1.

### 3.2.2 (vi) The arbitral Tribunal's approach in the round

At the very least it can be said that this arbitral tribunal, as with a number of others in recent times, has taken a clearly proactive approach to fact-finding in engaging with the parties, mediating in their dispute regarding the disclosure of evidence, requesting information itself and even appointing an independent expert to review and redact information in order to reach a solution that would satisfy both parties and, most importantly, give

---

[167] Ibid. paras 80–6.

the Tribunal the best chance of achieving as close an approximation of the truth as possible. The appointment of the independent expert to adjudicate on issues of disclosure of information is particularly innovative and appears to have worked well in the present case and to the satisfaction of both States – illustrating that more proactive tribunals are not immediately threatening to States and can in fact help to illicit further information required for the proper administration of justice. The Tribunal also relied heavily on independent experts' advice and cited expert advice referred to in the submissions of the parties – a practice not often seen in the ICJ.[168] Admittedly some bargaining was necessary in order to ensure that both parties were happy with the solution reached but this is to be expected in the course of international litigation. The Tribunal's proactive approach facilitated the evidentiary compromise and could serve as a model for other international courts and tribunals considering being more proactive in their approach to fact-finding.[169]

### 3.2.3  Abyei Arbitration

The Abyei Arbitration is similarly noteworthy for its approach to issues of fact-finding including requesting information, active involvement in the proceedings and the appointment of experts.

### 3.2.3 (i)  Introduction

The Abyei Arbitration took place at the Permanent Court of Arbitration in 2009 under the PCA's Optional Rules for Arbitrating Disputes Between Two Parties of Which Only One is a State. The arbitration was a politically significant one concerning a dispute over territorial boundaries between the State of Sudan and the newly formed State of South Sudan. The dispute was brought before an arbitral tribunal due to the non-State nature of the Sudan People's Liberation Movement/Army (SPLM/A) at the time. Although the International Court of Justice has a long history with territorial disputes, it would have been unable to deal with this dispute since its Statute does not permit non-State parties to appear before it.[170]

---

[168] Riddell, 'Scientific Evidence in the International Court of Justice – Problems and Possibilities' 255.
[169] *Guyana v. Suriname Arbitration* paras 90–107.
[170] Brooks Daly, 'The Abyei Arbitration: Procedural Aspects of an Intra-state Border Arbitration' 23 *Leiden Journal of International Law* 801, 803; Article 34(1) states that 'only States may be parties in cases before the Court'.

Following decades of civil war the Protocol on the Resolution of the Abyei Conflict was signed in May 2004; however, it did not contain any agreement in relation to the boundaries of the Abyei area. Instead, the Protocol provided for the establishment of the Abyei Boundaries Commission (ABC) to 'define and demarcate the Area of the nine Ngok Dinka Chiefdoms transferred to Kordofan in 1905'[171] consisting of members appointed by the parties and five independent experts appointed by the US, UK and IGAD.[172] The ABC was to prepare a report that would be final and binding upon the parties.[173] However, the award was immediately disputed by the parties and the 2008 Abyei Road Map contained an obligation on both parties to refer the dispute to arbitration.[174]

The task of the resulting Arbitral Tribunal was twofold: firstly, to effectively conduct judicial review to determine whether or not the ABC had exceeded its powers,[175] and secondly, if it was found to have done so, to 'proceed to delimit the boundaries of the area of the nine Ngok Dinka Chiefdoms transferred to Kordofan in 1905, based on the submissions of the parties'[176] or to declare that the report of the ABC was valid.[177]

### 3.2.3 (ii)  Evidence : the Tribunal's request for certain documents

The SPLM/A alleged that it had been denied access to a number of documents and requested of the Tribunal 'full and unhindered access to the SPLM/A and counsel to the relevant archival documents at the Survey Department'.[178] In turn the Tribunal requested that the documents in question be produced. Under Article 24(3) of the PCA Rules the Tribunal requested that the Government of Sudan supply the Tribunal and the SPLM/A with a detailed list of documents including a full record

---

[171] Abyei Protocol, Article 5(1); see Understanding on Abyei Boundaries Commission (Abyei Appendix) 2004.
[172] Abyei Protocol Article 5(2), Abyei Appendix Article 2.
[173] Abyei Appendix Article 5.
[174] The Road Map for Return of IDPs and Implementation of Abyei Protocol signed in Khartoum, 8 June 2008; see para 134.
[175] Arbitration Agreement, Article 2(a); see Vaughan Lowe and Antonios Tzanakopoulos, 'The Abyei Arbitration' in Lise Bosman and Heather Clark (eds), *The Abyei Arbitration (Sudan/Sudan People's Liberation Movement/Army)* The Permanent Court of Arbitration Award Series (The Hague: The Permanent Court of Arbitration, 2012) para 19.
[176] Arbitration Agreement, Article 2(c).
[177] Arbitration Agreement, Article 2(b); Award, para 6.
[178] Letter to the Tribunal 17 March 2009.

of maps and records as specified.[179] The Tribunal laid out a detailed procedure regarding what information it desired, and the options that the Government of Sudan had in producing it, including a procedure for objecting to disclosure.[180]

The Tribunal also invited the SPLM/A to request any other documents it needed,[181] which the SPLM/A did on a number of occasions.[182] Nevertheless, the SPLM/A continued to argue that it had been denied complete access to the Sudan Survey Department and Sudan National Records Office and urged the Tribunal to draw adverse inferences from Sudan's failure to provide unfettered access to this information.[183] Sudan refuted these allegations throughout, accusing the SPLM/A of 'an unfettered fishing expedition' and arguing that the SPLM/A's 'own failure to exercise due diligence is no justification for a late request to seek access to such a potentially wide array of documents'.[184]

On the other side, Sudan claimed that a number of its witnesses had been harassed and threatened,[185] allegations which the SPLM/A promised it had investigated and found to have no basis in fact.[186] Furthermore the SPLM/A continued to protest that its legal representatives had been 'wholly obstructed from viewing a single relevant document' and 'prohibited from carrying out any of their own research'.[187] After a long exchange of letters between the parties the Government of Sudan stated that it had already provided a number of the requested maps to the Tribunal and to the SPLM/A and that others could not be located.[188] Throughout this time the Tribunal played an active role, prompting the production of the requested evidence.[189]

---

[179] In the Matter of an Arbitration Before a Tribunal Constituted in Accordance with Article 5 of the Arbitration Agreement Between the Government of Sudan and the Sudan People's Liberation Movement/Army on Delimiting Abyei Area and the Permanent Court of Arbitration Optional Rules for Arbitrating Disputes Between Two Parties of Which Only One is a State between the Government of Sudan and the Sudan People's Liberation Movement/Army, Final Award, 22 July 2009, see Transcript of 24 November 2008 Procedural Hearing 34–5.
[180] Ibid.; see Transcript of 24 November 2008 Procedural Hearing 34–5.
[181] Award para 46.   [182] Award paras 49, 53.
[183] Award para 57; *Abyei Arbitration Award* para 61; see SPLM/A letter dated 3 April 2009 2–3; see also SPLM/A letter dated 8 April 2009 2.
[184] Award paras 49, 52, 23 March 2009.   [185] Award para 63.   [186] Award paras 64–5.
[187] *Abyei Arbitration Award*; letter to the Government of Sudan and Tribunal, 26 March 2009.
[188] Ibid. para 55; letter of 30 March 2009.
[189] See for example the Presiding Arbitrator's request to the Government of Sudan to respond to the points made on 3 April.

In response to the possibility of drawing adverse inferences, the Tribunal made an astute distinction in order to avoid addressing the issue directly. The Tribunal stated that it believed that the SPLM/A was not asking the Tribunal to draw adverse inferences at this precise moment but rather the SPLM/A was putting the Government of Sudan 'on notice' that it might seek adverse inferences if its requests for information were not complied with.[190] In doing so the Tribunal stated that '[i]n light of the arguments presented at oral pleadings, the Tribunal will decide, in the fullness of these proceedings, whether any adverse inferences or other appropriate conclusions should be drawn'.[191]

Both parties presented arguments regarding admissibility and weight of evidence produced.[192] The Tribunal, however, ultimately accorded no weight to allegations of intimidation, obstruction of access to documents and drew no adverse inferences,[193] a point lamented by Judge Al-Khasawneh in his dissent.[194] During the oral pleadings Judge Al-Khasawneh asked four witnesses of the Government of Sudan if they had been intimidated by agents of the SPLM/A; however, ultimately nothing came of these allegations with the Award describing the witnesses as giving 'varying answers'.[195] As he has been in previous cases,[196] Judge Al-Khasawneh was vehemently critical of the Tribunal's approach to both fact-finding and fact-assessment.[197] Judge Al-Khasawneh even went so far as to accuse the Tribunal of doing the very thing it had accused the ABC of, namely exceeding its mandate, by delimiting boundaries 'without the reasoning required of it by Experts'.[198] In particular, in relation to the reasoning for the eastern and western boundaries and their intersection with the northern boundary, Al-Khasawneh described the authority for the Tribunal's delimitation as one source, and that that

---

[190] *Abyei Arbitration Award* para 61, 11 April 2009, Communication from the Tribunal to the parties.
[191] Ibid. para 61, 11 April 2009, Communication from the Tribunal to the parties.
[192] Award para 306 onwards; for arguments on oral tradition see para 372.
[193] Lowe and Tzanakopoulos, 'The Abyei Arbitration' 60.
[194] Dissent of Judge Al-Khasawneh paras 31, 200.
[195] *Abyei Arbitration Award* para 66; see witness testimony of Mr Zakaria Atem Diyin Thibek Deng Kiir at GoS Oral Pleadings, 21 April 2009, Transcr. 43/04 – 44/05, Mr Majid Yak Kur at GoS Oral Pleadings, 21 April 2009, Transcr. 54/13 – 55/09, Mr Ayom Matit Ayom at GoS Oral Pleadings, 21 April 2009, Transcr. 51/04 – 51/19 and Mr Majak Matet Ayom at GoS Oral Pleadings, 21 April 2009, Transcr. 51/25 – 52/12.
[196] See Joint Dissenting Opinion in *Pulp Mills*.
[197] Dissent of Judge Al-Khasawneh paras 10, 15, 22(e).
[198] Dissent of Judge Al-Khasawneh para 5.

source was 'the imprecise, non-contemporaneous remarks made by Howell in 1951 which the majority quoted out of context and misinterpreted'.[199]

### 3.2.3 (iii) Experts appointed by the Tribunal

On 16 April 2009 the Tribunal passed Procedural Order No.2, which provided for the appointment of Douglas Vincent Belgrave and Bill Robertson as experts to provide assistance to the Tribunal in the course of this arbitration.[200] The task of the experts was to be, should the Tribunal find that the ABC had exceeded its mandate, to assist the Tribunal in delimiting the boundaries of the nine Ngok Dinka Chiefdoms transferred to Kordofan in 1905 in accordance with the Arbitration Agreement.

### 3.2.3 (iv) Experts and witnesses appointed by the parties

The parties presented witnesses to the Tribunal. The Government of Sudan had criticised the use of witness evidence in this case, which the Tribunal agreed with in cases of oral evidence passed down through generations; however, it went on to state that 'depriving witness evidence per se of all probative value would be unjustifiable'[201] and that it would 'accordingly admit oral evidence and will assign it the weight proper to it in each instance. It will be duly taken into account, in particular, in so far as it corroborates other sources of evidence'.[202] Furthermore, throughout the course of proceedings, both the Government of Sudan[203] and the SPLM/A[204] produced experts to speak to their case. In appointing its own experts and hearing both witnesses and expert opinion put forward by the parties it can be said that the approach of the Tribunal is reminiscent of the similarly more proactive approach to fact-finding taken in the *Abyei* and *Kishenganga* arbitrations, as we will see in the following section.

---

[199] Dissent of Judge Al-Khasawneh para 6; see P. P. Howell, 'Notes on the Ngork Dinka of Western Kordofan', 32 *Sudan Notes and Records* 239, 242, cited in Award at paras 701ff.
[200] See Procedural Order No. 2.   [201] *Abyei Arbitration Award* para 717.
[202] Ibid. para 718.
[203] Pursuant to Procedural Order No. 1, the Government of Sudan presented the following witnesses to answer questions propounded by the Tribunal: Mr Ayom Matet Ayom, Mr Majak Matit Ayom, Mr Majid Yak Kur.
[204] As notified on 20 March 2009 and 30 March 2009, the SPLM/A presented the following experts and witnesses for direct examination and for cross-examination by the Government of Sudan: Mr Deng Chier Agoth, Professor J. A. Allan, Dr Peter Poole, Professor Martin Daly, Mr Richard Schofield.

### 3.2.3 (v)  Abyei in the round

What can be said about the fact-finding approach of the arbitral tribunal in the Abyei Arbitration? Some commentators have characterised the approach of the tribunal in the *Abyei* Arbitration as providing 'passive treatment of scientific fact-finding' since the tribunal interpreted its mandate so as to not require 'an analysis of the substantive correctness' of the science and stated that it would not 'engage at the outset in an omnibus re-operating of the ... appreciation of evidence'.[205] However, whether or not the tribunal had the scientific expertise to be able to engage with such disputed scientific facts or whether an arbitral tribunal was the best place to do so is somewhat doubtful. Rather, the approach of the tribunal in establishing experts and engaging with the parties is anything but passive, especially compared to the practice of the International Court of Justice.

There are a number of proactive aspects of its fact-finding process. For instance, in the dispute over access to documents between the parties, the Tribunal played a proactive role in handling the requests and bringing the dispute to a mutually agreeable compromise. In addition the Tribunal was proactive in requesting information, asking questions and appointing its own experts in addition to those appointed by the parties. Although the Tribunal was diplomatic – or, some might say, hesitant – in its approach to drawing adverse inferences, and whilst Al-Khasawneh's vociferous dissent suggests that the fact-finding process is far from perfect, it can nevertheless be said that the Tribunal was readily willing to engage with the parties in the fact-finding process and ready to utilise some of its fact-finding powers to establish a solid factual basis for the resolution of the dispute. A similar willingness to engage with the facts can be seen in the third and final arbitration examined in this chapter, that of the recent *Kishenganga* arbitration.

## 3.2.4   Kishenganga

### 3.2.4 (i)   Introduction

The recent Partial Award of the Kishenganga Indus Waters Arbitration (*Kishenganga*) constituted in accordance with the Indus Waters Treaty of 1960 between India and Pakistan contains a number of notably proactive

---

[205] *Abyei Arbitration Award* 410, 411; D'Aspremont and Mbengue, 'Strategies of Engagement with Scientific Fact-Finding in International Adjudication' 17.

fact-finding elements. Conducted under the auspices of the PCA, the dispute concerns the Kishenganga Hydro-Electric Project (KHEP) and centres around two legal questions. The first relates to whether India's proposed diversion of the river Kishenganga (Neelum) into another tributary breaches India's legal obligations owed to Pakistan. The second question concerns the technical issue of whether, under the Treaty, India may deplete or bring the reservoir level of a so-called run-of-river plant below Dead Storage Level (DSL) in any circumstances except in the case of an unforeseen emergency.[206]

### 3.2.4 (ii)  Adoption of Rules of Procedure

Under Procedural Order No. 1 of 21 January 2011, and in accordance with Paragraph 16 of Annexure G, the parties agreed the Supplemental Rules of Procedure for the arbitration. The Court noted that the parties had expressed two viable options: firstly, the PCA Optional Rules for Arbitrating Disputes Between Two States, or secondly, the Rules of Procedure similar to those used by arbitral tribunals established under UNCLOS in proceedings administered by the PCA. After hearing the parties' views at the first meeting the Court issued Procedural Order No. 2 on 16 March 2011 adopting the Supplemental Rules of Procedure.[207]

### 3.2.4 (iii)  Site visits

Interestingly, at the first meeting of the parties, even before the Rules of Procedure had been adopted or the scope of the dispute set in stone, the parties agreed on the need for the Court to conduct a site visit in the course of proceedings.[208] The parties agreed that the Court should visit the site of the Pakistan Neelum-Jhelum Hydro-Electric Plant (NJHEP) as well as the KHEP.[209] The parties agreed that the only presentations made to the Court during the site visit were to be those of experts limited to

---

[206] See Pakistan's Request for Arbitration para 4; for a detailed account of the factual and historical background of the dispute see Ahmad, 'The Indus Waters Kishenganga Arbitration and State-to-State Disputes'.

[207] See Procedural Order No. 2 para 1.1. Note that this Order has not been published in full and as such there is only a limited amount that can be said about the Rules of Procedure.

[208] In the Matter of the Indus Waters Kishenganga Arbiration before the Court of Arbitration Constituted in Accordance with the Indus Waters Treaty 1960 between the Government of India and the Government of Pakistan Signed on 19 September 1960, between the Islamic Republic of Pakistan and the Republic of India, Partial Award, 18 February 2013 para 8.

[209] Procedural Order No. 3 was passed concerning the itinerary of the visit, the share of the costs to be apportioned and the size of the delegations amongst other matters.

objective, technical issues, meaning that legal issues and argumentation were not permitted to be put forward during the visit.[210]

Furthermore the Court conducted a second site visit, at the request of Pakistan, on 6 December 2011. After circulating a draft of Procedural Order No. 7 to canvass the thoughts of the parties the Court issued it on 16 January 2012, stating that from 3 to 6 February 2012 three members of the Court, Sir Franklin Berman, Professor Wheater and one member of the Secretariat, would visit the site. The visit would be documented by video and pictures to be shown to the rest of the Court and experts not part of the delegations of the parties would make brief presentations to the members of the Court visiting.

The parties were reassured that the procedure adopted regarding the content of the presentations made to the visiting Court and warned the parties against participating in *ex parte* discussions with members of the Court – a problematic issue faced by the ICJ in recent times.[211] The second site visit consisted of a visit to the Neelum valley and inspection of the gauge-discharge observation site at Dudhnial and a water-pumping station at Athmuqam – videos of the site visit and the presentations made to the visiting Court were presented to the parties in accordance with Procedural Order No. 7.

### 3.2.4 (iv) Information requested of the parties

From the outset the Court played an active role in proceedings. For instance, on 27 August 2011 Professor Wheater, the umpire appointed by the Rector of Imperial College London, requested information from India regarding technical aspects of the KHEP dam including cross-sections of the dam, drawings of the dam elevation and India's Environmental Impact Assessment, amongst other things.[212] The Chairman asked India to furnish the information requested by Professor Wheater by 2 September 2011 and Pakistan to comment on the information submitted by India by 7 September 2011.[213]

---

[210] *Kishenganga Partial Award* para 5 onwards. Furthermore, as a result of the ordering of Interim Measures the Court passed Procedural order No. 6 and ordered two inspections to monitor the implementation of the Interim Measures; Procedural Order No. 6 Concerning the Joint Report dated 19 December 2011, submitted pursuant to paragraph 152(2) of the Order on Interim Measures.

[211] See 27 January 2012 Registrar Message to the Parties Regarding Procedural Order No. 7, ibid, para 85.

[212] See Interim Measures Hearing Tr. (Day 3), 27 August 2011, 201:6 to 202:25.

[213] Interim Measures Hearing Tr. (Day 3), 27 August 2011, 294:10–16.

As we can see already, the Arbitral Tribunal actively participated in the proceedings, requesting information and taking charge of the fact-finding process. Subsequently India informed the Court that the majority of the information requested of it had already been given to Pakistan and that any information that had not been given to Pakistan would be put before the Court with India's Counter-Memorial.[214] On 7 September 2011 Pakistan submitted its comments on India's letter to the Court and provided the Court with two additional documents that had not already been made available to the Court.[215] Furthermore, a substantive part of the Partial Award is dedicated to the Court's finding that it had insufficient data on record to determine a precise minimum downstream flow.[216] The parties did not dispute that such a minimum was to be set but could not agree on what this minimum should be and as such this task fell to the Court. However the Court felt it had insufficient data to make such a judgment. Accordingly, the Court took the decision to be proactive and to request further information from the parties.

This is significant in that, as opposed to the reactive approach of the ICJ where judgments are made on the basis of the information submitted by States the vast majority of the time, in this case the Court was willing to admit that it had a factual deficiency and was willing to take steps to remedy it.[217] The Court requested further information from the parties and deferred its judgment on this matter in a detailed request, listing the specific information required of each of the parties.[218] The Court's request is wide-ranging, stipulating that the data 'should be accompanied by full information on the assumptions underlying these analyses'.[219] The Court went on to state the strict time limits placed on the submission of the information to the tribunal.[220]

### 3.2.4 (v) Information requested by the parties

In the phase of the written submissions, after the submission of Pakistan's Memorial and India's Counter-Memorial[221] each party made a

---

[214] 2 September 2011, Letter to the Court.
[215] *Kishenganga Partial Award* para 60. In the words of the Court, '[t]he evidence presented by the Parties does not provide an adequate basis for such a determination, lacking sufficient data ... Accordingly, the Court finds itself unable, on the basis of the information presently at its disposal, to make an informed judgment'.
[216] Ibid. para 445.   [217] Ibid.   [218] Ibid. para 458.
[219] Ibid. paras 460–3; see Decision D, 201.
[220] Ibid. 120 days from the issuance of the Partial Award.
[221] On 27 May 2012 and 23 November 2011 respectively.

number of requests for documents and further information – an interesting procedural practice, especially considering how the arbitral tribunal dealt with these requests. Requests of this type are more akin to the common law procedure of discovery and are commonplace in international commercial arbitration but are much less common in international inter-State adjudication. It is for this reason that the practice of the Court in this case is particularly interesting.

By email Pakistan requested that India produce a number of documents that had been referred to in India's Counter-Memorial.[222] Meanwhile India requested that Pakistan produce additional information on the purpose of the construction of Adit 1 and the range of uses it could be put to in relation to KHEP,[223] and later on 13 January 2012 requested that Pakistan provide a copy of the Environmental Impact Assessment (EIA) and other assessments for the NJHEP and technical details of the four upstream projects planned.[224] These queries were resolved satisfactorily at the merits stage of proceedings.[225]

In relation to one particular letter requested, the CWPC letter, Pakistan had requested that it be disclosed in full since it was central to India's case, and, importantly, that the Court was competent to do so under Paragraph 20 of Annexure G of the Treaty.[226] On the other hand, India argued that the letter itself was not relevant to the case at hand, that it did not rely on it 'in terms of Rule 11(i)(a) of the Supplementary Procedural Rules' and that lastly the full disclosure of the unredacted letter risked 'prejudice to India', also making reference to the Official Secrets Act 1923 in force in both India and Pakistan.[227] The requests between the parties for the disclosure of information prompted the Court itself to intervene and notify the parties of the procedure that would cover Pakistan's application for production of the CWPC letter:

> India is requested to provide to all Members of the Court (through the Registrar) a full copy of [the CWPC] letter at India's earliest convenience, but *in no case later* than Tuesday, February 7, 2012. By no later than

---

[222] *Kishenganga Partial Award* para 91; specifically an unredacted version of a letter from 1960 from the Chairman of India's Central Water and Power Commission (the CWPC Letter), a letter dated 13 January 1958 referred to in the CWPC letter, the preliminary hydro-electric survey of the Indus basin and letter of 13 January and revised environmental impact assessments conducted in 2006 (EIAs). This request was later reiterated on 21 January; see para 95.
[223] Email communication 5 January 2012, ibid. para 92.   [224] Ibid. para 93.
[225] Hearing Tr. (Day 5), 24 August 2012, at 145:15 to 146:8, ibid. para 102.
[226] See Procedural Order No. 8.   [227] See Procedural Order No. 8.

## 3.2 RECENT INTER-STATE ARBITRATIONS

Tuesday, February 7, 2012, India is to provide its views on any applicable principle of state secrecy or privilege that the Court should take into account in deciding Pakistan's disclosure application. Pakistan is invited to comment on India's submission by no later than Friday, February 10, 2012.[228]

In reply to Pakistan and the Court's prompting, India provided a full, unredacted copy of the CWPC letter along with a copy of the Official Secrets Act 1923 (India) and a copy of the Official Secrets Act 1923 (Pakistan) – each party restating their respective positions.[229]

In order to resolve this impasse the Court passed Procedural Order No. 8 on 14 February 2012. Significantly, the Court stated that it 'believes that any Party offering a document in evidence should provide the full document' and noted that indeed, under Paragraph 20 of Annexure G and Article 13(2) of the Supplemental Rules of Procedure, it had the power to '*require* from the Parties the production of all papers and other evidence it considers necessary'[230] either *proprio motu* or at the request of one of the parties. In attempting to balance its views that a party should disclose information in full with India's concerns regarding official secrets, the Court proposed a compromise solution of seeking an examination of the material *in camera* before making a judgement as to whether it should be disclosed in full to the other party.[231] After reviewing the document the Court found that it was not directly relevant to the issues currently in dispute and that 'the non-disclosure of the redacted passages will not hamper Pakistan's ability to respond to the arguments made in India's Counter-Memorial'.[232] This practice can be seen as similar as the approach of the Court in the *Guyana/Suriname* arbitration without the formal appointment of an independent expert to review the evidence. Nevertheless we can see active engagement from the Court in eliciting and procuring information from the parties through compromise.

### 3.2.4 (vi) Expert witnesses

Under paragraph 3.2 of Procedural Order No. 9 on 15 June 2012 the parties indicated the names of both the experts and the witnesses whom they intended to cross-examine. Due to the fact the oral proceedings are

---

[228] *Kishenganga Partial Award* para 97, 1 February 2012 (emphasis added).
[229] Ibid. on 7 and 9 February 2012 (emphasis added).
[230] See Procedural Order No. 8, at 3.1.   [231] See Procedural Order No. 8, at 3.4.
[232] See Procedural Order No. 8, at 3.5.

not publicly available it is not possible to comment in any great detail on the value added to the tribunal's fact-finding process by the cross-examination of expert witnesses or the exact format that such examination followed. However, at the very least it can be said that in conducting cross-examination of both witnesses and experts, by all accounts a valuable element of the proceedings,[233] the procedural approach of the arbitral tribunal, and of the parties themselves, is notably more proactive than the ICJ.

### 3.2.4 (vii) The Kishenganga arbitration in the round

The arbitral tribunal in *Kishenganga*, like the preceding two, has taken a proactive approach to fact-finding.[234] From the outset the tribunal showed a willingness to become actively involved in the fact-finding process through the agreement to undertake a site visit (and a later follow-up visit). Furthermore the tribunal was forthright in requesting information from the parties that it felt it required in order to establish a solid factual foundation upon which to decide the case. In relation to the disputed documents, the arbitral tribunal was also similarly proactive in mediating the dispute and although it stopped short of going as far as the tribunal in *Guyana/Suriname* in appointing an independent expert, it did take extra steps to examine the information *in camera* before making a judgement on its relevance to the case at hand. This approach appears to have been acceptable to both parties. And whilst the tribunal did not appoint any experts of its own in this case, this can more likely be attributed to the composition of the Panel itself which was deliberately made up of arbitrators with relevant expertise in the required areas (and the fact that experts were appointed by the parties themselves). As such, there is much to consider in the approach of the tribunal when considering potential lessons for the ICJ.

## 3.3 Chapter 3 summary

What can be gleaned from this brief survey of the practice of the WTO adjudicative bodies and recent inter-State arbitrations? First of all, it can be

---

[233] Foster, 'New Clothes for the Emperor? Consultation of Experts by the International Court of Justice' 3; *Kishenganga Partial Award*; see also *Guyana v. Suriname Arbitration*; *Abyei Arbitration Award*.

[234] Jacur, 'Remarks on the Role of Ex Curia Scientific Experts in International Environmental Disputes' 450.

said that the approach of the two most popular means of settling international disputes today to fact-finding is generally more proactive than the ICJ. However, this fact should not be surprising in itself. These tribunals have different constitutive instruments, operate as part of different institutional structures (or as part of no strict institutional structure, as the case may be) and certainly do not carry the same symbolic value nor bear the same burden in terms of progressive development of international law as the ICJ does. Indeed, in some instances the differences between the tribunals are more clearly apparent; in particular in relation to the fact that there is no permanent bench of arbitrators (despite the PCA being nominally 'permanent') or in relation to the flexibility regarding the Rules of Procedure that arbitrating States enjoy. Nevertheless, the tribunals have more similarities than differences. All are tribunals dealing with States, applying international law and playing an important role in the peaceful settlement of international disputes.

As such, the differences between the approaches of the tribunals to the issue of fact-finding cannot simply be dismissed as inevitable given their genetic make up. Rather, many of the differences identified are the result of a more or less proactive attitude to fact-finding. But what can be said are the main differences? There are a number of aspects of the fact-finding process that are particularly distinctive:

1. First of all, both the WTO adjudicative bodies and inter-State arbitrations more actively engage with the case before them through asking questions and requesting information. In both cases the tribunals come close to asserting a power to compel the disclosure of evidence.
2. Secondly, the WTO adjudicative bodies have (with limited success) attempted to assert a clear burden of proof through the *prima facie* case requirement to take more control over the fact-finding process.
3. Thirdly, both the WTO adjudicative bodies and inter-State arbitration both regularly hear and examine witnesses put before them by the parties and more significantly, appoint their own experts in seeking to better evaluate the evidence put before them.
4. Fourthly, in addition to the (already remarkably proactive in comparison to the ICJ) step of requesting information from the parties, both the WTO adjudicative bodies and inter-State arbitrations have also drawn adverse inferences from a party's failure to produce the requested information.
5. Fifthly, one arbitral tribunal undertook a site visit (and necessary follow-up visit). The site visit mechanism is one which has been

seldom used by the ICJ but one which by all accounts was significant in the arbitration in question.

These aspects of the fact-finding processes of the tribunals examined in this chapter stand out as being significantly different from the approach taken by the ICJ. In fact, in these respects the tribunals examined mark themselves out as clearly more proactive in terms of fact-finding than the ICJ. It is this conclusion that begs the question of whether by adopting a similarly proactive approach to fact-finding, such as being more assertive in its requests for information, the ICJ could perhaps remedy some the current fact-finding deficiencies examined in the previous chapter. It is this question, the possibility of seeing a Court more proactively engaging in the process of fact-finding, and the potential obstacles facing the Court were it to choose to do so, that is the focus of the following chapters.

# 4

# Winds of change: the possibility of reform

Richard B. Lillich famously argued that the Court often fails 'to take advantage of existing procedures to help unearth the facts that may be the key to the resolution of disputes'.[1] This point was made and developed at length in Chapters 1 and 2. However, it is the conclusions that Lillich drew from this state of affairs that are the subject of this chapter, namely that the Court should 'be far more aggressive in seeking the facts' and utilising the fact-finding tools it already possesses.[2] This chapter seeks to draw on the practice of the other international tribunals examined in Chapter 3 and suggests that there are a number of avenues open to the Court that could potentially remedy some of its current fact-finding weaknesses:

1. The first relates to the possibility of making greater use of the fact-finding powers that the Court already possesses. Section 4.1 explores the possibility of the Court taking a teleological approach to its Statute and Rules and the so-called duty of collaboration in asking whether the Court could construe its fact-finding powers to compel the production of evidence, as opposed to merely requesting it.
2. Secondly, the possibility of better utilising the Court's power to order provisional measures under Article 41 of its Statute is examined.
3. Thirdly, relating to both the fact-finding and fact-assessment processes, Section 4.3 explores the possibility of increased use of experts, the refinement of the current procedure for the presentation of expert evidence and greater use of cross-examination as a way of aiding the Court in effectively assessing the facts put before it by the parties.

---

[1] R. B. Lillich, *Fact-Finding before International Tribunals: Eleventh Sokol Colloquium* (Irvington-on-Hudson, NY: Transnational, 1992) 76.
[2] Ibid.

Subsequently Chapter 5 examines the merits of taking a more proactive approach to fact-finding as facilitated in the manner set out in the present chapter.

## 4.1 Developing a power to compel the disclosure of evidence

The first avenue the Court could explore in taking a more proactive approach to the facts relates to the possibility of making greater use of the fact-finding powers the Court already possesses. This section explores the possibility of the Court taking a teleological approach to its Statute and Rules and relying on the so-called duty of collaboration in asking whether the Court could potentially construe its fact-finding powers to compel the production of evidence, as opposed to merely requesting it.

### 4.1.1 As things stand: discovery and the unclear binding nature of Article 49 ICJ Statute

As we saw in Chapter 1, the Court possesses considerable fact-finding powers including the ability to request information from the parties under Article 49 of its Statute. However, in practice the Court has not made any significant use of this fact-finding power. Instead, the consistent practice of the Court has been to allow the parties to retain almost exclusive control over the fact-finding process whilst it has played a reactive role in this process.[3]

But what of the suggestion that the Court could interpret its Article 49 powers to seek information as being binding on the parties? Tams states that whilst this would undoubtedly increase the effectiveness of the Court in its dispute settlement role, *de lege lata*, 'the more convincing view is that the parties are under no legal obligation to comply with

---

[3] In the absence of a prosecutor no explicit duty of disclosure exists in this regard as it does before international criminal tribunals such as the ICTY. Rule 66 of the ICTY's Rules of Evidence and Procedure states that the Prosecution is under an obligation to provide the Defence with all material concerning the indictment in the accused's case within thirty days of the accused's first appearance. Further, paragraph B states that when the Defence requests, the Prosecution must allow access to 'books, documents, photographs and tangible objects in the Prosecutor's custody or control' which will be used as evidence in the trial, belonged to the accused or could assist the Defence in preparing for the trial. Rule 67(B) provides the corresponding right for the Prosecution in relation to information in the possession of the Defence. Rule 68 also provides an additional obligation on the Prosecutor to disclose exculpatory material.

## 4.1 THE DISCLOSURE OF EVIDENCE

requests under Art. 49',[4] since, where this duty is imposed on States, the relevant statutory instruments or Rules of Procedure will usually state this clearly or heavily imply such a duty.[5] Indeed, the wording of Article 49 merely states that the Court can 'call upon' parties to submit evidence and as such has been described as a 'rather meagre substitute for real powers for procuring evidence, which the ICJ does not possess'.[6]

The argument could be made that States are under an obligation to comply with requests for information under Article 49 of the Statute as a result of the fact that the UN Charter imposes an obligation on States to comply with 'decisions' of the Court. However, as Brown has demonstrated, it is unlikely that orders requesting information under Article 49 could be regarded as decisions in themselves, highlighting that the consequences for not complying with requests under Article 49 are set out expressly in that provision, namely the possibility of 'formal note' being taken of such a refusal, not a breach of the Charter.[7]

A legal obligation for parties to comply with requests for information is regularly imposed on parties before other international courts and tribunals. Some have a specific power set out in their constitutive instrument,[8] whilst others such as the ICTY and ICTR derive such a power from a special source. To elaborate, the Appeals Chamber of the ICTY stated in the *Blaškić* case that it possessed a power to compel the production of information in Article 29 of the Court's Statute arising from 'the provisions of Chapter VII and Article 25 of the United Nations Charter and from the Security Council Resolution adopted pursuant to these provisions'.[9] The ICTY at the time described this power as 'novel and indeed unique' – arising as it did from the Security Council's Chapter VII powers.[10] Other international tribunals such as the adjudicative bodies of the WTO have established a binding power through judicial interpretation – an issue to which we shall return presently.

---

[4] Tams, 'Article 49' 1107; citing *Canada-Aircraft (Complaint by Brazil)*, Appellate Body Report, reproduced in Dispute Settlement Reports (1999), Vol III, 1377 para 188.
[5] Ibid.    [6] Ibid.
[7] Chester Brown, *A Common Law of International Adjudication* (Oxford University Press, 2007) 106.
[8] See for instance Article 86 Rome Statute, Article 24(3) Rules of Procedure of Iran–US Claims Tribunal and other arbitral tribunals such as Article 55 of the German–Polish Mixed Arbitral Tribunal and Article 90 of the German-French Mixed Arbitral Tribunal; see Tams, 'Article 49' footnote 47.
[9] *Prosecutor v. Blaškić* 100 ILR 688, 699.    [10] Ibid.

Nevertheless, international legal scholarship has traditionally regarded the ICJ's powers to request information from the parties as lacking binding legal force. For instance, Highet has stated that the Court's most significant impediment to functioning decisively in evidentiary positions is its inability to compel the production of evidence or subpoena witnesses.[11] Similarly, Alford Jr stated that whilst the Court may request information from the parties and international organisations, without a power to compel production, 'the Court tends to rely heavily upon the evidence submitted without positive efforts to police the truth of the facts'.[12]

As well as not making any significant use of its Article 49 ICJ Statute power to request information, the Court has not developed a practice of granting discovery requests (whereby one party may request that the Court order the other party to produce documentation relevant to the case before it) as generally found in common law jurisdictions. One exception is the *ELSI* case in which counsel for Italy complained that the United States had not put forward crucial evidence and requested that the United States make available to the Court a financial statement of the year 1967 of Raytheon/ELSI's auditors which the United States had referred to in its oral argument but had not produced.[13] In mentioning but not producing the information, the United States appeared to be in breach of Article 56(4) of the Court's Rules which prohibit any reference during the oral proceedings to information that has not been put before the Court under Article 43 of the Statute or that is not readily available to the public.[14]

Italian counsel asked the Chamber to request the financial statement be disclosed in accordance with Article 49 of the Statute and Article 62(1) of the Rules, and the President requested the United States to do so.[15] The United States complied with the request for disclosure promptly, and the document proved to be significant to the outcome of the case.[16] Italy's

---

[11] Highet, 'Evidence, the Court, and the Nicaragua Case' 10.
[12] Alford Jr, 'Fact Finding by the World Court'.
[13] In fact Italy made an issue of the fact that the United States had not put forward the evidence of its own volition and had to be asked to disclose it, saying the evidence 'was not filed voluntarily with the Applicant's pleadings, although one might have expected that they would have been considered rather important, in the interests of justice and the amicable resolution of a matter of this kind; Verbatim Record C 3/CR 89/8 of 23 February 1989 19.
[14] See Article 56(4) of the Court's Rules.
[15] Verbatim Record C 3/CR 89/4 of 16 February 1989 45.
[16] See *ELSI Case* 26 para 19 and 53 para 79.

request for information was described by one commentator as 'unprecedented' in the history of the Court, a form of (indirect) discovery, in providing 'an effective substitute for more forthright discovery powers'.[17] What the Court would have done had the United States refused to comply with the Court's request is unclear and this remains the sole example of the Court agreeing to a request for information. For instance, as we saw in Chapter 2, in the *Bosnian Genocide* case the Court refused to order Serbia to produce the minutes of the Serbian Supreme Defence Council, which were believed to be the evidence that would prove that the army of the *Republika Srpska* was under the control of Serbia, stating that the Court had sufficient evidence before it, including ICTY records.[18] Relatedly, in the recent preliminary objections phase of the *Croatian Genocide* case, the Court refused a similar request made by Croatia, stating that it was 'not satisfied that the production of the requested documents was necessary for the purpose of ruling on preliminary objections'.[19] As such the practice of the Court shows that it has not routinely either been asked to make orders for discovery or consented to granting them.[20] Given the lack of practice in this area it is not surprising that the Court has not laid out any guidelines as to what conditions must be met to ensure the granting of a discovery order.[21]

Nevertheless, these traditional conceptions of the Court's powers to request information, and its limited use of any form of discovery procedure, do not tell the whole story. In fact, in light of the practice of other international courts and tribunals, the Court could feasibly interpret its powers to insist upon the disclosure of evidence. In this regard, the practice of the WTO adjudicative bodies merits attention.

### 4.1.2 *'Should' means 'shall'? The curious case of Article 13 WTO DSU*

As we saw in Chapter 3 at Section 3.1.2.1, Article 13 of the WTO Dispute Settlement Understanding formally grants Panels a broad power to request information from parties appearing before them. Article 13 provides the Panels with an investigative power that is not limited

---

[17] Highet, 'Evidence, The Chamber, and the ELSI Case' 60.
[18] *Bosnian Genocide Case* 129 para 206.
[19] *Croatian Genocide Preliminary Objections*, 416 paras 13–15.
[20] Benzing, 'Evidentiary Issues' 1249.   [21] Ibid.

to scientific or technical evidence or even to expert evidence.[22] In fact, the Appellate Body (AB) has held that Panels can seek information from any relevant source it so chooses[23] and that in principle there are no limits to this discretionary authority.[24] In the words of the AB in *Canada – Civilian Aircraft*, Panels are 'vested with ample and extensive discretionary authority to determine *when* it needs information to resolve a dispute and *what* information it needs'.[25] On the face of it, it would appear that the use of the term 'should' rather than 'shall' in Article 13.1 gives requests an exhortatory character as opposed to binding legal effect.[26] Consequently, requests for information made of parties under Article 13 would not be compulsory, and similarly individuals would be under no binding obligation to provide information (nor would Members themselves be obliged to require individuals provide the requested information).[27]

However, despite the fact that a literal reading of Article 13 does not appear to impose a binding legal obligation on the parties to comply with requests for information, there has been some suggestion in recent times that Article 13 nevertheless places a binding duty on parties. For instance, in *Canada – Civilian Aircraft* the AB stated that although the term 'should' has an exhortatory character, it could also 'express a duty or obligation.'[28] As such, consideration of the facts of the *Canada – Civilian Aircraft* case is warranted.

Brazil raised a preliminary motion requesting documentary discovery at the very beginning of the case (even before any submissions had been made) asking the Panel to undertake extensive 'additional fact-finding'.[29]

---

[22] Pauwelyn, 'The Use of Experts in WTO Dispute Settlement'.
[23] *Argentina – Measures Affecting Imports of Footwear, Apparel and Other Items*, Appellate Body Report, 27 March 1998, WT/DS56/AB/R para 84.
[24] See *Canada – Measures Affecting the Export of Civilian Aircraft*, Appellate Body Report, WT/DS70/AB/R, 2 August 1999 para 185.
[25] *Canada – Measures Affecting the Export of Civilian Aircraft*, Appellate Body Report, WT/DS70/AB/R, 2 August 1999 para 192 (emphasis in original). In this same case the Appellate Body held that a *prima facie* case did not need to be established before a panel had the right to seek information about the allegations; see para 185.
[26] Lichtenbaum, 'Procedural Issues in WTO Dispute Resolution' 1252.    [27] Ibid.
[28] *Canada – Measures Affecting the Export of Civilian Aircraft*, Appellate Body Report, WT/DS70/AB/R, 2 August 1999 para 187; see Behboodi, '"Should" means "Shall": A Critical Analysis of the Obligation to Submit Information Under Article 13.1 of the DSU in the Canada – Aircraft Case'.
[29] Specifically, Brazil requested 'the complete details of all operations of the Export Development Corporation, the Canada Account, the Technology Partnerships Canada and its predecessor programs, the Canada-Québec Subsidiary Agreement on Industrial Development, and the Société de Développement Industruel du Québec with regard to the civil aircraft industry, including all grants, loans, equity infusions, and loan guarantees, or any

## 4.1 THE DISCLOSURE OF EVIDENCE

In the course of the case Brazil argued that Canada was under a legal obligation to disclose the information requested of it and averred that it was under a duty to fully co-operate with the tribunal.[30]

Canada, meanwhile, refused to comply with Brazil's wide-ranging requests for information, accusing Brazil of having 'embarked on a fishing expedition and cast a drift-net – and has asked the Panel to pilot the ship.'[31] Crucially, Canada did not deny that it had a duty of collaboration with the tribunal, but argued that this duty only came into effect with regard to countering the legal arguments and evidence produced against it.[32] In other words, Canada argued that the duty of collaboration only came into effect when the other party had made a *prima facie* case against it, and that in cases where the other party is arguably engaging in a 'fishing expedition' for information, this duty did not apply.[33] The duty of collaboration is one that we will return to examine in greater detail in Section 4.1.4.

Canada also argued, relying on *Japan – Agricultural Products*, that Article 13 DSU does not permit the Panel to engage in fact-finding for the purpose of making the case of a claimant.[34] As such, Canada refused to co-operate with what it called a 'shot-gun' request for information and argued that there was nothing in GATT or WTO jurisprudence that substantiated the position that a responding party can be subject to a process of discovery.[35]

However, the AB upheld that Panel's right to make binding requests, arguing that if Article 13 DSU were to be interpreted as representing merely a non-binding request for information, the Panel's 'right to seek information' would be rendered meaningless.[36] As such, the AB pointed

---

other direct or indirect financial contribution of any kind'; see Letter from the Government of Brazil to Mr David de Pury, Chairman of the Panel, 23 October 1998.

[30] *Canada – Measures Affecting the Export of Civilian Aircraft*, Appellate Body Report, WT/DS70/AB/R, 2 August 1999 para 186 onwards.

[31] Reply Submission of Canada, 30 October 1998 para 3.

[32] Brazil's Appellant's Submission para 53.

[33] Further, in the *Argentina – Footwear* Panel report, the Panel discussed the duty to collaborate, citing the work of Kazazi in this regard, who had previously argued that the duty of collaboration did not arise until one party had presented a *prima facie* case; Kazazi, *Burden of Proof and Related Issues: A Study on Evidence before International Tribunals* 573.

[34] See *Japan – Measures Affecting Agricultural Products*, Appellate Body Report, WT/DS76/AB/R, 19 March 1999 paras 129–30.

[35] Reply Submission of Canada, 30 October 1998 para 6.

[36] *Canada – Measures Affecting the Export of Civilian Aircraft*, Appellate Body Report, WT/DS70/AB/R, 2 August 1999 para 187; the AB also relied on Article 3.10 obligation to engage in proceedings in 'good faith'; See AB Reports in *EC – Hormones*, *US – Shrimp*, *Canada – Aircraft* para 184.

to the wording of Article 13.1 that WTO Members were under a duty to 'respond promptly and in full' to requests for information made by the Panels,[37] suggesting that this stipulation added further weight to the argument that 'should' ought to be read as 'shall' in this provision.[38] The AB went on to state that:

> To hold that a Member party to a dispute is not legally bound to comply with a panel's request for information relating to that dispute, is, in effect, to declare that Member legally free to preclude a panel from carrying out its mandate and responsibility under the DSU. So to rule would be to reduce to an illusion and a vanity the fundamental right of Members to have disputes arising between them resolved through the system and proceedings for which they bargained in concluding the DSU. We are bound to reject an interpretation that promises such consequences.[39]

As such, the AB 'transformed the right of a panel to *seek* information ... into a right to *obtain* such information' in order to ascertain the facts of a dispute.[40]

Perhaps unsurprisingly, the AB's interpretation of the fact-finding power contained in Article 13 DSU has come in for criticism. For instance, Kuyper has pointed out that inferring a binding duty to provide evidence from the obligation to act in good faith is somewhat unsound since any refusal to do so, whilst providing a satisfactory basis upon which to draw adverse inferences, does not warrant taking the extra step of extrapolating a duty to provide information, a duty described as 'an unnecessary logical step and construed on the basis of rather flimsy contextual analysis'.[41] Furthermore, as one commentator has stated, 'where judicial or arbitral bodies can impose upon States a duty to disclose evidence, the statutory instruments or procedural rules will say so, or will at least clearly imply it'.[42] The question in this case is whether Article 13 can be read as clearly implying a duty to

---

[37] *Canada – Measures Affecting the Export of Civilian Aircraft*, Appellate Body Report, WT/DS70/AB/R, 2 August 1999 para 187.
[38] Marceau and Hawkins, 'Experts in WTO Dispute Settlement' 499.
[39] *Canada – Aircraft*, Appellate Body Report para 189.
[40] Behboodi, '"Should" means "Shall": A Critical Analysis of the Obligation to Submit Information Under Article 13.1 of the DSU in the Canada – Aircraft Case' 585. In addition, the *Argentina – Footwear* case made a different argument regarding the duty of a party to disclose information that was in their sole possession; *Argentina – Measures Affecting Imports of Footwear, Textiles, Apparel and Other Items*, Panel Report, WT/DS56/R, 25 November 1997 para 6.40.
[41] Kuyper, 'The Appellate Body and the Facts' 321.   [42] Tams, 'Article 49' 1107.

disclose requested information or not – a question not definitively answered in the case law.

Further, another commentator has questioned the dangerous precedent created by such an interpretation, asking 'how are government lawyers and private sector counsel to advise their clients as to the nature and scope of their obligation? How are future negotiators to be counselled on drafting treaty language?'[43]

It would appear at the very least, however, that Panels and the AB conceive of Article 13 as granting a power to compel the production of evidence in a way that is notably more proactive than the ICJ, for instance.[44] Although the AB's reasoning in this case may be far from satisfactory, the end result of asserting a power to compel the disclosure of information did not provoke outrage from WTO Members. It is suggested that the same result can be achieved for the ICJ through less problematic legal reasoning, as the following section will set out.

### 4.1.3 Developing a power to compel the disclosure of evidence for the ICJ

Judge Owada, in the *Oil Platforms* case, argued that the Court has in the past been overly concerned with the sovereign nature of the parties before it and the desire to not appear to favour one party over another. In other words, the Court's preoccupation with appearing impartial has meant that it has under-utilised its Article 49 ICJ Statute power to request information from the parties. Judge Owada argued that the Court, as a court of justice, must act like one in the course of judicial proceedings and do all that it can to address the problems caused by the Court's traditional reactive approach to fact-finding.[45] In order to do so, he argued that 'the only way to achieve this would have been for the Court to take a more proactive stance on the issue of evidence and that of fact-finding'.[46]

---

[43] Behboodi, '"Should" means "Shall": A Critical Analysis of the Obligation to Submit Information Under Article 13.1 of the DSU in the Canada – Aircraft Case' 578.

[44] Lichtenbaum, 'Procedural Issues in WTO Dispute Resolution' 1252; *Argentina – Measures Affecting Imports of Footwear, Textiles, Apparel and Other Items*, Panel Report, WT/DS56/R, 25 November 1997 paras 6.52–6.54.

[45] *Oil Platforms (Islamic Republic of Iran v. United States of America)*, Judgment, ICJ Reports 2003 161; Dissenting Opinion of Judge Owada at 321.

[46] Ibid. Dissenting Opinion of Judge Owada at 321.

The need for a more proactive approach extends beyond the facts of the *Oil Platforms* case to all cases where the Court's traditionally reactive approach to fact-finding is a hindrance to the proper administration of justice (see Chapter 2). Drawing on the practice of the WTO adjudicative bodies, there is little preventing the Court from requesting information from the parties again in the future and insisting that its powers to do so are compulsory, in the right circumstances.[47] Such circumstances would include where the information requested is in the sole possession of one party, where the other party has made a *prima facie* case and where it can demonstrate that it has made reasonable efforts to obtain the information requested, conditions to which we shall return in Section 4.1.4(iv).

The Court's extensive fact-finding powers and the broad wording of Article 49 of the Statute and Article 62 of the Rules permit an interpretation of the Court's powers that holds that it has the power to compel production and draw adverse inferences from any unexplained refusal to do so. Quite simply, the open wording of Article 49 of the Court's Statute and the corresponding Article 62 of the Rules mean that the Court would not need to engage in the type of linguistic gymnastics that the WTO adjudicative bodies were forced into in order to construe its power to seek information as binding on the parties to the case before it. Article 49 of the Statute states plainly that the Court 'may, even before the hearing begins, call upon the agents to produce any document or to supply any explanations' whilst Article 62 of the Rules relatedly states that the Court 'may at any time call upon the parties to produce such evidence or to give such explanations as the Court may consider to be necessary for the elucidation of any aspect of the matters in issue, or may itself seek other information for this purpose.' Quite plainly, interpreting the Court's power to 'call upon' agents or parties to produce evidence it 'considers to be necessary for the elucidation of any aspect of the matters in issue' is less of a stretch compared to interpreting that a party 'should' produce information to mean that it 'shall' do so.

Whilst, admittedly, international courts and tribunals that possess such compulsory powers of production usually have this power explicitly laid out in statutory form, the trailblazing example of the WTO adjudicative bodies could act as a precedent for the Court. Furthermore, any purposive interpretation of its Article 49 powers to request information, in line with the principle of effectiveness, point to the conclusion that the

---

[47] Highet, 'Evidence, The Chamber, and the ELSI Case'.

argument that the Court can issue binding requests for information is not completely implausible.

A purposive interpretation of the provisions that contain the Court's fact-finding powers is permitted as part of the customary rule for treaty interpretation as set out in Article 31(1) of the 1969 Vienna Convention on the Law of Treaties (VCLT). This 'general rule of interpretation' states that that '[a] treaty shall be interpreted in good faith and in accordance with the ordinary meaning to be given to the terms of the treaty in their context and in the light of its object and purpose.' The WTO has given the most concise statement of the 'general rule of interpretation' set out in Article 31(1) of the VCLT in recent times in the *US – Shrimp* case, stating that:

> A treaty interpreter must begin with, and focus upon, the text of the particular provision to be interpreted. It is in the words constituting that provision, read in their context, that the object and the purpose of the states parties to the treaty must first be sought. Where the meaning imparted by the text itself is equivocal or inconclusive, or where confirmation of the correctness of the reading of the text itself is desired, light from the object and purpose of the treaty as a whole may be usefully sought.[48]

Whilst the ICJ has also stated that the ordinary meaning is the starting point for treaty interpretation which the interpretation must be based 'above all upon the text of the treaty',[49] the reference in Article 31(1) to the 'object and purpose' introduces an element of purposive, teleological interpretation.[50] Accordingly, despite the fact doing so is far from an exact science,[51] purposively interpreting its existing powers to request information to insist upon the production of evidence is an option open to the Court.

---

[48] *Import Prohibition of Certain Shrimp and Shrimp Products*, Appellate Body Report, WT/DS58/AB/R, 12 October 1998 para 114; see also I. Sinclair, *The Vienna Convention on the Law of Treaties* (2nd edn, Manchester University Press, 1984) 130.

[49] *Territorial Dispute (Libyan Arab Jamahiriya/Chad), Judgment, ICJ Reports 1994* 6 para 41.

[50] Jan Klabbers, 'Treaties, Object and Purpose', Max Planck Encyclopedia of Public International Law, opil.ouplaw.com.ezproxy.eui.eu/home/EPIL; Richard Gardiner, *Treaty Interpretation* (Oxford University Press, 2008) 194.

[51] See the difficulties noted in Jan Klabbers, 'Some Problems Regarding the Object and Purpose of Treaties' 8 *Finnish Yearbook of International Law* 138; Isabelle Buffard and Karl Zemanek, 'The "Object and Purpose" of a Treaty: An Enigma?" 3 *Austrian Review of International and European Law* 311; Ulf Linderfalk, 'On the Meaning of the "Object and Purpose" Criterion, in the Context of the Vienna Convention on the Law of Treaties, Article 19' 72 *Nordic Journal of International Law* 429.

This is especially so given the fact that purposive interpretation has 'traditionally played a part in the interpretation of constitutions of international organisations (and their implied powers) and other multilateral, "legislative" conventions' as well as the fact that in international law purposive interpretation is closely linked to the principle of effectiveness.[52] Crucially, the ICJ has in its case law consistently 'harnessed' the principle of effectiveness to the purposive interpretation of treaties. As such, any ambiguity or uncertainty may be interpreted in line with the object and purpose of the treaty as a whole in order to 'enable the treaty to have appropriate effects'.[53] An example of this can be seen in the *Territorial Dispute* case where the Court applied the principle of effectiveness with regards to the object and purpose of the treaty in seeking to delimit a settled boundary.[54] The Court interpreted the treaty provision so as best to give practical effect to the object and purpose of the treaty, and stated that doing otherwise 'would be contrary to one of the fundamental principles of interpretation of treaties, consistently upheld by international jurisprudence, namely that of effectiveness'.[55]

Drawing on such reasoning, the Court could purposively interpret its own fact-finding powers and assert that the way to best give effect to these powers is that they be considered binding on the parties. The Court's Statute (being without a preamble), Rules and the relevant provisions of the UN Charter provide little more than the fact that Court is both a principal organ and principal judicial organ of the United Nations.[56] Despite this, it is clear that the object and purpose of Article 49 of the Court's Statute, for example, is to ensure that the Court has all the facts it needs to make sound legal determinations, and if the Court felt that the most effective way to establish such facts was to compel the production of evidence it is difficult to imagine an argument that State parties could advance without somehow appealing to traditional privileges of State sovereignty and the control over the fact-production process

---

[52] Mark E. Villiger, 'Article 31 – General Rule of Interpretation' in Mark E. Villiger (ed), *Commentary on the 1969 Vienna Convention on the Law of Treaties* (The Hague: Martinus Nijhoff, 2009) 427; ILC, Report on the Draft Articles on the Law of Treaties, *Yearbook of the International Law Commission 1966*, Vol II, 219.

[53] Ibid.    [54] *Territorial Dispute* 25.

[55] Ibid.; the Court citing *Lighthouses Case between France and Greece, Judgment*, 1934, PCIJ Series A/B, No. 62, 27; *Namibia Advisory Opinion* 35 para 66; *Aegean Sea Continental Shelf Case* 22 para 52.

[56] See Articles 7(1) and 92 of the UN Charter.

that States have enjoyed in the past.[57] In short, through taking a teleological approach to this power the Court can begin to assert that parties must comply with its requests for information. Bolstering this interpretation is the related duty of collaboration.

### 4.1.4 The duty of collaboration and the burden of proof

#### (i) Definition

In the recent *Argentina – Footwear* case a Panel of the WTO adjudicative bodies, considering whether it should allow a request from the US to order the production of documents from Argentina, stated that the very idea of the peaceful settlement of international disputes by adjudication is founded on the notion of co-operation between the parties and that to this end there existed a 'rule of collaboration' with regard to the production of evidence.[58] It is this rule or duty that is considered in the following section.

However, before we can turn our attention to the duty of collaboration that is the topic of the following section, a preliminary word is needed about the burden of proof before the ICJ. Like the majority of international courts and tribunals[59] the burden of proof before the Court has always generally been said to lie with the party seeking to establish its case in accordance with the principle of *actori incumbit probatio*.[60] In this regard the status of the party as applicant or defendant is not *necessarily* determinative. In reality the Court does not operate a strict

---

[57] One possible exception is national security or 'prejudice to governmental interest' as recognised by Judge Jessup in his Separate Opinion in the *Barcelona Traction Preliminary Objections* case at para 97; the United Kingdom successfully argued that it was not bound to submit documents on the basis of 'naval secrecy' in the *Corfu Channel Case* 4; furthermore, in the *Bosnian Genocide Case* para 205 the Court noted that the requested documents had been redacted on grounds of national security in the course of refusing Bosnia's request for the Court to formally seek these documents.

[58] *Argentina – Measures Affecting Imports of Footwear, Textiles, Apparel and Other Items*, Panel Report, WT/DS56/R, 25 November 1997 para 6.40; similarly in *India – Patent Protection for Pharmaceutical and Agricultural Chemical Products*, Appellate Body Report, WT/DS50/AB/R, 19 December 1997 para 94.

[59] *Bosnian Genocide Case* para 204: '[o]n the burden or onus of proof, it is well established in general that the applicant must establish its case and that a party asserting a fact must establish it'; *Nicaragua Case* para 101: 'it is the litigant seeking to establish a fact who bears the burden of proving it.'

[60] *Pulp Mills Case* para 162; Sir Gerald Fitzmaurice, *The Law and Procedure of the International Court of Justice* (Cambridge: Grotius, 1986) 576; Wolfrum, 'International Courts and Tribunals, Evidence'.

burden of proof and it may be the case that in relation to different legal issues before the Court, different parties bear the burden at different times.[61] For instance, in the *Guinea v. Congo* case it was for one party to establish that local remedies were exhausted or that extenuating circumstances existed that avoided this requirement – whilst at the same time it was for the other side to prove that these local remedies had not been exhausted.[62] Similarly, in *Rights of US Citizens in Morocco*, the Court determined that the United States bore the burden of proving that its citizens had certain rights in the French Zone of Morocco, despite the fact that France was formally the applicant party in this case.[63] The Court's operation in this way means that when cases are brought before it through mutual agreement it has no need to alter its approach to the burden of proof.[64]

Additionally, the Court recently held in the *Pulp Mills* case that the burden (at least in the context of this particular case) does not shift in relation to the precautionary principle, stating that 'while a precautionary approach may be relevant in the interpretation and application of the provisions of the Statute, it does not follow that it operates as a reversal of the burden of proof'.[65] Similarly, the Court has not in the past stressed a strict standard of proof.[66] But what is the significance of there not being a strict burden of proof before the Court?

---

[61] See the argument made criticising the generally vague attitude to the burden of proof before the Court and supporting a variable burden depending on the facts of the case in *I.C.J. Pleadings, Pulp Mills*, CR 2009/15, 28 September 2009 10 para 15.

[62] *Case Concerning Ahmadou Sadio Diallo (Republic of Guinea v, Democratic Republic of the Congo), Judgment*, 30 November 2010 para 56: '[i]n short, when it comes to establishing facts such as those which are at issue in the present case, neither party is alone in bearing the burden of proof'. See also Higgins, 'Speech by H. E. Judge Rosalyn Higgins, President of the International Court of Justice to the Sixth Committee of the General Assembly'.

[63] *Case concerning rights of nations of the United States of America in Morocco, Judgment of August 27th, 1952, ICJ Reports 1952* 176; see Kolb, *The International Court of Justice* 931.

[64] See for instance *The Minquiers and Ecrehos case, Judgment of November 17th, 1953, ICJ Reports 1953* 47, 52.

[65] *Pulp Mills Case* para 164; Boyle and Harrison, 'Judicial Settlement of International Environmental Disputes: Current Problems' 267. It should be noted, however, that the Court's position in this regard is far from uncontested and that several scholars have argued persuasively to the contrary, the leading work in this regard being C. E. Foster, *Science and the Precautionary Principle in International Courts and Tribunals: Expert Evidence, Burden of Proof and Finality*, in particular chapters 5 and 6 for these purposes.

[66] See Valencia-Ospina, 'Evidence before the International Court of Justice' 203. As Fitzmaurice stated, the view in international law has always been that important international litigation should not depend on 'accidents of a largely procedural or formal situation'; see

## 4.1 THE DISCLOSURE OF EVIDENCE

Whilst the party alleging a claim generally bears the burden of proof in accordance with the principle of *actori incumbit probatio*, this party does not bear the burden of production of evidence alone. Once jurisdiction has been established in the case before the Court each party is under an obligation to collaborate with the Court in the establishment of a sound factual foundation upon which the Court can make legal determinations. And indeed, the Court most recently in the *Pulp Mills* case explicitly stated that both States were to co-operate in the production of evidence in order to assist the Court in order to resolve the dispute before it.[67]

The Court specifically mentioned that the parties ought to co-operate in the provision of evidence to the Court beyond that which supports their own case. It is this sort of statement and conception of the role of States in the fact-finding on which the Court could seize in order to take a more proactive approach to the facts. In doing so the ICJ could become more like other courts that have become more assertive in their own function and more assertive in emphasising the duty of collaboration whilst no longer seeing themselves as being at the mercy of the whims of States or of their sovereignty.

It has long been argued by international legal scholars that in light of the absence of an explicit power which would enable the Court to compel the production of evidence like those that exist in domestic law, States 'have a more extensive obligation to produce all evidence within their control than that normally imposed upon litigants in municipal proceedings'.[68] For instance, in Georges Scelle's report to the International Law Commission in 1950 as Special Rapporteur on Arbitral Procedure stated that 'il est ... un principe certain, c'est que les Etates en litige ont l'obligation de collaborer de bonne foi à l'administration de la preuve'.[69]

---

Fitzmaurice, *The Law and Procedure of the International Court of Justice* 576; Kolb, *The International Court of Justice* 944.

[67] *Pulp Mills Case* paras 162, 163, 168.

[68] Sandifer, *Evidence Before International Tribunals* 112; see also Wolfrum, 'International Courts and Tribunals, Evidence'; J. F. Lalive, 'Quelques remarques sur la preuve devant la Cour permanente et la Cour internationale de justice' 7 *Annuaire Suisse de Droit International* 77, 85 ; C. F. Amerasinghe, *Evidence in International Litigation* (Leiden, Boston: Martinus Nijhoff, 2005) 66.

[69] Arbitral Procedure, Document A/CN.4/18 Rapport par Georges Scelle, *Yearbook of the International Law Commission* (1950), Vol II, 134 [It is a certain principle, that litigating States have an obligation to collaborate in good faith in the administration of the evidence].

This obligation has often been termed the 'duty of collaboration', but what exactly is it? The duty of collaboration can be broadly defined as the obligation placed on States appearing as parties before international courts and tribunals to provide information necessary for the establishment of the facts of the case and the proper administration of justice more generally.[70] The duty of collaboration arises when States agree to submit their disputes to international adjudication.[71] As such, the rationale underpinning the duty of collaboration has much to do with the sovereign nature of the States appearing before the Court and the fundamentally important principle of consent in international law. As V. S. Mani famously stated, '[a]djudication cannot take place in a vacuum; it can function properly only if the parties are willing to co-operate with the tribunal by furnishing it with all necessary and relevant facts by way of evidence'.[72]

Once consent has been given to international adjudication it is a widely held position that parties are obligated to act in good faith and to put evidence before the tribunal 'so as to enable it to arrive at a viable and fair resolution of the conflicting claims'.[73] The duty of collaboration falls on both the claimant and defendant States, or any party appearing before the Court, and is meant to benefit all parties in this non-discriminatory manner.[74] The duty has a positive aspect, this being the duty to co-operate with the other party and with the Court to achieve the settlement of the dispute through the judicial process,[75] including the establishment of the factual foundation of the case. Similarly, there is a negative aspect to this duty, in that States are obligated not to destroy or deliberately obstruct access to information within their sole possession.[76] Whilst the rule of collaboration is not specifically mentioned in either the Court's Statute or Rules, the rule is contained in other international legal instruments.

---

[70] Sandifer, *Evidence before International Tribunals* 117; Mosk, 'The Role of Facts in International Dispute Resolution' 137.

[71] V. S. Mani, *International Adjudication: Procedural Aspects*, Vol 4 (The Hague: Kluwer Law International, 1980) 198.

[72] Ibid.; see also Kolb, *The International Court of Justice* 942.

[73] Mani and Mani, *International Adjudication: Procedural Aspects*; see also Benzing, 'Evidentiary Issues' 1247.

[74] Kazazi, *Burden of Proof and Related Issues: A Study on Evidence Before International Tribunals* 121.

[75] Benzing, 'Evidentiary Issues' 1247; citing A. Peters, 'International Dispute Settlement: A Network of Cooperational Duties' 14 *European Journal of International Law* 1.

[76] Benzing, 'Evidentiary Issues' 1247.

(ii) The duty of collaboration in international instruments

The 1907 Hague Convention contains a mention of the duty in relation to the Permanent Court of Arbitration. Article 75 lays down that States are under a duty 'to supply the tribunal, as fully as they consider possible, with all the information required for deciding the case.' The Draft on Arbitral Procedure produced by the International Law Commission in 1958 stated in Article 21 that:

> The parties shall cooperate with the tribunal in the production of evidence and shall comply with the measures ordered by the tribunal for this purpose. The tribunal shall take note of the failure of any party to comply with its obligations under this paragraph.[77]

This was developed even further in Article 10 of the 1962 Permanent Court of Arbitration Rules of Arbitration and Conciliation for Settlement of International Disputes between Two Parties of Which Only One Is a State, which states that 'the parties undertake to facilitate the work of the Commission and particularly to furnish it to the greatest possible extent with all relevant documents and information'.[78]

Similarly Rule 33(3) of the Rules of Procedure for Arbitration Proceedings (Arbitration Rules) of ICSID 1986 states that:

> The parties shall cooperate with the Tribunal in the production of evidence and in the other measures provided for in paragraph (2). The Tribunal shall take formal note of the failure of a party to comply with its obligations under this paragraph and of any reasons given for such failure.[79]

Further, Article 2 of the 1991 Resolution of the Institut de Droit International, on the subject of non-appearance, made reference to the duties of a State appearing before the Court. The Resolution states that 'in considering whether to appear or to continue to appear in any phase of proceedings before the Court, a State should have regard to its duty to co-operate in the fulfilment of the Court's judicial functions'.[80]

---

[77] Draft on Arbitral Procedure adopted by the International Law Commission at its Fifth Session, (1958), Article 21(2) in II *Yearbook of the International Law Commission*, A/CN.4/SER.A/1958/Add.1, 9 para 20; 20. Article 21 (formerly Article 15) could be placed before Article 20, for it is concerned with the general subject of the hearing of evidence before the closure of proceedings.

[78] Article 10, superseded by rules based on the UNICTRAL rules, www.pca-cpa.org/showfile.asp?fil_id=194.

[79] Rule 33(3) of the Rules of Procedure for Arbitration Proceedings (Arbitration Rules) of ICSID 1986.

[80] Institut de Droit International, Session of Basel, 1991, Non-Appearance before the International Court of Justice, Rapporteur, Arangio-Ruiz, Preamble.

In addition, Article 6 of Annex VII of UNCLOS relating to arbitral proceedings under the Convention provides explicitly for the duties of the parties to the dispute, stating that parties are under a duty to facilitate the work of the arbitral tribunal; a clear statement of the duty of collaboration. Subsection (a) provides that the parties are under a duty to provide the tribunal with 'all relevant documents, facilities and information' and subsection (b) provides that parties are under a duty to 'enable it when necessary to call witnesses or experts and receive their evidence and to visit the localities to which the case relates'.

However, these statutory documents reveal little about the content of the obligation. For more useful insight into the duty of collaboration it is to the case law of various international courts and tribunals that we must look.

### (iii) The duty of collaboration in international jurisprudence

The development of this duty can be traced throughout the history of international dispute settlement. The classic example most often cited is the *Parker* case before the Mexican Claims Commission, in which the Commission said:

> It is the duty of the respective Agencies to cooperate in searching out and presenting to this tribunal all facts throwing any light on the merits of the claim presented. The Commission denies the 'right' of the respondent to merely wait in silence in cases where it is reasonable that it should speak.[81]

It is interesting to note the similarity of the wording of this famous formulation of the duty of collaboration to the most recent high-profile invocation in the *Pulp Mills* case before the Court, to which we shall return.[82] The Commission also said that States were bound to make full disclosure of the facts reasonably within their knowledge or that can reasonably be ascertained by them, regardless of whether they are exculpatory or otherwise.[83] The Commission emphasised the relationship

---

[81] RIAA, Vol IV, 39.
[82] Contrast: 'It is ... to be expected that the Applicant should, in the first instance, submit the relevant evidence to substantiate its claims. This does not, however, mean that the Respondent should not co-operate in the provision of such evidence as may be in its possession that could assist the Court in resolving the dispute submitted to it'; *Pulp Mills Case* paras 162, 163, 168.
[83] *American–Mexican General Claims Commission, William A Parker (USA) v. United Mexican States*, Award of 31 March 1926, RIAA 4 (1951) 35, 39 para 6.

## 4.1 THE DISCLOSURE OF EVIDENCE

between the duty of collaboration and the principle relating to burden of proof, *actori incumbit probatio*, stating that:

> Whilst ordinarily it is incumbent upon the party who alleges a fact to introduce evidence to establish it, yet before this Commission this rule does not relieve the respondent from its obligation to lay before the commission all evidence within its possession to establish the truth, whatever it may be.[84]

As such, whilst it may be the case that the onus falls on the claimant State in cases before international tribunals, the burden in the production of evidence is not that State's burden alone. The duty of collaboration complements the rule of *actori incumbit probatio* 'and in cases where the full application of the latter may result in unreasonable consequences or impede the due process of the proceedings, the rule of collaboration plays a balancing role'.[85] The respondent State, in some cases, may be under a duty to collaborate with the court or tribunal in the establishment of the factual record. And indeed it has been argued that the duty of collaboration is not a mere formality; it is not enough that the party deny the claims made against it, rather, the party must justify its denial and put before the Court documents that are in its sole possession.[86]

Admittedly, the exact extent to which States must comply with requests for information is not entirely clear. As Feller stated with regard to the position taken by the Mexican Claims Commission, '[t]o the cynical observer of the habits of lawyers all this may seem nothing more than a pious wish.'[87] And indeed, the practice of international courts and tribunals since the *Parker* case does not indicate that a clear legal obligation on States to this full effect has been definitively established, with States being reluctant to put information damaging to their case before the tribunal in full knowledge of the fact that the Court plays an almost completely reactive role and that this information would be unlikely to come before the Court were they to withhold it.[88]

There is some evidence in recent case law of international tribunals that the duty of collaboration is one which could potentially be utilised to

---

[84] Ibid. 35, 39 para 6.
[85] Kazazi, *Burden of Proof and Related Issues: A Study on Evidence before International Tribunals* 121.
[86] Ibid.   [87] Ibid.
[88] See the position of the British Government in *Corfu Channel Case*; Mosk, 'The Role of Facts in International Dispute Resolution' 100.

bolster the obligation to provide requested evidence.[89] Should the Court choose to do so, it could rely on the duty of collaboration in order to enforce a power to compel the production of evidence. Indeed a number of States have advocated a rule of collaboration in their submissions to the Court.[90] Further, the ICJ itself recently made reference to the duty of collaboration in the *Pulp Mills* case, stating that:

> It is ... to be expected that the Applicant should, in the first instance, submit the relevant evidence to substantiate its claims. This does not, however, mean that the Respondent should not co-operate in the provision of such evidence as may be in its possession that could assist the Court in resolving the dispute submitted to it.[91]

As stated above, the sentiment expressed by the Court, namely that the party bearing the burden of proof does not bear the sole burden with regard to the production of evidence, is expressed in not dissimilar terms to the famous statement of the US–Mexican Claims Commission in the *Parker* case. Robert Kolb has argued that the duty of collaboration is especially pertinent in relation to the ICJ owing to nature of disputes before the Court the facts of which 'are often unique, often spread over a long period of time, and ... frequently difficult and uncertain of access.'[92] This being so, it is suggested that the duty of collaboration is one which could aid the Court in its fact-finding process and recent statements such as the one in the *Pulp Mills* case suggest that this is a course of action that the Court would not necessarily rule out.

Another prominent recent discussion of the duty of collaboration came in the aforementioned *Argentina – Footwear* case in which a Panel of the WTO adjudicative bodies stated that the very idea of the peaceful settlement of international disputes by adjudication is founded on the notion of co-operation between the parties, and that to this end there existed a 'rule of collaboration' with regard to the production of evidence.[93] Furthermore, in

---

[89] Mosk, 'The Role of Facts in International Dispute Resolution' 100; Kazazi, *Burden of Proof and Related Issues: A Study on Evidence before International Tribunals* 136; Riddell and Plant, *Evidence before the International Court of Justice* 98.
[90] I.C.J. Pleadings, The Wall A.O., CR 2004/1, 23 February 2004 para 57; see argument of Palestine that '[a]s a matter of policy a Member State should not be allowed to undermine the judicial function of the Court by refusing to place facts it considers essential before the Court, and then benefit from this situation by seeking to use it as a means of denying the Court jurisdiction.'
[91] *Pulp Mills Case* para 163.     [92] Kolb, *The International Court of Justice* 943.
[93] *Argentina – Measures Affecting Imports of Footwear, Textiles, Apparel and Other Items*, Panel Report, WT/DS56/R, 25 November 1997 para 6.40; similarly in *India – Patent*

## 4.1 THE DISCLOSURE OF EVIDENCE

the context of National Treatment, it has been argued that placing the onus of production on the party deemed to be 'better informed', in light of the duty of collaboration, could help to alleviate some of the informational issues facing adjudicators.[94] Being heavily influenced by law-and-economics literature, it has been argued that the best way to minimise the possibility of judicial mistakes, as well as ensuring the adjudicative body has the most accurate picture of the facts upon which to make judicial determinations, is to place the onus of production on the better-informed party. In fact, Foster has suggested that such arguments can be traced back to Jeremy Bentham, who famously stated that 'he should have the burden on whom it would sit lightest'.[95] Such 'better-informed' parties are defined as those who have access to information that the other party does not, or those who can gain access to information at a substantially lower cost. In theory, this would achieve the result that 'information that would otherwise not be available will be presented'.[96] Such proposals also arise in the in the anti-dumping context. These proposals advocate that in the case where a party does not answer the questions put to it by the Panel or in some way impedes the establishment of the factual record, the Panel may instead base its decision on the best facts available.[97]

Similarly, and most recently, in the context of the Annex V SCM Agreement mechanism, the AB stated that any interpretation of the information-gathering power contained in this provision that would frustrate the collection of evidence would be contrary not only to

---

*Protection for Pharmaceutical and Agricultural Chemical Products*, Appellate Body Report, WT/DS50/AB/R, 19 December 1997, the AB stated that parties should be 'fully forthcoming from the very beginning both as to the claims involved in the dispute and as to the facts relating to those claims ... Claims must be stated clearly. Facts must be disclosed freely', para 94.

[94] See Grossman, Horn and Mavroidis, 'Legal and Economic Principles of World Trade Law: National Treatment' 125; see also Mavroidis, *Trade in Goods* 295.

[95] John Bowring, *The Works of Jeremy Bentham*, Vol VI, 139, 136; C. E. Foster, 'Burden of Proof in International Courts and Tribunals' 29 *Australian Year Book of International Law* 27, 46.

[96] Grossman, Horn and Mavroidis, 'Legal and Economic Principles of World Trade Law: National Treatment' 126.

[97] Cameron and Orava, 'GATT/WTO Panels between Recording and Finding Facts' 229. Note the additional obligations placed on States to comply with Investigating Authorities in the context of Anti-Dumping and Subsidies; see Article 6.8 Anti-Dumping Agreement and Article 12.7 Subsidies and Countervailing Measures Agreement; under these provisions the Investigating Authorities are competent to make determinations on the basis of the facts available to them and specifically allow for the drawing of adverse inferences in the case of failure to produce requested information.

'WTO Members' manifest intention to promote the early and targeted collection of information' but also, crucially, contrary to 'the duty of cooperation to which a responding Member is subject'.[98]

In international arbitration too there have been recent pronouncements on the duty of collaboration. For instance, in the *Guyana/Suriname* arbitration discussed in Chapter 3 the Tribunal explicitly reminded the parties of the importance of the principle of collaboration in the course of international proceedings, citing Articles 5 and 6 of Annex VII of UNCLOS as well as Articles 7(1) and (2) of the Tribunal's own Rules of Procedure in support of this position.[99] As stated above, it is significant that the Tribunal set out in clear terms that once consent has been expressed the parties have a duty to collaborate with the Tribunal in the interests of the proper administration of justice.

Of course there are potential drawbacks to insisting that States are under a duty of collaboration to put information within their sole possession before the Court such as the fact that it may not be clear when information is 'within the sole possession' of one party or when the other has done all it can to secure the information.[100] Relatedly, there exists the danger that insisting on the duty of collaboration might encourage a flurry of speculative cases, or that any duty would disproportionately affect States with less resources.[101] In addition, commentators such as Benzing have argued that imposing such a duty on parties to provide evidence 'would mean a virtually unlimited duty of the parties to disclose all relevant facts and evidence, even in relation to evidence adverse to the interests of the party in possession of the particular document.'[102] Nevertheless, the implication that the insistence on any such duty of collaboration resulting in practice to 'a virtually unlimited duty' is an exaggeration since the duty is in fact subject to a number of conditions which restrict the number of situations in which States can be compelled to comply with this duty.

---

[98] *US - Measures Affecting Trade in Large Civil Aircraft (Second Complaint)*, Appellate Body Report, WT/DS353/AB/R, 12 March 2012 para 520.
[99] *Guyana v. Suriname Arbitration*.
[100] Lichtenbaum, 'Procedural Issues in WTO Dispute Resolution' 1254.
[101] Mavroidis, *Trade in Goods* 295.
[102] *The Parker Case* 35, 39 para 6; see also Commission appointed under Art. 26 of the ILO Constitution, *Complaint by the Government of Portugal Concerning the Observance by the Government of Liberia of the Forced Labour Convention*, 1930 (No. 29), Decision of 25 February 1963, ILR 36 (1968) 351, 378–9; Benzing, 'Evidentiary Issues' 1247.

(iv) A duty of collaboration that is conditional

Whilst the Court in fact has the right to insist that the parties, being under a duty of collaboration, co-operate with the Court in the fact-finding process,[103] this duty is not absolute. Rather, it is subject to a number of conditions, illustrated well by the Panel in *Argentina – Footwear*, which was careful to emphasise the two relevant conditions, namely: (i) that it only applies to the disclosure of evidence in the *sole possession* of the other party. The fact that States may be compelled to place before the Court any information within its sole possession is one with a long lineage with the Court stating in its very first case that a 'State may, up to a certain point, be bound to supply particulars of the use made by it of the means of information and inquiry at its disposal'.[104] Secondly, (ii) the duty does not arise until 'the claimant has done its best to secure evidence and has actually produced some prima facie evidence in support of its case'.[105]

As a result of these conditions it is clear that parties do not have the right to full compulsory discovery of the kind generally found in domestic common law legal systems, but rather a narrower power to insist on collaboration in the production of evidence subject to strict conditions. This distinction and the limitations on these powers make the prospect of the Court insisting on such a power before the ICJ a more realistic prospect, compared to the alternative of a more all-encompassing power of discovery.

In sum, what can be said about the operation of the duty of collaboration in international judicial practice to date? Whilst the Court's Statute

---

[103] Behboodi, '"Should" means "Shall": A Critical Analysis of the Obligation to Submit Information Under Article 13.1 of the DSU in the Canada – Aircraft Case' 582.
[104] *Corfu Channel Case* 18.
[105] *Argentina – Measures Affecting Imports of Footwear, Textiles, Apparel and Other Items*, Panel Report, WT/DS56/R, 25 November 1997 para 6.40; see Behboodi, '"Should" means "Shall": A Critical Analysis of the Obligation to Submit Information Under Article 13.1 of the DSU in the Canada – Aircraft Case' 582. Furthermore these criteria are reminiscent of the treatment of this issue before the Iran–US Claims Tribunal which has developed a number of safeguards against so-called fishing requests. In guarding against such requests, the practice emerged that the request made is firstly 'necessary', 'warranted' or 'appropriate' and that, secondly, the party had already taken 'all reasonable steps' to obtain the requested information; *Weatherford International Inc. and the Islamic Republic of Iran*, Case No. 305, Chamber Two, Order of 15 Februuary 1985; *Brown & Root Inc. and the Islamic Republic of Iran*, Case No. 432, Chamber One, Order of 4 January 1993. See, for example, Order of March 14, 1983 in *William Stanley Shashoua and Government of the Islamic Republic of Iran, et al.*, Case No. 69, Chamber One.

and Rules do not explicitly mention the duty of collaboration, and whilst Article 43(2) of the Statute appears only to require that States put information before the Court 'in support of their arguments',[106] nevertheless the argument that both parties appearing before the Court are under a duty of collaboration in relation to the production of evidence is strong.[107] The number of international instruments and support in international jurisprudence lend weight to this argument. To this end, if the Court were to choose to do so, subject to the conditions of sole possession, previous attempts to obtain information and the establishment of a *prima facie* case, the Court can insist that both parties are under a duty to put relevant information before the Court. Subsequent refusals to do so could result in the drawing of adverse inferences against that party (an issue examined in Section 4.2.6).[108]

Whilst it has been demonstrated that the Court could insist that parties to a case before it are under a duty to put relevant information before the Court, it is easy to see the shortcomings of such an approach. In cases of refusal to co-operate it would appear that the only option left open to the Court is to draw adverse inferences – a power that the Court already possesses. As such, the utility of insisting upon the compulsory nature of its power to order the production of evidence by the parties is open to question. This is an issue that will be addressed in greater detail in Chapter 5 Section 5.3 along with other shortcomings of the reforms proposed in this chapter. Presently, however, with the Court relying to such a significant extent on the consent of States, the assertion of the duty to collaborate undoubtedly provides the Court with another means by which to attempt to ensure the participation of those parties to a case before it in order to establish as close an approximation of the facts as possible.

## 4.2 Provisional measures

The following section argues that provisional measures are a further potential means of making binding requests for information. The Court's previous interpretation of its provisional measures powers and Article

---

[106] Benzing, 'Evidentiary Issues' 1247.
[107] Foster, 'Burden of Proof in International Courts and Tribunal' 46.
[108] Sean D. Murphy, 'The Experience of the Eritrea-Ethiopia Claims Commission' 106 *Proceedings of the Annual Meeting (American Society of International Law)* 237; Eritrea-Ethiopia Claims Commission, Rules of Procedure, Art 1.

41 of its Statute represents a model for the kind of creative restyling that the Court could and should undertake in order to remedy some of the deficiencies in the Court's current approach to fact-finding.[109] To elaborate, Article 41 of the Court's Statute, dealing with the Court's power to order provisional measures, states:

1. The Court shall have the power to indicate, if it considers that circumstances so require, any provisional measures which ought to be taken to preserve the respective rights of either party.
2. Pending the final decision, notice of the measures suggested shall forthwith be given to the parties and to the Security Council.[110]

The Court's power to order provisional measures is discretionary and exceptional.[111] This power is discretionary due to the fact that the Court is under no obligation to order provisional measures when requested to do so – Article 41 of the Statute stating that the Court need only provide provisional measures 'if it considers that circumstances so require'. The Court retains broad and unfettered discretion in this regard. Further, the power is exceptional due to the fact Article 41 of the Statute imposes strict constraints on when this power can be exercised, namely only in situations 'to preserve the respective rights of either party'.

Whilst the Court's power may be discretionary and exceptional, its binding force was for a long time somewhat uncertain due to the fact Article 41 does not explicitly state that such measures are binding on parties in cases that come before the Court. Although the Court's power to indicate provisional measures lies in the Statute, the Rules clarify the extent of this power, providing for example that the Court has the power

---

[109] This creative restyling terminology is inspired by the proposals of the late Antonio Cassese; see Cassese, 'It is High Time to Restyle the Respected Old Lady'.

[110] And indeed such measures are made in the form of an order; see Rüdger Wolfrum, 'Interim (Provisional) Measures of Protection', *Max Planck Encyclopedia of Public International Law* 4. The term used here will be 'provisional measures', in line with Article 46 of the Court's Statute. It should be noted, however, that the Rules of the Permanent Court of International Justice, and the rules of the ICJ until 1978, used the term 'interim measures of protection'. However, since the Rules were revised in 1978 to bring them into line with the Court's Statute, provisional measures shall be the terminology used here. See H. Thirlway, 'The Indication of Provisional Measures by the International Court of Justice' in R. Bernhardt (ed), *Interim Measures Indicated by International Courts* (Max-Planck-Institut für ausländisches öffentliches Recht und Völkerrecht: Springer-Verlag, 1994) 3, 119 onwards.

[111] Wolfrum, 'Interim (Provisional) Measures of Protection' para 4. This discretionary and exceptional nature is in line with the status of provisional measures in other international courts and tribunals; see Article 290 UNCLOS.

to make such provisional measures *proprio motu*[112] and that it may indicate provisional measures not specifically requested by the parties.[113]

The long-running academic debate surrounding the binding nature of provisional measures before the ICJ centred around the wording of Article 41 of the Court's Statute which refers to the power to 'indicate' provisional measures that 'ought to be taken'. The fact that Article 41 does not employ imperative terminology and the fact that the ordinary meaning of the term 'indicate' does not imply any obligations 'led most scholars to conclude that there [was] no question of a binding provisional measures order'.[114] However, the Court has since clarified that its power to order provisional measures under Article 41 is indeed binding upon the parties.[115]

In the course of the *LaGrand* case Germany argued that the United States had failed 'to take all measures at its disposal' to ensure that Walter LaGrand was not executed for the crimes he had been convicted of pending the final judgment of the Court, as the provisional measure had stipulated.[116] The United States, on the other hand, argued that the drafting history of Article 41 did not support the argument that provisional measures were binding on the parties. The Court ultimately held that, after considering the object and purpose of the Statute, and the English and French versions of the text, provisional measures under Article 41 of the Statute were binding on the parties.[117]

### 4.2.1 What is the object of provisional measures?

The Court in the *Fisheries Jurisdiction* case laid down its authoritative statement regarding the object of provisional measures, namely that the Court's power to order provisional measures 'presupposes that irreparable prejudice should not be caused to rights which are the subject of a dispute in judicial proceedings'.[118] As such it is clear to see why

---

[112] Article 75(1) Rules.   [113] Article 75(2) Rules.
[114] A. Tzanakopoulos, 'Provisional Measures Indicated by International Courts: Emergence of a General Principle of International Law' 57 *Revue Hellénique de droit international* 53, 58; H. Lauterpacht, *The Development of International Law by the International Court of Justice* (Cambridge University Press, 1958) 253.
[115] *LaGrand (Germany v. United States of America)*, Judgment, ICJ Reports 2001 466 paras 102–9.
[116] Ibid. para 103.   [117] Ibid. para 103.
[118] *Fisheries Jurisdiction (Federal Republic of Germany v. Iceland)*, Interim Measures of Protection, Order of 17 August 1972, ICJ Reports 1972 30, 34 para 22.

## 4.2 PROVISIONAL MEASURES

provisional measures are often termed 'protective measures'; due to the fact that they have been traditionally conceived of as having the sole object of protecting the parties' rights in international law and the integrity of the judicial process as a whole.[119]

Provisional measures seek to ensure that the rights of parties existing at the time of the request for the order are protected through ensuring that neither party takes any action (or omission) that would frustrate the object of the adjudicative process.[120] Not all international courts and tribunals have explicit powers to order provisional measures,[121] although some have insisted on the inclusion of such a power in their Rules of Procedure. Practice in this regard has suggested to some commentators that international courts and tribunals believe the power to order provisional measures to be an inherent judicial power.[122]

The need for the power to order provisional measures stems from the fact that once the case is brought, it may be some years before the judgment is handed down. The power to order provisional measures allows the tribunal to keep a handle on the dispute in the intervening period to ensure that the judicial process is not frustrated by either party in the meantime.[123] As Judge Ndiaye has said of provision measures in the context of ITLOS, the actions of one party can threaten the entire judicial process and as such:

> The role of provisional measures is, therefore, to prevent those unfortunate consequences from happening, to ensure the effectiveness of the

---

[119] S. Rosenne, *Provisional Measures in International Law: The International Court of Justice and the International Tribunal for the Law of the Sea* (Oxford University Press, 2005) 3.

[120] Wolfrum, 'Interim (Provisional) Measures of Protection' para 7; Igor V. Karaman, *Dispute Resolution in the Law of the Sea*, Vol 72 (The Hague: Martinus Nijhoff, 2012) 95.

[121] For instance inter-State arbitrations under the PCA and Panels under the WTO adjudicatory system; see Brown, *A Common Law of International Adjudication* 123.

[122] Sir Gerald Fitzmaurice argued that international courts and tribunals should have the power to order provisional measures 'in order to ensure that justice is done and that the eventual decision of the Court on the merits is not stultified by intermediate action on the part of one or other party rendering such decision unenforceable or unavailing'; see Fitzmaurice, *The Law and Procedure of the International Court of Justice* 542; see also the extensive discussion in Brown, *A Common Law of International Adjudication* 125.

[123] Brown, *A Common Law of International Adjudication* 121; see also Bernard Oxman, 'Jurisdiction and the Power to Indicate Provisional Measures' in Lori F. Damrosch (ed), *The International Court of Justice at a Crossroads* (Dobbs Ferry, NY: Transnational, 1987) 323; Maurice Mendelson, 'Interim Measures of Protection in Cases of Conntested Jurisdiction' 46 *British Yearbook of International Law* 259.

decision-making process, and to help maintain the *status quo* with regard to situations contested in the meantime, which the other party is allegedly seeking to alter.[124]

The most common course of action ordered by the Court is to oblige the parties to co-operate and enter into negotiations to resolve the dispute at hand,[125] and to order that the parties do nothing that would aggravate or complicate the dispute.[126] Further, provisional measures have the purpose of preserving the integrity of the judicial process, or 'the effective functioning of the system and the proper administration of justice', for which the Court itself is responsible.[127]

### 4.2.2 When can provisional measures be made?

A combination of the wording of Article 41 of the Court's Statue and the case law of the Court have indicated that a number of conditions must be met for the Court to be able to order provisional measures.

First of all, the Court has established that it must have *prima facie* jurisdiction in order to consider ordering provisional measures.[128] The Court must convince itself that on the face of it the facts of the case indicate that the Court has jurisdiction over the dispute and that the

---

[124] Karaman, *Dispute Resolution in the Law of the Sea* 96.
[125] Jean d'Aspremont, 'The Recommendations Made by the International Court of Justice' 56 *International and Comparative Law Quarterly* 185, 188 footnote 22; *The Mox Plant* case, International Tribunal of the Law of the Sea, order, para 89; *Land Reclamation Malaysia v. Singapore (Provisional Measures, ITLOS) Order of 8 October 2003*, Order para 106; see also Shigeru Oda, 'Provisional Measures, The Practice of the International Court of Justice' in V. Lowe and M. Fitzmaurice (eds), *Fifty Years of the International Court of Justice* (Cambridge University Press, 1996) 551.
[126] d'Aspremont, 'The Recommendations Made by the International Court of Justice' 188; *Nuclear Test (Australia v. France), Order, ICJ Reports 1973* 106; *Nuclear Test (New Zealand v. France), Order, ICJ Reports 1973* 142; *Case Concerning Military and Paramilitary Activities in and against Nicaragua (Nicaragua v. United States of America), Order, ICJ Reports 1984*; *Armed Activities Case* para 47. See the interesting argument by Thirlway, 'The Indication of Provisional Measures by the International Court of Justice' 14 in this regard that provisional measures in this respect are closely intertwined with the broader principle that parties before the Court must not frustrate the object and purpose of a treaty during the stage between the signature of the treaty and its coming into force; see Article 18, Vienna Convention on the Law of Treaties 1969.
[127] Kolb, *The International Court of Justice* 616.
[128] Paolo Palchetti, 'The Power of the International Court of Justice to Indicate Provisional Measures to Prevent the Aggravation of a Dispute' 21 *Leiden Journal of International Law* 623, 630.

rights sought to be preserved are the rights that will be at the heart of the dispute at the merits stage.[129] Secondly, the Court must be convinced that there is the chance of irreparable harm.[130] The Court's jurisprudence indicates that it will make an assessment on the risk of rights being irreparably harmed on the basis of probability, a standard short of certainty.[131]

Finally, the Court must be convinced of the urgency of the situation. Provisional measures must be required as a matter of urgency.[132] As such, this suggests that the temporal element relates to urgency at the time of the request, and not only 'pending the final decision'.[133] Multiple orders for provisional measures can be made.[134]

It is conceivable that these conditions may be met in cases regarding the preservation of evidence. There is no reason to doubt that there may be situations where the Court has *prima facie* jurisdiction, such as where there is a danger that evidence may be at risk of destruction, that the danger of irreparable harm and urgency requirements may be met.[135] And indeed there are examples in the Court's case law in which it has utilised provisional measures in relation to evidence.

### 4.2.3 Provisional measures and evidence

The Court's power to order provisional measures to ensure the protection of parties' rights is broad enough to cover the proper conduct of the judicial process[136] and to ensure that the Court is able to render a judgment that is effective.[137] To this end, the preservation of evidence 'without which a party might not be able to prove its claim and the

---

[129] Ibid.
[130] See for instance *Nuclear Tests Case 1974* 139; *Tehran Hostages Case* para 36; *Bosnian Genocide, Provisional Measures* para 34 amongst others; see Wolfrum, 'Interim (Provisional) Measures of Protection' para 14.
[131] Brown, *A Common Law of International Adjudication* 140; *Certain Criminal Proceedings in France (Republic of the Congo v. France), Provisional Measure, Order of 17 June 2003, ICJ Reports 2003* 102 para 35.
[132] *Certain Criminal Proceedings in France*
[133] Brown, *A Common Law of International Adjudication* 143.
[134] See *Bosnian Genocide* case where Bosnia made two requests, [1993] ICJ Rep 3 and [1993] ICJ Rep 325; and *Pulp Mills* case where the Court made two separate provision measures orders, on 13 July 2006 and 29 November 2006.
[135] R. Higgins, 'Interim Measures for the Protection of Human Rights' 36 *Columbia Journal of Transnational Law* 91, 108.
[136] Wolfrum, 'Interim (Provisional) Measures of Protection' para 7.
[137] Brown, *A Common Law of International Adjudication* 121.

tribunal might not be able to settle the dispute' is a legitimate aim of provisional measures.[138]

Expanding more specifically on the Court's ability to order measures that protect the integrity of the judicial process, significantly, there is some precedent for the use of provisional measures in this manner. In the *Cameroon v. Nigeria* case the Court referred to the fact-finding mission to the Bakassi Peninsula proposed by the Secretary-General[139] in ordering the parties to 'take all necessary steps to conserve evidence relevant to the present case within the disputed area'.[140] Furthermore, crucially, the Court ordered the parties to 'lend every assistance to the fact-finding mission which the Secretary-General of the United Nations has proposed to send',[141] although the Court did not ultimately refer to the Secretary-General's report in the final judgment.[142]

That the Court, in an order binding on the parties, ordered co-operation with the Secretary-General's fact-finding mission is significant in demonstrating the use of provisional measures to safeguard the judicial process as a whole and to aid the Court in its fact-finding task. In this regard the order in the *Cameroon v. Nigeria* case can be seen as precedent for the more extensive use of provisional measures by the Court in taking a more proactive approach to the facts. For example the Court is competent to include in a provisional measure the obligation to preserve specific evidence that lies in the sole possession of that party and that has been specifically requested by the other party. Again, there is some precedent for such action.

For instance, before the PCIJ in the *Denunciation of the Treaty of 2 November 1865 between China and Belgium* case, President Huber ordered, specifically referring to Article 41 of the Court's Statute, that property and shipping not be sequestered or seized and be protected from 'any destruction other than accidental'.[143] Similarly, the ICJ in the *Frontier Dispute* case ordered that both parties 'should refrain from any act likely to impede the gathering of evidence material to the

---

[138] See *Denunciation of the Treaty of 2 November 1985 between China and Belgium*, PCIJ, Ser. A, No. 8, Order of 8 January 1927, II ('as regards property and shipping'); Brown, *A Common Law of International Adjudication* 122.
[139] *Land and Maritime Boundary between Cameroon and Nigeria, Provisional Measures, Order of 15 March 1996*, ICJ Reports 1996 13.
[140] Ibid.   [141] Ibid.
[142] *Land and Maritime Boundary between Cameroon and Nigeria Case.*
[143] See Order of 8 January 1927, in *Denunciation of the Treaty of 2 November 1865 between China and Belgium*, Ser A., No. 8, 1927.

present case'[144] and in the *Land, Maritime and Frontier Dispute* case the Court ordered that the parties 'take all necessary steps to conserve evidence relevant to the present case within the disputed area'.[145]

Further, there is evidence of the use of provisional measures for preservation in other international courts and tribunals. For instance, in the *Biwater Gauff v. Tanzania* case the ICSID arbitral tribunal ordered the preservation and provision of documentation in respect of a number of pieces of evidence requested by the company.[146] There is some evidence of this in other areas of international law such as the *AGIP v. Congo* case in which the ICSID arbitral tribunal granted a discovery order in a provisional measure.[147] Additionally, a particularly high-profile recent example of the use of provisional measures in relation to evidentiary matters arose during the provisional measures stage of the *Land Reclamation* case between Malaysia and Singapore.

In this case provisional measures were sought by Malaysia to prevent the continuation of land reclamation works being carried out by Singapore that were alleged to adversely affect the marine environment in the Straights of Johor, the body of water that separates Malaysia from Singapore.[148] On 4 July 2003 Malaysia requested the establishment of an arbitral tribunal under Annex VII of UNCLOS to delimit the boundary between the territorial waters of the two States, to determine whether Singapore's land reclamation activities had breached its obligations under UNCLOS and to seek cessation of these activities. However, before the arbitral tribunal could render its decision Malaysia sought provisional measures from ITLOS, as it was entitled to under Article 290(5) of UNCLOS.[149] Malaysia's request for provisional measures attempted to bring a immediate halt to Singapore's land reclamation activities and to impose an obligation on Singapore to provide Malaysia with all relevant information on their planned works, afford Malaysia the opportunity to comment on these works and for Singapore to agree to negotiate with Malaysia.[150]

---

[144] *Frontier Dispute, Provisional Measures, Order of 10 January 1986, ICJ Reports 1986* 3, B.
[145] *Bosnian Genocide Case*.
[146] See *Procedural Order No. 1, 31 March 2006, Biwater Gauff v. Tanzania*, ICSID Tribunal case no. ARB/05/22.
[147] *AGIP v. Congo*, 1 ICSID Rep 306, 311 (1979); *Bosnian Genocide Case* paras 66, 451, 467.
[148] *Land Reclamation Malaysia v. Singapore (Provisional Measures, ITLOS) Order of 8 October 2003*.
[149] Article 290(5) UNCLOS.
[150] See Request for Provisional Measures Submitted by Malaysia, 4 September 2003, www.itlos.org/fileadmin/itlos/documents/cases/case_no_12/request_malaysia_eng.1.pdf.

During the course of proceedings Professor James Crawford made passing reference to a meeting between the two States which had taken place on 22 August 2003 at which a proposal for a 'jointly-funded assessment process' had been discussed and remarked that it remained the Malaysian delegation's position that this should be put in place.[151] In response, Professor Koh, in making Singapore's closing statement to the tribunal, remarked that Singapore was willing to co-operate with Malaysia on a range of matters including co-operating to 'co-commission and co-finance a new scientific study by independent experts'.[152] In its Order of 8 October 2003 the Tribunal subsequently noted that Singapore had accepted Malaysia's proposal to this end[153] and prescribed that the two States 'shall ... enter into consultations forthwith in order to ... establish promptly a group of independent experts'.[154] Whilst this measure only imposes an obligation on the parties to enter into consultations with regards to the establishment of the group of experts, it is nonetheless remarkable that the Tribunal would indicate such a provisional measure which relates specifically to the gathering of evidence as opposed to the preservation of the rights of the parties per se. This fact appeared unremarkable to the judges, avoiding mention in any of the eight declarations and separate opinions made. It is perhaps even more remarkable that the Tribunal indicated this provisional measure *proprio motu* since this was not a measure that had originally been sought by Malaysia, but had merely been mentioned before the Court in passing.

Additionally, it is important to note that this group of experts (GOE) was in fact subsequently established and that it had a very real impact on the resolution of the dispute between the two States. Whilst the report of the GOE is not publicly available, after the group had submitted its final report the States signed a Settlement Agreement on 26 April 2005 which specifically states that the parties 'have considered and reviewed the GOE's Final Report and accepted its recommendations' and which terminates the arbitral proceedings before the PCA.[155] Consequently, in taking a proactive approach to the fact-finding process in indicating a

---

[151] *Land Reclamation Malaysia v. Singapore (Provisional Measures, ITLOS) Order of 8 October 2003*; 27 September 2003, 9.30am, Oral Proceedings, Verbatim Record 18 line 19.
[152] Ibid. 27 September 2003, 9.30am, Oral Proceedings, Verbatim Record 37 line 36; Professor Koh subsequently stated that Singapore had accepted this proposal from Malaysia at the meeting in August and had reiterated its support in its 'Note' of 2 September 2003; see 39 line 2.
[153] Ibid. para 86.     [154] Ibid. operative paragraph 1.
[155] *Malaysia/Singapore Award, Annex 2.*

provisional measure *proprio motu* ITLOS has not only set an important precedent upon which the ICJ could draw but also materially contributed to the resolution of the dispute.

Through making a request for information through provisional measures under Article 41 of the Court's Statute, coming either from the other party or from the Court itself, the Court has the ability to make its requests binding on the parties. In doing so, the Court would be able to circumvent the unclear legal issue as to whether its power to request information from the parties under Article 49 of its Statute (see Chapter 1 at Section 1.1.4) is legally binding on the parties or merely recommendatory. Since the Court has been reluctant to make requests for information in the past, and has not regularly drawn adverse inferences in those few cases it has requested information, having the weight of the binding authority of provisional measures behind it, the Court could more easily take a more proactive approach to securing the facts necessary to make sound legal determinations in cases that come before it.

### 4.2.4 The obstacle to using provisional measures as part of a more proactive approach to fact-finding

There is a potential obstacle to the Court more often utilising its power to indicate provisional measures to secure the protection and production of evidence – namely the requirement that the provisional measures can only be made to preserve the rights of the parties before the Court that will form the basis for the merits of the case. As Palchetti has stated, '[t]he Court does not have the power to protect *proprio motu* rights of the parties that are not in dispute in the case before it; this would constitute an *ultra petita*'.[156] In practice the Court has always stressed that the measures in question were related to the dispute rights in the case at hand.

That having been said, Palchetti's argument is open to question. First of all, the history of the Court's use of provisional measures in relation to evidence can be said to have the underlying rationale of protecting the judicial process rather than protecting the rights of individual parties per se. As such, they are not designed to protect a right that is in dispute in the case, but rather to protect the integrity of the judicial process, and as such it is hard to see how the Court could be acting *ultra petita* in

---

[156] Palchetti, 'The Power of the ICJ to Indicate Provisional Measures' 622.

such cases.[157] Consequently, in cases where the Court uses interim measures to protect or order the production of evidence, the fact the orders do not relate to a right that is in dispute in the case at hand is inconsequential. As Kolb has stated, 'measures indicated by the Court of its own volition can be slightly further removed from the subject matter of the dispute than measures to protect disputed substantive rights ... since damage to the procedure will unfailingly, albeit indirectly, affect the parties' substantive rights too'.[158] In sum, the Court is not precluded from couching its requests for information in provisional measures in this respect. However, the prospect of the Court making binding requests for information, or orders to preserve existing evidence, in light of States' traditional control over the fact-finding process, raises the possibility that States will simply not comply with such requests.

### 4.2.5 Legal consequences of non-compliance with provisional measures

There have been a number of recent examples of non-compliance with provisional measures in the practice of the Court. For example, in the *Armed Activities* case the Court found that Uganda had failed to comply with its provisional measure of 1 July 2000.[159] However, since the Democratic Republic had only requested a declaration to this effect and had not sought damages the Court did not make an award of compensation for the breach that it had found to have been committed. Similarly in the *Bosnian Genocide* case the Court found Serbia to have breached the provisional measures of 8 April 1993 and 13 September 1993.[160] And in this case Bosnian and Herzegovina did seek monetary compensation for Serbia's failure to comply with the Court's provisional measures. However, ultimately the Court opted to make a declaratory statement to the effect that Serbia had breached its obligations rather than ordering monetary compensation.[161]

Nevertheless, the Court's reluctance to award monetary compensation is arguably inconsequential in the context of provisional measures relating to evidence. In such cases, what is sought is not a declaratory

---

[157] See Kolb, *The International Court of Justice* 946, stating that 'good faith requires above all else, the presevation of the subject matter of the dispute. The parties must not take steps which might deprive the Court's proceedings of their value, or gravely affect them in some other way.'
[158] Ibid.    [159] *Armed Activities Case* paras 264, 345(7).
[160] *Bosnian Genocide Case* paras 66, 451, 467.    [161] Ibid. paras 469, 471(1).

statement or compensation but rather the production or protection of documents, for instance (although admittedly it would in some cases be difficult to establish whether the evidence had been preserved, or in other words whether the measure had been complied with).[162] In such cases where it could be established that the measure had not been complied with, a better course of action for the Court would be to draw adverse inferences from any failure of the parties to comply with (binding) provisional measures. Although the Court has not in the past shown a clear preference for drawing adverse inferences from refusals to providing requested information or to comply with provisional measures, developing such a practice in the future could be a key part of the Court's taking a more proactive approach to fact-finding in order to remedy the current weaknesses of its current practice.

### 4.2.6 Failure to comply with provisional measures and duty of collaboration generally: adverse inferences

It has been suggested that the Court may be able to address the problems caused by its traditionally reactive approach to fact-finding through creative use of Article 49 of its Statute which enables it to take 'formal note' of any refusal to produce requested material (and subsequently draw adverse conclusions from any refusal to do so).[163] The practice of drawing adverse inferences is commonplace in the practice of both domestic and international judicial bodies.[164] As such, it has been

---

[162] Although this issue is beyond the scope of the present work, such a situation would require a similarly proactive approach from the Court in order to establish whether the order had been breached.

[163] Halink, 'All Things Considered: How the International Court of Justice Delegated its Fact-Assessment to the United Nations in the Armed Activities Case' 19; Halink cites *Bosnian Genocide Case* para 205. See also Teitelbaum, 'Recent Fact-Finding Developments at the International Court of Justice' 130, in which Teitelbaum argues that the Court drew 'conclusions' from (although did not take formal note of) Serbia and Montenegro's failure to produce documents in the *Bosnian Genocide* case.

[164] See Principles 17.3, 21.3 ALI/UNIDROIT Principles of Transnational Civil Procedure; Sandifer, *Evidence Before International Tribunals* 150; J. A. Ragosta, 'Unmasking the WTO – Access to the DSB System: Can the WTO DSB Live up to the Moniker World Trade Court?' 31 *Law and Policy in International Business* 739, 764. Judge Jessup, in *Barcelona Traction Preliminary Objections*, stated that, despite the fact that the Court's Statute does not explicitly provide for the power to draw adverse inferences, 'if a party fails to produce on demand a relevant document which is in its possession, there may be an inference that the document "if brought, would have exposed facts unfavourable to the party"'.

suggested that it is an inherent judicial function.[165] However, despite some support for this position from the bench,[166] the Court has never done so in practice. Is it feasible to envisage that the Court could make greater use of adverse inferences to entice the parties to disclose the necessary information?

An example of the Court's historical reluctance to draw adverse inferences can be seen in the approach of the Court in the *Corfu Channel* case, in which the United Kingdom refused to produce specific information requested by the Court, namely Admiralty orders.[167] However, the Court in this case declined to draw specific adverse inferences from the United Kingdom's refusal to comply with the Court's request. Similarly, in the *Bosnian Genocide* case, Bosnia and Herzegovina requested Serbia and Montenegro to produce documents under Article 49 of the Court's Statute; however, the Court did not accede to Bosnia and Herzegovina's request,[168] merely stating that 'it [had] not failed to note the Applicant's suggestion that the Court may be free to draw its own conclusions'[169] but that 'the Court observes that the Applicant has extensive documentation and other evidence available to it, especially readily accessibly ICTY records'.[170]

Judge Al-Khasawneh heavily criticised the Court for its reasoning in this respect, arguing that the documents would have in all likelihood 'shed light on the central questions of intent and attributability' in the case and that the Court's reasoning behind not requesting the information 'is worse than its failure to act'.[171] One commentator referred to

---

[165] Grando, *Evidence, Proof, and Fact-Finding in WTO Dispute Settlement* (Oxford University Press, 2009) 264.

[166] This position has found support from the Court in the form of Judge Owada, who has argued that the Court must not be so cautious about appearing impartial and that Article 49 is potentially a useful tool for 'levelling the playing field' in relation to the evidence presented by both parties before the Court (such as in cases where some States retain exclusive access to some information that it does not let the other party see). See Dissenting Opinion of Judge Owada in the *Oil Platforms Case* 321.

[167] *Corfu Channel Case* 32, the request being reproduced in *Pleadings, Oral Arguments, Preliminary Objection, Merits* Vol 8, 428, and the refusal at *Pleadings, Oral Arguments, Documents, Preliminary Objection, Merits* Vol. V, 255; Benzing, 'Evidentiary Issues' 1251.

[168] I.C.J. Pleadings, Bosnian Genocide, CR 2006/43, 8 May 2006 28 para 60.

[169] Para 206; Teitelbaum, 'Recent Fact-Finding Developments at the International Court of Justice' 131.

[170] *Bosnian Genocide Case* para 206.

[171] Ibid.; see Dissenting Opinion of Judge Al-Khasawneh at para 35, and the Dissenting Opinion of Judge Mahiou at paras 53–63.

the argument made by Judge Owada in the *Oil Platforms* case (see Section 4.1.3 above) and stated that the Court found itself in a similar position in the *Bosnian Genocide* case – namely faced with a 'curable problem' that could have been solved through a more proactive approach to the facts.[172]

Accordingly, in such situations the Court can feasibly make greater use of its powers under Article 49 of its Statute to request the required information. The fact that the request for information has come from the parties rather than from the Court *proprio motu* is not significant since neither Article 49 of the Court's Statute nor Article 62 of its rules lay down any stipulation outlawing this practice. In fact, Article 66 of the Court's Rules states that the Court may at any time 'either *proprio motu* or at the request of a party' utilise its fact-finding powers in the course of obtaining evidence – it is presumed that the same lack of distinction between requests from the parties and action *proprio motu* exists in relation to requests for information and the drawing of adverse inferences.

Chapter 3 highlighted that adjudicative bodies of the WTO have drawn adverse inferences from the refusal of one party to provide information requested of it by the other party or Panel in a number of cases.[173] This is so despite the fact there is only one reference to adverse inferences in the WTO Agreements (namely Article 7(7) Annex 5 of the SCM Agreement). Drawing on the case law of various international courts and tribunals, only unexplained refusals to co-operate can warrant the drawing of adverse inferences.[174] For example, in *Argentina – Footwear* the Panel drew an adverse inference from Argentina's refusal to provide information requested by the United States, stating this refusal taken together with the evidence presented by the United States favoured

---

[172] Teitelbaum, 'Recent Fact-Finding Developments at the International Court of Justice' 133.

[173] See for example *Canada – Measures Affecting the Export of Civilian Aircraft*, Appellate Body Report, WT/DS70/AB/RW, 2 August 1999 para 203.

[174] *Levitt v. Iran (1991)* 27 Iran-US CTR 145 (Appendix BRA-II) at para 64 ('the Respondents have failed to submit the majority of the documents requested and have so *without adequate reasons for this failure*'); In the *Aerial Incident of 27 July 1955* case Israel protested that the Bulgarian Government was deliberately withholding material facts requested of it by Israel during the course of proceedings. Consequently Israel took the step of similarly withholding evidence in response, 'reserving all its rights in the matter of evidence, including the right to make appropriate applications to the Court under Article 49 of the Statute'. See *Aerial Incident of 27 July 1955 Case, Pleadings* 98.

their position.[175] Whilst the power to draw adverse inferences more generally flows from the duty of collaboration found in international adjudication (see Section 4.2.6 above), the ICJ has a much more explicit power to draw adverse inferences than the WTO adjudicative bodies and that, as such, it could make greater use of this power in order to bring before it information that it requires for the resolution of the case at hand.[176]

As argued in Chapter 3, the practice of drawing adverse inferences is a potentially helpful tool that could be utilised by the Court to flush out the facts required to establish the factual foundations of the case that have not been placed before them by the parties themselves.[177] The real value of adverse inferences is 'its capacity to induce cooperation' rather than the inference itself.[178] Crucially, it should be stressed that the drawing of adverse inferences does not shift the burden of proof from the claimant to the defendant State. Rather, the drawing of adverse inferences is a constituent part of the evaluation of the facts in the course of the judicial body's important fact-assessment role.

Whilst a party may undoubtedly run the risk of an adverse inference being drawn as a result of it not providing evidence to counter-claims made against it, 'this is not a true burden of proof, and the use of an additional label to describe what is an ordinary step in the fact-finding process is unwarranted'.[179] As such, instead of conceiving of the burden of proof constantly shifting between one party and the other, the burden remains on the party seeking to establish a claim (except where a party invokes a specific exception) and matters such as the drawing of adverse

---

[175] *Argentina – Measures Affecting Imports of Footwear, Textiles, Apparel and Other Items*, Panel Report, WT/DS56/R, 25 November 1997 para 6.40.

[176] Mavroidis, 'Development of WTO Dispute Settlement Procedures' 174. It has been argued that the practice of drawing adverse inferences more accurately squares with the good faith obligation to co-operate with the proceedings that is placed on all Members rather than imposing on them a binding duty to disclose information by construing 'should' and 'shall'; see Section 3.1.2.1. above; Kuyper, 'The Appellate Body and the Facts' 321.

[177] Collins, 'Institutionalized Fact-Finding at the WTO' 372; Cameron and Orava, 'GATT/WTO Panels Between Recording and Finding Facts'.

[178] Grando, *Evidence, Proof, and Fact-Finding in WTO Dispute Settlement* 266; Kuyper, 'The Appellate Body and the Facts' 321.

[179] See the Supreme Court of Canada in *Snell v. Farrell* (1990) 2 SCR 311, 107 NBR (2d) 94, 72 DLR (4th) 289, 110 NR 200,4 CCLT (2d) 229; Grando, *Evidence, Proof, and Fact-Finding in WTO Dispute Settlement* 85.

inferences ought to be left to the judicial body to manage in the course of their judicial function.[180]

Of course there are drawbacks to the practice of drawing adverse inferences such as the fact that where neither the Court nor the other party are aware of information that has been withheld the power is rendered useless.[181] Nonetheless, if the Court is to take a more proactive approach to the facts that will involve the Court making requests for information and facilitating the production of evidence more often, the Court may encounter some resistance from some States. In this regard, despite the obvious difficulties, the practice of drawing adverse inferences when information that has been requested is willingly withheld without justification could be one that is of great potential value for the Court.

Further, blatant refusals to comply with requests directly from the Court were it to insist on its right that the information be produced are likely to be a generally rare occurrence. It is in the party's best interest to co-operate with the Court and to comply with what is asked of it in order to give itself the best chance of prevailing in the case at hand. As Highet has stated:

> [I]f a state wishes to prevail in a litigation, it had better do what is asked of it by the tribunal, sovereignty or no sovereignty ... Of course, states are always ... free to conduct their cases as they see fit, but if they wish to win, they should ... exercise that freedom consistent with any preferences indicated by the Court or chamber.[182]

And indeed Highet's advice to States regarding their litigation strategy still rings true today. Turning now from the use of provisional measures and the duty of collaboration, the remainder of this chapter will focus on an issue which has become a prominent focus of attention in recent years, namely the Court's use of expert evidence. In doing so, proposals will be set out for the development of a clear strategy for the use of expert evidence which will better ensure the proper administration of justice.

## 4.3 Developing a clear strategy for the use of experts before the court

The third way in which the Court could take a more proactive approach to fact-finding in order to address the weaknesses identified in Chapter 2

---

[180] As Grando argues, 'courts would be wise to refrain from stating that the burden of proof, even in the sense of the tactical burden, shifts'; ibid.
[181] Cameron and Orava, 'GATT/WTO Panels between Recording and Finding Facts'.
[182] Highet, 'Evidence, The Chamber, and the ELSI Case' 63.

is through better use of experts before the Court. This is a possibility that has been explicitly advocated by a number of judges in the recent jurisprudence of the Court and by a number of voices in international legal scholarship.[183] For instance, in the *Pulp Mills* case Judge Yusuf made a plea to the Court to adapt the way it deals with factually complex cases and to develop 'a clear strategy which would enable it to assess the need for an expert opinion at an early stage of its deliberations on a case',[184] arguing that such cases are increasingly going to come before the Court and, as such, states 'will need to see that the facts related to their case are fully understood and appreciated by the Court'.[185]

In order to improve the Court's fact-finding process the Court must 'display greater readiness to use, indeed exhaust, the possibilities granted by its Statute, in an open and fair way'.[186] In the words of Mbengue, the Court must '[interweave the] legal process with knowledge and expertise'[187] by playing a more active role in weighing the facts in order to determine whether factual assertions are 'sufficiently supported or reasonably warranted', for instance.[188] The Court, being 'endowed with considerable discretion and two well-defined procedures to use outside sources of expertise'[189] is more than capable of developing such a clear strategy in relation to the consultation of experts in which both the bench and experts alike respect the functional autonomy of the other.[190]

---

[183] See for instance Foster, 'New Clothes for the Emperor? Consultation of Experts by the International Court of Justice' 4; Tullio Treves, 'Law and Science in the Interpretation of the Law of the Sea Convention: Article 76 Between the Law of the Sea Tribunal and the Commission on the Limits of the Continental Shelf' 3 *Journal of International Dispute Settlement* 483; M. M. Mbengue, 'International Courts and Tribunals as Fact-Finders: The Case of Scientific Fact-Finding in International Adjudication' 34 *Loyola of Los Angeles International and Comparative Law Review* 53; Del Mar, 'Weight of Evidence Generated through Intra-Institutional Fact-finding before the International Court of Justice'; Karel Wellens, 'Happy Birthday to the 'Respected Old Lady' ESIL Newsletter Vol 18, June 2015.
[184] *Pulp Mills Case*, Declaration of Judge Yusuf at para 14.
[185] Ibid., Declaration of Judge Yusuf at para 14.
[186] Simma, 'The International Court of Justice and Scientific Expertise'.
[187] *Pulp Mills Case*, Joint Dissenting Opinion of Judges Al-Kasawneh and Simma at para 3.
[188] *EC – Measures Concerning Meat and Meat Products*, Appellate Body Report, WT/DS26/AB/R, WT/DS48/AB/R, 16 January 1998 para 186; Mbengue, 'Scientific Fact-finding by International Courts and Tribunals' 524.
[189] Simma, 'The International Court of Justice and Scientific Expertise'.
[190] Jacur, 'Remarks on the Role of Ex Curia Scientific Experts in International Environmental Disputes' 453.

## 4.3 THE USE OF EXPERTS BEFORE THE ICJ

The following subsection proposes such a clear strategy for the use of experts before the Court. First of all, the Court ought to make greater use of pre-hearing conferences in order to ensure that the proceedings are as streamlined as possible. Secondly, the end of the use of *experts fantômes* and the practice of presenting experts as counsel once and for all is advocated in order to foster a culture of examination and cross-examination of experts in open court. Thirdly, it is proposed that the Court appoint its own experts to assist it in cases in which the facts are of such a nature so as to be beyond what any judge could reasonably be expected to comprehend. Being armed with its own expert advice, the Court will be better placed to play an active role in questioning and examining the experts put forward by the parties and to deal with disputes between the parties over the disclosure of evidence. Each element of the strategy will be examined in turn.

### 4.3.1 Fostering a culture of examination and cross-examination in open court

The first part of a clear strategy for the use of experts – to make regular use of pre-hearing conferences – is straightforward and does not require much explanation. At the moment pre-hearing conferences are 'limited to participation of the representatives of the parties and the President' and are 'off the record'.[191] The suggestion that the Court make greater use of pre-hearing conferences, as other international tribunals do, in order to improve the use of expert evidence before the Court, is one which has been made by a number of commentators.[192]

Making pre-hearing conferences a regular feature of all cases before the Court could be achieved through an order under Article 48 of the Court's Statute and could have a number of potential benefits to the Court. First of all, the parties could indicate whether or not they intend to put forward experts in the course of proceedings and discuss the potential appointment of a Court-appointed expert to assist the Court. At this juncture the Court could discuss any potential objections that the parties

---

[191] See Rosenne, 'Fact-Finding Before the International Court of Justice' 247.
[192] Holtzmann has argued that pre-trial conferences dramatically reduce the volume and duplication of evidence in international arbitration and there is no reason to say that they would not similarly benefit the international adjudicative process; Howard M. Holtzmann, *Streamlining Arbitral Proceedings: Some Techniques of the Iran-United States Claims Tribunal* (The Hague: Kluwer Law International, 2007).

had to a particular expert and deal with such issues at this early stage. Secondly, the Court could hear claims for the disclosure of documents and assess whether or not to make use of its provisional measures power to order the preservation or production of evidence, as explored at Section 4.2. Furthermore, and perhaps most crucially for our purposes, the parties could establish points of common ground and points of disagreement. Establishing some form of consensus would enable better use to be made of the Court's time during the oral proceedings, avoiding, for example, the need for cross-examination of experts on points which are not contested or relevant.[193]

In addition to this preliminary issue, developing a clear strategy for the use of expert evidence before the Court requires that an immediate end be brought to the use of *experts fantômes* as examined in Chapter 2 at Section 2.1.2 and the practice of experts appearing as counsel in order to encourage a culture of examination and cross-examination of experts in open court.[194]

As argued in Chapter 2, the current practice of not informing the parties that the Court is seeking expert assistance whilst circumventing the procedure for doing so as set out in the Court's Statute and Rules denies parties the right they would have otherwise had under Article 67 (2) of the Rules to comment on the expert evidence if such an expert had been properly appointed under Article 50 of the Court's Statute.[195] This practice has been criticised in recent cases by members of the Court such as Judges Al-Khasawneh and Simma, who have argued that this practice is unacceptable in cases in which complex factual issues form part of the crux of the case.[196] Whilst these judges were correct to highlight the problem of informal resort to experts, it is argued that they do not go far enough in their assessment of the situation. Owing to the fact that the use of informal expert evidence is inherently problematic, the practice of the

---

[193] Foster, *Science and the Precautionary Principle in International Courts and Tribunals* 79; see Rosenne, 'Fact-Finding Before the International Court of Justice' 247; David Neuberger, 'Expert Witnesses', Lord Neuberger at the annual Bond Solon Expert Witness Conference Expert Witnesses para 29, www.supremecourt.uk/docs/speech-141107.pdf.

[194] Certain parts of the following chapter were considered in relation to the issue of procedural fairness in another work by the present author, namely J. G. Devaney, 'Evidentiary Fairness in International Non-Criminal Tribunals' in A. Sarvarian and A. Zidar (eds), *Procedural Fairness in International Courts and Tribunals* (London: British Institute of International and Comparative Law, 2015)

[195] Tams, 'Article 50' 1118.

[196] *Pulp Mills Case*, Dissenting Opinion of Judges Al-Khasawneh and Simma at para 14; see also Simma, 'The International Court of Justice and Scientific Expertise' 231.

## 4.3 THE USE OF EXPERTS BEFORE THE ICJ

Court in seeking informal advice from experts should be brought to an immediate and final halt in the interests of the proper administration of justice.[197]

In addition to bringing an end to the practice of informal consultation of experts, there is another practice which the Court ought to, and to some extent has already begun to, discontinue: that of parties presenting experts as counsel. This practice, highlighted as a weakness of the Court's fact-finding procedure in Chapter 2 at Section 2.1.1, has been commonplace in the practice of the Court, despite being the subject of criticism in international legal scholarship and posing problems for the Court in practice.[198]

For instance, in the *ELSI* case, Giuseppe Bisconti, a lawyer who had advised the U.S. corporation at the heart of the case was included as a member of the United States team before the Court. Problems arose in the course of his submission during the oral proceedings as it became clear that the lawyer was not only addressing the Court as counsel for the United States but also speaking to his own knowledge as legal advisor to the American corporation. President Ruda upheld Italy's complaint that Bisconti was not only appearing as counsel but also as a witness and as such should be treated as a witness subject to cross-examination and ordered that such cross-examination take place.[199]

A similar issue arose before the ITLOS in the provisional measures stage of the *Land Reclamation* case. Whilst Malaysia called one expert, Professor Falconer, who was subsequently cross-examined, another, geomorphologist Professor Sharifah, made a statement as a member of Malaysia's defence team and as such could not be cross-examined.[200] Ultimately the difficulty was overcome by ensuring that the expert made the solemn declaration required of experts under Article 79(b) of the Rules which meant that the expert could be examined as an expert by counsel of Singapore.[201] It should be noted, however, that Malaysia technically retained discretion over whether it wished to do so or not.

---

[197] Tams, 'Article 50' 1118.
[198] Watts, 'Enhancing the Effectiveness of Procedures of International Dispute Settlement', 21 *Max Planck Yearbook of United Nations Law* 21, 30.
[199] See *ELSI Case*; Watts, 'Enhancing the Effectiveness of Procedures of International Dispute Settlement' 30.
[200] See ITLOS/PV03/01, verbatim record of the sitting of 25 September 2003 25; *Land Reclamation Malaysia v. Singapore (Provisional Measures, ITLOS) Order of 8 October 2003*.
[201] Treves, 'Law and Science in the Interpretation of the Law of the Sea Convention' 486.

Had Malaysia preferred to keep Professor Sharifah as part of its delegation and not agreed to her subsequently making the declaration under Article 79(b), cross-examination could have been avoided. Despite such academic criticism and practical issues, such practice has been common in the jurisprudence of the Court.

This practice in the past left States with a decision to make – for whilst the State may benefit from avoiding having their expert subjected to awkward questions, there is no doubt that the perception of the individual as an independent expert is affected.[202] As one commentator remarked:

> [A]n advocate is clearly partisan, putting forward what are known to be not so much his personal views as simply the best arguments he can think of in support of his client's case, whereas an expert is known to be putting forward his own beliefs and opinions as to matters within his range of expertise, and is relying on his known authority in his own field.[203]

Whilst States consider the tactical pros and cons of each option, the decision is more important for the Court in that the decision to retain experts as counsel rather than putting them forward as experts subject to cross-examination deprives the Court of an important means of drawing out the facts, and circumvents the procedure laid down in Article 50 of the Statute and the Rules for the examination of experts.[204] The possibility of experts being cross-examined in the course of the oral proceedings is an essential part of the adjudicative process, since, through the process of cross-examination, experts can be scrutinised in a way that is simply not possible when they appear as counsel.[205]

### 4.3.1 (i) Cross-examination: from white elephant to indispensable weapon in the Court's arsenal

Cross-examination facilitates examination of the three main issues in relation to expert evidence: its relevance, probative value, and the reliability of the expertise.[206] In the absence of rules of admissibility and in light of the Court's relaxed approach to qualifications (see Sections 1.3.2 and 2.1.1) much emphasis falls on fact-assessment – the process through which the Court attributes probative weight to the evidence placed before

---

[202] Foster, *Science and the Precautionary Principle in International Courts and Tribunals* 89.
[203] Watts, 'Enhancing the Effectiveness of Procedures of International Dispute Settlement' 29.
[204] Tams, 'Article 51' 1303.   [205] ICTY Rules, Rule 90(H); ICTR Rules, Rule 90(G).
[206] Singh, 'Expert Evidence' 601.

it, including expert evidence. In this respect, the examination of an expert witness and subsequent cross-examination regarding the expert's methodology and supporting evidence can be extremely useful to the Court in determining the probative value and relevance of the evidence presented by one party.[207]

Further, the adversarial nature of the cross-examination process is particularly helpful in relation to the testimony of experts due to its ability to expose underlying assumptions and contingencies 'thereby preventing an uncritical acceptance of alleged truths'.[208] Cross-examination allows the Court to test experts and witnesses on evidence they have already given in written form to ask questions with regard to gaps in their testimony. Furthermore, experts' credentials, biases and scientific research are all likely to be called into question during cross-examination, with experts expected to answer immediately rather than given time to prepare written statements away from the spotlight of cross-examination.[209] The President of the Supreme Court of the United Kingdom, Lord Neuberger, recently spoke of the virtues of both parties conducting cross-examination in an adversarial setting, highlighting its ability to ensure the best use of cross-examination:

> The fact that an expert witness, witness 1, knows that he has to face an expert witness, witness 2, on the other side, and that witness 2 will presumably be briefing the advocate who is to cross-examine witness 1, should help concentrate the mind of witness 1 on ensuring that his evidence is at least credible. Unless there is equality of arms when it comes to expert witnesses, witness 1 will be sorely tempted, sometimes sub-consciously no doubt, to over-egg his evidence, or at least not to take quite as much care as he might have done if he knew that there was someone as expert as he was testing and challenging his evidence.[210]

Lord Neuberger succinctly highlights the benefits of cross-examination compared to, for example, the appointment of one single joint expert, as is sometimes the practice in common law systems.[211] Foster has cited Professor Vaughan Lowe's cross-examination of the Malaysian expert witness Professor Falconer before the ITLOS in the *Land Reclamation*

---

[207] *Prosecutor v. Blagojević and Jokić*, IT-02-60-T, Judgment, 17 January 2005 27.
[208] Sheila Jasanoff, 'What Judges Should Know about the Sociology of Science' 32 *Jurimetrics* 345, 1577.
[209] Foster, *Science and the Precautionary Principle in International Courts and Tribunals* 101.
[210] Neuberger, 'Expert Witnesses' para 31; ibid., para 29.
[211] Ibid. para 31; ibid., para 29.

case as a clear example of the value of cross-examination for the fact-finding process.[212] Lowe sought to call into question the testimony of Malaysia's expert as a whole, arguing that his expertise as well as the scope of the report presented were limited. Professor Lowe also forced the expert to confirm that he had been compensated for his services, calling his impartiality into question.[213] Such developments are highly unlikely to occur where experts appear as counsel and are not subject to the scrutiny of the opposing party. As such, the Court's fact-finding process is impoverished without cross-examination; indeed one commentator has even gone so far as to state that the absence of cross-examination is 'harmful for the good administration of justice'.[214]

On a positive note it would appear that there is already evidence of a shift away from the practice of experts appearing as counsel. The strong words of the Court in the *Pulp Mills* case clearly indicated a shift in what the Court experts:

> [T]hose persons who provide evidence before the Court based on their scientific or technical knowledge and on their personal experience should testify before the Court as experts, witnesses or in some cases in both capacities, rather than as counsel, so that they may be submitted to questioning by the other party as well as the Court.[215]

Judge Greenwood further stated that the Court had unequivocally indicated that this 'unhelpful' and 'unfair' practice should not be repeated in future cases.[216] Judge Greenwood went on to state emphatically that '[t]he distinction between the *evidence* of a witness or expert and the *advocacy* of counsel is fundamental to the proper conduct of litigation before the Court'.[217]

Bringing an end to the practice of presenting experts as counsel will not have seismic effects on the way that the Court operates and certainly does not require amendment of the Court's Statute. In fact, insisting that experts are put forward and examined in open Court is envisaged in the Court's Statute and Rules and as such States should merely consistently

---

[212] *Land Reclamation (Provisional Measures)* Oral Proceedings 25 September 2003 35.
[213] *Land Reclamation (Provisional Measures)* Oral Proceedings 25 September 2003 35.
[214] Hamamoto, 'Procedural Questions in the Whaling Judgment' 12; Foster, *Science and the Precautionary Principle in International Courts and Tribunals* 101.
[215] *Pulp Mills Case* para 167; see also Joint Dissenting Opinion of Judges Al-Khasawneh and Simma, para 6.
[216] Ibid., Separate Opinion of Judge Greenwood at 231 para 27 onwards.
[217] Ibid., Separate Opinion of Judge Greenwood at 231 para 27 onwards.

conform to the procedure for the examination of experts before the Court that exists but which has been underused to date. Further, the Court would not need to change its current relaxed approach to qualifications of experts (see Chapter 2 at Section 2.1.1) since any cross-examination would necessarily draw out any problematic issues with regards to the credentials of an expert.[218]

It should be made clear that the procedure for hearing party-appointed experts and party-appointed witnesses is the same and as such the two can be discussed together. The procedure for both is set out in Articles 57, 58, 63, 66, 70 and 71 of the Rules of the Court which addresses procedural issues such as the timing and language of hearings.[219] Witnesses have been heard in a number of cases before the Court,[220] although the Court's experience with cross-examination has been much criticised in the past. For instance, the process of examining witnesses in the *South West Africa* case involved the testimony of fourteen 'witness-experts' produced by South Africa over the course of two months of hearings. However, Highet remarked that these witnesses 'might as well have never come to The Hague', as their testimony added so little to the case and delayed the proceedings to such an extent.[221] Such criticism, it has been argued, may have dissuaded the Court from encouraging more widespread use of witness testimony.[222]

However, witnesses have been heard by the Court in subsequent cases and a number of witnesses were put forward in the recent *Croatian Genocide* case.[223] The experience of international criminal tribunals provide a counter-example to the Court's experience in the *South West Africa* case and demonstrate that a large number of witnesses can be heard without derailing the judicial process. For instance in the *Tadić* case the ICTY heard 126 witnesses and examined over 461 exhibits.

---

[218] See *I.C.J. Pleadings, Whaling in the Antarctic*, CR 2013/7, 3 July 2013 31, where during cross-examination Australia sought to call the independence of Japan's expert Professor Walløe into question.
[219] Most important of these provisions is Article 58 of the Rules which requires parties to 'communicate to the Registrar, in sufficient time before the opening of the oral proceedings, information regarding any evidence which it intends to produce or which it intends to request the Court to obtain'.
[220] Highet has argued that *Corfu Channel* and *Nicaragua* are the 'outstanding examples of the use of witnesses and experts to arrive at a decision in the International Court'; Highet, 'Evidence, the Court, and the Nicaragua Case' 22; see also Highet, 'Evidence and Proof of Facts' 357.
[221] Highet, 'Evidence, the Court, and the Nicaragua Case' 22. [222] Ibid.
[223] See the oral proceedings on 4 and 5 March 2014 in *Croatian Genocide Case*.

Similarly, large numbers of witnesses were heard in the *Kupreškić* case, in which 157 witnesses were called and 700 exhibits produced, and in the *Blaškić* case, in which 161 witnesses were called and 1,423 exhibits produced.[224] Further, most recently before the ICC in the *Lubanga* case the Chamber heard sixty-seven witnesses over several months, including four expert Chamber witnesses.[225]

In practice, experts and witnesses have tended to testify between the first and second round of oral proceedings. The Statute and the Rules 'provide only very little information about the legal regime governing the examination of exerts and witnesses' specifying only that '[w]itnesses and Experts shall be examined by the agents, counsel or advocates of the parties under the control of the President. Questions may be put to them by the President and by the judges. Before testifying, witnesses shall remain out of court'.[226]

Although brief, these provisions clarify a number of important issues such as conveying that the examination of witnesses and experts will be primarily conducted by the parties themselves,[227] and overseen by the Court through the President, with the judges able to pose questions should they so wish.[228] Although leaving many questions unanswered, such as how long the period of examination should be, the Court has developed a 'reasonably well established' practice in the limited number of cases in which experts and witnesses have been presented by the parties.[229] The approach taken by the Court in the very first case, *Corfu Channel*, has been particularly influential in this regard.[230] This practice

---

[224] Richard May and Marieke Wierda, 'Evidence before the ICTY' in Richard May and others (eds), *Essays on ICTY Procedure and Evidence in Honour of Gabrielle Kirk McDonald* (The Hague: Martinus Nijhoff, 2000) 250.

[225] Judgment, *Thomas Lubanga* (ICC-01/04-01/06-2842), Trial Chamber 1, 14 March 2012 at 11; Rosalynd C. E. Roberts, 'The Lubanga Trial Chamber's Assessment of Evidence in Light of the Accused's Right to the Presumption of Innocence' 10 *Journal of International Criminal Justice* 923, 924.

[226] See Articles 58 and 65 of the Rules of the Court; Tams, 'Article 51' 1305.

[227] Ibid.; Couvreur, 'Le Règlement Juridictionel' 381.

[228] Tams, 'Article 51' 1305; Couvreur, 'Le Règlement Juridictionel' 381.

[229] *Corfu Channel Case* 87; Tams, 'Article 51' 1307; Riddell and Plant, *Evidence before the International Court of Justice* 312; Rosenne and Ronen, *The Law and Practice of the International Court, 1920-2005* 1309-21.

[230] *Corfu Channel Case*; Tams, 'Article 51' 1306; Rosenne, *Procedure in the International Court* 140. Article 63(2) Rules provides for the examination of witnesses 'otherwise than before the Court itself' - this provision has never been used but would be where witnesses are examined during site visits under Article 66 of the Rules or by Commissions of Inquiry under Article 50 ICJ Statute.

## 4.3 THE USE OF EXPERTS BEFORE THE ICJ

generally consists of four phases: examination-in-chief by the party calling the expert or witness; cross-examination by the other party; re-examination by the original party; then a round of questioning from the judges.[231] The Court's procedure is significantly more flexible than that of any domestic court:

> There is no limit to the number of questions that may be put. The Court has one wish, and that is that as much light as possible should be case upon the matter discussed by the Court, and secondly the Court wishes to give the Parties every opportunity to defend their points of view.[232]

Following the Court's remarks in the judgment in the *Pulp Mills* case, commentators have argued that it is likely that cross-examination 'can be expected to take on an increased importance and absorb a greater proportion of the Court's time'.[233] And this seems to have been the case as the recent *Whaling in the Antarctica* case saw the examination and cross-examination of party-appointed witnesses generally in line with the procedure for examining witnesses laid out above. The *Whaling in the Antarctic* case represented an important post-*Pulp Mills* indication of how the Court envisaged handling experts in cases that come before it in the future. The case saw the submission of individual opinions by three party-appointed experts at the written stage of proceedings, followed by cross-examination on the opinions expressed.[234] Australia called Professor Mangel and Dr Gales, who were examined by Professor Philippe Sands QC and subsequently cross-examined by Professor Vaughan Lowe QC. Presenting opposing expert evidence for Japan was Professor Walløe, who was also cross-examined.

The cross-examination was overseen by the President, who called counsel from each side to conduct the cross-examination. The President broadly set out the procedure for cross-examination at the beginning of the proceedings.[235] Each expert was first examined by an agent of the party calling him (the 'examination-in-chief' lasting up to a maximum of

---

[231] See Rosenne, *The Law and Practice of the International Court 1985* 1310.
[232] President of the Court, *Corfu Channel*, Pleadings, Vol III, 428–9; for a fuller examination of cross-examination before the Court see Tams, 'Article 51' 1307; Talmon, 'Article 43' 1149 paras 144–54.
[233] Foster, 'New Clothes for the Emperor? Consultation of Experts by the International Court of Justice' 2, 7; *Pulp Mills Case* para 167–8; ibid., Separate Opinion of Judge Greenwood at 28.
[234] I.C.J. Pleadings, *Whaling in the Antarctic*, CR 2013/7, 26 June 2013 66 para 25; see *I.C.J. Pleadings, Whaling in the Antarctic*, CR 2013/7, 27 June 2013 paras 12, 13.
[235] I.C.J. Pleadings, *Whaling in the Antarctic*, CR 2013/7, 27 June 2013 38.

thirty minutes), after taking the declaration under Article 64(b) of the Court's Rules. The examination was to take the form of either answers in response to questions asked by agents or in the form of a prepared statement. In fact, Japan's expert Professor Walløe was asked by Professor Lowe to present a twenty-minute statement to the Court rather than answering questions put to him by counsel, as Australia had done.[236] The opposing party was then given the opportunity to cross-examine the expert for up to sixty minutes, confined to any statement already made either in written or oral form by the expert. The party who called the witness was then asked if it wished to have the opportunity to re-examine the expert for up to a further thirty minutes. Afterwards, the judges put their own questions to the experts.

The cross-examination carried out by Professors Sands and Lowe QC was extensive and the maximum time allotted for examination was utilised.[237] Subsequently the judges took advantage of their right to ask questions of the experts called by the parties and (at times multiple) questions were asked of Australia's expert Professor Mangel by Judges Bennouna, Cançado Trindade, Greenwood, Donohue, Keith, and Owada.[238] A similarly large number of questions were asked of Japan's expert, with Judges Greenwood, Cançado Trindade, Yusuf, Bennouna, Keith and Charlesworth all asking questions.[239]

However, the Court's vision for how cross-examination ought to play out in cases before it post-*Pulp Mills* has been dealt a blow by subsequent events which have served to highlight that further regulation of this procedure is necessary. In the recent joined cases between Nicaragua and Costa Rica several problematic incidents arose relating to the cross-examination of experts presented by the parties. These cases similarly involved particularly complex scientific issues and the oral proceedings were dominated by the examination of party-appointed experts. At the

---

[236] See I.C.J. Pleadings, *Whaling in the Antarctic*, CR 2013/7, 3 July 2013 17.
[237] See I.C.J. Pleadings, *Whaling in the Antarctic*, CR 2013/7, 27 June 2013, 39–50 for the examination by Professor Sands for Australia, and 51–63 for the cross-examination by Professor Lowe for Japan. See I.C.J. Pleadings, *Whaling in the Antarctic*, CR 2013/7, 3 July 2013, 15 onwards, for examination by Professor Lowe and 23–48 for cross-examination by Mr Gleeson.
[238] I.C.J. Pleadings, *Whaling in the Antarctic*, CR 2013/7, 27 June 2013 63, 64, 67, 69 and 70 respectively.
[239] See I.C.J. Pleadings, *Whaling in the Antarctic*, CR 2013/7, 3 July 2013 49–50, 50–3, 53–5, 55–7, 57–9 respectively; all except Charlesworth had back-and-forth exchanges evidencing some interaction with the proceedings.

## 4.3 THE USE OF EXPERTS BEFORE THE ICJ

start of proceedings the President laid out the procedure to be followed in the same manner as the *Whaling* case.[240]

Unhappily for the Court the cross-examination of these witnesses did not proceed as smoothly as it had done in the *Whaling* case. For example, Samuel Wordsworth QC, representing Costa Rica, at various times in the course of the proceedings in both cases objected to the manner in which an expert was cross-examined by counsel for Nicaragua. Amongst Wordsworth's objections were the use of leading questions[241] and the lack of distinction between re-examination and examination-in-chief by counsel for Nicaragua.[242]

Wordsworth repeatedly objected to counsel for Nicaragua Mr Paul Reichler's line of questioning during his re-examination of an expert, accusing him of attempting to conduct another examination-in-chief, or, in other words, of trying to gain a procedural advantage. Whilst Reichler rebuffed such suggestions, the President nevertheless was forced to intervene and issue a reminder of the procedure that the Court had set out at the beginning of the proceedings and to urge counsel to restrict their line of questioning to those issues that were the subject of the cross-examination.[243] That the President was forced to do so ought to be concerning for the Court.

Whilst this may well not be an issue in every case that comes before the Court, the point remains that in order for cross-examination to function properly all involved must know exactly what is required of them – witnesses, experts, counsel and judges alike. As such, it would appear that the Court's current relaxed approach of generally sketching out the procedure at the beginning of the case does not provide enough guidance to those not familiar with the process of cross-examination (or those seeking to exploit the room for manoeuvre left by the general nature of the Court's approach). This issue undoubtedly requires attention and the Court ought to consider issuing a Practice Direction to provide specific guidance to the parties in order to ensure the proper administration of justice.[244]

---

[240] Ibid., *Pleadings, Oral Arguments*, CR/2015/3, 14 April 2015 20.
[241] Ibid., *Pleadings, Oral Arguments*, CR/2015/6, 17 April 2015 34.
[242] *Nicaragua v. Costa Rica, Joined Cases, Pleadings, Oral Arguments*, CR 2015/9, 20 April 2015 10.
[243] *Nicaragua v. Costa Rica, Joined Cases, Pleadings, Oral Arguments*, CR 2015/9, 20 April 2015 12.
[244] Neuberger, 'Expert Witnesses' para 3.

Nevertheless, when it comes to cross-examination of experts before the Court, the main benefit far outweighs the costs, namely that compared to the practice of prior written statements or of experts appearing as counsel and avoiding examination, cross-examination provides the Court with 'a critical method of testing the truthfulness, accuracy and reliability' of the expert's evidence.[245] The Court is provided with the opportunity to see experts speaking to their opinions, to clarify areas of uncertainty and ultimately to avoid the 'merry contradiction' of which Judge Simma has spoken.[246] Accordingly, the practice of experts appearing as counsel should be halted once and for all, and experts and witnesses alike should be put forward for cross-examination owing to the fact that this process is a crucial part of the judicial process. However, in order to avoid the kind of problematic issues relating to cross-examination seen in recent times this may require the introduction of a Practice Direction to further clarify the procedure for cross-examination.

The second necessary step in creating a clear strategy for the use of experts before the Court is for the Court to more regularly appoint its own experts to assist it in the handling of complex facts; it is to this issue that we now turn our attention.

### 4.3.2 Court-appointed experts

In addition to hearing party-appointed experts in open court subject to cross-examination, the appointment of the Court's own experts would assist the Court in creating a clear strategy for the use of expert evidence in a number of ways. First of all, a Court-appointed expert could act as an aid regarding the comprehension of factually complex evidence. An independent expert, appointed by the Court, in line with the practice of other international courts and tribunals as set out in Chapter 3, could assist the Court in understanding technical issues of methodology and advise as to the important nuances that exist in the particular field to

---

[245] Roberts, 'The Lubanga Trial Chamber's Assessment of Evidence in Light of the Accused's Right to the Presumption of Innocence' 936.

[246] John Jackson, 'Finding the Best Epistemic Fit for International Criminal Tribunals Beyond the Adversarial–Inquisitorial Dichotomy' 7 *Journal of International Criminal Justice* 17, 32; see also the 'Decision on the Defence Motions to Summon and Protect Defence Witnesses, and on the Giving of Evidence by Video-Link, *Tadić* (IT-94-1-T), Trial Chamber, 25 June 1996 at 11: '[t]he physical presence of a witness at the seat of the International Tribunal enables the judges to evaluate the credibility of a person giving evidence in the courtroom. Moreover, the physical presence ... may help discourage the witness from giving false testimony'.

which the parties' experts have spoken.[247] The appointment of the Court's own expert would be particularly helpful in aiding the Court in ensuring more effective questioning which in turn would help the Court to be more proactive in its approach to fact-finding and ensure that the Court was able to wring the most out of the experts presented by the parties and expose any weaknesses in their evidence. Secondly, drawing on the practice of other international courts and tribunals, the Court could appoint its own expert to assist the Court in issues related to the disclosure of evidence that may arise in the course of proceedings.

### 4.3.2 (i) An aid in the comprehension of factually complex evidence

This first advantage is important given the fact that the greater cross-examination of party-appointed experts will not be entirely unproblematic. To elaborate, the adversarial process of cross-examination, whilst helpful in testing the credibility of experts, testing bias, and drawing out information to fill gaps in the evidentiary record, is not conducive to achieving consensus between the experts appointed by the parties. In fact it has been said that cross-examination 'often undermines the commonly held assumptions upon which consensus is built and thus further promotes the impression that there is little about which the experts agree', even if in fact there is very little disagreement between the parties' experts.[248] As Lord Neuberger has said, cross-examination 'can be good theatre, but the rather gladiatorial and artificial nature of the cross-examination process may not be the best way of arriving at the truth'.[249] As such, in emphasising the differences in opinions between experts, there is the danger that cross-examination has what has been termed a 'neutralizing effect' on expert testimony which is portrayed as being 'merrily contradictory' and which, ultimately, does not assist the court.[250]

---

[247] The role of Court-appointed experts is envisaged as being to serve the function described by Lord President Cooper in *Davie v. Magistrates of Edinburgh*: 'Their duty is to furnish the Judge ... with the necessary scientific criteria for testing the accuracy of their conclusions, so as to enable the Judge ... to form their own independent judgment by the application of these criteria to the facts proved in evidence' 1953 S.C. 34 at 40; see also Couvreur, 'Le Règlement Juridictionel' 382.

[248] Joseph Sanders, 'Expert Witness Ethics' 76 *Fordham Law Review* 1539, 1577; Jasanoff, 'What Judges Should Know About the Sociology of Science' 1577.

[249] Neuberger, 'Expert Witnesses' para 31.

[250] See Jeffrey L. Harrison, 'Reconceptualizing the Expert Witness: Social Costs, Current Controls on Proposed Responses' 18 *Yale Journal on Regulation* 253, 263; Simma, 'The International Court of Justice and Scientific Expertise' 231; Samuel R. Gross, 'Expert Evidence' *Wisconsin Law Review* 1113, 1166.

Of course, such issues are apparent in all domestic legal systems which make use of cross-examination. In the legal literature of such States there are often calls to move away from this adversarial procedure in order to counter some of the difficulties that cross-examination causes.[251] Civil legal systems have a long tradition of making use of court-appointed experts to assist the court with complicated matters of evidence particularly in civil cases.[252]

Greater use of Court-appointed experts was described as the most compelling option open to the Court in the face of scientific or factual disagreement by a number of judges in the *Pulp Mills* case.[253] Judge Yusuf, for example, was of the view in the *Pulp Mills* case that the Court should have sought expert assistance as provided in Article 50 of the Court's Statute and is critical of the Court's approach to the factual complexity of the case.[254] As we saw in Chapter 1, Article 50 of the Court's Statute allows the Court to '*at any time*, entrust an individual, body, bureau, commission, or other organization that it may select, with the task of carrying out an enquiry or giving an expert opinion'.[255]

Whilst States are not provided with the explicit right to cross-examine such an expert opinion,[256] through Article 67 of the Rules of the Court parties are given the opportunity to express their opinion on the inquiry or expert opinion – granting them at least a voice on their findings.[257] The opportunity for the parties to comment upon the evidence provided by the Court's expert is crucially important in terms of the proper administration of justice and is just one of the safeguards that the Court must ensure are in place when appointing its own expert – a point to which we will return throughout the discussion of this issue.

---

[251] O'Donnell, 'Judicialising History or Historicising Law' 317; Remme Verkerk, 'Comparative Aspects of Expert Evidence in Civil Litigation' 13 *International Journal of Evidence and Proof* 167, 172; Eric Barbier de la Serre and Anne-Lise Sibony, 'Expert Evidence Before the EC Courts' 45 *Common Market Law Review* 941.

[252] de la Serre and Sibony, 'Expert Evidence before the EC Courts' 946.

[253] *Pulp Mills Case*, Joint Dissenting Opinion of Judges Al-Kasawneh and Simma at para 8.

[254] Ibid., Declaration of Judge Yusuf at 1.

[255] Article 50 of the Court's Statute, ibid., Dissenting Opinion of Judges Al-Khasawneh and Simma at para 8 (emphasis added).

[256] Article 51 ICJ Statute, Rule 67(2) ICJ Rules; Tams, 'Article 50' 1127; Yaël Ronen, 'Participation of Non-State Actors in ICJ Proceedings' 11 *The Law and Practice of International Courts and Tribunals* 77, 81.

[257] In addition, Articles 64 and 65 which refer generally to 'witnesses and experts' arguably also apply to Court-appointed experts.

## 4.3 THE USE OF EXPERTS BEFORE THE ICJ

In light of the experience of, for example, the WTO adjudicative bodies (see Chapter 3 at Section 3.1.2.5), the best means of examining experts is on an individual basis as opposed to expert groups.[258] Whilst the WTO adjudicative bodies have the power to establish a so-called expert review groups under Article 13 of the DSU it has never done so. It was argued that one of the reasons that an expert review group had not been established in the WTO context to date was due to the requirement in DSU Appendix 4 paragraph 6 that such groups prepare a report of their findings and that such a report could be seen as 'transforming the expert group into a form of a "tribunal within a tribunal"'.[259] In other words, Panels have been reluctant to tie their hands, both in terms of the flexibility of the process and limiting their discretion as to the ultimate factual determination.[260] And indeed this may also be the case with the ICJ which may have very real concerns of having the final factual determination taken out of its hands. Whilst any commission of inquiry established under Article 50 of the Court's Statute would not be able to formally bind the Court, the very production of a report of a number of experts, which would carry a great deal of epistemic weight, may be different to distinguish or depart from.[261] As such the Court's position as the final arbiter of fact may be called into doubt.

In addition, there is the suggestion that the production of a report by a group of experts could result in a 'vague and monolithic consensus position' – a common criticism of the collegiate process of adjudication.[262] Considerations of cost and time also play a role and it has been suggested that it may be easier to simply call upon one exert rather than establishing an expert review group given the time constraints imposed by the DSU.[263] For these reasons the appointment of an individual expert or a small number of experts may be preferable for the Court as opposed to a commission of inquiry.

---

[258] Foster, 'New Clothes for the Emperor? Consultation of Experts by the International Court of Justice' 15.
[259] Pauwelyn, 'The Use of Experts in WTO Dispute Settlement' 328. Such concerns have been voiced in the context of international criminal law; see Derham and Derham, 'From ad hoc to Hybrid' 27.
[260] This argument has also been put forward to explain the lack of use of commissions of experts before the European Court of Justice; see de la Serre and Sibony, 'Expert Evidence before the EC Courts' 961.
[261] Pauwelyn, 'The Use of Experts in WTO Dispute Settlement' 328.     [262] Ibid.
[263] See DSU Article 12.9; ibid.

One obvious way that the appointment of the Court's own expert would benefit the Court would be in assisting the bench to become actively involved in proceedings and ask questions.

The practice of the Court to date in relation to the asking of questions from the bench generally accords with the Court's reactive approach to fact-finding set out in Chapter 1. In other words, the Court has on the whole limited itself to individual judges asking questions from the bench during the oral proceedings.[264] Former Judge Mohammed Bedjaoui remarked upon the Court's reluctance to engage with the proceedings in accordance with its reactive approach. Judge Bedjaoui accurately describes the practice of the judges in not making regular use of their powers to ask questions or request information, but rather 'for the most part those on the bench remain silent, like a jury listening to arguments in order to weigh their merits. Hence, their passivity during the hearings is combined with impassivity'.[265]

Foster notes that practice before the ICJ differs substantially from that of the WTO adjudicative bodies which regularly put longer questions to the parties and are able for example 'to pursue the development of a thorough understanding of all aspects of the case by means of specific, direct questions to the parties after each of the oral hearings, or substantive meetings with the parties'.[266] Whilst the Court, through Articles 60 and 61 of its Rules, has the power to direct the oral proceedings and indicate which points it believes it has heard enough, the Court has been reluctant to undertake this 'exceedingly delicate' task for fear of creation the 'impression that it is inclined towards the party most sharing its view of that relevance'.[267]

Although the Court certainly remains reluctant to interrupt counsel in the presentation of their oral evidence, more recent cases have evidenced a significant number of judges asking questions of counsel and experts after they have made their presentation. For instance, in the *Whaling* case

---

[264] Riddell and Plant, *Evidence before the International Court of Justice* 88; see for instance the technical and scientific questions asked of both Argentina and Uruguay by Judge Simma; *I.C.J. Pleadings, Pulp Mills.*, CR 2009/15, 17 September 2009 67 para 1.

[265] Mohammed Bedjaoui, 'The Manufacture of Judgments at the International Court of Justice' 3 *Pace Yearbook of International Law* 29, 42.

[266] Foster, *Science and the Precautionary Principle in International Courts and Tribunals* 88. See for instance *Brazil – Measures Affecting Import of Retreaded Tyres*, Complaint by the European Communities (WT/DS332), Appellate Body Report, DSR 2007: IV, 1527; Panel Report DSR 2007: V, 1649.

[267] Bedjaoui, 'The Manufacture of Judgments at the International Court of Justice' 44.

a number of judges engaged in proceedings and asked questions, such as Judge Greenwood, who asked a question of Australia,[268] and Judge Donoghue, who asked two technical sample size questions regarding Japan's whaling programme.[269] This level of questioning is to be welcome given the fact that, especially in after the appointment of the Court's own expert, the ICJ is particularly well placed to question counsel and examine witnesses and should do so more regularly.

This is so due to the fact that, compared to judges in some domestic legal systems, those sitting on the bench at the ICJ are well acquainted with the facts. As Damaška states, 'the interrogation process – to be effective – requires the questioner to be familiar with the subject matter of inquiry'.[270] In this vein, ICJ judges, with consistently voluminous amounts of documentary evidence at their fingertips and the aid of their own expert, can be said to be sufficiently informed to ask useful, probing questions of counsel and witnesses.

Ultimately, in light of the practice of other international courts and tribunals, a more active dialogue between the Court, the parties and the experts 'would provide the opportunity for them to discover more about the essence of the issue under dispute and to help deal with issues requiring particular clarification'.[271] Consequently, as part of developing a broader strategy for the use of expert evidence before the Court, the appointment of the Court's own expert could ensure both that judges become the 'savvy consumers of scientific evidence' that they need to be and that a solid factual foundation is established through the proper administration of justice.

### 4.3.2 (ii) Facilitating the disclosure of evidence

A second advantage that increased use of Court-appointed experts would have for the Court is the role that experts can play in disputes over the disclosure of evidence, as has been demonstrated in other international courts and tribunals in Chapter 3. Increased use of Court-appointed experts would be particularly useful in cases such as the *Bosnian* and *Croatian Genocide* cases in which the Court refused to order the

---

[268] I.C.J. Pleadings, Whaling in the Antarctic, CR 2013/7, 27 June 2013, 2 July 2013 63–4.
[269] I.C.J. Pleadings, Whaling in the Antarctic, CR 2013/7, 27 June 2013, 2 July 2013 64.
[270] Mirjan Damaška, 'The Uncertain Fate of Evidentiary Transplants: Anglo-American and Continental Experiments' 45 *The American Journal of Comparative Law* 839, 850.
[271] Foster, *Science and the Precautionary Principle in International Courts and Tribunals* 134.

236   WINDS OF CHANGE: THE POSSIBILITY OF REFORM

production of redacted evidence from the other party and justified this decision through somewhat oblique reasoning (see above at Section 2.1.3). Again, drawing inspiration the practice of other international courts and tribunals, the appointment of the Court's own expert would allow it to better handle such disputes which appear to be becoming increasingly commonplace in practice today.

Recalling a number of examples set out in Chapter 3 serves to illustrate the usefulness of tribunal-appointed experts in this role. For instance, in the *Guyana v. Suriname* arbitration examined in Section 3.2.2 the tribunal appointed an independent expert to assess the claims of Guyana with regard to the disclosure of a number of redacted documents in the possession of Suriname.[272] The appointment of an expert to fulfil this role appears to have worked well in this case and to the satisfaction of both States.

In the same vein, other inter-State arbitrations have become actively involved in disputes over the disclosure of documents. Whilst these arbitrations did not all adopt the approach taken in the *Guyana v. Suriname* case, they all displayed a willingness to engage proactively in the resolution of the dispute one way or another. For instance, in the *Kishenganga* arbitration the Court proposed a compromise solution of seeking an examination of the material *in camera* before making a judgment as to whether it should be disclosed in full to the other party.[273]

A similar sequence of events took place in the more recent arbitration between Mauritius and the United Kingdom conducted under the auspices of the Permanent Court of Arbitration. In the course of this arbitration Mauritius challenged the redactions made to a number of documents by the United Kingdom.[274] Mauritius was persistent in seeking an explanation for the redaction of the documents[275] and subsequently the Tribunal intervened by taking the step of writing to the parties and 'urging' the United Kingdom to remove all aforementioned redactions 'not strictly required on grounds of irrelevancy or legal professional privilege' and to justify its decisions one way or another.[276] Despite several attempts to assure Mauritius that it was not unduly

---

[272] Order No. 3, 2.0. and 3.2.3.     [273] See Procedural Order No. 8, at 3.4.
[274] *In the Matter of the Chagos Marine Protected Area Arbitration before an Arbitral Tribunal Constituted under Annex VII of the United Nations Convention on the Law of the Sea between the Republic of Mauritius and the United Kingdom of Great Britain and Northern Ireland, Award, 18 March 2015* para 35.
[275] Raising this issue consistently throughout the proceedings, see ibid. paras 35, 36 and 37.
[276] Ibid. para 38.

withholding information and that all redactions could be justified,[277] Mauritius continued to express concerns regarding the United Kingdom's reasons for non-disclosure of certain sections of documents. As a result, Mauritius invited the Tribunal to request the United Kingdom to provide unredacted copies of the documents concerned for what it termed *ex parte* review to achieve a determination that the reasons the UK had given were justified.

The Tribunal duly obliged and requested the United Kingdom to disclose to it those documents, which were set out in Annex 185, to the Tribunal. The United Kingdom subsequently agreed and arranged for the documents to be delivered to the British Consulate-General in Istanbul where the Tribunal could examine the documents.[278] The Tribunal's role in the fact-finding process in this regard is significant and notably proactive. The Tribunal then proposed a procedure consisting of a preliminary review by the Presiding Arbitrator followed by the Tribunal as a whole to confirm 'that the contents of each redaction qualify for non-disclosure on grounds recognized by the Tribunal'.[279] Ultimately, upon inspecting the documents the President determined that the United Kingdom's reasons for not providing unredacted versions of the relevant documents were justified and that there would be no need for the rest of the Tribunal to attend and that the Tribunal was justified in finding that the documents in question need not be redacted.[280]

What the preceding examples serve to illustrate is that more proactive tribunals are not immediately threatening to States and can in fact help to facilitate the disclosure of further information required for the proper administration of justice. For this reason it is argued that the appointment of an expert by the Court to handle disputes over the disclosure of documents as the tribunal in *Guyana v. Suriname* did would be advantageous for the Court and would not unduly wrest control over the production of evidence from the parties to the case before the Court.

### 4.3.2 (iii) Necessary safeguards for the appointment of the Court's own expert

Of course, the use of independent experts also has potential drawbacks. To elaborate, Court-appointed experts must be sure not to disrupt the nature of the judicial process. It is for these reasons that in the WTO context, where Panel-appointed experts are common, written

---

[277] Ibid. paras 38, 39, 40.   [278] Ibid. para 45.   [279] Ibid. para 47.
[280] Ibid. para 49.

instructions to experts have increasingly included an explicit request to refrain from expressing their views on the law.[281] In addition, such concerns have also led to the development of the so-called ultimate issue rule in other contexts in international adjudication as an attempt to ensure the integrity of adjudicators as final arbiters of fact and law.

The prospect of increased use of experts by the Court will undoubtedly raise concerns regarding whether the Court would be potentially delegating its judicial function to the expert. This issue has arisen in other contexts and sparked widespread academic debate.[282] Ultimately, however, such concerns are not sufficient reason to detract from the advantages that greater use of experts would bring. Today in other contexts, as in the past,[283] the 'ultimate issue rule' has come to govern the relationship between the bench and experts.

Essentially the ultimate issue in any case is the disputed legal issue which represents the very reason the tribunal was convened. The rule holds that despite the fact that an expert has been appointed, and although their determinations may prove significant to the outcome of the case, an expert should never be the person left to make a final legal determination, such as whether a person is criminally responsible for committing a crime – that task remains with the adjudicator.[284]

---

[281] Foster, *Science and the Precautionary Principle in International Courts and Tribunals* 78; *Japan – Measures Affective Agricultural Products*, Appellate Body Report, WT/DS76/AB/R, 22 February 1999 para 129; Boyle and Harrison, 'Judicial Settlement of International Environmental Disputes: Current Problems' 273.

[282] Foster, 'New Clothes for the Emperor? Consultation of Experts by the International Court of Justice' 14; Jacur, 'Remarks on the Role of Ex Curia Scientific Experts in International Environmental Disputes' 444; Boyle and Harrison, 'Judicial Settlement of International Environmental Disputes: Current Problems' 271.

[283] Historically the ultimate issue principle has operated in a number of Common Law jurisdictions. Although this rule has been formally abolished in many jurisdictions the general principle that experts must not speak to the crucial legal issues of the case is still influential; see Foster, *Science and the Precautionary Principle in International Courts and Tribunals* 146.

[284] See *Prosecutor v. Kordic and Cerkez*, Case No IT-95-14, Transcript, 29 January 2000 13–89; see also Special Court for Sierra Leone, *Prosecutor v. Brima et al.*; Gert-Jan Alexander Knoops, 'The Proliferation of the Ultimate Issue Rule Pertaining to Expert Witnesses Testimony before International and Internationalized Criminal Courts: Pitfalls and Paradoxes' in Giuliana Ziccardi Capaldo (ed), *The Global Community Yearbook of International Law and Jurisprudence 2001*, Vol 1; *Prosecutor v. Casimir Bizimungu et al. (Decision on the Admissibility of the Expert Testimony of Dr Binafair Nowrojee)* ICTR-99-50-T, 8 July 2005. 'The judge ... can determine equally well ... [and] thus the special legal knowledge of the judge [renders the witness' opinion unnecessary]', see Deon J. Nossel, 'The Admissibility of Ultimate Issue Expert Testimony

For instance, the ICTY Trial Chamber has in the past upheld the objection of the defence and prevented reliance on an evidentiary report which related to the ultimate issue of the case, saying that this was the exclusive competence of the Trial Chamber.[285] Similarly the *Prosecutor v. Brima et al.* case[286] before Trial Chamber II of the Special Court for Sierra Leone stated that whilst any information that was relevant was admissible under Rule 89(C), it would disregard any information presented by the experts which 'draws any conclusions or inferences which the Trial Chamber will have to draw, or makes any judgments which the Trial Chamber will have to make'.[287]

In the *Pulp Mills* case Judge Yusuf specifically addressed this issue, playing down concerns for two main reasons. First of all, in addition to ensuring that parties were provided with the opportunity to comment on the evidence of the Court's expert, Judge Yusuf argued that it was for the expert merely to elucidate and 'clarify the scientific validity of the methods used to establish certain facts', but importantly, that it was not for the expert to weigh the probative value of the facts.[288] Secondly, the judge sought to assuage fears over the use of experts by highlighting that 'the elucidation of facts by the experts is always subject to the assessment of such expertise and the determination of the facts underling it *by the Court*'.[289] Judge Yusuf also provided guidance as to how the Court should utilise experts in such situations, namely not by entrusting the clarification of 'all the facts submitted to it' in a wholesale manner, but rather by identifying specific areas in which the Court needs specific assistance or clarification before employing experts'.[290]

In the context of international criminal law commentators have argued that issues such as individual criminal responsibility should not be

---

by Law Enforcement Officers in Criminal Trials' 93 *Colum Law Review* 231, citing J. Wigmore, *Evidence in Trials at Common Law* (3rd Edn, 1952) 103.

[285] See *Prosecutor v. Kordic and Cerkez*, IT-95-14, Transcript, 28 January 2000 13–89; see also *Prosecutor v. Kovacevic* IT-97-24-T, Transcript, 6 July 1998 13305–7, in which the Trial Chamber held that expert opinion contained many 'conclusions, drawing inferences, drawing conclusions, which is the duty of the Trial Chamber to consider and to draw if appropriate or reject' which would 'invade the right, power and duty of the Trial Chamber to rule upon this issue'.

[286] *Prosecutor v. Brima et al.*, Case 16, Transcripts, 14 October 2005 38.

[287] Knoops, 'The Proliferation of the Ultimate Issue Rule Pertaining to Expert Witnesses Testimoney before International and Internationalized Criminal Courts' 289.

[288] *Pulp Mills Case*, Declaration of Judge Yusuf at para 10.

[289] Ibid., Delcaraiton of Judge Yusuf at para 10 (emphasis added).

[290] Ibid., Declaration of Judge Yusuf at para 11.

determined by expert witnesses and that they should not assist the tribunal in question in making such determinations, which remain within the sole purview of the tribunal itself.[291] That the ultimate issue rule operates in this way is essential in safeguarding the rights of the accused and preventing extra-judicial bodies from having inappropriate influence over tribunals.[292] Utilising the ultimate issue rule, judges are capable of critically considering the assistance provided by the Court-appointed expert and taking this into account when making both factual and legal determinations.[293] As Moreno has stated, '[j]udges do not need to become trained scientists to achieve accurate and consistent legal decision-making in cases involving scientific evidence. They need to become savvy consumers of the scientific evidence that comes before them'.[294]

### 4.3.3 Summary: a clear strategy for the use of experts before the Court

In short, it has been argued that a further means through which the Court could take a more proactive approach in order to address the weaknesses in its fact-finding procedure set out in Chapter 2 is to develop a clear strategy for dealing with the use of experts before the Court. This would potentially involve a more proactive approach to asking questions of parties from the bench and cross-examination of party-appointed witnesses to draw out the information needed to make solid factual determinations. Further, the Court could make greater use of its powers to appoint its own experts under Article 50 of the Statute, which would serve a number of purposes including helping the Court to deal with complex facts, more effectively questioning party-appointed experts and even including the establishment of a procedure for the resolution of disputes over the disclosure of evidence between the parties. In this vein the Court ought to ensure, in addition to allowing the parties the opportunity to comment on the evidence of its expert, it retains the final determination of both law and facts accordance with the 'ultimate issue rule'.

---

[291] Knoops, 'The Proliferation of the Ultimate Issue Rule Pertaining to Expert Witnesses Testimoney before International and Internationalized Criminal Courts' 291.
[292] Ibid. [293] Simma, 'The International Court of Justice and Scientific Expertise'.
[294] Joelle Moreno, 'Einstein on the Bench?: Exposing What Judges Do Not Know About Science and Using Child Abuse Cases to Improve How Courts Evaluate Scientific Evidence' 64 *Ohio State Law Journal* 531, 549.

## 4.4 Chapter 4 summary: realistic measures to achieve a more proactive approach to fact-finding

This chapter focused on a small number of issues related to the Court's procedural operation that could realistically be adapted, should the Court so choose, to in order to remedy some of the current weaknesses in its procedure. It was argued that, in addition to making greater use of pre-hearing conferences, the Court could viably develop a power to compel the production of evidence through purposively interpreting its current fact-finding powers and by relying on the duty of each party to collaborate in the production of evidence. Similarly, it was argued that the Court could make greater use of provisional measures to giving binding force to its requests for information, subject to a number of conditions. Further, a substantial part of the chapter focused on the Court's use of experts and set out a number of ways in which the Court could develop a clear strategy for better use of expert evidence in cases that come before it in order to remedy some of the weaknesses of its fact-finding procedure, as set out in Chapter 2.

This chapter has chosen to focus on a small number of changes that could realistically be made through orders or practice directions, crucially without amendment of the Court's Statute, and that are based on the practice of other inter-State courts and tribunals. The value of drawing on the comparative exercise undertaken in Chapter 3 is that all the suggestions made in this chapter are currently in operation with regard to a similar inter-State Court – lending additional realism and credibility to the suggestions. Nevertheless, even if the Court were to decide to adopt a more proactive approach to the facts, perhaps through utilising one of the means proposed in this chapter, there are a number of potential obstacles and limitations facing the Court. It is these obstacles and limitations that are the subject of the final chapter.

# 5

# A more proactive approach to fact-finding

## (i) Introduction

In assessing the relative merits of a more proactive approach to fact-finding, this final chapter shows that whilst the Court's current approach is not without its advantages, the criticisms of this approach explored in detail in Chapter 2 are justified. As such, the chapter then moves on to consider a more proactive approach to fact-finding. In doing so, Chapter 5 first illustrates in practical terms what the more proactive approach set out in Chapter 4 would look like. Whilst a case was made for such reforms in the preceding chapter, Chapter 5 considers the limitations of the Court's fact-finding powers that have been advocated and ruminates on the merits of the Court's current reactive approach to fact-finding. Having considered the limitations of the Court's fact-finding powers, it is clear that taking a more proactive approach to fact-finding is no panacea for the current problems that the Court faces. Nevertheless, it is maintained that implementing the proposals set out in Chapter 4 would ultimately leave the Court better placed to make accurate factual determinations upon which the law could be decided.

## 5.1 Positive aspects of the Court's current reactive approach

At this point it should be reiterated that at no stage has it been argued that the Court has ever unjustifiably taken a position whereby it has avoided focusing on factual issues in favour of solely addressing the law. As stated above, if one has not been in the Court's position it is often difficult to imagine how one could prove that a decision taken by the Court to focus on legal issues and not conduct further fact-finding was the wrong decision. It may be that the Court had sound reasons for not conducting its own fact-finding, such as considerations of judicial economy or the fact that resolution of those factual issues was not central to

## 5.1 POSITIVE ASPECTS OF THE ICJ'S CURRENT APPROACH   243

the resolution of the dispute at hand.[1] Rather, it was argued that instead of talking in terms of the Court using 'avoidance techniques' in order to negate the need to engage with the facts, the most that can be said is that the Court has very clearly displayed a number of tendencies which, taken together, demonstrate a consistently reactive approach to the facts in cases that have come before it.

In addition, it should be made clear that the reactive approach is not without its benefits. For instance, it could be said that by focusing on the legal issues in a particular case the Court reduces the possibility of the case being distinguished on the facts in the future, therefore increasing the (already extremely significant) legal value of the Court's pronouncements.[2] In addition, there are a number of practical reasons why it may be sensible for the Court to place the emphasis on the parties in terms of fact-finding. This is the case since the Court is often significantly removed from the facts of the dispute, both in terms of distance and time. Given that the highly political nature of cases before the Court means that it may take many years for the proceedings to begin, the value of 'descending' on the site to conduct its own fact-finding is somewhat dubious. As such, it makes more sense for the parties themselves, who are generally closer to the facts, to put such evidence before the Court, than for the Court (limited as its resources are) to embark on a fact-finding expedition from the Hague.

Staying with the nature of the cases that come before the Court, the sheer breadth of legal and factual issues, number of witnesses and expanse of territory can often in some way justify the Court's reactive position. For instance, in cases such as *Armed Activities, Bosnian Genocide* and *Croatian Genocide*, the disputes in question involved a dizzying array of factual and legal issues which took place on the territory of a number of different States and over the course of many years. In such circumstances the Court's decision to rely on information submitted by the parties, established in cases before other international tribunals such as the ICTY or in UN Commissions of Inquiry is eminently understandable.

---

[1] The Court has referred to the principle of judicial economy as 'an element of the requirements of the sound administration of justice'; see *Croatian Genocide Preliminary Objections* para 89.

[2] This is so despite the Court's legal pronouncements having no binding force apart from between the parties to the case before it under Article 59 of the Court's Statute, and despite there existing no formal doctrine of *stare decisis*, the Court's pronouncements have always been accorded significant respect by States, scholars and other international tribunals; see Shahabuddeen, *Precedent in the World Court* (Cambridge University Press, 1996).

Furthermore, as stated above, many States see it as part of their privilege as sovereign States to choose what evidence they put before the Court. The traditional argument is that States prefer to retain as much control over the evidentiary process as possible, and that as such they would be hostile to the Court taking greater control over the process and becoming more actively involved.[3] For instance, Foster has argued that 'international disputants will generally want to bear primary responsibility for mustering the evidence in support of their cases and presenting it to an international court'.[4] It has been argued that the presentation of the case being left to the parties themselves is fundamentally important regarding the parties' perception of the fairness of the procedure.[5] As such, it would appear to make little sense for the Court to duplicate the fact-finding efforts of the parties. Ultimately, in such cases the Court's decision to accept the evidence put before it by the parties and to concentrate on the points of contention as defined by the parties could in the circumstances turn out to be the most prudent option available to the Court.

Indeed, it has not at any stage been argued that the Court should completely disregard all evidence submitted to it by the parties in favour of undertaking wide-ranging fact-finding of its own accord; this is simply not practicable. Rather, it has been argued that there are a number of deficiencies in the way the Court currently operates and that the practice of other international courts and tribunals in some way provides helpful reference points when considering reform in order to ensure that the Court makes factual determinations that are as accurate as they possibly can be.

These deficiencies have presented the Court with real problems, and as such, despite the positive aspects of the Court's current approach to fact-finding (which undoubtedly exist), it is maintained that there is a pressing need for the Court to consider reform. As Chapter 2 set out in detail, the Court's reactive approach to fact-finding can be a recipe for an unsure factual foundation upon which to make legal judgments.[6] The Court's approach to expert evidence and use of *experts fantômes*, cross-examination, and over-reliance on UN Commissions of Inquiry all have problematic aspects which undermine the Court's fact-finding process. Furthermore, in cases where a party fails to appear before the Court, its

---

[3] J. K. Cogan, 'The 2010 Judicial Activity of the International Court of Justice' 105 *American Journal of International Law* 477.
[4] Foster, *Science and the Precautionary Principle in International Courts and Tribunals* 80.
[5] Ibid.
[6] Alvarez, 'Are International Judges Afraid of Science?: A Comment on Mbengue' 87.

reactive approach to fact-finding is found wanting due to the fact that it only has the evidence of one party upon which to make its findings of fact. Without conducting its own investigations into the factual background of the case at hand the Court's reactive approach, which makes the Court dependent on States to submit the facts to it, is a handicap. Drawing on the practice of other international courts and tribunals, Chapter 4 set out a number of proposals which the Court could adopt in an attempt to remedy the current deficiencies of the Court's current approach to the fact-finding process. As such, it is useful at this stage to consider how the Court's approach to fact-finding would look if it were to adopt a more proactive approach to fact-finding.

## 5.2 How to deal with factually complex cases before the Court

Early consultation between the parties regarding those factual issues upon which there is agreement and those which are likely to be contentious could help to focus the Court's attention on the areas where it is most needed.[7] At the moment pre-trial conferences are 'limited to participation of the representatives of the parties and the President' and are 'off the record'.[8] The suggestion that the Court make greater use of pre-hearing conferences is one that certainly could benefit the operation of the Court.[9] The reform of this process would not be problematic and could be achieved through an order under Article 48 of the Court's Statute.

Any party requiring access to information held by the other party (subject to the conditions of sole possession, previous attempts to obtain information and the establishment of a *prima facie* case)[10] could make this known to the Court.[11] At this early stage the Court could consider utilising its provisional measures powers, which are broad enough to cover the proper conduct of the judicial process to ensure that the Court is able to render a judgment that is effective.[12] To this end, the preservation of evidence 'without which a party might not be able to prove its claim and the tribunal might not be able to settle the dispute' is a

---

[7] Foster, *Science and the Precautionary Principle in International Courts and Tribunals* 79; see Rosenne, 'Fact-Finding before the International Court of Justice' 247.
[8] See Rosenne, 'Fact-Finding before the International Court of Justice' 247.
[9] Holtzmann, *Streamlining Arbitral Proceedings* .   [10] See Section 4.1.4(iv).
[11] See Section 4.1.
[12] See Section 4.2; Wolfrum, 'Interim (Provisional) Measures of Protection' para 7; Brown, *A Common Law of International Adjudication* 121.

legitimate aim of provisional measures.[13] During the initial stages of the proceedings, however, the initiative for placing information before the Court would by and large remain with the parties.

In cases of non-appearance the Court would take a more proactive approach to fact-finding and attempt to test the applicant States' claims itself.[14] Being proactive in cases of non-appearance by employing 'whatever means and resources may enable it to satisfy itself whether the submissions of the applicant State are well-founded in fact and law'[15] is the only way to properly ensure parties' due process rights. Instances of non-appearance have occurred in some of the most politically significant cases in the history of the Court and as long as the Court's jurisdiction operates on a consensual basis it can never be ruled out that at any time the Court may again be faced by the difficulties that non-appearance poses to its reactive approach to fact-finding.[16]

Should the parties wish to present expert evidence, such experts should be put before the Court subject to examination and cross-examination. In no circumstances should experts appear as counsel.[17] In doing so the Court will reap the benefits of cross-examination of the expert evidence and avoid the 'merry contradiction' of two (equally well-qualified) experts with opposing views.[18] Relatedly, in such situations the Court should seriously consider the appointment of its own expert to assist it in the evaluation of the technical or factually complex elements of the dispute.[19] At no time should the Court consult *experts fantômes* as this practice is contrary to the proper administration of justice.[20] During the cross-examination of the parties' experts, and with the assistance of the Court's own expert, the Court, having access to copious amounts of documentary evidence, should be encouraged to put questions to the parties on issues on which it feels require further clarification or elaboration as the Court is entitled to do under Article 61 of the Court's Rules.

If at any time the Court encounters resistance from the parties it should display greater willingness to draw adverse inferences from this

---

[13] See *Sino-Belgium Case*, Order of 8 January 1927, II ('as regards property and shipping'); Brown, *A Common Law of International Adjudication* 122.
[14] Riddell and Plant, *Evidence before the International Court of Justice* 223; *Nuclear Tests Case 1974* para 15 and 257 para 16.
[15] *Nicaragua Case* para 59.   [16] Von Mangoldt and Zimmermann, 'Article 53' 1353.
[17] See Section 4.3.1.
[18] Simma, 'The International Court of Justice and Scientific Expertise' 231.
[19] See Article 50 of the Court's Statute as elaborated in Article 62(2) of the Rules.
[20] See Section 4.3.1.

lack of co-operation. Whether a party has refused to comply with a provisional measure indicated by the Court or an order for the disclosure of information (this order being compulsory, in line with the interpretation of Article 49 ICJ Statute set out in Chapter 4 at Section 4.1.), the Court should utilise its Article 49 ICJ Statute power to draw adverse inferences in a way that it has hitherto been reluctant. As stated above, the real utility of such action is in inducing disclosure rather than the actual inference itself.

These proposed reforms are relatively small in number and could realistically be made through orders or practice directions, crucially without amendment of the Court's Statute, and are based on the practice of other inter-State courts and tribunals. The value of drawing on the comparative exercise undertaken in Chapter 3 is that all the proposals made are currently in operation with regard to a similar inter-State Court – lending additional realism and credibility to the suggestions. However, it must be conceded that, even if the Court were to follow this exact procedure, a more proactive approach from the Court, which makes greater use of the Court's fact-finding powers, is no panacea. In relation to all of the avenues that it is suggested the Court could take in improving its fact-finding process, there are obstacles.

## 5.3 The limits of the Court's fact-finding powers

There are a number of significant limits to the proposals designed to improve the Court's approach to fact-finding as set out in Chapter 4. It is important to emphasise that the proposals set out in Chapter 4 do not represent blind faith in the increased use of all of the Court's fact-finding powers as the answer to those problems that it currently faces. A number of examples serve to illustrate this point.

First of all, although States have not voiced their opposition to the progressive interpretation of the equivalent fact-finding power in the context of the WTO, there of course remains the possibility that States could reject similar moves by the ICJ in relation to interpreting Article 49 of its Statute as being binding on the parties as advocated in Chapter 4.[21] In such circumstances, owing to the consensual nature of the Court's jurisdiction, the threat of States 'taking their business elsewhere' (or more problematic still, seeking to resolve the dispute through non-pacific

---

[21] See Section 4.1.

means) could influence the Court in future decisions as to whether to uphold this progressive interpretation of Article 49.

Furthermore, even if the Court were to insist that its Article 49 power is compulsory, should any party refuse to co-operate (whether it be with a request for information contained in a provisional measure or under Article 49 specifically, or more general non-co-operation with the Court) the only option left to the Court is to draw adverse inferences. However, the power to draw adverse inferences is one that the Court explicitly possesses (again in Article 49 ICJ Statute) and as such the utility of insisting upon the compulsory nature of its power to order the production of evidence by the parties is open to question.[22]

In addition, it is unclear to what extent greater use of the Court's fact-finding powers will help to remedy those problems the Court faces in cases of non-appearance as discussed in the second half of Chapter 2. To elaborate, it was argued in Chapter 2 that in cases of non-appearance the Court should be more proactive in utilising those fact-finding powers that it already possesses, such as requesting information from an existing UN Commission of Inquiry or requesting the establishment of such an inquiry to assist it.[23] However, recent practice of UN Commissions of Inquiry has illustrated that even where additional fact-finding is carried out, lack of consent from the State involved in the investigation can amount to a near-insurmountable obstacle. It is of course the State's own sovereign prerogative to withhold such consent and this prerogative continues to limit the extent to which the Court and the United Nations more generally can be proactive in its fact-finding.[24]

A clear example of this can be seen in the experience of the UN Human Rights Council's Gaza inquiry in 2009. Israel's refusal to co-operate with the Goldstone Inquiry is a clear example of how non-co-operation can present serious difficulties in terms of fact-finding.[25] Goldstone himself has recently spoken of the difficulties presented by Israel's non-co-operation,

---

[22] For a full account see M. Benzing, *Das Beweisrecht vor internationalen Gerichten und Schiedsgerichten in zwischenstaatlichen Streitigkeiten*, Vol 215 (Berlin, Heidelberg: Springer, 2010).

[23] See Section 2.2.

[24] Article 2(7) sets out that '[n]othing contained in the present Charter shall authorize the United Nations to intervene in matters which are essentially within the domestic jurisdiction of any state or shall require the Members to submit such matters to settlement under the present Charter; but this principle shall not prejudice the application of enforcement measures under Chapter VII'.

[25] HRC Resolution A/HRC/12/48, 25 September 2009.

## 5.3 THE LIMITS OF THE ICJ'S FACT-FINDING POWERS 249

which he states, along with the subsequent emergence of further information, caused him many 'sleepless nights' and cast doubt upon a number of the factual determinations made in the Goldstone Inquiry which ultimately caused Goldstone to 'row back' on a number of the inquiry's factual determinations in a now infamous *Washington Post* opinion-editorial.[26] Non-co-operation necessarily entails greater reliance on secondary sources such as press reports and interviews with individuals who claim to have witnessed certain events which, whilst still useful to some extent, are of less probative value than primary fact-finding.[27] Such practice cautions against reliance on factual determinations made in fact-finding inquiries which were not granted consent to visit the area under investigation (and indeed, in practice consent is denied on a regular basis).[28] As such, the extent to which increased use of the Court's fact-finding powers will actually result in more information coming before the Court is unclear.

Moreover, there are a number of the Court's fact-finding powers that were not advocated by the present author in relation to the improvement of the Court's fact-finding process. For instance, as stated above, greater use of the Court's power to conduct site visits under Article 44(2) of its Statute is not advocated. Whilst there is little doubt that such site visits provide helpful background to the complex facts of a case, questions remain regarding their use as a fact-finding tool capable of bringing important new information before the Court.[29] Ultimately, the utility of a group of judges who are not experts making site visits under Article 44(2) ICJ Statue in cases involving particularly complex or technical facts is doubtful.

Similarly, it should be noted that increased use of the Court's competence to establish a commission of inquiry under Article 50 of the Court's

---

[26] Richard J. Goldstone, 'Quality Control in International Fact-Finding Outside Criminal Justice for Core International Crimes' in Morten Bergsmo (ed), *Quality Control in Fact-Finding* (Florence: Torkel-Opsahl, 2013) 50.
[27] See Section 1.4.
[28] Chinkin, 'U.N. Human Rights Council Fact-Finding Missions: Lessons from Gaza' 488. Such refusal of admittance is in fact commonplace in practice; see Weissbrodt and McCarthy, 'Fact-Finding by International Nongovernmental Human Rights Organizations' 59: 'the great bulk of human rights fact-finding by both IGOs and NGOs is accomplished without on-site visits'. See also, for example, Israel's refusal to allow the Human Rights Council's fact-finding mission to visit the Occupied Palestinian Territory under HRC Resolution S-1/1. Similarly, the high-level fact-finding mission to Darfur was unable to obtain visas from the Government of Sudan. HRC Res 4/8, 30 March 2007. See also, for example, HRC Resolution S-17/1, 23 August 2011; see First Report A/HRC/S-17/1/2/Add.1 and Second Report A/HRC/19/69, 22 February 2012.
[29] Walter, 'Article 44' 1048.

Statute as it did in the *Corfu Channel* case is not advocated. This reluctance can be attributed to the fact that other inter-State tribunals such as the WTO and inter-State arbitrations have displayed a preference for reliance on individual experts rather than commissions of inquiry or expert review groups. This can be attributed to a fear of creating a 'tribunal within a tribunal'.[30] As stated above, the Court may be loath to fetter its own discretion, both in terms of the flexibility of the fact-finding process and limiting its discretion as to the ultimate factual determination by establishing a commission of inquiry under Article 50 of its Statute. On the other hand, individual experts offer the Court greater control over the fact-finding process and avoid the Court being presenting with a report representing the common findings of a group of experts which would carry great epistemic weight and would be extremely hard to contradict or nuance. In addition, of course, this reluctance is also the result of resource constraints which obviously limit the Court's ability to establish a commission of inquiry under Article 50 of its Statute. Both financial and time restraints would appear to favour the appointment of an individual expert as opposed to a commission of inquiry under Article 50 of the Court's Statute.[31] Time and resource constraints are fundamentally important to the Court and must not be overlooked at any stage when considering reform of the Court's procedure.

The practice of other international courts and tribunals as examined in Chapter 3 also cautions against advocating greater resort to witness testimony. The problematic handling of witnesses and the dubious value that such witnesses have brought to international proceedings to date, coupled with the fact that the Court has never called a witness *proprio motu* under Article 50 of its Statute, prevented this this particular reform from being advocated.[32] In the same vein, the WTO's experience in utilising the burden of proof raises fears that manipulating the burden of proof before the ICJ would complicate rather than improve the Court's fact-finding process.[33] To date the Court has somewhat shied away from

---

[30] See Section 3.1.2.5.
[31] See DSU Article 12.9; Pauwelyn, 'The Use of Experts in WTO Dispute Settlement' 328.
[32] Article 50 states that '[t]he Court may, at any time, entrust any individual, body, bureau, commission, other organization that it may select, with the task of carrying out an enquiry or giving an expert opinion'. See Section 1.1.5; Higgins, 'Speech by H. E. Judge Rosalyn Higgins, President of the International Court of Justice to the Sixth Committee of the General Assembly'; Talmon, 'Article 43' paras 133–6.
[33] See the lengthy section on the WTO's experience with the burden of proof in Section 3.1.4.

making explicit statements on the burden and standard of proof in cases that have come before it. Whilst increasingly complex cases coming before the Court may lead some to call for a clearer articulation of the burden of proof, the practice of the adjudicative bodies of the WTO should be a cautionary tale for the Court as attempts to utilise the burden of proof have brought an element of uncertainty to proceedings.[34]

The Court's Article 30(2) ICJ Statute power to appoint an assessor as an independent expert to assist judges in technical matters, crucially without the right to vote, has been advocated by some commentators.[35] However, such proposals are not advocated for two simple reasons. First of all, in contrast to the other proposals put forward in Chapter 4, such provisions in the constitutive instruments and rules of procedure of other international courts and tribunals have never been utilised and as such there is no relevant practice upon which to draw to support the claim that any moves in this direction would benefit the Court as they have benefitted other international tribunals.[36] Secondly, assessors in their role in aiding the Court in specific factual matters without having a vote in the proceedings is ultimately similar to that of a Court-appointed expert.[37] Given that increased use of such experts is so strongly advocated in Chapter 4 the need for the appointment of assessors in addition is rendered less necessary.

One proposal that deserves closer attention is that of making more regular use of Article 34(2) of the Court's Statute. Article 34(2) provides that the Court may request of public international organisations information relevant to cases before it and represents another fact-finding tool

---

[34] Ibid.
[35] C. Payne, 'Mastering the Evidence: Improving Fact-Finding by International Courts' 41 *Environmental Law Journal* 1191, 1217; see Federal Rules of Civil Procedure 53 (c)(1). Such masters were appointed by the U.S. Supreme Court in almost every case between 1961 and 1992; now authorised by Federal Rules of Civil Procedure, Rule 53, and corresponding State measures; see Federal Rules of Civil Procedure 53, e.g. Massachusetts Rules of Civil Procedure 53; the appointment of assessors is explicitly provided for in Article 30(2) of the Court's Statute and similar provisions exist in the constitutive instruments of other international courts and tribunals such as Article 289 UNCLOS; see Myron H. Nordquist, *United National Convention on the Law of the Sea*, Myron H. Nordquist, S. Rosenne and Louis B. Sohn (eds), Vol V, Articles 279–320, Annexes VI, VI, VII, VIII and IX, Final Act, Annex I, Resolutions I, II, III and IV, (The Hague, Martinus Nijhoff 1989) 51; Gudmundur Eiriksson, *The International Tribunal for the Law of the Sea* (The Hague: Martinus Nijhoff, 2000) 67; Neuberger, 'Expert Witnesses' para 29.
[36] Treves, 'Law and Science in the Interpretation of the Law of the Sea Convention' 485; Annex VII is different in that Arts 2 and 3 stipulate qualifications for experts.
[37] Foster, *Science and the Precautionary Principle in International Courts and Tribunals* 127.

for the Court.[38] Although the Court has not made significant use of this provision to date, greater use of this provision could provide the Court with additional information that would not have been put before it by the parties.[39] To elaborate, in taking a more proactive approach to the facts, under Article 34(2) the Court could request the Human Rights Council or the UN Secretary-General, for instance, to establish a commission of inquiry to provide it with more information in relation to factual issues that have arise in cases that come before the Court.

Utilising Article 34(2) as such it could be foreseen that the Court could exert control over a number of procedural issues relating to the establishment of the fact-finding inquiry, including specifying on exactly which issues it requires further assistance. Furthermore, this procedure would have the additional benefit of being a relatively inexpensive way of bringing additional information before the Court due to the fact that the costs incurred would be borne by the General Assembly or the Secretary-General.

However, whilst Article 34(2) of the Court's Statute is, at least in theory, another means by which the Court can bring information not submitted by the parties before the Court, in reality jurisdictional constraints mean that Article 34(2) is unlikely to ever meaningfully alter the way in which information comes before the Court. Such constraints significantly limit the number of contentious cases as well as advisory opinions that the Court is asked to adjudicate.[40] In addition to such jurisdictional problems there are of course the dangers associated with executive-administrative finality, as discussed at length in Chapter 2.

Ultimately the preceding sections have sought to demonstrate two points. First of all, not all of the Court's fact-finding powers are advocated as ways in which the Court could address the weaknesses in its

---

[38] The corresponding Rules of the Court, Article 69(1) to (3), state that the Court can 'at any time prior to the closure of the oral proceedings, either *proprio motu* or at the request of one of the parties ... request a public international organization ... to furnish information relevant to a case before it'; Chinkin and Mackenzie, 'Intergovernmental Organizations as "Friends of the Court"' 140.

[39] For a fuller discussion of the merits of taking the course of action considered in this subsection, see Devaney, 'Killing Two Birds with One Stone'.

[40] In accordance with this provision the General Assembly and the Council can request an advisory opinion on 'any legal question' and under Article 96(2) any other organ or specialised agency, if so authorised by the Assembly, can request an opinion on any question 'arising within the scope of their activities'; B. Simma, 'Article 92' in B. Simma (ed), *The Charter of the United Nations: A Commentary* (2nd edn, Oxford University Press, 2002).

current fact-finding process. Secondly, those reforms that are proposed which involve greater use of certain fact-finding powers are limited in nature and are not a perfect solution to the problems the Court currently faces. In short, not only does the Court's current reactive approach to fact-finding have its merits, but the Court's fact-finding powers are also limited in nature. Nevertheless, it is maintained that the reforms proposed in Chapter 4, were they to be adopted, have the potential to materially improve the fact-finding process before the International Court of Justice.

# Epilogue

The central argument of this book, that taking a more proactive approach to fact-finding will enable the Court to address a number of current weaknesses in its approach to fact-finding, is not merely academic. The proposals advocated in Chapter 4 are designed to be capable of implementation by the Court in practice. Inspiration for these reforms is drawn from the practice of other inter-State tribunals and it is important to remember that today the ICJ is just one of several means for settling inter-State disputes. Furthermore, jurisdiction remains largely consensual in international law and as such it is necessary to consider how the proposed reforms, and the resulting more proactive approach, could affect the appeal of the Court to States deciding how they wish to settle an inter-State dispute.

Due to the popularity of the WTO Adjudicatory Bodies and the renaissance of inter-State arbitration (as well as continued use of more traditional fora) there is more inter-State dispute settlement today than ever before. Although not all inter-State arbitrations are conducted in public, there now exists a large body of international practice upon which to draw. The practice of the WTO Adjudicatory Bodies and inter-State arbitrations illustrate that more proactive tribunals do not necessarily provoke a defensive response from States in order to protect their own sovereignty, by, for instance, resisting requests for information or simply refusing to appear. In fact there appears to be no discernable connection between a tribunal taking a more proactive approach to fact-finding and non-appearance or non-compliance. Of course, the possibility remains that the increased visibility that comes with being a party to a case before the World Court would prompt States to behave differently, but in the absence of any evidence to support such a suggestion, until a more proactive approach is taken such speculation as to the reaction of States will inevitably remain just that: speculation. Consequently, the Court has reason to be bold in pursuing a course of action that the evidence presented in Chapter 3 suggests could address a number of fact-finding problems that it currently faces.

Throughout the preceding chapters other inter-State tribunals such as ITLOS and the international criminal tribunals were referred to in relation to a number of discrete areas, most often to provide context or a point of comparison in relation to the argument being made. However, it is clear that the issue of judicial fact-finding is equally in need of academic attention in other areas. For instance, international investment law is one of the most exciting and active areas of international law at present. Consideration of issues of evidence and fact-finding before investment tribunals would undoubtedly raise pertinent issues. Similarly, whilst there has been some discussion of the use of evidence before international criminal tribunals,[1] further academic attention is merited, especially given the fact that individual liberty is at stake in such cases.

The proposed reforms are few in number and could realistically be adopted should the Court choose to do so. The rationale behind the modest, realistic nature of the proposals is summed up well by former President of the Court Rosalyn Higgins, who has stated that '[o]ne hasn't to be grandiose, but if we can help in particular cases, in coping with what otherwise could be disintegrating into violence, it's very good'.[2]

The reforms proposed would provide the Court with a power to compel the production of evidence through purposively interpreting its current fact-finding powers, relying on the duty of each party to collaborate in the production of evidence or by couching its requests within provisional measures which are binding on the parties (subject to a number of conditions). Furthermore, the reforms proposed in Chapter 4 would provide the Court with a clear strategy for better use of expert evidence which would assist the Court in cases involving particularly complex or technical evidence, which Chapter 2 showed present the Court with very real difficulties and threaten the proper administration of justice. This issue provides just one example of how fruitful the comparative exercise undertaken in Chapter 3 was in terms of providing models for reform of the Court's problematic approach to fact-finding. For instance, the *Guyana/Suriname* arbitration provided a clear example of the value of a tribunal-appointed expert in cases where the discovery of

---

[1] Combs, *Fact-Finding without Facts*; K. A. A. Khan, C. Buisman and C. Gosnell, *Principles of Evidence in International Criminal Justice* (Oxford University Press, 2010).
[2] J. Joor and H. V. Stuart, *The Building of Peace, A Hundred Years of Work on Peace through Law: The Peace Palace 1913–2013* (The Hague: Eleven International, 2013) 405.

certain information is disputed,[3] whilst the *Kishenganga* arbitration provided a useful alternative in this respect, demonstrating how discussions between the parties with the adjudicators *in camera* can similarly lead to satisfactory results in terms of the disclosure of contested information.[4]

As highlighted above, these select reforms would not require amendment of the Court's Statute – a process that would be difficult if not impossible. Of course, the ultimate decision as to whether the Court reforms its fact-finding process lies with the Court itself. Those who sit on the bench of the World Court may well decide to carry on regardless, dealing with cases that are consistently complex in terms of the facts, unconvinced of the benefits of taking a more proactive approach to fact-finding. Or, and this is perhaps more likely, whilst there may be some within the Court who recognise a need for reform, the institutional culture of the Court may prove resistant to change. Nevertheless, at the very least serious reconsideration of how the Court deals with facts is warranted. Otherwise, in the words of the late Antonio Cassese, 'there is a risk that more cases will go elsewhere (e.g. to arbitral courts or to specialized tribunals...) and the Court will become a less attractive institution.'[5]

---

[3] Order No. 4 1(a) 1(b) and 2(a); See *Guyana v. Suriname Arbitration* paras 64–70; see also Procedural Order No. 8, at 3.1.

[4] See Procedural Order No. 8, at 3.4, 3.5.

[5] Cassese, 'It is High Time to Restyle the Respected Old Lady' 239; or, as Wellens has stated, 'in the years to come the Respected Old Lady cannot simply afford to maintain its overly passive judicial policy'; K. Wellens, 'Happy Birthday to the "Respected Old Lady"' ESIL Newsletter, Vol 18.

# BIBLIOGRAPHY

Abi-Saab G, 'Independence of the Judiciary from Political Organs' in Boisson de Chazournes L, Romano C and Mackenzie R (eds), *International Organizations and International Dispute Settlement: Trends and Prospects* (Ardsley NY, Transnational 2002)

Ahmad J, *'The Indus Waters Kishenganga Arbitration* and State-to-State Disputes' 29(2013) Arbitration International 507

Åhman J, *Trade, Health, and The Burden of Proof in WTO Law* (Alphen aan den Rijn, Netherlands, Kluwer Law International 2012)

Akande D and Tonkin H, 'International Commissions of Inquiry: A New Form of Adjudication?' EJIL: Talk! 6 April 2012

Alexandrov SA, 'Non-appearance before the International Court of Justice' 33 (1995) Columbia Journal of Transnational Law 41

Alford Jr NH, 'Fact Finding by the World Court' 4 (1959) Villanova Law Review 37

Alvarez J, 'Are International Judges Afraid of Science?: A Comment on Mbengue' 34 (2012) Loyola of Los Angeles International and Comparative Law Review 12

Alvarez JE, *Burdens of Proof* (ASIL, ASIL Newsletter: Notes from the President 2007)

Amerasinghe CF, *Evidence in International Litigation* (Leiden, Boston, Martinus Nijhoff 2005)

Arangio-Ruiz V, 'The ICJ Statute, the Charter and Forms of Legality Review of Security Council Decisions' in Vorah LC (ed), *Man's Inhumanity to Man, Essays in Honour of Antonio Cassese* (The Hague, Kluwer Law International 2003)

Bantekas I and Ntah S, *International Criminal Law* (London, Cavendish 2003)

Barceló J, 'Burden of Proof, Prima Facie Case and Presumption in WTO Dispute Settlement' 42 (2009) Cornell International Law Journal 23

Bassiouni MC, 'Appraising UN Justice-Related Fact-Finding Missions' 5 (2001) Washington University Journal of Law and Policy 35

Beckman R, 'The Philippines v. China Case and the South China Sea Disputes' Asia Society, LKY SPP Conference, South China Sea: Central to Asia-Pacific Peace and Security, New York, 13–15 Mar 2013: Centre for International Law

'The UN Convention on the Law of the Sea and the Maritime Disputes in the South China Sea' [American Society of International Law] 107 (2013) The American Journal of International Law 142

Bedjaoui M, 'The Manufacture of Judgments at the International Court of Justice' 3 (1991) Pace Yearbook of International Law 29

*The New World Order and the Security Council: Testing the Legality of its Acts* (The Hague, Martinus Nijhoff Publishers 1994)

'La "Descente sur les lieux" dans la pratique de la Cour International de Justice et de sa devancière' in Rest A, Hafner G et al. (eds) *Liber Amicorum Professor Ignaz Seidl-Hohenveldern* (The Hague, Martinus Nijhoff 1998)

Behboodi R, '"Should" Means "Shall": A Critical Analysis of the Obligation to Submit Information Under Article 13.1 of the DSU in the Canada-Aircraft case' 3 (2000) Journal of International Economic Law 563

Benzing M, *Das Beweisrecht vor internationalen Gerichten und Schiedsgerichten in zwischenstaatlichen Streitigkeiten*, Vol. 215 (Berlin, Heidelberg, Springer 2010)

'Evidentiary Issues' in Zimmermann A et al. (eds), *The Statute of the International Court of Justice* (2nd edn, Oxford University Press 2012)

Bergsmo M (ed), *Quality Control in Fact-Finding* (Florence, Torkel Opsahl 2013)

Berman F, 'Remarks by Frank Berman' 106 (2012) Proceedings of the Annual Meeting (American Society of International Law) 162

Bernárdez ST, 'Article 48' in Zimmermann A (ed), *The Statute of the International Court of Justice: A Commentary* (Oxford University Press 2006)

Bilder RR, 'The Fact/Law Distinction in International Adjudication' in Lillich R (ed), *Fact-finding before International Tribunals* (Irvington-on-Hudson NY, Transnational 1992)

Boas G, 'Admissibility of Evidence under the Rules of Procedure and Evidence of the ICTY: Development of the "Flexibility Principle"' in May R et al. (eds), *Essays on ICTY Procedure and Evidence in Honour of Gabrielle Kirk McDonald* (The Hague, Martinus Nijhoff 2001)

Böckstiegel K-H, 'The Relevance of National Arbitration Law for Arbitrations Under the UNCITRAL Rules' 1 (1984) Journal of International Arbitration 223

Boisson de Chazournes L, 'Introduction: Courts and Tribunals and the Treatment of Scientific Issues' 3 (2012) Journal of International Dispute Settlement 479

Bothe M, 'The WHO Request' in Boisson de Chazournes L and Sands P (eds), *International Law, the International Court of Justice and Nuclear Weapons* (Cambridge University Press 1999)

'Fact-finding as a Means of Ensuring Respect for International Humanitarian Law' in Heinegg W and Volker E (eds) *International Humanitarian Law Facing New Challenges* (Berlin, New York, Springer 2007)

Bowring J, *The Works of Jeremy Bentham* (Edinburgh, William Tait 1843) Vol. 6, 139

Boutruche T, 'Credible Fact-Finding and Allegations of International Humanitarian Law Violations: Challenges in Theory and Practice' 16 (2011) Journal of Conflict and Security Law 105

Boyle A and Harrison J, 'Judicial Settlement of International Environmental Disputes: Current Problems' 4 (2013) Journal of International Dispute Settlement 245

Bronckers M and McNelis N, 'Fact and Law in Pleadings before the WTO Appellate Body' in Weiss F (ed), *Improving WTO Dispute Settlement Procedures: Issues and Lessons from the Practice of Other International Courts and Tribunals* (London, Cameron May 2000)

Brower CN, 'The Anatomy of Fact-Finding Before International Tribunals: An Analysis and a Proposal Concerning the Evaluation of Evidence' in Lillich RB (ed), *Fact-Finding Before International Tribunals* (Irvington-on-Hudson NY, Transnational 1992)

'Evidence before International Tribunals: The Need for Some Standard Rules' 28 (1994) The International Lawyer 47

Brower CN and Brueschke JD, *The Iran-United States Claims Tribunal* (The Hague, Boston, London, Martinus Nijhoff 1998)

Brown C, *A Common Law of International Adjudication* (Oxford University Press 2007)

Brownlie I, 'The Justiciability of Disputes and Issues in International Relations' 42 (1967) British Yearbook of International Law 123

Buffard I and Zemanek K, 'The "Object and Purpose" of a Treaty: An Enigma?' 3 (1998) Austrian Review of International and European Law 311

Cameron J and Orava SJ, 'GATT/WTO Panels between Recording and Finding Facts: Issues of Due Process, Evidence, Burden of Proof, and Standard of Review in GATT/WTO Dispute Settlement' in Weiss F (ed), *Improving WTO Dispute Settlement Procedures: Issues and Lessons from the Practice of Other International Courts and Tribunals* (London, Cameron May 2000)

Cardozo BN, *The Nature of the Judicial Process* (Yale University Press 1921)

Cassese A, 'Fostering Increased Conformity with International Standards: Monitoring and Institutional Fact-Finding' in Cassese A (ed), *Realizing Utopia: The Future of International Law* (Oxford University Press 2012)

'The International Court of Justice: It is High Time to Restyle the Respected Old Lady' in Cassese A (ed), *Realizing Utopia: The Future of International Law* (Oxford University Press 2012)

Charney JI, 'Disputes Implicating the Institutional Credibility of the Court: Problems of Non-Appearance, Non-Participation, and Non-Performance' in Damrosch L (ed), *The International Court of Justice at a Crossroads* (Dobbs Ferry NY, Transnational 1987)

Chinkin C, 'U.N. Human Rights Council Fact-Finding Missions: Lessons from Gaza' in Arsanjani M et al. (eds), *Looking to the Future: Essays on International Law in Honour of W Michael Reisman* (Boston, Martinus Nijhoff 2011)

Chinkin CM and Mackenzie R, 'Intergovernmental Organizations as "Friends of the Court"' in Chazournes L (ed), *International Organizations and*

*International Disputes Settlement - Trends and Prospects* (Ardsley NY, Transnational 2002)

Christoforou T, 'Settlement of Science-based Trade Disputes in the WTO: A Critical Review of the Developing Case Law in the Face of Scientific Uncertainty' 8 (1999) New York University Environmental Law Journal 622

'WTO Panels in Face of Scientific Uncertainty' in Weiss F (ed), *Improving WTO Dispute Settlement Procedures: Issues and Lessons from the Practice of Other International Courts and Tribunals* (London, Cameron May 2000)

Cogan JK, 'The 2010 Judicial Activity of the International Court of Justice' 105 (2011) American Journal of International Law 477

Collins D, 'Institutionalized Fact-Finding at the WTO' 27 (2006) University of Pennsylvania Journal of International Economic Law 367

Combs NA, *Fact-finding Without Facts: The Uncertain Evidentiary Foundations of International Criminal Convictions* (Cambridge University Press 2010)

Couvreur P, 'Le Règlement Juridictionel' in Institut du droit économique de la mer (ed), *Le processus de délimitation maritime étude d'un cas fictif: colloque international Monoco 27–29 mars 2003* (Paris, Pedone 2004) 380

Cronin-Furman KR, 'The International Court of Justice and the United Nations Security Council: Rethinking a Complicated Relationship' 106 (2006) Columbia Law Review 435

Crook J, 'The Case Concerning Armed Activities on the Territory of the Congo (Democratic Republic of Congo v. Uganda) and Its Implications for the Rules on the Use of Force' (2006, American Society of International Law Briefing at Tillar House)

D'Aspremont J, 'The Recommendations Made by the International Court of Justice' 56 (2007) International and Comparative Law Quarterly 185

D'Aspremont J and Mbengue MM, 'Strategies of Engagement with Scientific Fact-Finding in International Adjudication' (Amsterdam Law School Research Paper No. 2013-20)

Daly B, 'The Abyei Arbitration: Procedural Aspects of an Intra-state Border Arbitration' 23 (2010) Leiden Journal of International Law 801

Damaška M, 'The Uncertain Fate of Evidentiary Transplants: Anglo-American and Continental Experiments' 45 (1997) The American Journal of Comparative Law 839

De la Serre E and Sibony A, 'Expert Evidence before the EC Courts', 45 (2008) Common Market Law Review 4

de Vabres HD, *L'action publique et l'action civile dans les rapports de droit pénal international* (Leiden, Boston, Brill, Nijhoff, 1929)

De Wet E, *The Chapter VII Powers of the United Nations Security Council* (Oxford, Hart Publishing 2004)

Del Mar K, 'Weight of Evidence Generated through Intra-Institutional Fact-Finding before the International Court of Justice' 2 (2011) Journal of International Dispute Settlement 393

Delbrück J, 'Review of *Fact-Finding before International Tribunals*, Edited by Richard B. Lillich' 88 (1994) American Journal of International Law 191

'Article 24' in Simma B (ed), *Charter of the United Nations: A Commentary* (Oxford University Press 2002)

Derham R and Derham N, 'From Ad Hoc to Hybrid – the Rules and Regulations Governing Reception of Expert Evidence at the International Criminal Court' 14 (2010) International Journal of Evidence and Proof 25

Devaney JG, 'Killing Two Birds with One Stone: Can Increased Use of Article 34(2) of the ICJ Statute Improve the Legitimacy of UN Commissions of Inquiry & the Court's Fact-Finding Procedure?' STALS Research Paper 2/2013

Distefano G and Henry E, 'The International Court of Justice and the Security Council: Disentangling Themis from Ares' in Bannelier K, Christakis T and Heathcote S (eds), *The ICJ and the Evolution of International Law: The enduring impact of the Corfu Channel Case* (Oxford, New York, Routledge 2012)

Dupuy F and Dupuy P-M, 'A Legal Analysis of China's Historic Rights Claim in the South China Sea' 107 (2013) The American Journal of International Law 124

Dupuy P-M, 'Article 34' in Zimmermann A (ed), *The Statute of the International Court of Justice: A Commentary* (Oxford University Press 2006)

Eiriksson G, *The International Tribunal for the Law of the Sea* (The Hague, Martinus Nijhoff 2000)

Elkind JB, *Non-Appearance before the International Court of Justice: Functional and Comparative Analysis* (The Hague, Boston, Martinus Nijhoff 1984)

Elsen TJH, *Litispendence between the International Court of Justice and the Security Council* (The Hague, TMC Asser Instituut 1986)

Fassbender B, 'Review essay: Quis judicabit? The Security Council, its powers and its legal control' 11 (2000) European Journal of International Law 219

Feldman T, 'A Tale of Two Closures: Comments on the Palmer Report Concerning the May 2010 Flotilla Incident' EJIL: Talk! 20 September 2011

Fitzmaurice G, 'The Problem of the "Non-Appearing" Defendant Government' 51 (1981) British Yearbook of International Law 89

Fitzmaurice SG, *The Law and Procedure of the International Court of Justice* (Cambridge, Grotius 1986)

Foster CE, 'Burden of Proof in International Courts and Tribunals' 29 (2010) Australian Year Book of International Law 27

*Science and the Precautionary Principle in International Courts and Tribunals: Expert Evidence, Burden of Proof and Finality* (Cambridge University Press 2011)

'New Clothes for the Emperor? Consultation of Experts by the International Court of Justice' 5 (2014) Journal of International Dispute Settlement 139

Francioni F, 'Multilateralism à la carte: the Limits to Unilateral Withholdings of Assessed Contributions to the UN Budget' 11 (2000) European Journal of International Law 43

'Integrating Scientific Evidence into Environmental Law: the International Dimension' in Grassi, S et al. (eds) *Scientific Evidence in European Environmental Rule-Making* (The Hague, Kluwer 2003)

'Access to Justice, Denial of Justice and International Investment Law' 20 (2009) European Journal of International Law 729

Franck T, 'Fact-Finding in the I.C.J.' in Lillich RB (ed), *Fact-Finding before International Tribunals* (Irvington-on-Hudson NY, Transnational 1992)

*Fairness in International Law and Institutions* (Oxford, Clarendon Press 2002)

Franck TM and Farley HS, 'Procedural Due Process in Human Rights Fact-Finding by International Agencies' 74 (1980) American Journal of International Law 308

Fry JD, 'Non-Participation in the International Court of Justice Revisited: Change or Plus Ca Change' 49 (2010) Columbia Journal of Transnational Law 35

Gaja, G, 'A New Way for Submitting Observations on the Construction of Multilateral Treaties to the ICJ' in Fastenrath, U et al. (eds) *From Bilateralism to Community Interest: Essays in Honour of Bruno Summa*, (Oxford University Press 2011)

'Relationship of the ICJ with Other International Courts and Tribunals' in Zimmermann A et al. (eds), *The Statute of the International Court of Justice* (2nd edn, Oxford University Press 2012)

Gao Z and Jia BB, 'The Nine-Dash Line in the South China Sea: History, Status, and Implications' 107 (2013) The American Journal of International Law 98

Gardiner R, *Treaty Interpretation* (Oxford University Press 2008)

Gatowski SI et al., 'Asking the Gatekeepers: A National Survey of Judges on Judging Expert Evidence in a Post-Daubert World' 25 (2001) Law and Human Behavior 433

Gattini A, 'Evidentiary Issues in the ICJ's Genocide Judgment' 5 (2007) Journal of International Criminal Justice 889

Gill TD, 'Legal and Some Political Limitations on the Power of the UN Security Council to Exercise its Enforcement Powers under Chapter VII of the Charter' 26 (1995) Netherlands Yearbook of International Law 33

Gill TD and Rosenne S, *The World Court: What It Is and How It Works*, Vol 41 (The Hague, Martinus Nijhoff 2003)

Goldstone RJ, 'Quality Control in International Fact-Finding Outside Criminal Justice for Core International Crimes' in Bergsmo M (ed), *Quality Control in Fact-Finding* (Florence, Torkel-Opsahl 2013)

Goldstone RJ and Hamilton RJ, 'Bosnia v. Serbia: Lessons from the Encounter of the International Court of Justice with the International Criminal Tribunal for the Former Yugoslavia' 21 (2008) Leiden Journal of International Law 95

Gowlland-Debbas V, 'The Relationship between the International Court of Justice and the Security Council in the Light of the Lockerbie Case' 88 (1994) The American Journal of International Law 643

'Article 7' in Zimmermann A (ed), *The Statute of the International Court of Justice: A Commentary* (Oxford University Press 2006)

Grace R and Bruderlein C, 'On Monitoring, Reporting, and Fact-finding Mechanisms' 1 (2012) European Society of International Law Reflections 1

Grando M, 'Allocating the Burden of Proof in WTO Disputes: A Critical Analysis' 9 (2006) Journal of International Economic Law 615

*Evidence, Proof, and Fact-Finding in WTO Dispute Settlement* (Oxford University Press 2009)

Gray C and Kingsbury B, 'Developments in Dispute Settlement: Inter-State Arbitration Since 1945' 63 (1992) British Yearbook of International Law 97

Gross SR, 'Expert Evidence' (1991) *Wisconsin Law Review* 1113

Grossman GM, Horn H and Mavroidis PC, 'Legal and Economic Principles of World Trade Law: National Treatment' IFN Working Paper No 917, 2012

Guilfoyle D, 'The Mavi Marmara Incident and Blockade in Armed Conflict' 81 (2011) British Yearbook of International Law 171

'The Palmer Report on the Mavi Marmara Incident and the Legality of Israel's Blockade of the Gaza Strip' EJIL: Talk! 6 September 2011

Halink S, 'All Things Considered: How the International Court of Justice Delegated Its Fact-Assessment to the United Nations in the Armed Activities Case' 40 (2007) New York University Journal of International Law & Policy 13

Hamamoto S, 'Procedural Questions in the Whaling Judgment: Admissibility, Intervention and Use of Experts' Japanese Society of International Law, The Honorable Shigeru Oda Commemorative Lectures 1

Harrison JL, 'Reconceptualizing the Expert Witness: Social Costs, Current Controls on Proposed Responses' 18 (2001) Yale Journal on Regulation 253

Helland E and Klick J, 'Does Anyone Get Stopped at the Gate? An Empirical Assessment of the Daubert Trilogy in the States' 20 (2012) Supreme Court Economic Review 1

Henckaerts J and Wiesener C, 'Human Rights Obligations of Non-State Armed Groups: A Possible Contribution from Customary International Law?' in Kolb R and Gaggioli G (eds), *Research Handbook on Human Rights and Humanitarian Law* (Cheltenham, Edward Elgar 2013)

Higgins R, 'The Place of International Law in the Settlement of Disputes by the Security Council' 64 (1970) The American Journal of International Law 1

*Problems and Process: International Law and How We Use It* (Oxford, Clarendon Press 1995)

'Interim Measures for the Protection of Human Rights' 36 (1997) Columbia Journal of Transnational Law 91

Speech by H. E. Judge Rosalynn Higgins, President of the International Court of Justice (At the 58th Session of the International Law Commission, 2006)

'Speech by H.E. Judge Rosalyn Higgins, President of the International Court of Justice to the Sixth Committee of the General Assembly' (Sixth Committee of the General Assembly, 2 November 2007)

'Introductory Remarks by Rosalyn Higgins' 106 (2012) *Proceedings of the Annual Meeting (American Society of International Law)* 229

Highet K, 'Evidence and Proof of Facts' in Damrosch LF (ed), *The International Court of Justice at a Crossroads* (Irvington-on-Hudson NY, Transnational 1987)

'Evidence, the Court, and the Nicaragua Case' 81 (1987) The American Journal of International Law 1

'Evidence, The Chamber, and the ELSI Case' in Lillich RB (ed), *Fact-Finding before International Tribunals* (Ardsley-on-Hudson NY, Transnational 1992)

Holtzmann HM, 'Fact-Finding by the Iran–United States Claims Tribunal' in Lillich RB (ed), *Fact-Finding before International Tribunals* (Irvington-on-Hudson NY, Transnational 1991)

*Streamlining Arbitral Proceedings: Some Techniques of the Iran-United States Claims Tribunal* (The Hague, Kluwer Law International 2007)

Howse R, 'The Most Dangerous Branch? WTO Appellate Body Jurisprudence on the Nature and Limits of the Judicial Power' in Cottier T, Mavroidis PC and Blatter P (eds), *The Role of the Judge in International Trade Regulation: Experience and Lessons for the WTO*, Vol 4 (University of Michigan Press 2009)

Hudson M, *The Permanent Court of International Justice 1920–1942* (New York, MacMillan 1943)

Hutcheson J, 'Judgment Intuitive The Function of the Hunch in Judicial Decision' 14 (1928) Cornell Law Quarterly 274

Imwinkelried EJ, 'Evaluating the Reliability of Nonscientific Expert Testimony: A Partial Answer to the Questions Left Unresolved by Kumho Tire Co. v. Carmichael' 52 (2000) Maine Law Review 19

Iynedjian M, 'The Case for Incorporating Scientists and Technicians into WTO Panels' 42 (2008) Journal of World Trade 279

Jacheć-Neale A, 'Fact-Finding' in Wolfrum R (ed) *Max Planck Encyclopedia of Public International Law* (online edition) http://opil.ouplaw.com/home/EPIL

Jackson J, 'Finding the Best Epistemic Fit for International Criminal Tribunals Beyond the Adversarial–Inquisitorial Dichotomy' 7 (2009) Journal of International Criminal Justice 17

Jacur FR, 'Remarks on the Role of *Ex Curia* Scientific Experts in International Environmental Disputes' in Boschiero N et al. (eds), *International Courts and the Development of International Law* (Berlin, Springer, Asser Press 2013)

Jasanoff S, 'What Judges Should Know about the Sociology of Science' 32 (1992) *Jurimetrics* 345

Jennings SR, 'International Lawyers and the Progressive Development of International Law' in Makarczyk J (ed), *Theory of International Law at the Threshold of the 21st Century: Essays in Honour of Krzystof Skubiszewski* (The Hague, Kluwer Law International 1996)
Jiménez de Aréchaga E, 'Le traitement des différends internationaux par le Conseil de Sécurité' 85 (1954-I) Recueil des cours, 1
Jolowicz JA, *On Civil Procedure* (Cambridge University Press 2000)
Joor J and Stuart HV, *The Building of Peace, A Hundred Years of Work on Peace through Law: The Peace Palace 1913–2013* (The Hague, Eleven International 2013)
Karaman IV, *Dispute Resolution in the Law of the Sea*, Vol 72 (The Hague, Martinus Nijhoff 2012)
Kazazi M, *Burden of Proof and Related Issues: A Study on Evidence before International Tribunals*, Vol 1 (The Hague, Martinus Nijhoff 1996)
Keith K, 'The International Court of Justice and Criminal Justice' 59 (2010) International and Comparative Law Quarterly 895
Kelsall T, *Culture Under Cross-examination: International Justice and the Special Court for Sierra Leone* (Cambridge University Press 2009)
Kelsen H, *The Law of the United Nations: A Critical Analysis of Its Fundamental Problems* (New York, Frederick A. Praeger 1950)
Khan KAA, Buisman C and Gosnell C, *Principles of Evidence in International Criminal Justice* (Oxford University Press 2010)
Klabbers J, 'Some Problems Regarding the Object and Purpose of Treaties' 8 (2006) Finnish Yearbook of International Law 138
  'Treaties, Object and Purpose' in Wolfrum R (ed) *Max Planck Encyclopedia of Public International Law* (online edition) http://opil.ouplaw.com/home/EPIL
Klein N, *Dispute Settlement in the UN Convention on the Law of the Sea*, Vol 39 (Cambridge University Press 2005)
Knoops G-JA, 'The Proliferation of the Ultimate Issue Rule Pertaining to Expert Witnesses Testimony before International and Internationalized Criminal Courts: Pitfalls and Paradoxes' in Capaldo GZ (ed), *The Global Community Yearbook of International Law and Jurisprudence 2001*, Vol 1 (2006–7)
Kolb R, *The International Court of Justice* (Oxford, Hart 2013)
Kuyper PJ, 'The Appellate Body and the Facts' in Bronckers M and Quick R (eds), *New Directions in International Economic Law, Essays in Honour of John H. Jackson* (The Hague, Kluwer Law International 2000)
Labuda P, 'What Lies Beneath the 'G' Word? Genocide-Labelling and Fact-Finding at the UN' EJIL: Talk! 28 May 2015
Lalive JF, 'Quelques remarques sur la preuve devant la Cour permanente et la Cour internationale de justice' 7 (1950) Annuaire Suisse de Droit International 77

Lamb S, 'Legal Limits to United Nations Security Council Powers' in Goodwin-Gill G and Talmon S, *The Reality of International Law Essays in Honour of Ian Brownlie*, (Oxford University Press 1999)

Lauterpacht H, 'The So-Called Anglo-American and Continental Schools of Thought in International Law' 12 (1931) British Yearbook of International Law 31

*The Development of International Law by the International Court* (Cambridge University Press 1958)

*Aspects of the Administration of International Justice* (Cambridge University Press 1991)

Lichtenbaum P, 'Procedural Issues in WTO Dispute Resolution' 19 (1997) Michigan Journal of International Law 1195

Lillich R (ed), *Fact-finding Before International Tribunals* (Irvington-on-Hudson NY, Transnational 1992)

Linderfalk U, 'On the Meaning of the "Object and Purpose" Criterion, in the Context of the Vienna Convention on the Law of Treaties, Article 19' 72 (2003) Nordic Journal of International Law 429

Lowe V and Tzanakopoulos A, 'The Abyei Arbitration' in Bosman L and Clark H (eds), *The Abyei Arbitration (Sudan/Sudan People's Liberation Movement/Army)* (The Permanent Court of Arbitration Award Series, The Permanent Court of Arbitration 2012)

Ludes FJ and Gilbert HJ (eds), *Corpus Juris Secundum: A Complete Restatement of the Entire American Law, Vol 31 A: Evidence* (St Paul, West Publishing 1964)

Lugard M, 'Scope of Appellate Review: Objective Assessment of the Facts and Issues of Law' 1 (1998) Journal of International Economic Law 323

MacCormick N, *Legal Reasoning and Legal Theory* (Oxford, Clarendon Press1978)

Mackenzie R et al., *The Manual on International Courts and Tribunals* (2nd edn, Oxford University Press 2010)

Mani VS, *International Adjudication: Procedural Aspects*, Vol 4 (The Hague, Kluwer Law International 1980)

Marceau GZ and Hawkins JK, 'Experts in WTO Dispute Settlement' 3 (2012) Journal of International Dispute Settlement 493

Marriott AL, 'Evidence in International Arbitration' 5 (1989) Arbitration International 280

Martenczuk B, 'The Security Council, the International Court and Judicial Review: What Lessons from Lockerbie?' 10 (1999) European Journal of International Law 517

Mathias S et al., *The International Court of Justice at 60: Performance and Prospects* (Proceedings of the Annual Meeting, American Society of International Law, Vol. 100, Annual 2006)

Matsushita M, Schoenbaum TJ and Mavroidis PC, *The World Trade Organization*, Vol 127 (Oxford University Press 2006)

Mavroidis PC, 'Amicus Curiae Briefs before the WTO: Much Ado About Nothing' in von Bogdandy A, Mavroidis PC and Mény Y (eds), *European Integration and International Co-ordination: Studies in Transnational Economic Law in Honour of Claus-Dieter Ehlermann* (The Hague, Kluwer Law International 2002)

'Development of WTO Dispute Settlement Procedures' in Ortino F and Petersmann E (eds), *Development of WTO Dispute Settlement Procedures*, Vol 18 (The Hague, Kluwer Law International 2004)

*Trade in Goods* (2nd edn, Oxford University Press 2012)

Mavroidis PC, Bermann GA and Wu M (eds), *The Law of the World Trade Organization (WTO): Documents, Cases & Analysis* (Eagea MN, West 2010)

May R and Wierda M, 'Evidence before the ICTY' in May R et al. (eds), *Essays on ICTY procedure and evidence in honour of Gabrielle Kirk McDonald* (The Hague, Martinus Nijhoff 2000)

Mbengue MM, 'International Courts and Tribunals as Fact-Finders: The Case of Scientific Fact-Finding in International Adjudication' 34 (2012) Loyola Los Angeles International & Comparative Law Review 53

'Scientific Fact-finding by International Courts and Tribunals' 3 (2012) Journal of International Dispute Settlement 509

McCabe MP, 'Arbitral Discovery and the Iran-United States Claims Tribunal Experience' 20 (1986) The International Lawyer 499

McWhinney E, *Judicial Settlement of International Disputes: Jurisdiction, Justiciability, and Judicial Law-Making on the Contemporary International Court* (The Hague, Martinus Nijhoff 1991)

Mendelson M, 'Interim Measures of Protection in Cases of Contested Jurisdiction' 46 (1972) British Yearbook of International Law 259

Moreno J, 'Einstein on the Bench?: Exposing What Judges Do Not Know about Science and Using Child Abuse Cases to Improve How Courts Evaluate Scientific Evidence' 64 (2003) Ohio State Law Journal 531

Mosk R, 'The Role of Facts in International Dispute Resolution' 203 (2003) Receuil des Cours - Collected Courses at the Hague Academy 11

Müller D, 'The Question Question' in Milanović M and Wood M (eds), *The Law and Politics of the Kosovo Advisory Opinion* (Oxford University Press, 2015)

Murphy SD, 'The Experience of the Eritrea–Ethiopia Claims Commission' 106 (2012) Proceedings of the Annual Meeting (American Society of International Law) 237

Niyungeko G and Salmon JAS, *La preuve devant les juridictions internationales* (Louvain-la-Neuve, Belgium, Bruylant 2005)

Nordquist MH et al., *United National Convention on the Law of the Sea* (The Hague, Martinus Nijhoff 1989)

Öberg MD, 'The Legal Effects of Resolutions of the UN Security Council and General Assembly in the Jurisprudence of the ICJ' 16 (2005) European Journal of International Law 879

O'Donnell T, 'Naming and Shaming: The Sorry Tale of Security Council Resolution 1530 (2004)' 17 (2006) European Journal of International Law 945
  'Judicialising History or Historicising Law: Reflections on *Irving v. Penguin Books and Lipstadt*' 62 (2012) Northern Ireland Legal Quarterly 291
Oda S, 'Provisional Measures, The Practice of the International Court of Justice' in Lowe V and Fitzmaurice M (eds), *Fifty Years of the International Court of Justice* (Cambridge University Press 1996)
Oxman B, 'Jurisdiction and the Power to Indicate Provisional Measures' in Damrosch LF (ed), *The International Court of Justice at a Crossroads* (Dobbs Ferry NY, Transnational 1987)
Palchetti P, 'Opening the International Court of Justice to Third States: Intervention and Beyond' 6 (2002) Max Planck Yearbook of United Nations Law 139
  'The Power of the International Court of Justice to Indicate Provisional Measures to Prevent the Aggravation of a Dispute' 21 (2008) Leiden Journal of International Law 623
Palmeter D and Mavroidis PC, *Dispute Settlement in the World Trade Organization: Practice and Procedure* (Cambridge University Press 2004)
Pauwelyn J, 'Evidence, Proof and Persuasion in WTO Dispute Settlement: Who Bears the Burden?' 1 (1998) Journal of International Economic Law 227
  'The Use of Experts in WTO Dispute Settlement' 51 (2002) International and Comparative Law Quarterly 325
Payne C, 'Mastering the Evidence: Improving Fact-Finding by International Courts' 41 (2011) Environmental Law Journal 1191
Peat D, 'The Use of Court-Appointed Experts by the International Court of Justice' 84 (2014) British Yearbook of International Law 271
Peel J, 'Risk Regulation Under the WTO SPS Agreement: Science as an International Normative Yardstick?' Jean Monnet Working Paper 02/04
  *Science and Risk Regulation in International Law* (Cambridge University Press 2013)
Pellet A, 'Strengthening the Role of the International Court of Justice as the Principal Organ of the United Nations' 3 (2004) The Law and Practice of International Courts and Tribunals 159
Petculescu I, 'The Review of the United Nations Security Council Decisions by the International Court of Justice' 52 (2005) Netherlands International Law Review 167
Peters A, 'International Dispute Settlement: A Network of Cooperational Duties' 14 (2003) European Journal of International Law 1
Quintana JJ, 'Procedural Developments at the International Court of Justice' 10 (2011) The Law & Practice of International Courts and Tribunals 135
Ragosta JA, 'Unmasking the WTO – Access to the DSB System: Can the WTO DSB Live up to the Moniker World Trade Court' 31 (1999) Law & Policy in International Business 739

Ramcharan BG, *International Law and Fact-Finding in the Field of Human Rights* (The Hague, Martinus Nijhoff 1982)

Reichler PS, 'The Impact of the Nicaragua Case on Matters of Evidence and Fact-Finding' 25 (2012) Leiden Journal of International Law 149

Reisman WM, 'Respecting One's Own Jurisprudence: A Plea to the International Court of Justice' 83 (1989) The American Journal of International Law 312

Reisman WM and Freedman EE, 'The Plaintiff's Dilemma: Illegally Obtained Evidence and Admissibility in International Adjudication' 76 (1982) American Journal of International Law 737

Riddell A, 'Scientific Evidence in the International Court of Justice – Problems and Possibilities' 20 (2009) Finnish Yearbook of International Law 229

Riddell A and Plant B, *Evidence before the International Court of Justice* (London, British Institute of International and Comparative Law 2009)

Roberts RCE, 'The Lubanga Trial Chamber's Assessment of Evidence in Light of the Accused's Right to the Presumption of Innocence' 10 (2012) Journal of International Criminal Justice 923

Rodenhäuser T, 'Progressive Development of International Human Rights Law: The Reports of the Independent International Commission of Inquiry on the Syrian Arab Republic' EJIL: Talk! 13 April 2013

Rohan CM, 'Rules Governing the Presentation of Testimonial Evidence' in Khan KAA, Buisman C and Gosnell C (eds), *Principles of Evidence in International Criminal Justice* (Oxford University Press 2010)

Romano C, 'The Role of Experts in International Adjudication' in *Le droit international face aux enjeux environmentaux, Colloque d'Aix-en-Provence 2009*, Société Française Pour le Droit International (Paris, Pedone 2010)

'Trial and Error in International Judicialization' in Romano C, Alter K and Shany Y (eds), *The Oxford Handbook of International Adjudication* (Oxford University Press 2013)

'A Taxonomy of International Rule of Law Institutions' 2 (2011) Journal of International Dispute Settlement 241

Ronen Y, 'Participation of Non-State Actors in ICJ Proceedings' 11 (2012) The Law and Practice of International Courts and Tribunals 77

Rosenne S, *The Law and Practice of the International Court* (1st to 4th edns, The Hague, Martinus Nijhoff 1987–2005)

*Procedure in the International Court: A Commentary on the 1978 Rules of the International Court of Justice* (The Hague, Martinus Nijhoff 1983)

'Fact-Finding before the International Court of Justice' in Rosenne S, Essays on International Law and Practice (Leiden, Martinus Nijhoff 2007) 235

*Provisional Measures in International Law: The International Court of Justice and the International Tribunal for the Law of the Sea* (Oxford University Press 2005)

*Essays on International Law and Practice* (The Hague, Martinus Nijhoff Publishers 2007)

Rosenne S and Ronen Y, *The Law and Practice of the International Court, 1920–2005* (4th edn, The Hague, Martinus Nijhoff 2006)

Rosenne S and Sohn LB, *United Nations Convention on the Law of the Sea, 1982: A Commentary*, Vol 5 (The Hague, Martinus Nijhoff 1989)

Saks MJ, 'Banishing ipse dixit: The impact of Kumho Tire on forensic identification science' 57 (2000) Washington & Lee Law Review 879

Samson E, 'Is Gaza Occupied? Redefining the Status of Gaza under International Law' 25 (2010) American University Law Review 915

Sanders J, 'Expert Witness Ethics' 76 (2007) Fordham Law Review 1539

Sandifer DV, *Evidence before International Tribunals*, Vol 13 (University Press of Virginia 1975)

Sandoval JG and Sweeney-Samuelson E, 'Adjudicating Conflicts over Resources: The ICJ's Treatment of Technical Evidence in the Pulp Mills Case' 3 (2011) Gottingen Journal of International Law 447

Scheinin M, 'Improving Fact-Finding in Treaty-Based Human Rights Mechanisms and in the Special Procedures of the Human Rights Council' in Bergsmo M (ed) *Quality-Control in Fact-Finding* (Florence, Torkel Opsahl 2013)

Schill S W, 'The Overlooked Role of Arbitration in International Adjudication Theory' 4 ESIL Reflections 4 May 2015

Schofield C and Carleton C, 'Technical Considerations in Law of the Sea Dispute Resolution' in Elferink A and Rothwell DR (eds), *Oceans Management in the 21st Century: Institutional Frameworks and Responses* (The Hague, Martinus Nijhoff 2004)

Schwarzenberger G, *International Law – As Applied by International Courts and Tribunals* (London, Stevens & Sons 1968)

Schwebel SM, *Three Cases of Fact-Finding by the International Court of Justice in International Law* (Cambridge University Press 1994)

'Speech of the President of the International Court of Justice to the General Assembly, A/52/PV.36, 27 October 1997

Schwisfurth T, 'Article 34' in Simma B (ed), *The Charter of the United Nations: A Commentary* (2nd edn, Oxford University Press 2002)

Scobbie I, 'Discontinuance in the International Court: The Enigma of the Nuclear Tests Cases' 41 (1992) International and Comparative Law Quarterly 808

'Unchart(er)ed Waters?: Consequences of the Advisory Opinion on the Legal Consequences of the Construction of a Wall in the Occupied Palestinian Territory for the Responsibility of the UN for Palestine' 16 (2005) European Journal of International Law 941

'Regarding/Disregarding: The Judicial Rhetoric of President Barak and the International Court of Justice's Wall Advisory Opinion' 5 (2006) Chinese Journal of International Law 269

Shahabuddeen M, *Precedent in the World Court*, Vol 13 (Cambridge University Press 1996)

Shany Y, 'Know Your Rights! The Flotilla Report and International Law Governing Naval Blockades' EJIL: Talk! 12 October 2010

'Faraway, So Close: The Legal Status of Gaza after Israel's Disengagement' 8 (2005) *Yearbook of International Humanitarian Law* 369

Shaw MN, 'The Security Council and the International Court of Justice: Judicial Drift and Judicial Function' in Muller AS (ed), *The International Court of Justice: Its Future Role After Fifty Years*, Vol 3 (The Hague, Martinus Nijhoff 1997)

Shelton D, 'The Participation of Non-Governmental Organisations in International Judicial Proceedings' 88 (1994) American Journal of International Law 611

Shifman BE, 'Revitalization of the Permanent Court of Arbitration' 23 (1995) International Journal of Legal Information 284

Shoyer AW and Solovy EM, 'The Process and Procedure of Litigating at the World Trade Organization: A Review of the Work of the Appellate Body' 31 (1999) Law & Policy of International Business 677

Simma B, 'Article 92' in Simma B (ed), *The Charter of the United Nations: A Commentary* (2nd edn, Oxford University Press 2002)

'The International Court of Justice and Scientific Expertise' 106 (2012) Proceedings of the Annual Meeting (American Society of International Law) 230

Simons M, 'Serbia's Darkest Pages Hidden from Genocide Court' *The New York Times* (New York, 8 April 2007), www.nytimes.com/2007/04/08/world/europe/08iht-serbia.5.5192285.html?_r=1&pagewanted=all

'Genocide Court Ruled for Serbia Without Seeing Full War Archive' *The New York Times* (New York, 9 April 2007), www.nytimes.com/2007/04/09/world/europe/09archives.html?_r=1&pagewanted=all

Sinclair I, 'Some Procedural Aspects of Recent International Litigation' 30 (1981) International and Comparative Law Quarterly 338

*The Vienna Convention on the Law of Treaties* (2nd edn, Manchester University Press 1984)

Singh A, 'Expert Evidence' in Khan KAA, Buisman C and Gosnell C (eds), *Principles of Evidence in International Criminal Justice* (Oxford University Press 2010)

Singh N, *The Role and Record of the International Court of Justice* (The Hague, Martinus Nijhoff 1989)

Steger D, 'Amicus Curiae: Participant or Friend? The WTO and NAFTA Experience' in von Bogdandy A et al. (eds), European Integration and International Coordination: Studies in Honour of Claus-Dieter Ehlermann (The Hague, Kluwer 2011) 419

Steger DP and Van den Bossche P, 'WTO Dispute Settlement: Emerging Practice and Procedure' 92 (1998) Proceedings of the American Society of International Law 79

Stein T and Richter S, 'Article 36' in Simma B and Mosler H (eds), *The Charter of the United Nations: A Commentary* (Oxford University Press 1996)
Stuyt AAM, *Survey of International Arbitrations: 1794–1989* (The Hague, Martinus Nijhoff 1990)
Talmon S, 'The Security Council as World Legislature' 99 (2005) The American Journal of International Law 175
　'Article 43' in Zimmermann A et al. (eds), *The Statute of the International Court of Justice* (2nd edn, Oxford University Press 2012)
Tams CJ, 'Article 49' in Zimmermann A (ed), *The Statute of the International Court of Justice: A Commentary* (Oxford University Press 2006)
　'Article 50' in Zimmermann A (ed), *The Statute of the International Court of Justice: A Commentary* (Oxford University Press 2006)
　'Article 51' in Zimmermann A (ed), *The Statute of the International Court of Justice: A Commentary* (Oxford University Press 2006)
Tams CJ and Devaney JG, 'Applying Necessity and Proportionality to Anti-Terrorist Self-Defence' 45 (2012) Israel Law Review 91
Tams CJ and Sloan J (eds), *The Development of International Law by the International Court of Justice* (Oxford University Press 2013)
Teitelbaum R, 'Recent Fact-Finding Developments at the International Court of Justice' 6 (2007) The Law and Practice of International Courts and Tribunals 184
Terris D, Romano CP and Swigart L, *The International Judge: An Introduction to the Men and Women Who Decide the World's Cases* (Oxford University Press 2007)
Thirlway H, 'Dilemma or Chimera – Admissibility of Illegally Obtained Evidence in International Adjudication' 78 (1984) American Journal of International Law 622
　*Non-appearance before the International Court of Justice* (Cambridge University Press 1985)
　'Normative Surrender and the Duty to Appear before the International Court of Justice: A Reply' 11 (1989) Michigan Journal of International Law 912
　'The Indication of Provisional Measures by the International Court of Justice' in Bernhardt R (ed), *Interim Measures Indicated by International Courts* (Max-Planck-Institut für ausländisches öffentliches Recht und Völkerrecht, Springer-Verlag 1994)
Thomson L, 'The ICJ and the Case Concerning the G/N Project: The Implications for International Watercourses Law and International Environmental Law' Centre for Energy, Petroleum, Mineral Law and Policy, Annual Review (1999) Article 8, wwwdundeeacuk/cepmlp/car/html/car3_article8htm
Tomuschat C, 'Uniting for Peace', United Nations Audiovisual Library of International Law, www.un.org/law/avl

Treves T, 'Law and Science in the Interpretation of the Law of the Sea Convention: Article 76 between the Law of the Sea Tribunal and the Commission on the Limits of the Continental Shelf' 3 (2012) Journal of International Dispute Settlement 483

Tzanakopoulos A, 'Provisional Measures Indicated by International Courts: Emergence of a General Principle of International Law' 57 (2004) Revue Hellénique de droit international 53

Ulfstein G, 'Awarding Compensation in a Fragmented Legal System: The Diallo Case' 4 (2013) Journal of International Dispute Settlement 477

'Treaty Bodies and Regimes' in Hollis D (ed), *Oxford Guide to Treaties* (Oxford University Press 2012)

Unterhalter D, 'Allocating the Burden of Proof in WTO Dispute Settlement Proceedings' 42 (2009) Cornell International Law Journal 209

'The Burden of Proof in WTO Dispute Settlement' in Janow ME, Donaldson V and Yanovich A (eds), *The WTO: Governance, Dispute Settlement & Developing Countries* (Huntington NY, Juris 2008)

Valencia-Ospina E, 'Evidence before the International Court of Justice' 1(1999) International Law Forum du droit international 202

Van den Bossche P and Zdouc W, *The Law and Policy of the World Trade Organization* (3rd edn, Cambridge University Press 2013)

Van den Hout T, 'Resolution of International Disputes: The Role of the Permanent Court of Arbitration – Reflections on the Centenary of the 1907 Convention for the Pacific Settlement of International Disputes' 21 (2008) Leiden Journal of International Law 643

Van den Wyngaert C, 'International Criminal Courts as Fact (and Truth) Finders in Post-Conflict Societies: Can Disparities with Ordinary International Courts be Avoided?'100 (2006) Proceedings of the Annual Meeting, American Society of International Law, 55

van Haersolte-van Hof JJ, 'The Revitalization of the Permanent Court of Arbitration' 54 (2007) Netherlands International Law Review 395

Verkerk R, 'Comparative Aspects of Expert Evidence in Civil Litigation' 13 (2009) International Journal of Evidence and Proof 167

Viseur Sellers P, 'Rule 89 (C) and (D): At Odds or Overlapping with Rule 96 and Rule 95?' in May R et al. (eds), *Essays on ICTY Procedure and Evidence in Honour of Gabrielle Kirk McDonald* (The Hague, Martinus Nijhoff 2001)

Von Mangoldt H and Zimmermann A, 'Article 53' in Simma B et al. (eds), *The Statute of the International Court of Justice* (Oxford University Press 2006)

Walter C, 'Article 44' in Zimmermann A (ed), *The Statute of the International Court of Justice: A Commentary* (Oxford University Press 2006)

Watson GR, 'Constitutionalism, Judicial Review, and the World Court' 34 (1993) Harvard International Law Journal 1

Watts SA, 'Burden of Proof and Evidence before the ICJ' in Weiss F (ed), *Improving WTO Dispute Settlement Procedures: Issues and Lessons from the Practice of Other International Courts and Tribunals* (London, Cameron May 2000)
'Enhancing the Effectiveness of Procedures of International Dispute Settlement' 21(2001) Max Planck Yearbook of United Nations Law 21
Weckel P, 'Le Chapitre VII de la Charte et son application par le Conseil de Sécurité' 37 (1991) Annuaire français de droit international 165
Weissbrodt D and McCarthy J, 'Fact-Finding by International Nongovernmental Human Rights Organizations' 22 (1981) Virginia Journal of International Law 1
Wellens K, 'Happy Birthday to the "Respected Old Lady"' ESIL Newsletter Vol 18, June 2015
Wilkinson S, 'Standards of Proof in International Humanitarian and Human Rights Fact-Finding and Inquiry Missions', Geneva Academy of International Humanitarian Law and Human Rights 2012
Wolfrum R, 'International Courts and Tribunals, Evidence' Max Planck Encyclopedia of Public International Law
Wolfrum R, 'Interim (Provisional) Measures of Protection' in Wolfrum R (ed) *Max Planck Encyclopedia of Public International Law* (online edition) http://opil.ouplaw.com/home/EPIL
Yang G, Mercurio B and Li Y, *WTO Dispute Settlement Understanding: A Detailed Interpretation*, Vol 7 (The Hague, Kluwer Law International 2005)

# INDEX

AB. *See* Appellate Body
ABC. *See* Abyei Boundaries Commission
Abyei arbitration, 165–70
  adverse inferences and, 168
  background about, 165–6
  evidence, request for, in, 166–9
  experts and witnesses appointed by parties in, 169
  experts appointed by Tribunal in, 169
  Al-Khasawneh and, 168–9
  passive approach in, 170
  proactive approach in, 170
  in round, 170
  tasks of, 166
Abyei Boundaries Commission (ABC), 166
*actori incumbit probatio* principle
  burden of proof and, 191–2
  collaboration and, 196–7
admissibility
  illegally obtained evidence and, 37–8
  limitations, 36–8
  negotiations between parties and, 37
  reactive approach and, 35–8
  Rule 89 of ICTY and, 35
adverse inferences
  AB and Panels and, 148–50
  Abyei arbitration and, 168
  Iran-US Claims Tribunal and, 156–7
  proactive approach to, 246–7
  provisional measures and, 213–17
*Aegean Sea Continental Shelf* case
  non-appearance and, 119–20
  procedure and, 42
*Aerial Spraying* case, 11, 99
agents, 79–80

Agreement on Subsidies and Countervailing Measures (SCM Agreement), 139–40
Agreement on the Application of Sanitary and Phytosanitary Measures (SPS Agreement), 139–40
Alford, Neill, Jr., 1
Annex V SCM Agreement, 199–200
Anti-Dumping Agreement, 199
Appellate Body (AB)
  adverse inferences and, 148–50
  *Argentina-Footwear* case and, 198–9
  Article 13 DSU and, 183–7
  burden of proof and, 143–8
  criticism of, 186–7
  crosscutting evidentiary issues affecting, 143–50
  evidence before, 141–3
  *prima facie* case and, 144–8
  question asking and, 234
*Argentina-Footwear* case, 148
  AB and, 198–9
  collaboration and, 185, 191, 198–9, 201
  conditional collaboration and, 201
  disclosure and, 186
  The Panels and, 198
*Armed Activities* case, 5
  fact-assessment, 47–8
  MONUC and, 96
  Panel of Experts and, 106
  provisional measures and, 212–13
  Security Council and, 62–3, 69
  Special Rapporteur of the Commission on Human Rights and, 96
  UN, deference to, in, 96–7

*Arrest Warrant* case, 3
Articles. *See* Court's Statute; Dispute Settlement Understanding; Iran-US Claims Tribunal; Rules of Court; United Nations Charter
assessors, 251

*Barcelona Traction* case, 42, 191
Beazley, P. B., 21
Bedjaoui, Mohammed, 234
Belgrave, Douglas Vincent, 169
Bentham, Jeremy, 199
Berman, Frank, 4
binding resolutions, 64–8
*Blaškić* case, 181
*Bosnian Genocide* case, 5
  Article 49 and, 183, 214–15
  fact-assessment, 48
  *Fall of Srebrenica* Report and, 94–5
  national security and, 191
  provisional measures and, 212–13
  redacted evidence and, 88–91
  UN, deference to, in, 94–5
*Botswana/Namibia* case, 78–9
British Admiralty Chart, 85–7
burden of proof
  AB and Panels and, 143–8
  *actori incumbit probatio* principle and, 191–2
  *Guinea v. Congo* case and, 192
  *Pulp Mills* case and, 192–3
  *Rights of US Citizens in Morocco* case and, 192
*Burkina Faso/Mali* case, 37

*Cameroon v. Nigeria* case, 85–7, 208
*Canada Aircraft* case
  Article 13 and, 184–6
  *Japan-Agricultural Products* case and, 185
*Case Concerning the Frontier Dispute*, 21–2
Cassese, Antonio, 256
Central Water and Power Commission (CWPC), 174–5
*Certain Expenses* case, 61–2

Chagos Marine Protected Area Arbitration, 236–7
Chapter VII, of Charter, 68–9
Charter interpretation, 56–8
China, 124–5
*Chorzów Factory* case, 37
collaboration
  *actori incumbit probatio* principle and, 196–7
  Annex V SCM Agreement and, 199–200
  Anti-Dumping Agreement and, 199
  *Argentina-Footwear* case and, 185, 191, 198–9
  conclusions, 201–2
  conditional duty of, 201
  definitions surrounding, 194
  Draft on Arbitral Procedure and, 195
  drawbacks, 200
  duty of, 191–202
  duty of, in international instruments, 195–6
  duty of, in international jurisprudence, 196–200
  evidence and, 197–8
  *Guyana/Suriname* arbitration and, 200
  Hague Convention and, 195
  Institut de Droit International and, 195
  Mani and, 194
  National Treatment and, 198–9
  negative and positive aspects of, 194
  *Parker* case and, 196–8
  PCA and, 195
  proactive approach to, 246–7
  provisional measures and, 213–17
  *Pulp Mills* case and, 193, 196–8
  Rule 33 of ICSID and, 195
  Scelle and, 193
  sovereignty and, 194
  UNCLOS and, 196
  *The Wall* advisory opinion and, 198
commissions of inquiry
  Article 50 and, 23–5
  proactive approach and, 249–50
  terminology surrounding, 93

## INDEX

Common Law jurisdictions, ultimate issue rule and, 238
confidentiality, DSU and, 130
contemporaneity, 50
*Continental Shelf* cases, 31–2
*Corfu Channel* case, 4
  experts and, 225
  national security and, 191
  non-appearance and, 119, 122
  site visit and, 16–17
  witnesses and, 80, 225
Council of the International Civil Aviation Organization (ICAO), 26
Court's Statute
  Article 30, 251
  Article 34
    power to request information from public international organisations, 25–7
    proactive approach and, 251–2
  Article 36, 8–9
  Article 41, 202–4
  Article 44, 16–18
  Article 48, 16
  Article 49, 8
    Article 62 and, 188
    binding nature of, 180–3
    *Bosnian Genocide* case and, 183, 214–15
    *Croatian Genocide* case and, 183
    disclosure and, 180, 188
    *ELSI* case and, 182–3
    national security and, 191
    *Oil Platforms* case and, 188–215
    power to request information and, 19–20
    proactive approach to, 247–8
    purposive interpretation and, 190–1
    Tams and, 180–1
  Article 50
    commissions of inquiry, 23–5
    court-appointed experts and, 21–3, 232
    power to establish inquiry, 20–5
    power to request information and, 19–20
    power to seek expert evidence, 20–5
    proactive approach and, 249–50
  Article 53
    *Aegean Sea Continental Shelf* case and, 119–20
    *Corfu Channel* case and, 119, 122
    independent verification of facts and, 117–18
    *jura novit curia* principle and, 116–17
    *Nicaragua* case and, 121–2
    non-appearance and, 115–18
    PCIJ and, 116
    reactive approach and, 117–18
    *Tehran Hostages* case and, 120–1
criticisms
  of AB, 186–7
  abundant, complex, or technical facts, 74–112
  deference to UN fact-finding, 93–112, 109
  experts appearing as counsel, 78–83
  factual inaccuracies, 83–8
  insufficient evidence, 115–25
  non-appearance, 115–25
  other problems, 88–93
  overview of, 73–4
  *Pulp Mills* case, 91–3
  as warranted, 125–6
*Croatian Genocide* case
  Article 49 and, 183
  redacted evidence and, 90
cross-examination
  benefits of, 222–4
  disadvantages of, 231–2
  experts and, 82–3, 219–32
  experts appearing as counsel and, 82–3
  as indispensable weapon, 222–30
  Neuberger on, 231–2
  party-appointed witnesses and, 225–7
  proactive approach to, 246
  problems surrounding, 228–9
  *Whaling in the Antarctic* case and, 227–8
  witnesses, physical presence of, and, 230

CWPC. *See* Central Water and Power Commission

Damaška, Mirjan, 235
Dannatt, Richard, 88–9
Democratic Republic of Congo. *See* United Nations Mission in the Democratic Republic of Congo
disclosure
  *Argentina-Footwear* case and, 186
  Article 49 and Article 62 and, 188
  Chagos Marine Protected Area Arbitration and, 236–7
  of evidence, 180–202, 235–7
  facilitating, 235–7
  *Guyana/Suriname* arbitration and, 160–1
  ICTY and, 180
  power to compel, 180–202
discovery requests, 182
Dispute Settlement Body (DSB)
  overview about, 129
  question asking and, 234
Dispute Settlement Understanding (DSU)
  Article 11, 131–2
  Article 12, 131
  Article 12.7, 130
  Article 13, 133
    AB and, 183–7
    binding nature of, 184
    *Canada Aircraft* case and, 184–6
    criticism regarding, 186–7
    curious case of, 183–7
    information gathering and, 133–4
    information requests under, 135–6
    The Panels and, 133–4, 183–7
    power to mandate individual experts and expert review groups, 136–8
    should means shall and, 183–7
  Article 17, 141–3
  confidentiality and, 130
  general provisions, 130–2
  overview about, 129–30
documentary evidence
  explosion of, 4

*Gabčikovo-Nagymaros* case and, 33–4
  Practice Directions and, 3–4
  predominance of, 31–5
documentary overload, 3–4
Draft on Arbitral Procedure, 195
DSB. *See* Dispute Settlement Body
DSU. *See* Dispute Settlement Understanding

*EC-Hormones* case, 137
ELSI case
  Article 49 and, 182–3
  discovery requests in, 182
  expert as counsel in, 221–2
equality of parties
  international adjudication and, 12, 13
  *Nicaragua* case and, 13
European Court of Justice, 233
evidence. *See also* rules of evidence
  AB and, 141–3
  Abyei arbitration and, 166–9
  assessment guiding principles, 45–51
  collaboration and, 197–8
  complexity of, 76–7
  defined, 11
  developing power to compel disclosure of, 187–91
  disclosure of, 180–202, 235–7
  documentary, 3–4, 31–5
  domestic legal systems and, 11–12
  illegally obtained, 37–8
  informal expert, 83–4
  insufficient, 115–25
  international adjudication and, 12–13
  international legal systems and, 12–13
  one source of, 107–8
  power to compel disclosure of, 180–202
  provisional measures and, 207–11
  redacted, 88–91
  SPLM/A requesting, 166–9
  weighing of, 43–51
evidential, 5
evidentiary, 5
examination, 219–30. *See also* cross-examination

executive-administrative finality, 50
experts. *See also* Panel of Experts
  Abyei arbitration and, 169
  appearing on behalf of parties, 133
  Article 13 DSU and, 136–8
  *Corfu Channel* case and, 225
  cross-examination and, 219–32
  cross-examination disadvantages and, 231–2
  examination and, 219–30
  *Gulf of Maine* case and, 21
  Guyana/Suriname arbitration and, 160–4, 236
  hydrographic, 160
  independent, 162–4
  informal, 83–4, 220–1
  Iran-US Claims Tribunal use of, 157
  Kishenganga arbitration, 175–6
  overview of strategy for use of, 217–19
  party-appointed, 22–3, 225–7
  party-appointed witnesses and, 225–7
  power to seek evidence from, 20–5
  pre-hearing conferences and, 219–20
  proactive approach to, 246
  reform and, 217–40
  special permanent expert bodies, 139–40
  task of, 80
  UN Commission of Experts, 95
  as witnesses, 80–1
experts, appearing as counsel
  agents and, 79–80
  Article 64 and, 82–3
  case examples of, 78–9
  consistent practice of, 78
  criticisms related to, 78–83
  cross-examination and, 82–3
  *ELSI* case and, 221–2
  proactive approach to, 246
  *Pulp Mills* case and, 78–9, 224
  witnesses and, 79–80
experts, court-appointed
  as aid in comprehension, 231–5
  Article 50 and, 21–3, 232
  Article 62 and, 21–3
  Article 67 and, 232
  Articles 64 and 65 and, 232
  benefits of utilizing, 230–1
  disclosure of evidence and, 235–7
  drawbacks, 237–40
  expert groups and, 233
  *Guyana/Suriname* arbitration and, 236
  judge asking questions and, 234–5
  proactive approach to, 246
  *Pulp Mills* case and, 232
  role of, 231
  rules of evidence and, 21–3
  safeguards, 237–40
  strategy for use of, 240
  ultimate issue rule and, 237–40

fact-assessment
  guiding principles, 45–51
  ICJ practice of, 46–51
  weighing of evidence and, 43–51
fact-finding
  of ICJ, 15–27
  judicial organ and, 55
  PCIJ and, 15–16
  proactive approach to, 51–71
  reactive approach to, 27–43
  reluctance to engage with complexity of, 27–30
  science and, 76
facts
  advisory opinions and, 10
  centrality of, 8–10
  Lauterpacht on weighing, 43
  weighing of evidence and, 43–51
  why they matter, 11–13
factually complex cases
  contestation in, 2–4
  as court's bread and butter, 1–6
*Fall of Srebrenica* Report
  *Bosnian Genocide* case and, 94–5
  Special Rapporteur of the Commission on Human Rights and, 95
  UN Commission of Experts and, 95
*Fisheries Jurisdiction* case
  non-appearance and, 116–17
  provisional measures and, 204–5
fishing requests, 201
Fitzmaurice, Gerald, 117–18, 205

Foster, C. E., 76
Franck, Thomas, 28, 45
Free Syrian Army, 110–11
functional distinction, 68–70
functional parallelism
  *Nicaragua* case and, 58–61
  principle organs and, 58–61
  Security Council and, 58–61
  *Tehran Hostages* case and, 58–61

*Gabčikovo-Nagymaros* case
  documentary evidence and, 33–4
  experts appearing as counsel in, 78–9
  science and, 33–4
  site visit in, 16–18
Gales, Dr., 227–8
Gattini, A., 12
Gaza Flotilla Incident, 104–6
general acceptance concept, 57–8
General Assembly
  binding resolutions and, 64–8
  *The Wall* advisory opinion and, 63–4
*Georgia v. Russia* case, 49
*German Interests in Polish Upper Silesia* case, 4
Goldstone, R. J., 89–90
Goldstone Panel
  dubious legal issues and, 104–6
  international law determination and, 103–6
  procedural legitimacy and, 102
*LaGrand* case, 204
*Guinea v. Congo* case, 192
*Gulf of Maine* case, 21
*Guyana/Suriname* arbitration, 158–65
  background about, 159–60
  collaboration and, 200
  court-appointed experts and, 236
  documents disclosure dispute in, 160–1
  hydrographic expert appointed in, 160
  independent expert in, 162–4
  Marker "B" and, 160
  Tribunal's approach in round, 164–5
  Tribunal's fact-finding approach, 162
  UNCLOS and, 159–60

Hague Convention, 195
Hamilton, R. J., 89–90
Higgins, Rosalyn
  admissibility and, 35–8
  reform proposals and, 255
*Hostages* case, 62
HRC. *See* Human Rights Commission
Hudson, Manley, 30
Human Rights Commission (HRC), 110–11
hydrographic expert, 160

ICAO. *See* Council of the International Civil Aviation Organization
ICJ. *See* International Court of Justice
ICSID. *See* International Centre for Settlement of Investment Dispute
ICTY. *See* International Criminal Tribunal for the former Yugoslavia
illegally obtained evidence, 37–8
independent experts, 162–4
informal expert, 83–4, 220–1
Institut de Droit International
  collaboration and, 195
  non-appearance and, 118
interest, 50
interim measures
  Kishenganga arbitration and, 171–2
  of protection, 203
international adjudication
  equality of parties and, 12–13
  rules of evidence and, 12–13
International Centre for Settlement of Investment Dispute (ICSID), 76–7
  Article 45, 116
  Rule 33, 195
  Rule 89, 35
International Court of Justice (ICJ). *See also* powers, of ICJ
  fact-assessment and, 46–51
  fact-finding of, 15–27
  facts, centrality of, and, 8–10
  as principle organ, 54
  role in cases of non-appearance, 124–5
  UN, deference to, by, 93–112

International Criminal Tribunal for the
   former Yugoslavia (ICTY)
  compelling information production,
    181
  disclosure and, 180
  redacted evidence and, 88–91
  Rule 89 of, 35
international investment law, 255
international law
  dispute resolution and, 6–8
  Goldstone Panel and, 103–6
  rules of evidence in, 12–13
International Law Commission, 195
inter-State arbitrations
  Abyei arbitration, 165–70
  conclusions, 176–8
  fact-finding and -assessment in
    recent, 150–76
  fact-finding provisions, 158–9
  Guyana/Suriname, 158–65
  history surrounding, 151
  Iran-US Claims Tribunal and, 153–8
  Kishenganga arbitration, 170
  pending, 151
  revitalisation of, 150–3
Iran-US Claims Tribunal
  adverse inferences, 156–7
  Article 24, 155–6
  experts, use of, 157
  explained, 153–4
  facts investigations and, 154–5
  fishing requests and, 201
  influence of, 153–8
  production of documents–Article
    24(3), 155–6
  production orders enforcement, 156
  in round, 158

Japan-Agricultural Products case, 185
Jennings, Robert, 83–4
judges
  asking questions, 234–5
  backgrounds of, 6–8
  roles of, 11–12
judicial economy, 243–5
judicial organ
  binding resolutions and, 64–8
  Chapter VII of Charter and, 68–9

  Charter interpretation and, 56–8
  conclusions, 70–1
  fact-finding and, 55
  functional distinction and, 68–70
  functional parallelism and, 58–61
  general acceptance concept and, 57–8
  hierarchy absence with, 61–2
  independence of, 55–6, 69–70
  as interdependent, 56
  *Kosovo* advisory opinion and, 66–7
  political considerations and, 55–6
  principle of legality and, 58
  principle organs, functional
    distinction from, 54–8
  recommendations and, 65
*jura novit curia* principle, 116–17

Keith, K., 44
Al-Khasawneh, Awn Shawkat, 90
  Abyei arbitration and, 168–9
  *Pulp Mills* case and, 91–3
KHEP. *See* Kishenganga Hydro-Electric
   Project
Kishenganga arbitration, 170, 236
  background about, 170–1
  CWPC letter and, 174–5
  expert witnesses, 175–6
  information requested by parties,
    173–5
  information requested of parties, 172–3
  interim measures and, 171–2
  Partial Award in, 173
  proactive approach in, 176
  Procedural Order No. 8 and, 175
  in round, 176
  rules of procedure adoption in, 171
  site visits in, 171–2
Kishenganga Hydro-Electric Project
   (KHEP), 170–1
*Kosovo* advisory opinion, 66–7
*Kumho Tyre* case, 76–7

Land, Island and Maritime Frontier
   Dispute, 33
Land Reclamation case
  expert as counsel in, 221–2
  Lowe and, 223–4
  provisional measures used in, 209–11

282

INDEX

Lauterpacht, Hersch
  rules of evidence and, 12–13
  weighing of facts and, 43
legal significance, 50
*Legality of Threat or Use of Nuclear Weapons* advisory opinion, 28–9
Lillich, Richard B., 179–80
Lowe, Vaughan, 223–4, 227–8

Mahiou, Ahmed, 90
Mangel, Professor, 227–8
Mani, V. S., 194
Marker "B," 160
Mauritius, 236–7
*Mavrommatis* case, 41–3
Mbengue, M. M., 75
Mexican Claims Commission, 196–8
Minna Datum, 85–7
MONUC. *See* United Nations Mission in the Democratic Republic of Congo
Mosk, R., 1

*Namibia* advisory opinion, 52
*Namibia* case, 10. *See also* Botswana/Namibia case
national security, 191
National Treatment, 198–9
Neelum valley, 171–2
Neuberger, David, 223, 231–2
*Nicaragua* case
  commissions of inquiry and, 23, 25
  equality of parties and, 13
  fact finding in, 33
  fact-assessment, 46–7
  functional parallelism and, 58–61
  non-appearance and, 121–2
  site visit and, 16–17
NJHEP. *See* Pakistan Neelum-Jhelum Hydro-Electric Plant
non-appearance
  *Aegean Sea Continental Shelf* case and, 119–20
  Article 45 and, 116
  Article 53 and, 115–18
  cases of, 118–24
  *Corfu Channel* case and, 119, 122
  criticisms related to, 115–25

defined, 115–25
*Fisheries Jurisdiction* case and, 116–17
Fitzmaurice and, 117–18
history and, 118–19
ICJ role in cases of, 124–5
independent verification of facts and, 117–18
Institut de Droit International and, 118
*Nicaragua* case and, 121–2
*Nuclear Tests* case and, 119
Philippines and China and, 124–5
proactive approach to, 246
*Tehran Hostages* case and, 120–1
*The Wall* advisory opinion and, 122–4
*Northern Cameroons* case, 62–3
*Nuclear Tests* case, 119

Office of the High Commissioner for Human Rights (OHCHR), 101–2
*Oil Platforms* case, 188–215
Orentlicher, Diane, 90
Owada, Hisashi, 188–215

Pakistan Neelum-Jhelum Hydro-Electric Plant (NJHEP), 171–2
Palchetti, P., 211–12
Palmer Report, 103–6
Panel of Experts
  *Armed Activities* case and, 106
  Porter Report and, 106–7
  Security Council and, 106, 109
  Uganda and, 109
The Panels
  adverse inferences and, 148–50
  *Argentina-Footwear* case and, 198
  Article 11 DSU and, 131–2
  Article 12 DSU and, 131
  Article 12.7 DSU and, 130
  Article 13 DSU and, 133–4, 183–7
  burden of proof and, 143–8
  conclusions, 176–8
  crosscutting evidentiary issues affecting, 143–50
  evidentiary practice before, 132–3
  expert groups and, 233
  experts appearing on behalf of parties, 133

general provisions, 130-2
information requests by, 135-6
information that can be gathered by, 133-4
power to ask questions, 134-56
power to mandate individual experts and expert review groups, 136-8
*prima facie* case and, 144-8
question asking and, 234
special permanent expert bodies and, 139-40
parallelism. *See* functional parallelism
*Parker* case, 196-8
party-appointed experts, 22-3, 225-7
party-appointed witnesses, 225-7
PCA. *See* Permanent Court of Arbitration
PCIJ. *See* Permanent Court of International Justice
Pellet, A., 64-8
Permanent Court of Arbitration (PCA)
  Abyei arbitration and, 165-70
  collaboration and, 195
  Iran-US Claims Tribunal and, 153-8
  Kishenganga arbitration, 170
  revitalisation of, 150-3
  Scott on, 150
  UNCITRAL Rules and, 153
  UNCLOS cases and, 152
Permanent Court of International Justice (PCIJ)
  Article 53 of Court's Statute and, 116
  fact-finding powers and, 15-16
  indisputable facts and, 2
  *Prince of Pless* case and, 98-9
  reactive approach of, 30
Permanent Group of Experts, 139-40
Philippines, 124-5
Philips Report, 104-6
Porter Commission Report
  over-reliance on, 108-9
  Panel Reports and, 106-7
powers
  limits of, 247-53
  of PCIJ, 15-16
powers, of ICJ, 15-27
  to compel evidence disclosure, 180-202

to establish inquiry, 20-5
to intervene in and ask questions, 18-19
to intervene in and direct proceedings, 18-19
to make orders, 16
to make site visits, 16-18
to order provisional measures, 202-3
to request information from parties, 19-20
to request information from public international organisations, 25-7
to seek expert evidence, 20-5
powers, of WTO, 133-41
  to ask questions, 134-56
  conclusions about, 140-1
  information gathering, 133-4
  information requests, 135-6
  to mandate individual experts and expert review groups, 136-8
  special permanent expert bodies and, 139-40
Practice Directions, 3-4
pre-hearing conferences
  benefits of, 219-20
  experts and, 219-20
pre-trial conferences, 245-6
*prima facie* case, 144-8
*Prince of Pless* case, 98-9
principle of legality, 58
principle organs
  binding resolutions and, 64-8
  Chapter VII of Charter and, 68-9
  Charter interpretation and, 56-8
  conclusions, 70-1
  cooperation among, 68-9
  equality of, 54-5
  fact-finding and, 55
  functional distinction and, 54-8, 68-70
  functional parallelism and, 58-61
  general acceptance concept and, 57-8
  hierarchy absence between, 61-2
  ICJ as one of, 54
  judicial organ functional distinction from, 54-8
  *Kosovo* advisory opinion and, 66-7

principle organs (cont.)
  political considerations and, 55–6
  principle of legality and, 58
  relationship with, 53
  roles of, 61–8
  traditional roles of, 53–4
proactive approach
  Abyei arbitration and, 170
  Article 34 and, 251–2
  Article 49 and, 247–8
  Article 69 and, 252
  assessors and, 251
  to collaboration, 246–7
  commissions of inquiry and, 249–50
  to experts, 246
  to fact-finding, 51–71
  to factually complex cases, 245–7
  Kishenganga arbitration and, 176
  limits of fact-finding powers and, 247–53
  *Namibia* advisory opinion and, 52
  to non-appearance, 246
  non-cooperation and, 248–9
  overview, 242
  pre-trial conferences and, 245–6
  realistic measures to achieve, 241
  site visits and, 249
  sovereignty and, 248
  States' reactions to, 254
  *The Wall* advisory opinion and, 52, 52
  witness testimony and, 250–1
Procedural Order No 8. and, 175
procedure, 50
Procedures for Developing Information Concerning Serious Prejudice, 139–40
proof. *See also* burden of proof
  defined, 11
  standard of, 104
*Prosecutor v. Brima et al.* case, 239
*Prosecutor v. Kordic and Cerkez* case, 239
provisional measures
  adverse inferences and, 213–17
  as binding, 203–4
  *Cameroon v. Nigeria* case and, 208
  case examples of use of, 208–9
  collaboration duty and, 213–17
  conclusions, 211
  conditions for ordering, 206–7
  as discretionary and exceptional, 203
  evidence and, 207–11
  *Fisheries Jurisdiction* case and, 204–5
  international courts and tribunals and, 205
  *Land Reclamation* case and, 209–11
  non-compliance legal consequences, 212–13
  object of, 204–6
  obstacle to use of, 211–12
  power to order, 202–3
  reform and, 202–17
  terminology and, 203
*Pulp Mills* case, 2, 5–6
  burden of proof and, 192–3
  collaboration and, 193, 196–8
  court-appointed experts and, 232
  criticism surrounding, 91–3
  experts appearing as counsel in, 78–9, 224
  fact determination and, 10
  fact-assessment, 48
  ultimate issue rule and, 239
purposive interpretation
  Article 49 and, 190–1
  *Territorial Dispute* case and, 190
  traditional role of, 190
  of treaties, 189

*Qatar v. Bahrain* case, 84–5

reactive approach
  admissibility and, 35–8
  Article 53 and, 117–18
  benefits of, 29
  classical approach to international judicial function and, 41–3
  conclusions, 72
  contributing factors, 30–43
  Court's pronouncements and, 243
  documentary evidence and, 31–5
  to fact finding, 27–43
  factual complexity and, 243
  factual inaccuracies resulting from, 83–8

other problems arising from, 88–93
of PCIJ, 30
positive aspects of, 242–5
proactive approach and, 51–71
redacted evidence and, 88–91
sovereign nature of parties and, 39–41
redacted evidence
   *Bosnian Genocide* case and, 88–91
   *Croatian Genocide* case and, 90
reform
   Article 13 DSU and, 183–7
   Article 49 of Court's Statute binding nature, 180–3
   collaboration duty and, 191–202
   Court's Statute and, 256
   experts and, 217–40
   modest, realistic nature of, 255
   overview, 179–80
   power to compel evidence disclosure, 180–202
   provisional measures, 202–17
Reichler, Paul, 228–9
relation to event, 50
resolutions
   binding, 64–8
   defined, 65
   dispute, 6–8
   General Assembly and Security Council, 63–4
Riddell, Anna, 84–7
*Rights of US Citizens in Morocco* case, 192
Robertson, Bill, 169
Rosenne, S., 6–8, 28
Rules of Court
   Article 58, 225
   Article 61, 18–19
   Article 62
      Article 49 and, 188
      court-appointed experts and, 21–3
      power to request information and, 19–20
   Article 63, 226
   Article 64, 82–3
   Article 67, 232
   Article 69
      power to request information from public international organisations, 25–7
      proactive approach and, 252
   Articles 64 and 65 and, 232
rules of evidence
   commissions of inquiry, 23–5
   court-appointed experts and, 21–3
   development of, 14–15
   fact finding powers and, 15–27
   generality, liberality and scarcity, 13
   international adjudication and, 12–13
   in international litigation, 12–13
   overview about, 14
   power to establish inquiry, 20–5
   power to intervene in and ask questions, 18–19
   power to intervene in and direct proceedings, 18–19
   power to make orders, 16
   power to make site visits, 16–18
   power to request information from parties, 19–20
   power to request information from public international organisations, 25–7
   power to seek expert evidence, 20–5
   procedure and, 14–15
   technical, 13

Sands, Philippe, 227–8
Scelle, Georges, 193
Schwarzenberger, Georg, 9
Schwebel, Stephen M., 4
science
   changeability of, 76
   defining, difficulty in, 76–7
   Foster on, 76
   *Gabčikovo-Nagymaros* case and, 33–4
   issues surrounding, 74–7
   as justiciable, 74
   legal fact-finding and, 76
   masses of information in, 4–6
   Mbengue and, 75
   Supreme Court, US, and, 76–7
   uncertainty and, 75–6
SCM Agreement. *See* Agreement on Subsidies and Countervailing Measures
Scott, James Brown, 150

Security Council
 Armed Activities case and, 62–3, 69
 binding resolutions and, 64–8
 functional parallelism and, 58–61
 inaccurate factual findings of, 70
 Panel of Experts and, 106, 109
 political considerations and, 55–6
 Uganda and, 109
 The Wall advisory opinion and, 63–4
Simma, Bruno, 91–3
site visits
 Corfu Channel case, 16–17
 Gabčikovo case, 16–18
 in Kishenganga arbitration, 171–2
 Nicaragua case, 16–17
 power to make, 16–18
 proactive approach and, 249
source, 50
South West Africa advisory opinion
 documentary evidence and, 4
 party-appointed witnesses and, 225–7
sovereignty
 collaboration and, 194
 equality of states and, 39–41
 proactive approach and, 248
special permanent expert bodies, 139–40
Special Rapporteur of the Commission on Human Rights
 Armed Activities case and, 96
 Fall of Srebrenica Report and, 95
SPLM/A. See Sudan People's Liberation Movement/Army
SPS Agreement. See Agreement on the Application of Sanitary and Phytosanitary Measures
Sudan People's Liberation Movement/Army (SPLM/A)
 evidence requested by, 166–9
 as non-State party, 165
Supreme Court, US, 76–7

Tams, C. J.
 Article 49 and, 3, 180–1
 on modernization of Court's conduct, 3
technological information, 4–6
Tehran Hostages case

functional parallelism and, 58–61
non-appearance and, 120–1
Temple at Preah Vihear case, 28
Territorial Dispute case, 190
Textiles Monitoring Body, 140
treaty interpretation
 Article 31 of VCLT and, 189
 purposive, 189
Trindade, Cançado, 5–6

Uganda
 Porter Commission Report and, 108–9
 Security Council Panel of Experts and, 109
ultimate issue rule
 Common Law jurisdictions and, 238
 court-appointed experts and, 237–40
 defined, 238
 Prosecutor v. Brima et al. case and, 239
 Prosecutor v. Kordic and Cerkez case and, 239
 Pulp Mills case and, 239
UN. See United Nations
uncertainty
 as common, 76
 science and, 75–6
UNCITRAL Rules. See United Nations Commission on International Trade Law Rules
UNCLOS. See United Nations Convention on the Law of the Sea
United Kingdom, 236–7
United Nations (UN)
 Armed Activities case and, 96–7
 Bosnian Genocide case and, 94–5
 Commission of Experts, 95
 consent of States and, 102–3
 credibility of, 101–2
 deference to, 93–112
 disinterested witnesses and, 100–1
 dubious legal issues and, 104–6
 HRC and, 110–11
 international law determinations and, 103–6
 legal issues cursory treatment and, 111–12

one source of evidence and, 107–8
over-reliance on, 107–8
Porter Commission Report and, 108–9
positive aspects of, 99–100
procedural legitimacy of, 102
purposes of, 99–100
standard of proof and, 104
*The Wall* advisory opinion and, 97–8
weaknesses in, 99–112
United Nations Charter
  Article 2, 248
  Article 7, 54
  Article 36, 58–61
United Nations Commission on International Trade Law Rules (UNCITRAL Rules)
  Iran-US Claims Tribunal and, 153–4
  PCA and, 153
United Nations Convention on the Law of the Sea (UNCLOS)
  cases, 152
  collaboration and, 196
  *Guyana/Suriname* arbitration and, 159–60
United Nations Mission in the Democratic Republic of Congo (MONUC)
  *Armed Activities* case and, 96
  evidentiary value of, 109–10
  unreliable aspects of, 107
United States (US). *See* Iran-US Claims Tribunal; *specific case*
US Civil War *Prize Cases*, 106
*US-Shrimp* case, 189
*US-Wheat Gluten* case, 149

VCLT. *See* Vienna Convention on the Law of Treaties
verification, 50
Vienna Convention on the Law of Treaties (VCLT), 189
  Article 31
    purposive interpretation and, 189
    *US-Shrimp* case and, 189
Vinuesa, Raúl Emilio, 92

*The Wall* advisory opinion
  collaboration and, 198
  General Assembly and Security Council resolutions and, 63–4
  legal judgment and, 61–2
  non-appearance and, 122–4
  proactive approach and, 52
  UN, deference to, in, 97–8
Walløe, Professor, 227–8
*Whaling in the Antarctic* case
  complexity in, 5
  cross-examination and, 227–8
  judges asking questions in, 234–5
Wheater, Professor, 172–3
witnesses
  Article 63 and, 226
  *Corfu Channel* case and, 225
  experts, appearing as counsel, and, 79–80
  experts as, 80–1
  party-appointed, 225–7
  physical presence of, 230
  proactive approach and, 250–1
  task of, 80
Wordsworth, Samuel, 228–9
World Trade Organization (WTO). *See also* Appellate Body; Dispute Settlement Body; Dispute Settlement Understanding; The Panels; powers, of WTO
  Article 31 of VCLT and, 189
  compelling information production, 181
  conclusions, 150, 176–8
  expert groups and, 233
  overview, 128–9
  powers, 133–41

Yusuf, Abdulqawi, 2, 239